The Political Presidency

The Political Presidency

PRACTICE OF LEADERSHIP

BARBARA KELLERMAN

New York   Oxford
OXFORD UNIVERSITY PRESS
1984

Library of Congress Cataloging in Publication Data
Kellerman, Barbara.
The political presidency.
Includes index.
I. Presidents—United States.
2. United States—Politics and government—1945–
3. Leadership. I. Title.
JK516.K37   1984   353.03'1   83-25128
ISBN 0-19-503457-0

Printing (last digit): 9 8 7 6 5 4 3 2 1

Printed in the United States of America

For
Kenneth Dana Greenwald
and
Thomas Dana Greenwald

"Who are these?"
"They are my sons."

In political activity, then, men sail a boundless and bottomless sea; and there is neither harbour for shelter nor floor for anchorage, neither starting place nor appointed destination. The enterprise is to keep afloat on an even keel; the sea is both friend and enemy; and the seamanship consists in using the resources of a traditional manner of behavior in order to make a friend of every hostile occasion.

Michael Oakeshott

Despite many attempts at analysis, from Machiavelli to the present day, political skill has remained among the more elusive aspects of power.

Robert Dahl

What are the qualities called for by so vast and intense a range of functions? Above all, I think [the president must have] the power to handle men, the ability almost intuitively to recognize the efficient human instrument for his purpose.

Harold Laski

Preface

The idea for this book grew out of what was widely perceived to be the failure of the Jimmy Carter presidency. When President Carter left office in January, 1981, *The New York Times* ran an article with the headline: "EXPERTS SEE '76 VICTORY AS CARTER'S BIG ACHIEVEMENT."[1] Some of our most respected academics and journalists had concluded that his "most memorable achievement was getting elected in the first place."

Yet, when pushed to describe Jimmy Carter's political shortcomings, everyone came up short. Although only 34 percent of the American people expressed actual approval of his performance in office (Ford had a 53 percent approval rating when he completed his term), we nevertheless continued to describe Carter as a man of "high moral principles," "a religious person," and one "sympathetic to the problems of the poor." The experts from the *Times* concurred: the man was intelligent and worked hard; he emerged from his term in the White House with his image of decency and integrity intact; and that term was, after all, four years without war or significant social unrest. In other words, even professional president-watchers were hard-pressed to pinpoint precisely why or how Jimmy Carter's administration had failed.

Instead, they resorted to rather vague generalizations about the times or the man. One said that it was just "one of those periods when presidents tend to disappear into the woodwork." Another volunteered about the outgoing president that he had never had that "fire-in-the-belly quality that people want in a political leader." And still another summed up the elusive quality of the Carter collapse by stating that "it was just one of those rare moments that historians will rack their brains to understand and explain."

In fact, the reasons for Jimmy Carter's political failure—and it was at least that, a *political* failure—still elude us. Lyndon Johnson was pushed into retirement by the domestic unrest resulting from what was seen to be *his* unpopular war. Richard Nixon was forced to resign because he manifestly violated his constitutional oath. Gerald Ford, it can be argued, was never really seen as more than a temporary, "substitute" president. And, to be sure, it could be said of Jimmy Carter that had it not been for the Iranian hostage crisis or high inflation, or, for that matter, had it not been for brother Billy, he might well have won a second term.

But in Carter's case the excuses for his overwhelming defeat seem lame. For on paper at least, he was and remained the boy scout president. With his moral virtues and his intellectual skills, he was "perhaps as admirable a human being as has ever held the job."[2] He embodied everything Americans normally prize: capacity, commitment, responsibility. Indeed, these virtues remained unchallenged, even after four difficult years in the White House. No one was claiming in 1980 that Carter was stupid, lazy, or dishonest.

What, then, had gone wrong? How is it that Carter was (and still is) seen to be, in some ill-defined way, inadequate as president? What was it, in short, that Carter was not?

I argue in this book that Carter conspicuously lacked the quality that is perhaps most essential to an effective presidency: political skill.

Let me explain. First, when I speak of an effective presidency, or effective presidential leadership, I am speaking here in terms of functional criteria only. I am *not* asking if the leadership was, for example, courageous, wise, or moral, or if it led the country down the proper path. I am asking only if it was effective in the sense that the president was able to accomplish what he wanted to accomplish. In particular, this book explores the president's realized and unrealized opportunities for directive leadership. It assumes that each president, on assuming office, has policy goals that are especially important to him, and toward which he wants to lead the rest of us. Thus, some key questions in evaluating an administration will be: Was the president able to get his way when he wanted to? If so, how did he do it? And if not, why not?

More specifically, my interest is in directive leadership under routine— or non-crisis—conditions.[3] Although the propostion will not be tested here, I am hypothesizing that the processes and skills that characterize directive leadership during periods of, for example, wars, depressions, or imminent nuclear threat are probably different from those that characterize routine directive leadership. One might even speculate that in America crisis leadership is easier. A crisis is massive and visible; as a widely experienced trauma, it focuses almost everyone's concern. There is consensus that something must be done and people are relieved, grateful even, that someone is taking responsibility for acting. More often than in less threatening circumstances, people are willing out of fear, anxiety, or enhanced social responsibility, to play the part of followers. (This is especially true when the threat is an external one.)

But under more ordinary conditions—conditions in which problems abound but no single problem is so great that it threatens the welfare of the entire community—there is, typically, no consensus on what constitutes a problem, on how to define those problems that manifestly exist, or even on which of the many pressing issues should take priority. Only rarely is there broad agreement on what problems ought to be addressed, in which order, or on what constitutes solutions. In short, most of the time American presidents must attempt to lead in situations in which there is no clearly agreed-upon national—or even majority—agenda.

Second, I will not use the term "political skill" to describe what it takes to *become* president; this term will refer to one aspect of *being* president. Thus, the "followers" we are directly concerned with are not "The American People," but those members of the political elite—Congress, for example—who will have to go along with, if not actively support, the president on each policy proposal. As a consequence, the term political skill refers to how well the president can lead or direct a relatively small and select group of people toward a particular goal.

Since directive presidential leadership is an interactive process heavily dependent on the informal use of sources of power, I believe that a president must have (1) the vision and motivation to define and articulate his agenda so as to broaden his base of support; and (2) some considerable ability to perform effectively in those interpersonal transactions necessary for bringing about his most important goals. He must engage in the persuading, bargaining, battling, compromising, co-opting, cooperating, committing, catering, and arm-twisting that is the essence of directive presidential leadership as it is defined in this book.

Other studies, notably Richard Neustadt's classic *Presidential Power,*[4] have explored how presidents can maximize their personal political power. Indeed, Neustadt's work led to the formulation of several maxims that, at least implicitly, address the subject of interpersonal activity. For example: A president cannot be "above the battle, or above politics, or simply work from within the confines of his own ideas." Or, "A sensitivity to the thoughts and feelings of others and an ability to create solutions that compromise contesting points of view are what distinguishes effective leadership from nonleadership."[5] This book, however, does not propose a grand strategy that presidents ought to employ. Instead, it takes a detailed look at what it is they actually do. Specifically, which tactics have presidents used—or failed to use—to get their own way? How do they manage, on a day-to-day basis, to get others to go along even some of the time?

Because the problems and processes of presidential leadership are by no means unique to the presidential office, this book begins with a broad-based discussion of leadership and followership in America. Political leadership cannot be understood apart from history and culture, and presidential leadership is similar to other leadership roles in contemporary American society. Thus, the five chapters that constitute Part I of the book place presidential leadership squarely in the context of the American national character and political culture and join three themes to form a comprehensive theory of presidential leadership. These themes are: leadership in America as a reflection of the American national character; presidential leadership as one variant of leadership as social exchange; and, emerging from these, presidential leadership as a set of behaviors that must include personal politicking.

Part II of the book looks at the practice of presidential leadership. It consists of six case studies written in light of the theory put forth in Part I. Each of our most recent presidents is analyzed in terms of how, and how well, they participated in making their own political fortune with regard to a single policy item in which they were strongly interested. These chapters gather evidence to support the proposition that a major gap in the presidential literature is the lack of an explicit and comprehensive discussion of the critical tie between the president as effective leader and the president as effective politician.[6]

This book is not intended to be the definitive analysis of presidential leadership. Rather, it isolates and very carefully considers one key aspect of that leadership—the attempt to direct influential "followers" to new ground. But, along the way, it inevitably becomes something else as well: a contemporary exploration of the much abused Aristotelian idea that effective politics is high art.[7]

June 1984   B. K.
New York

Acknowledgments

At the beginning there was advice and support from James MacGregor Burns, Bruce Mazlish, Bruce Miroff, and Lawrence Wrightsman. Toward the end Thomas Cronin and Edwin Hollander gave me the benefit of their good counsel; and the Rockefeller Foundation made it possible for me to sign off in Bellagio. I am especially grateful to the staffs of the Kennedy, Johnson, and Ford Libraries; to Isabel Brachfeld who collected material with consummate care and skill; and to Susan Rabiner who guided the project with a firm, sure hand.

My debt to Kenneth Greenwald is immeasurable. Both his encouragement and expert editing constitute major contributions.

Contents

I

A Theory of
Presidential Leadership

1

Leadership in America

> I hold it that a little rebellion now and then is a good thing, and as necessary in the political world as storms in the physical.
>
> *Thomas Jefferson*

We wail a good deal about America's crisis of leadership, a lament that suggests a collective wish for leaders more powerful as well as more competent. Yet the course of our public life reveals a suspicion of those officials—elected or appointed—who exercise what is seen as too much political power. We undercut those who get "too big for their britches" and, more often than not, finally turn down and out officeholders who would be strong leaders—those who persist too much in defining America's goals and in pushing us hard to reach them.

The truth is that Americans have never inclined much to hero-worship, certainly not in politics. We are ambivalent about our political leaders and wary of forceful leadership in both theory and practice. Even George Washington was a controversial figure in his own lifetime—he became a demigod only in death.[1] Abraham Lincoln also had to await those who never saw him in the flesh; only in this century did we come to acknowledge his greatness.[2]

We seem to prefer making our heroes out of popular figures. For a long time Davy Crockett was the most important and best known candidate for national hero-worship.[3] Now we give our admiration and adulation to the modern gods and goddesses of popular culture—rock stars, movie actors and actresses, and sports personalities. These acts of minor deification satisfy our wish to bestow greatness on someone other than ourselves, but not on those who may demand of us that we prove our devotion by following them politically. Of our political leaders, it may fairly be said that they engage us emotionally only rarely—for instance, in times of great national emergency, or when they are wounded or slain. Mostly, America has belied what is considered by some to be an innate need for authentic heroes and kings.[4]

It would be difficult to exaggerate the impact on our political life of this resistance to leadership, this need to contain the authority of our leaders.

It permeates our national traditions, customs, and ideals, and influences the character and form of our government. As much as anything else, our basic antiauthority and even antigovernment attitude defines our political culture.

The term political culture refers to those enduring and widespread ideas, habits, norms, symbols, and practices that are politically relevant, especially as they pertain to the legitimate use of power.[5] The concept is related to what Erich Fromm calls "social character," the nucleus of the character structure of most members of a group that developed "as the result of the basic experiences and mode of life common to that group."[6] Every nation's political culture, then, is a system peculiar unto itself that was shaped by national history and development and transmitted intergenerationally.* America's political culture with regard to leadership may be said to have three key characteristics: (1) *an antagonism toward govermental authority;* (2) *an ambivalence toward constituted leaders;* and (3) *an uncertainty about what constitutes effective and proper management in public life.*

In significant part, these characteristics grow out of our revolutionary heritage.[7] The very fact of a revolutionary movement in America had a transforming effect on the whole "discipline and pattern" of the society. These changes gradually became an irresistible force, especially in the decade before Independence. Before 1760, Americans continued to assume that theirs was a hierarchical society in which it was natural for some to be rich and some poor, some honored and some obscure, some powerful and some weak. The assumption was that "authority would continue to exist without challenge." But, as historian Bernard Bailyn notes, "the revolution brought with it arguments and attitudes bred of arguments endlessly repeated, that undermined these premises of the *ancient regime.*"[8]

There could be no clinging to the past during a decade in which defiance of the highest constituted powers "poured from the colonial presses and was hurled from half the pulpits of the land. The right, the need, the absolute obligation to *disobey legally constituted authority* had become the universal cry" (italics mine).[9] Rather than obedience, it was now resistance that was a "doctrine according to godliness."[10]

The newfound distrust of authority was felt so fervently that it could scarcely be confined to politics. Religious dissent followed and spread quickly. In New England a scion of the church went so far as to deny "all human authority in matters of faith and worship."[11] By 1776, it was the order of the day to question, to doubt, to challenge, and to engage in overt acts of defiance, all of which were considered justifiable disobedience to authority in all sectors of the society.

*Anthropologists refer to this socialization as "enculturation."

Of course, the impact of the increasing revolutionary fervor still fell most heavily on political life. What was not at all clear, however, during the decades just before and after Independence, was whether all this heated talk of liberty, equality, and common consent could constitute the principles of a stable form of government. After all, "What reasonable social and political order could conceivably be built and maintained where authority was questioned before it was obeyed, where social differences were considered to be incidental rather than essential to community order, and where superiority, suspect in principle, was not allowed to concentrate in the hands of a few but was scattered broadly through the populace?"[12]

The answers to this question naturally varied. Some saw the revolution as "the triumph of ideas and attitudes incompatible with the stability of any standing order." Others determined that it "was only where there was this defiance, this refusal to truckle, this distrust of all authority, political or social, that institutions would express human aspirations, not crush them."[13]

The task of squaring the "basic nonconformism with the stability required by property, investment, and law"[14] fell to the founding fathers. They assumed the responsibility of reconciling what seemed to be the irreconcilable strivings for both freedom and order. Not surprisingly, much of the debate centered on what was to be the highest office in the land: the presidency. The founding fathers' aversion to monarchy made the question of just how much authority would be granted the president one of the most contentious issues of the day. *The Federalist Papers,* that great collection of essays by Alexander Hamilton, James Madison, and John Jay in defense of the Constitution, strike at the heart of the matter. Hamilton, himself a proponent of a relatively powerful presidency ("Energy in the Executive is a leading character in the definition of good government"[15]), had the task of distinguishing between the president and the detested king of Great Britain. Note how even Hamilton felt obliged to point to constraints that would be placed on the holder of America's highest political office.

> The President of the United States would be an office elected by the people for *four* years; the king of Great Britain is a perpetual and *hereditary* prince. The one would be amenable to personal punishment and disgrace; the person of the other is sacred and inviolable. The one would have a *qualified* negative upon the acts of the legislative body; the other has an *absolute* negative. The one would have a right to command the military and naval forces of the nation; the other, in addition to this right, possesses that of *declaring* war, and of *raising* and *regulating* fleets and armies by his own authority.[16]

From the beginning, Americans thought it necessary to make clear that the presidency was unlike any other office or role. Just as with every other government official, the president's powers were to be vested in and derived from the people. This was an affirmation of our belief that "of all the rules within the liberal tradition, the one that the people should ultimately control is the most central."[17]

But, again, the same question arose: If authority was to be so carefully constrained, how and by whom was our public life to be managed? "The key figure in lending respectability and credibility to the new government, of course, was George Washington. . . . His presence in New York, the new capital after 1789, legitimized the administration of executive power and, really, the entire experiment in republican government."[18] (Moreover, Washington had the wit and wisdom to let potentially inflammatory matters of title and symbol be settled by the due course of time. John Adams, for example, proposed that the president be called "His Highness, the President of the United States of America, and Protector of their Liberties.")

But if Washington was able to resolve for the moment the tension between liberty and order, the antiauthority strain that was rooted in the American revolution did not disappear. Indeed, it manifestly persisted and, over time, became entrenched. Max Lerner has gone so far as to assert that, "American thinkers have been at their best in their antiauthoritarianism."[19] He mentions, for example, the dicta of Jefferson and Madison on freedom of thought, the pamphleteering of the Jacksonians, Calhoun's plea for a veto power by which political minorities could hold their place, Thoreau's doctrine of "civil disobedience," the "thunderbolts" of Henry Demarest Lloyd against Standard Oil, and William James' "pluralistic universe."

Naturally, America's antiauthoritarianism—the insistence on leveling—had profound implications for its political leadership. Alexis de Tocqueville noted:

> When it comes to the influence of one man's mind over another's, that is necessarily very restricted in a country where the citizens have all become more or less similar. . . and since they do not recognize any signs of incontestable greatness or superiority in any of their fellows, are continually brought back to their own judgment as the most apparent and accessible test of truth. So it is not only confidence in any particular man which is destroyed. There is a general distaste for accepting any man's word as proof of anything.[20]

The link between our ideology and our leadership emerges even more clearly from what has been referred to as the content of the American Creed. The enduring values or ideals of the American Creed are, in contrast to the values of most other societies, liberal, individualistic, democratic, egalitarian, and hence basically antigovernment and antiauthority in character.[21] Obviously, political leadership will be difficult in a system in which the governing ideology imposes limits on power and on the institutions of government. Necessarily, there is a "distaste for accepting any man's word as proof of anything" in a political culture whose central themes are opposition to power and suspicion of government as the most dangerous embodiment of power.[22]

It should be added that the culture of capitalism lends strong support in this regard to our political ideology. Louis Hartz concluded that in the nineteenth century Hamilton's grandiose capitalist dream was combined with the Jeffersonian concept of equal opportunity. "The result was to electrify the democratic individual with a passion for great achievement and to produce a personality type that was neither Hamiltonian nor Jeffersonian but a strange mixture of them both: the hero of Horatio Alger."[23]

Capitalism romanticizes, encourages, and rewards the entrepreneur above all, and entrepreneurs are, by definition, energetic individualists rather than conforming organization types.[24] Thus, "making it" in a capitalist society is to stake your private claim; "self-made individuals" make it on their own; and "free enterprise" is all about the right of individuals to accrue what they can for themselves in a free-for-all of unfettered opportunity. Capitalism goes hand in glove with a sociopolitical system that values the rights of the autonomous individual over the good of the group.[25] The heroic archetype of both is the self-interested go-getter, not the self-effacing team player. Thus, submitting to bosses or bureaucrats is part of neither the Capitalist Creed nor the American Creed. The economy is run according to the golden rule of capitalism: Each individual on his own and for himself. For better and for worse, it is a natural fit with a political culture that does not as a matter of course grant to anyone the right of unqualified leadership.*

The point is that there is a powerful connection between culturally celebrated attitudes and how we behave, between our creed and our culture. As will become increasingly evident throughout this book, the tactics of effective political leadership grow out of the specifics of the political culture. In this sense the ideals of the American Creed may be seen as the determinants of effective political leadership in this country.

I have asserted that our wariness toward power and authority is as old as the Republic and deeply ingrained. I would argue further that there are times when this bent is exaggerated. For a complicated mix of social, political, economic, and technological reasons, at certain moments—the 1960s, for example—our hostility toward established power increases and upheaval results.

---

*It has been said that the "ruggedness of American individualism derives from the fact that pioneering, buccaneering, in a word 'frontiering' has here been an attribute."[26]

General political turmoil is followed, in turn, by a quieter period, typically characterized by a pervasive sense of disappointment and promises unfulfilled. The late 1970s were just such a post-upheaval era. Our mood was pessimistic,[27] and we were soured on our leaders. Indeed, by the early 1980s Richard Reeves was able to conclude, after a journey of many months through the country, that leadership by individuals and small groups "is becoming a thing of the past in American democracy."[28]

As I suggested, the trend started at least fifteen years earlier. In a 1965 statement, John Gardner cautioned that "we are immunizing a high proportion of our most gifted young people against any tendencies to leadership." Although Gardner acknowledged that our colleges, graduate schools, and professional schools effectively prepare their students for the job market, he argued that this narrow professional conception left "little room for leadership in the normal sense. . . . Entry into what most of us would regard as the leadership roles in the society at large is discouraged."[29]

The growing disparagement of leadership was, of course, greatly accelerated by the Vietnam experience. Watergate eroded still further our trust in government and in our leaders. According to Gallup, 67 percent of those polled reported that the Watergate scandal reduced their confidence in the federal government "somewhat" (37 percent) or a "great deal" (30 percent).[30]

Thus, the antileadership vaccine, the disappointing close of a creedal passion period, and the exposure of corruption at the top level of American government combined to create a situation in which, as *Time* put it, political leadership was "the biggest issue." On the occasion of the 1976 *Time*-sponsored "Leadership Conference," the news weekly reported that our trust in government had declined from 76 percent in 1964 to 33 percent in 1976, and that 83 percent of American voters said that they did not "trust those in positions of leadership as much as they used to."[31]

The trend continued. In 1981 Gallup reported "further evidence of the poor public image of politicians in the United States." Members of Congress and state and local officeholders were—in terms of Gallup's "ethics scale"—"among the lowest rated of the occupations tested."[32]

Of course, some of this is the result of media overexposure. In recent years leaders and leadership have become hot topics. But there have also been more serious efforts to uncover what exactly political leadership is, why so many of our leaders seem to us to be so ineffectual, and why we have trouble recruiting "the best and the brightest" to fill leadership roles. In part, this push to examine political institutions and processes in the light of leadership theory is the result of an increasingly fragmented political community. Single issue politics has replaced party politics, and the old coalitions that made governing possible within our system of checks and balances have been weakened.

Moreover, there is nothing to replace them. It has been argued that what happened was the cracking of consensus politics. Consensus was to be, in the prevailing early 1960s view, the grand contemporary achievement of American politics. Confidence in our political leaders would overcome America's tendencies toward fragmentation and stalemate; through skilled leadership national energies would be concentrated on the realization of broadly supported public objectives. But the consensus constructed in the first half of the 1960s cracked in the second half. The phenomena that cracked it were, of course, the Vietnam War and racial polarization, along with the later addition of economic "stagflation." By the mid 1970s all the major premises of consensus politics—economic growth with stable prices, the absence of fundamental political conflict, the efficacy of expert problem solving, Cold War unity—had become problematical, and along with it the idea that leadership could be achieved through group consensus.[33]

The proposition that we may still be in a time of particular uncertainty about the proper role of political leaders is given further support by David Broder's 1980 book, *Changing of the Guard*.[34] Broder interviewed hundreds of people who constitute the new generation of American Leaders, "men and women who have spent the last 20 years bringing about the changes with which they are now confronted."[35] Above all, he looked at what has happened to leadership in two of our most venerable political institutions: the presidency and the Congress.

Broder writes that the first two post-Vietnam presidents—Gerald Ford and Jimmy Carter—"were notably ineffectual at leading the government or rallying public support."[36] In part, of course, this had to do with the personalities of the two men. But in Broder's conversation with Stuart Eizenstat, then a top aide to President Carter, six themes emerged that suggest systemic challenges to intellectual and political authority. Each of them implicitly addresses why modern political executives so often have trouble getting us to follow or even to participate.

1. There is a basic conflict between the public's desire for greater services and its resistance to government spending and regulation.
2. The task of reconciling these conflicts is impeded by the lack of tested doctrine to solve the most complicated policy riddles among competing groups.
3. The struggle for scarcer resources has heightened tensions among competing groups.
4. Increasingly well-organized economic interest groups have mobilized

their forces to defend, and even expand, their claims on the federal budget.

5. Congress has seen a fragmentation of its institutional authority as power has been dispersed among small subcommittees, each of which is vulnerable to interest group pressures from its own clientele.

6. The influence of party loyalty has been so diminished that appeals for unity based on that allegiance are of negligible impact.[37]

Legislators confirm the problems of contemporary political leadership. Christopher Dodd, then a member of Congress and later a Senator from Connecticut, commented that "it's awfully hard" to mobilize Democrats on any legislative issue. According to Dodd even younger members

> don't want to feel as though they have to be responsible to the leadership. They see *themselves* as being leaders. And that is why I question the ability of the institution to come to terms, in the long run, with the problem, unless we decide that some people have got to be the pawns or the foot soldiers and others are going to have to be the leaders.[38]

Interestingly, Broder chose to conclude *Changing of the Guard* not with a question about our willingness to follow, but with one about the willingness of our elected officials to lead. About our political leaders he asks: Do most of them have what it takes? He implies that our reluctance to exert power may equal our reluctance to bow to it: "So the challenge to the young people will not be to abolish bureaucracy or escape from it, but to tame it and to lead it. [But] there were some moments when I thought I heard them saying that that was a task from which they might shrink."[39]

Having argued that we are not at root antiauthority, I am obliged to equivocate by making explicit that this bias does not constitute the whole picture. As Michael Kammen points out in his Pulitzer-Prize-winning *People of Paradox,* the desire to reconcile our "restless pluralities" has resulted in a "matrix of paradoxy" in American life: "Conservatism *and* liberalism, individualism *and* corporatism, hierarchy *and* equalitarianism, emotionalism *and* rationalism, autonomy *and* co-operation."[40] However deep-seated and enduring our libertarian and egalitarian impulses, they do not characterize all of us all the time. We have not been altogether immune from the desire for even political heroes (especially during hard times), from the tendency to label "great" those presidents who have been most comfortable with power, or from the romantic notion, revived at least once every four years, that strong leaders on white horses will deliver us from whatever current evil threatens us. The trouble, as Kammen suggests, is that "Americans expect their heroes to be Everyman and Superman simultaneously."[41]*

---

*Kammen fails to note the delicious irony in that Superman is, simultaneously, Clark Kent.

But to concede that we can, under certain circumstances, be seduced by those who exercise power and authority with style and flair is not to weaken the point that we are more aptly characterized as distrustful of these types. This book follows from the premise that because of the content of the American Creed, leadership in America is difficult at best. In Max Lerner's words, "the bent is toward the deflation of authority in individuals."[42] Yet it is precisely *because* the American people tend to resist being led[43] that what I have labeled "the political presidency" becomes so fascinating a subject. Despite the impediments to leadership in our constitutional system, and in our national character, certain presidents have managed to be much more effective leaders than others.

2

Presidential Leadership

> The powers delegated by the proposed constitution to the
> Federal Government are few and defined.
>
> *James Madison*

The questions this book seeks to address are: Given the formal constraints
on the presidential office, and given the antiauthority ideals of the American Creed that make Americans disinclined to do much following, how, in
routine situations, does the Chief Executive ever manage to get anything
at all accomplished? How is it that attempts at presidential influence sometimes actually succeed?

In our political life there is a degree of symbolism from which the president more than any other leader stands to benefit. He has been graced, for
example, with some of the trappings of royalty—a palace, a retinue of ser-
vants, the modern equivalent of white horses and gilded carriage. But even
this first among equals merits precious little reverence and only the most
occasional submissiveness. Exactly how, then, does this most exalted of our
politcal leaders lead? To start formulating some answers, we must first look
at the presidential role.

To talk about the office of the president—as opposed to talking about the
president himself—is to talk of a particular defined role. All institutional
offices or positions have defined roles; indeed they *are* their roles. The new
treasurer of the local P.T.A. assumes his or her office with certain role con-
ceptions and demands already associated with the office, as does the vice
president in charge of public relations for General Motors, as does the president of the United States whose institutional context is the office of the
president in the executive branch of the federal government. A role is a
pattern of interaction defined by the answer to one question: Who expects
whom to do what in which situation?[1]

Leadership theorists have distinguished between leadership and headship: The leader is the one with influence over his or her followers; the head
is whoever occupies the institution's highest office. Our interest for the
moment is in the head—whoever fills the role of Chief Executive of the
United States. The presidential role provides images that justify the presi-

dent's authority; it motivates him to lead and others to follow.[2] I should point out, however, that the head does not necessarily satisfy our wish for a "leader." Great leaders do more than just satisfy role requirements; like great actors, they re-create their roles. And as great actors tend to change the plays within which they perform their roles (the very plays for which their roles were created), great leaders often change those very institutions that have created and refined the role the leader has inherited.[3]

Thus, the waters muddy very quickly. Is the presidency first a matter of personality (leadership), or of office (headship)? To what extent *must* the president respond to a particular set of role demands? How much of his authority does he derive from his position, and how much from his own personal sources of power?

Clinton Rossiter's classic text on the American presidency describes the office as consisting of ten different roles: the president as Chief of State, Chief Executive, Commander-in-Chief, Chief Diplomat, Chief Legislator, Chief of Party, Voice of the People, Protector of the Peace, Manager of Prosperity, and World Leader.[4] More broadly grouped, these compose the Foreign Affairs Presidency, the Domestic Presidency, and the Economic Presidency.[5] Such roles can also be seen as imposing certain task requirements. We expect our presidents to engage in the following types of activity: crisis management, symbolic and morale-building leadership, priority setting and program design, recruitment leadership, legislative and political coalition building, program implementation and evaluation, and general oversight.[6]

Who expects all this? We all do—the public at large, the political elite, and politically interested others from abroad, as well.

From whom? The president, the Chief Executive. Our demands on him are extraordinary. We require him over and over again to prove himself to us, to be "all things to all men."

To do what? To fill all of the above-mentioned roles. He must be an expert on everything from clean air to neutron bombs; he must be skilled as a backslapper and military tactitian; he must have moral fiber, vision, ambition, energy, brains, craftiness, and decency.

In which situation? In all of them. A man for all seasons. From missile crises to Easter egg hunts, the president is expected to fill the lead roles in all types of activities.

But the trouble with a tidy (albeit long) list of role categorizations is that it implies a tidy leadership. There is an implicit suggestion that the president's "followers" in each area of decision are a homogeneous lot and that, therefore, his tasks as leader are clear and unambiguous. Yet the nature of politics belies this image. In America especially, politics is the business of coping with scores of competing demands, and it is perhaps the democratic leader's primary task to mediate sociopolitical conflicts among constituencies that have *different* needs, wants, and expectations. In other words, the answer to the crucial "Who expects?" question is much more complicated than it first appears. Only on rare occasions—usually international crises—is there a consensus, even among the president's followers, on what is to be done. This circumstance, this "unstable pluralism," together with our antiauthority tradition, makes presidential leadership especially problematic.

Individuals in role conflict situations are uncomfortable. The cross-fire of competing claims is an obnoxious problem to be solved as quickly as possible.[7] Solutions include certain strategies of noncompliance (for example, making an excuse to avoid taking action);[8] repudiation of one group; playing off one group against another; stalling until the pressures subside; redefining the leader's (president's) role; or leading a double life (different images for different audiences).[9] In short, how presidents cope with shifting role conflicts is important, and it depends less on the formal definition of the Chief Executive's role than on the ways of coping that are congenial to any particular president's personality.

Finally, Presidents range from those who are role-determined leaders, individuals who fill their role in the manner of the punctilious bureaucrat, to those who are role-determining leaders, individuals who enact their presidential role in a highly personal style, exceeding (or falling short of) what is expected.[10] This distinction is similar to one made by organization theorists between *required* leadership and *discretionary* leadership. "Required leadership is that dictated by the leader's role . . . [while] discretionary leadership involves intervention with leadership behaviors beyond those prescribed by the role."[11] What we have is a situation in which the institutional context and presidential role set boundaries. And these boundaries entail a few nonnegotiable role demands—but there is leeway. Because of the ubiquity of role conflict, and because of the considerable room for discretionary or role-determining leadership, the presidential office is in fact quite plastic.

All roles derive their legitimacy from some source of authority. The presidential role gets its legitimacy from the Constitution, and, to some students of the presidency, that explains almost all. In *The American Presidency,* Richard Pious argues that "the key to an understanding of presidential power is to concentrate on the constitutional authority that the president asserts unilaterally through various rules of constitutional construction and interpretation. . . ."[12] Pious asserts that presidents *must* rely on their constitutional prerogatives because they have no other source of power: "They cannot obtain an electoral mandate, do not gain control of party machinery, fail to lead their legislative parties, and cannot obtain expertise from the advisory system that would permit them to lead Congress and the nation by force of argument."[13]

Pious's emphasis is quite different from that of Richard Neustadt in *Presidential Power*. Neustadt argues that precisely because the Constitution does so *little* to bestow presidential power, the Chief Executive has no choice but to rely on his own personal resources. "The constitutional convention of 1787 is supposed to have created a government of 'separated powers.' It did nothing of the sort. Rather it created a government of separated institutions *sharing* powers."[14] Since, according to Neustadt, neither the Constitution nor powers bestowed on the president by Congress establish clear authority, the president's sources of power are mainly the extraformal ones he can muster on his own.

If one were to accept Neustadt's argument, as I do, at least in modified form (that is, personal power is an essential component of effective presidential leadership*), what must a president have, or what must he be, if he is to muster the personal power he needs to lead?[16]

Neustadt wrote that presidential power is the power to persuade, and that the ability to persuade depends on effective bargaining. The skilled bargainer convinces others that it is in their own best interests to go along, to allow themselves to be persuaded. In order to perform this feat repeatedly, a president must have: a will for power, the skill to win over others to his support, a willingness to engage with others in political battle, and the ability to attract attention to himself and his goals. The last must involve a readiness to work hard on his own behalf as his own public relations operator, as well as being his own chief politician.[17]

What seems to count most is the ability to engage in skilled interpersonal activity. Neustadt's blueprint can be followed only by a president able to draw on considerable social skills, in particular vis-à-vis the political elite.

Other scholars of the presidency implicitly concur. One asserts that the most successful presidents are active-positive types, who have "relatively high self-esteem and relative success in relating to their environment."[18] Another looks for a "democratic style of authority" that may be characterized by the following qualities: (1) Presidents should be able to "hold discussions with those who work in their immediate circle, which would reflect democratic norms" and (2) Presidents should demonstrate "standard political skills . . . [which include] the ability to speak, to persuade, to maneuver and manipulate, to structure situations, and to secure agreement

*Paul Light makes the useful distinction between personal, political, and institutional *resources* and formal *prerogatives*. He writes that, "Formal prerogatives guarantee certain advantages, but they do not explain the vast differences between individual presidents."[15]

in the face of conflict."[19] And still others make the same point even when apparently avoiding the subject of personality. The following are the first two principles put forth "as a foundation for recommendations to strengthen the Presidency as an instrument of effective self government," but are they really divorced from the president's persona?

> 1. Presidential management is primarily a matter of working with others to achieve national purpose.... 2. The dominant approach by the President in dealing with others should be a collaborative one....[20]

What is striking about all these prescriptions is how much they have in common. Most students of the presidency believe that the office allows and even encourages role-determining leaders who, to be effective, must draw to some degree on personal sources of power. Mainly, this resource consists of what I would label interpersonal competence. There is the implicit suggestion that to be a directive leader, to accomplish at least some part of his own program, the president must be able to maneuver skillfully from within the world of other people. He must be able to use others for his own purpose.

To illustrate the point, we might return to Rossiter's roles. Of the ten listed, no less than seven imply an ability to get along with, manage, engage, impress, persuade, and rally other people: the president as Chief of State, Chief Executive, Chief Diplomat, Chief Legislator, Chief of Party, Voice of the People, and World Leader. And indeed crisis management, symbolic and morale-building leadership, recruitment leadership, legislative and political coalition building, program implementation, and evaluation all require skill at building and maintaining good working relationships with others.

What we can then say about the presidency is that those parts of it that have to do with headship have as their main source of power the president's constitutional authority. But those parts that involve leadership have as their main source of power the president's skill as an interpersonal actor.

Max Lerner has observed that our antiauthority political culture is disinclined to give the president the benefit of the doubt: "While the President is often cursed extravagantly, he is rarely praised extravagantly. This is what [has been] called the 'debunking of the chosen symbol'.... Except in rare instances ... the symbol is there to do a job under pitiless critical examination, not to be followed blindly and adoringly."[21] Thus, presidents who are intent on achieving certain goals had better be able to convince others to walk alongside.*

---

*This is not to deny that each president will in any case have some partisans or hard core followers whom they can almost always count on.

To further examine the nature of presidential leadership, we must consider the domain in which this leadership is exercised, and those leadership tactics that will be effective in an environment that presupposes democracy, and in which there is a resistance to being led.

This domain is one in which three elements combine to create a situation in which political leadership is made exceedingly difficult.

1. *Ideology.* We have already seen that the egalitarian ethic is particularly deeply rooted in our political culture. As Tocqueville observed of the United States.

   > [Should an innovator] arise, he would have great difficulty in making himself heard to begin with, and even more in convincing people.
   >
   > When conditions are almost equal, one man is not easily persuaded by another. . . . [There is no inclination in a democracy for men] to accept one of their number as a guide and follow him blindly; one hardly ever takes on trust the opinion of an equal of like standing with oneself.[22]

2. *Politics.* America is characterized by multilateral conflict, by an "unstable pluralism." All kinds of conflicts arise among as well as between classes, parties, interest groups, etc.[23]

3. *Structure.* There is no need to expand here on the ways in which our governmental structures and institutions tend to work in competition rather than in support of each other. Suffice it to say simply that the system of fragmented power combines with the prevailing political culture to create a climate that is inhospitable, if not downright hostile, to the expression of political leadership.

In his important book, *Power and Leadership in Pluralist Systems,* Andrew McFarland suggests that in order to lead in a situation of multilateral conflicts, the leader must minimize these conflicts by upgrading common interests. McFarland—who derives some of his thinking in this regard from Karl Mannheim's *Ideology and Utopia,* particularly Mannheim's notion of multi-perspective comprehension—labels this kind of leadership "dynamic mediation."[24] As interesting as the notion is theoretically, its applicability is questionable. Whether students of the presidency, for example, would agree that America's Chief Executives normally lead by upgrading common interests—as opposed to pandering to baser instincts—remains open to debate.

In any case, McFarland's attempt to grapple with how leaders in pluralist systems can actually lead is provocative, significant, and for some reason—possibly methodological and "scientific" in origin—quite unique.

Indeed, few if any students of the presidency have explored what actually constitutes noncrisis leadership in the American political culture.

The following analysis views leadership as *social exchange.* I hope that the discussion will shed light on precisely how and why the president's skills as an interpersonal actor must affect his success as a political leader, and also clarify how routine directive leadership might be exercised within the confines of the American Creed. Although this analysis is largely in general terms, bear in mind that the leadership processes that particularly interest us are those that take place between the *president and key members of the political elite.*

Edwin Hollander has defined leadership as the term is used in this book: a process of influence between leader and followers. Although the leader may have power, influence depends more on persuasion than on coercion. Thus, the leadership process involves a two-way influence relationship. Put another way, leadership is not just the job of the leader; it also requires the cooperation of others.[25] This emphasis on *influence*—on winning over to a particular idea or behavior without making an explicit threat or using force—is of special interest to those concerned with leadership in the American presidency.

Because leadership defined as influence is noncoercive, in any study of leadership, leaders must share the spotlight with followers. The attempt to influence can succeed only if the person trying to exert influence attends to the particular needs and wishes of his or her followers. Thus, leadership becomes a process, not a person, and it is *transactional.* It flows from leader to followers, and from the followers back to the leader.

Hollander states: "When leaders are effective, they give something and get something in return. This social exchange, or transactional approach to leadership, involves a trading of benefits. The leader provides a benefit in directing the group. . . . In return the group members provide the leader with status and the privileges of authority."[26] In short, although the will, feeling, and insights of the leader will have the greatest single impact on the course of events, those of followers count too.[27] For a leader to exert influence he must take into account not only the nature of the situation but also the characteristics, expectations, and motivations of those whom he would lead.

Hollander's definition of leadership is similar to a type of leadership James MacGregor Burns also labels "transactional." Hollander talks of a "social exchange, or transactional approach to leadership," while Burns writes that "the relations of most leaders and followers are *transactional*— leaders approach followers with an eye to exchanging one thing for another. . . . The exchange could be economic or political or psychological in nature."[28] Put in terms our founding fathers would have understood, both Hollander and Burns view leadership in terms of mutual payoffs.*

Given the requisite attention to followers, only a limited number of methods are available to those who would lead (that is, exercise influence). By definition none should be coercive; but it is nevertheless true that some exert more pressure than others. Moreover, we distinguish among methods of influence according to their "harshness," with milder methods preferred to harsher ones.[30] Persuasion, for example, is considered "better" than manipulation. Of course, the method used will depend on who the leader is, what role he or she fills, who the followers are, and what the situation is.

Methods of influence include:

1. *Control over the gains and costs to followers.* The president controls certain outcomes. He may, for example, offer a reward for a favor, or he may withhold the reward until he gets the behavior he wants. Acts of influence in these situations typically convey, with varying degress of explicitness, a direction ("do this"), and a consequence ("if you do, you will get my support for something *you* want").

2. *Persuasion.* This method relies on the president's altering his followers' perceptions, beliefs, and attitudes regarding the common good. It can be argued that persuasion is an especially appropriate mode of influence in democratic systems. Ideally, no extraneous inducement is offered, and the followers' response, or lack thereof, is entirely voluntary.

3. *Affective Control.* The relationship between leader and followers is such that the followers start with a desire or sense of obligation to accept attempts at influence made by the leader. All the president has to do is indicate his preferences while preserving the natural tendency in most of us to be seen as cooperative.

4. *Control over the Followers' Environment.* The methods of influence thus far involve a direct interaction between leader and followers. But another, more indirect method of influence is available. The president who wants to influence his followers may also do so by taking actions that do not directly affect them, but alter their environment instead; the leader modifies the environment by bringing additional pressures on the follower to induce the desired change of attitude or behavior. Because this method of influence can be used without the knowledge or consent of those affected, it may fairly be labeled manipulation.[31]

Broadly speaking, the methods of influence may be divided along two natural tones of division: rational/nonrational and direct/indirect.[32] In the

*Burns writes of another kind of leadership he labels transforming: "The result of transforming leadership is a relationship of mutual stimulation and elevation."[29] But he acknowledges that transforming leadership is rare. One could argue, moreover, that transforming leadership also entails mutual payoffs.

best of all possible worlds, democratic leadership would rely exclusively on tactics that are both rational and direct.

We return now to that other half of the dyad: the followers. What affects their willingness to follow the leader?

1. *The Desire To Receive Reward or Avoid Punishment.* Followers comply with the leader's request in order to obtain something they want, or to avoid something they do not want.

2. *Desire To Be Similar to an Admired Person.* Sometimes followers want to be identified with those who have gained widespread esteem. Thus, they model their beliefs, values, and behaviors on the leader who represents what Freud referred to as a common "ego ideal."[33]

3. *Desire To Abide by One's Values.* The reward in some leader–follower interactions is not so much a matter of gaining social recognition or monetary rewards as it is of reinforcing one's self-identity and confirming the notion of the sort of person one wants to be.[34]

4. *Group-oriented Desires.* Followers who are members of a group, and committed to a certain group outcome, are susceptible to attempts at influence made by the leader when these attempts are seen as trying to bring about the attainment of this outcome.

5. *Intrinsic Gratification.* Followers come to view the leader's direction as intrinsically rewarding. Once they internalize the leader's recommendation, they persist in the appropriate attitude or behavior even when the leader's attempts at influence cease.

6. *Dependency Needs.* This view of leadership has the leader standing in a paternal relationship to the led, utilizing many of the "unconscious attitudes built up in the follower during childhood as part of the relation to the father."[35] Although this dependency need is not dominant in the transactional leadership typical of our political life, it is not altogether absent.[36]

Having considered methods of influence, and what motivates followers to accept influence attempts, we turn finally to what fuels the influence process: sources of power.[37] What resources can leaders draw on in their exchange relationship with followers? Social psychologists have identified three different sources of power: instrumental, authoritative, and libidinal.[38] In terms of presidential power, the first refers to the executive's capacity to obtain compliance by applying the stick (for example, withholding federal funds) or awarding the carrot (granting federal funds). The second refers to his ability to persuade on the basis of his legal, moral, intellectual, or political authority. A constant source of authority is the Constitution; variable resources include information, expertise, and public and party (congressional) support. Libidinal power enables the president to enlist others in his cause based on his capacity to engender in them an emotional response. Libidinal responses can range from the simple wish to help, to admiration and affection, to an unhealthy submissiveness.[39] Quite obviously, the more sources of power a president has, and the greater they are, the stronger the likelihood that presidential influence will take place.[40]

Of course, all sources of power may all be used to coerce. They can effect involuntary submission and a loss of free will. In this book, however, sources of power constitute resources for transactional leadership, for the exercise of presidential influence in the context of the American Creed. Ideally, when transactional leadership occurs, both leader and followers stand to gain. The strong emphasis is on a *trading of benefits rather than on punishment.*[41]

Presidential leadership is a process in which at least two actors participate. Before the process is set in motion, the president has already been affected by his institutional role and by long- and short-range contexts. But finally the president's ability to lead, to direct, to exert influence, will depend on how he is perceived by his followers. Does he have the interpersonal proficiency to make the political elite think he has the will and skill to get them where they want, give them what they want, and make them feel the way they want to feel?

The presidential role has been shaped by the American Creed, and it is embedded in an antiauthority political and economic culture. The president who would lead, therefore, must do so in a situation of considerable constraints on power. In David McClelland's words: "A Martian observer might conclude that as a nation we are excessively, almost obsessively, worried about the abuse of power."[42] Thus, the president's success as a directive leader—the degree to which he accomplishes what he set out to accomplish—seems to depend to a considerable degree on his own personal capacities. And whether we like it or not, this boils down to his skill at leadership depending on his skill as a political operator.

3

Political Skill in America

> There's only one way to hold a district: you must study human nature and act accordin'. . . .
>
> To learn human nature you have to go among the people, see them and be seen. I know every man, woman, and child in the Fifteenth District, except them that's been born this summer—and I know some of them, too. I know what they like and what they are weak in, and I reach them by approachin' at the right side. . . .
>
> *George Washington Plunkitt*

Plunkitt was a Tammany boss when Tammany was supreme and was proud, even thrilled, to be a politician.[1] Political bosses would "preserve the nation." Plunkitt could not stand to think they might become extinct, dinosaurs in an age of primaries.

> Have you ever thought of what would become of the country if the bosses were put out of business and their places were taken by a lot of cart-tail orators and college graduates? It would mean chaos. It would be just like takin' a lot of dry-goods clerks and settin' them to run express trains on the New York Central Railroad. It makes my heart bleed to think of it.[2]

Plunkitt's warning notwithstanding, we now have what he dreaded. America has a politics peopled by college graduates instead of old-fashioned bosses; a politics in which amateurs—not professionals—determine who runs for office; a politics in which few go among the people anymore, "to see them and be seen"; and, worst of all, we now have a politics that denigrates the politician's art.

In Chapter 1 I argue that we have always been ambivalent about our political leaders but that recently this ambivalence has deteriorated into distrust and disdain. We lament "the crisis of American leadership" but at the same time are suspicious of those who are "hungry for power," and we assail the political processes that accomplish our public business. Even more than before, politics is dirty and politicians are suspect.

We have paid a price for this habit of seeing politics with a jaundiced eye. Not least among the costs is that politicians themselves too often demean precisely that behavior in which they engage. Henry Fairlie observes that Richard Nixon "despised his own very [political] skills, and so himself and others."[3] And Jimmy Carter, by playing the manager instead of the politician, also chose to separate and distance himself from what he saw as little more than a sullied kind of maneuvering. New York printer James Smith, who challenged Major Edward Koch in the 1981 Democratic mayoral primary, made the point clearly: "I am the only one running who is a nonpolitician," he proudly proclaimed, disparaging the very career he sought. "I am the only one offering the people a real choice!"

But who can blame politicians for their disclaimers? The reputation of politics has entered into a decline so precipitous that in his widely distributed text on the presidency, Thomas Cronin feels obliged to caution that "high-minded people who look down their noses at the politician should take another look. The art of politics is vital in a democratic society. Politics is the arena in which conflict gets managed, issues get clarified, and problems get resolved."[4] Speaking on public television recently, old Washington hand Clark Clifford warned similarly that politics "must not be denigrated. Politics is a very important part of our government. . . . It's the way our country runs. It's the lubricant that keeps the wheels going smoothly."[5] Nevertheless, "if past is prologue, presidents in the future will go to considerable lengths to portray themselves as unconcerned with [politics]. They will do so in large part because the public applauds the divorce between the presidency and politics."[6]

Why has politics lost so much of its panache? Why do politicians disdain to call themselves what they are—politicians? And why have so many of us lost our taste for the political process?*

Some of the reasons are well known and may be very briefly listed here.

First, there is the decline of the party, especially noticeable in its diminished importance in the presidential nominating process. The increase in the number and importance of primaries has reduced the need for obtaining the broadly based support of party leaders; hence there is less call for the interpersonal negotiating that characterized traditional political activity. In other words, intraparty politicking is no longer essential to electoral success. Instead, candidates out to win primaries typically depend on a small circle of proven loyalists, some of whom have no influence or reputation with any part of the electorate or party apparatus.

Second, the age of television has gradually introduced an ersatz politics, one in which politicians computerize their careers and press the flesh via

*For example, in the 1960 presidential election 62.8 percent of eligible voters went to the polls; in 1980 the turnout was only 53.9 percent.

the tube. They become removed from those whom they represent, and even from peers whose cooperation they will need in the business of running the government, should they win. Moreover, television demystifies; it spreads bad news fast. It also puts a premium on money rather than personal political skill.

Third, recent scandals at the highest level of American government have left an enduring legacy. Although politicians have always been suspect to an extent, their stock since Watergate has declined precipitously; now there may be more a presumption of venality than a suspicion.

But a much less obvious reason for the demise of politics as we once knew it also exists: No one seems to understand anymore what exactly politics entails, what it means to be politically skilled, and what constitutes politics' own virtues and rewards.

In an earlier day, when smoke-filled rooms were the norm, we seemed to understand better what practicing politics was about. Plunkitt boasted that "[We Tammany bosses] ain't all bookworms and professors. If we were, Tammany might win an election once in four thousand years."[7] To be a political animal was more a matter of good instincts, natural talent, and common sense than it was of raw intellect. Politics was an interpersonal activity based on an intuitive and also experiential knowledge of what made people tick. But now our politicians have law degrees. They are encased. They think it more advantageous to display themselves as being part of a special elite than as one of the people. And we seem to have lost all our appreciation for the art of politics—"the art of making the difficult and desirable possible."[8]

Scholars have been of little help here. For example, although the experts agree that the presidency is "an intensive experience in practical politics,"[9] students of that office have failed to identify exactly what "practical politics" really means. The interpersonal processes that literally constitute political activity remain obscure. As political scientist Robert Dahl put it:

> [Political skill] is generally thought to be of critical importance in explaining differences in the power of different leaders. . . . However, despite many attempts at analysis, from Machiavelli to the present day, political skill has remained among the more elusive aspects of power.[10]

Fairlie suggests that in fact politics and government "are not refined. They are rather brutish exercises of power and character." But, he continues: "Why I love politics, and admire politicians, and value democracy, is that this brutish exercise of power and character is so contained and civilized by them. There is an immediate urgency for us all in the Periclean ideal that politics is the highest art of a civilized people."[11]

Clifford, in conversation with Bill Moyers, takes a less exalted view, but one that nevertheless has politics as the fuel that makes our government run. Clifford makes vividly clear the equation between politicking and transactional leadership. Both sides are motivated because although both sides give something, they get something in return. Presidential politics amounts to a trading of benefits in which the effective president will indeed have "the power to handle men, the ability almost intuitively to recognize the efficient human instrument for his purpose."[12]

CLIFFORD: . . . Politics is our system.

MOYERS: Define it. What do you mean "politics"?

CLIFFORD: Ah, this is it. I mean that if a president fulfills his obligation, then he must have a program. And if he has a program, then he must try to get the Congress to pass the program. And in doing that, there occurs one of the most skillful areas—our most skillful, our most illustrious presidents have been good politicians: Abraham Lincoln, was, do you see; Teddy Roosevelt was; Franklin Roosevelt was; and Lyndon Johnson was.

MOYERS: Lyndon Johnson, in the beginning.

CLIFFORD: Oh, excellent in the beginning. So, you've got a program. You want to get it through. You have an energy program. You have civil rights programs. You have human rights programs. A president has to have a program. He absolutely flounders if he doesn't know politics.

MOYERS: Which is trading, which is compromise.

CLIFFORD: But sure.

MOYERS:—which is persuading.

CLIFFORD: Sure. Which is saying, "I have certain things that you want. But you have certain things that I want. And I will work out arrangements with you in which you will get some of what you want if you will give me some of what I want." And it goes very nicely. And what you do, too, is you invite congressmen to the White House for dinner. You know what it does? It puts 'em in great with their wives. Because the wives love to be invited to the White House, do you see. And they love to talk about it to their friends. "Well, I went to the White House last night. The President said this and the President said that." You make a friend of that senator. And after awhile, you can call him in. And President Johnson calls in a senator and he says, "Joe," and Joe says, "Yes, Mr. President." He says, "Does that law partner of yours still want to be a federal judge?" "Oh," he says, "he certainly does." "Well," he says, "you know I've been thinking about that lately and we're going to talk about that. But in the process of talking about that, I want to talk with you about the fact that I think we've got to increase our Social Security program." "Well, Mr. President, I've spoken against that." "Well, I know, Joe. But times have changed. And you think about it awhile, you see. Let a week go by, you call me." Joe calls him in a week and says, "Mr. President, I've been thinking about that and I think there's a lot of merit to your position. And I believe I can change on that Social Security. I want to come over and talk to you. And, incidentally, I talked to my partner, and he is just tickled to death." Now, people say, "Well, that's politics." That's the way the country runs. That's the way business runs. That's the way commerce runs. That's the way our government runs. [It] is that you're constantly trading assets back and forth to get your program.[13]

If effective presidential leadership in fact demands skilled politicking, it is important to shed light on what Dahl labeled so elusive: political skill.

Political skill has remained an elusive aspect of power because it has not been linked to social character or even to political culture. That is, it has not been looked at in context. Social character, you will recall, is that part of character shared among significant social groups and is the product of the experience of these groups.[14] When such groups constitute a nation, social character is referred to as national character.

"Of all the books that no one can write," Jacques Barzun once mused, "those about nations and national character are the most impossible."[15] The "quest for national character, culture or style plunges one into a tangle of complex historical considerations,"[16] and indeed the problem of scale for large heterogeneous states has moved most analysts to abandon at least the quantitative approach to measuring national character.[17] Yet there is still the widely shared perception that such a thing as national character does exist. Although the field of culture and personality has gone somewhat out of fashion in the last twenty-five years, and although different positions have generated divergent concepts and methods, there are, in fact, no serious theoretical disputes among contemporary culture and personality theorists. Most assume that some kind of adaptive fit exists between the personality characteristics of a population and the sociocultural environment of that population.[18]

As far back as 1758—nation-states in Europe were still in the throes of being formed—a German observed that "Every nation has its motive. In Germany it is obedience; in England freedom; in Holland trade; in France, the honor of the King." A century later, the idea was further refined: "Seminal ideas received in childhood, standards of feeling and thinking and living handed down from one overlapping generation to another, make the man English or French or German in the rudimentary outfit of his mind."[19]

To be sure, America is different.[20] It is, as I indicated, very much larger and more heterogeneous than any nineteenth century European nation. But if we can accept that national character is no more than the relatively enduring personality characteristics that are modal among the adult members of the society,[21] then there is no reason why we should be other than American in the "rudimentary outfit" of our collective mind. If indeed, as I am arguing, a consensual culture exists in this country that has been transmitted from generations, and is only modestly changed during its entire history, there must then be such a thing as the American national character.[22] Max Lerner, in *America as a Civilization,* observes: "For good or ill, America is what it is—a culture in its own right, with many characteristic lines of power and meaning of its own, ranking with Greece and Rome as one of the great distinctive civilizations of history."[23]

But what is the nature of American culture? What defines our national character? The answer remains elusive, and, although the precise reasons for this elusiveness are multifarious, one stands out as more important than the rest. Americans are, to reiterate Kammen's apt phrase, a "people of paradox." He continues: "Americans have managed to be both puritanical and hedonistic, idealistic and materialistic, peace-loving and war-mongering, isolationist and internationalist, conformist and individualist, consensus-minded and conflict-prone."[24]

Lerner has observed that in our impulses to polarize one may see proof that American life is deeply split, or one may prefer to see these same impulses as contradictory parts of a bewildering puzzle. Yet both he and Kammen offer an alternative view. They suggest that the tensions, paradoxes, biformities, and polar impulses form the essence of what we are, and of what distinguishes us from everyone else. Because of our heterogeneity, perhaps, it is the paradoxes, and their particular configurations, "which can be called peculiarly our own."[25]

I am proposing that the content or configuration of political skill is determined by the way in which the national character is realized in the political culture. What it takes to be politically skilled in America will differ at least somewhat from what it takes to be politically skilled in any other country.

If political skill is shaped by political culture, to understand the nature of political skill in America we must begin by returning briefly to the ideology that shaped that culture: the ideology of the American Creed. As we have discussed, in contrast to the values of most other societies, the values of the American Creed are antigovernment and antiauthority in character. We can assume, then, that the politician who would be skilled in such a climate must adhere to norms and practices that do not offend "followers" who have internalized America's antiauthority ideals. Thus, to be politically skilled in America is, among other things, to give at least the impression of a democratic leadership, of power shared.

But if power is shared too much and too often, there is no leadership. To lead is to exercise a greater degree of influence than others have—at least on some issues. The problem for an American president is to maintain a form of democratic leadership vis-à-vis the political elite while simultaneously fighting hard and well for what he believes to be right.

As we saw earlier, the way in which this balancing act can best be accomplished is through transactional leadership. Such leadership may reasonably be described as democratic because it entails social exchange: Power is divided, or at least it is experienced as such. We also saw that transactional leadership, by definition, is an activity that takes place between leaders and followers. To understand leadership in America, or at least the part of it that is an expression of political skill, we need to examine how people in this country generally behave in relation to each other. How do we present ourselves in our interpersonal encounters? What is our national style?

This question, with its attendant political implications, occupied Tocqueville in the 1840s, and a century later sociologist David Riesman sought to answer it. Riesman addressed the issue of the American national character in his book, *The Lonely Crowd*.[26] Because I draw on *The Lonely Crowd* to further my argument, let me briefly discuss what is widely considered Riesman's most important contribution.

Like Tocqueville (and in unwitting defiance of Barzun's caution), Riesman set out to portray the American national character. His particular interest was in the tension between attempting to adhere to one's own beliefs while conforming to the prevailing norms of society. In part, Riesman explored this tension by analyzing styles and processes of leadership. He proposed that there were two periods in American history when "a sharply defined ruling class emerged": circa 1800 (the election of 1836 was seen by Riesman as "the high point of oligarchic rule") and after the Civil War when "the captains of industry" emerged as our new governors. He argued that during these two periods the mood of the ruling class was one of "conscious leadership directed by conscious class consideration." It was a time for leadership by the "inner-directed man," the autonomous man who is guided in his behavior by his own personal sense of what to do and what not to do.*

But, Riesman continued, "the bullet that killed McKinley marked the end of the days of explicit class leadership." McKinley's death signaled the end of a time when leaders and led had mutual interests and shared goals, when, "because the goals were clear, the obvious job of the leader was to lead; of the led to follow." Riesman concluded that this "situation and these inner-directed motivations gave a clarity to the political and social scene in 1896 that it does not appear to have had in Tocqueville's day and has not had since."[27]

Riesman's central thesis is that during the first half of this century—and I would argue during the second half as well—both leaders and followers have been of a different sort: They have been "other-directed." Other-directed people are guided less by an inner sense of direction, less by the courage of their own convictions, and more by others. All their lives they pay close attention to other people who, in turn, serve as guideposts for how to think, feel, and behave. Naturally, for those who are other-directed, interpersonal activity takes on critical importance. Indeed it has been said

---

*Sometimes, the inner-directed man is actually an "above-directed" man, who did his duty as he believed God gave him the right to see it. The important point is that he did not look to the opinion of others for guidance in the matter of goals.

that for other-directed types, personal relationships become "the main highway to self-definition, to identity."[28]

It should be pointed out that the historiography of Riesman's analysis has been questioned. In particular, Seymour Martin Lipset—in an important essay titled "A Changing American Character?"—argues that other-directedness has been with us from the start. Riesman is right, Lipset writes, in showing how "bureaucratization and urbanization *reinforce* those social mechanisms which breed other-directedness." However, these mechanisms operate within an historic context that also generated such traits in a nonbureaucratic and nonurban society. "Other-direction, or, to put it less dramatically, sensitivity to the judgments of others, is an epiphenomenon of the American egalitarian ethos, the opportunities for rapid status mobility, and the general growth of an urban, bureaucratic society."[29]

But if Riesman's history has been challenged, his main argument—that we had come into a time heavily populated by other-directed types—remains convincing. In a 1972 reconsideration of *The Lonely Crowd,* Jonathan Yardly commented on how the book's definitions of social character and predictions about the development of American society still pertain: "The other-directed person is clearly the American of the 70's."[30] Indeed, Yardly hypothesized that other-directedness would be even more pervasive in the future: "The more populous we become, the more easily we travel about, the more quickly we are placed in communication with others—the more secure will be the hold of other direction on the American character."[31]

In any case, Riesman was not alone in his view of conformity (interpersonal sensitivity, if you will) as the hallmark of the twentieth century American social character. William Whyte, Jr.'s much discussed *The Organization Man* came to the same conclusion. Although Whyte's book was written in the 1950s, his point could as well be made today: Young people "don't see [the 'system'] as something to be bucked, but as something to be cooperated with."[32] And there is a striking similarity between the other-directed type and Erich Fromm's "marketing personality."*

> If we ask what the respective weight of skill and personality as a condition for success is, we find that only in exceptional cases is success predominantly the result of skill and of certain other human qualities like honesty, decency, and integrity. . . . The "personality factor" always plays a decisive role. Success depends largely on how well a person sells himself in the market, how well he gets his personality across, how nice a package he is.[33]

*Fromm's terminology was of course deliberately chosen. In Chapter 1 I pointed to the link between our antiauthority ideology and capitalism. Similarly, Fromm sees national character as an outgrowth of, among other things, the economic system. Riesman too sees our tendency to excessive sociability as resulting from the structure of the economy.

In light of what became of a certain B-movie actor, it is amusing to note that Fromm goes on to say that "the most important means of transmitting the desired personality pattern to the average man is the motion picture." The movie star is the marketing personality incarnate:

> Our motion-picture stars have no great works or ideas to transmit, but their function is to serve as the link an average person has with the world of the "great."[34]

Interestingly, Ronald Reagan is also brought to mind by Lerner's description of America's dominant ideals: "They are the ideals ... of being popular and charming, of being a success.... The dominant drive is social acceptance."[35]

Observers like Riesman, Whyte, Fromm, and Lerner are claiming that the American national character has evolved to the point where right and wrong are consensually decided, and how good or bad we are and what we ought to be is determined by what pleases others. Put another way, Americans have highly developed conventions of flexibility and conviviality. To be a successful interpersonal actor in this country is to undertake frequent prosocial or friendly communications, and it is to avoid unwarranted expressions of dominance. Quite simply, we are of a temper that is both democratic and friendly.[36]

Of course, all of this is perfectly appropriate to a society whose denizens have been labeled "joiners" and "belongers." Lerner claims that no other civilization shows as many "secret fraternal orders, businessmen's 'service clubs,' trade and occupational associations, social clubs, garden clubs, women's clubs, church clubs, theater groups, political and reform associations, veterans' groups, ethnic societies, and other clusterings of trivial or substantial importance."[37] Once again, although the point was made years ago, it still holds. We still think of groups as the cure for what ails us.* Thus, with regard to our social (national) character, the emphasis is manifestly on the word *social*.

If Riesman is correct in suggesting that twentieth century America is particularly conducive to other-directedness, it is nevertheless no accident that he appears to locate only a few inner-directed leaders in our entire history (for example, McKinley, Wilson). For to look closely is to see that the other-directed leader is in keeping with the American Creed while the inner-directed leader is not—as indeed Lipset's important point implies.

The values of the American Creed are liberal, individualistic, democratic, and egalitarian. Opposition to power and suspicion of government are central themes in American political thought. Thus, it may be assumed

---

*Nowadays, we are especially enamored of "self-help" groups that permeate our society in scores of different guises.

that our political culture encourages us to be suspicious of those leaders who would march to their own drummer, expecting others simply to follow, but supportive of those leaders who put a premium on at least appearing to take their cues from their followers.

Riesman clearly has mixed feelings about the leader who "has many of the characteristics of the artist and entertainer," about a president like FDR who "exploited" his charm. But it is precisely this kind of leader who adheres to the cautions on democratic leadership. Surely it is the other-directed governor rather than the inner-directed one who more closely follows the maxim that in a democratic commonwealth, "power [must] not only be shared, but subordinated to respect for the dignity of the human personality."[38]

What we get, in short, is what we are. Indeed, our most effective political leaders *embody* those parts of our national character that are the most salient. If our political culture has as its central themes opposition to power and suspicion of government, then it is altogether logical that those who seek to become political leaders cloak their more purely personal needs (for example, for power, achievement) and ambitions in the mantle of other-directedness. Thus, although America has a rich variety of leaders, at all levels, facing hundreds of different tasks in thousands of different situations, I would argue that in mainstream American politics effective leaders do *share* the quality of appearing to be considerably more other-directed than inner-directed.

To be sure, I do not mean to imply that there is no golden mean. There should be an intermediate position that posits a leader who, unlike the other-directed person, has strong convictions, but who, unlike the inner-directed person, can respond in an open way to the needs, beliefs, demands, and values of others. I am proposing that in our political culture even those who are most inner-directed must—if they are to succeed as political leaders—adopt other-directed manners. For it is other-directedness that conveys an interest in others, or at least an attentiveness to them. In other words, it is precisely the other-directed leader who gives the impression—not necessarily inauthentic, of course—of an inclusive, democratic leadership. This person appears, thereby, to emobdy our opposition to power based on one true light, whereas the autonomous inner-directed leader symbolizes what we as a people have, since even before the American revolution, been against.

In all of this, however, there is—as befits a "people of paradox"—a tension: between the individualism of the American Creed on the one hand and the conformity of American behavior on the other. Three resolutions to this tension may be put forth. The first suggests that what we in fact have is a collective or plural individualism. American individualism is the togetherness of several and not the isolation of one, or the absorption of all into a higher unity. Americans join many groups, but surrender themselves to none.[39] The second may be labeled the internal resolution. It rests within each one of us who is identified by the American national character, and it proposes that our conformity may actually be a step toward a more genuine individuality. By outwardly accepting the conventions of our groups, we may have greater "psychic energy to develop and fulfill our private potentialities as unique persons."[40] The third way of resolving the tension is external, and pertains particularly to leadership; it has to do with how we act out, or behave. One way for Americans to hold on to the ideal of individualism—especially in a bureaucratized society that demands increasingly routinized and conforming behavior in the workplace—is to resist political leadership. By refusing to "go along" in those situations in which they are not absolutely required to, Americans are able to retain a semblance of the individualistic ideal still held dear. Given this, the other-directed political leader, especially in routine situations, will be the most effective at conceiving and engaging in leadership as social exchange. In a culture in which a gap exists between the ideal of individualism and the extent to which conforming behavior is required in "real life," the political leader who can coax followership through shared rewards stands the greatest chance of success.

To clarify further the link between national character, political culture, and political skill, let us turn again to Fromm, who theorized that "The whole personality of the average individual is molded by the way people relate to each other, and it is determined by the socio-economic and political structure of the society."[41]

What constitutes political skill within a given group is similarly determined. America provides the example: It has a four-hundred-year-old written history that has resulted in a certain ideology and politics as well as particular social, political, and economic structures. As we have seen in this chapter, the American experience has also affected certain patterns of interpersonal relations and ways in which people present themselves in everyday life. All of these factors converge to shape—via their impact on national character and political culture—the nature of political skill. (Of course, what it takes to be politically skilled will vary somewhat over time, for even durables such as ideology and institutions evolve in response to changing conditions.)

This conception of the impact of the society on the nature of political skill is illustrated in Figure 1. But this figure refers only to the general influences on the nature of political skill. To complete the rescue of political

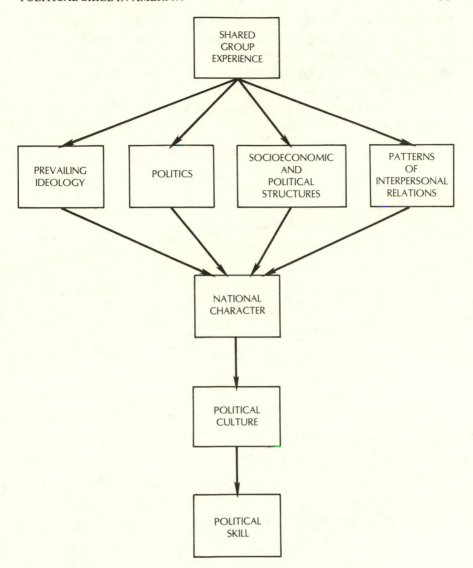

Figure 1. General Influences on the Nature of Political Skill

skill from the realm of the elusive, we must also consider specific influences. These grow out of the particular political role.

Role is a relatively regular pattern of interaction that can be described by who expects whom to do what in which situation. The American presidency is a role in that it is an institutional position of which it may be said that different groups expect the one who fills that position to accomplish different tasks. The president must then decide on the following questions:

What are the most pressing issues? How should these issues be addressed? What is the "right" thing to do in each case? Thus, what constitutes political skill in the American presidency will be affected by both the general influences outlined in Figure 1 and the specific influences determined by the exact nature of the presidential role at a given moment. All politicians in America have their craft shaped by the same general influences. But the specifics that determine the content of political skill depend on the particular political role each of them fills.

4

Political Skill:
Tactics and Requisites

> If Roosevelt could ride the whirlwind, it was because he him-
> self was always in motion. . . . Gay, laughing, confident, he
> dominated the life of the White House.
>
> *James MacGregor Burns on FDR*

To further uncover the nature of political skill in America, we must sort out what constitutes our political activity. What does it mean to be labeled politically skilled in this country?

Insofar as this book is concerned, to be politically skilled is to have the demonstrable ability to lead or direct toward a particular end, and to do so at a relatively low cost. Skill, then, is a capacity. Tactics are the form that capacity takes. These tactics are the content or substance of political skill and, as such, must be employed for political skill to be realized.

George C. Edwards III has written about what he calls presidential "leg-islative skills." He mentions a number of political tactics a president can employ to try to get Congress to do what he wants them to. Together, they make up a handy "shopping list" for those who would begin to understand "the political presidency." Note that each of the following tactics can be employed not only vis-à-vis members of Congress, but vis-à-vis any member of the political elite.[1] All are targeted directly at one or more persons and are designed to influence.

Preemption of Problems. The president anticipates his followers' concerns and acts to preempt them or ward them off.
Advance Notice. The president advises his followers of what he will do to give them a chance to review his action and accommodate them-selves to it.
Timing. The president times his leadership initiatives to fit the mood of the moment. The right moment depends on such factors as momen-tum, availability of sponsors, and opportunities for neutralizing the opposition.

Use of the Cabinet. The president briefs each cabinet member on initiatives that are pertinent to his or her area. Thus, cabinet members are enlisted as foot soldiers on behalf of presidential programs.

Personal Appeals and Access. The president takes it on himself to pick up the phone, or appeal face to face, to followers whose support he needs on a particular item.

Bargaining. The president trades favors to procure backing for policies and programs.

Arm Twisting. If necessary, the president applies pressure, through implicit or explicit threats, to get people to do what he wants them to.

Services. The president renders a variety of services and favors to create a general climate of good will and to win support on particular issues.

Personal Amenities. The president wins friends and influences people by engaging in the social courtesies that enhance professional relationships. These courtesies include small gifts and mementos, invitations to the White House or Camp David, and personal notes.

Compromise. The president meets his followers part way in order to get them to accept something that would otherwise be unpalatable. Compromise has to be used judiciously, however, at just the right moment and in just the right way, so that it is not seen as a sign of weakness.

Detachment. The president refrains from becoming identified too closely with particular parts of his program. In this way, failed initiatives can be considered professional disagreements instead of personal rejections, which lead to bitterness and anger.

Outside Support. The president exerts pressure on those who might influence those whom he would lead.

Three more tactics might be added to this list. The first is education. To some extent the notion of education is subsumed under the tactic of advance notice. But I am thinking here about more than letting others know what is in store. I perceive the president as teacher–leader who *educates, excites,* and *mobilizes* his would-be followers on behalf of his position.[2] I am thinking about a teaching president who enlightens and indeed arouses the public and the political elite about the existing situation, and who then gets both groups to focus on the particular resolution that he espouses. In fact, this instruction, this grafting of the private vision on to the collective mind should be the first tactic employed. For to the extent that followers have been helped to see the light, they will be the more likely to (1) join together, and (2) lend support. They will become—in spite of our antiauthority culture—cooperative (with each other as well as with the leader) and capable of being mobilized.

The second item to add to Edwards's list is impression management. Sociologist Erving Goffman's work on the presentation of self in everyday life is of interest here.[3] Put simply, the president must seem presidential. That is, he must—through some combination of guile and intuition—*convey the impression that he in particular is suited to the presidential role.* In view of the considerable political effectiveness of Ronald Reagan, it is interesting to recall that Goffman equates successful impression management with good acting. He writes of "belief in the part one is playing," of performances, settings, dramatic realizations, and dramaturgical loyalty, discipline, and circumspection. In short, the president *and* his team must put on a performance so convincing that they define the situation first by appearing to be perfectly cast, and then by getting all concerned to follow the script that they, in fact, have written.

Ingratiation is the third and final item to add to the political tactics list. Although it is actually an aspect of impression management, ingratiation is important enough to be mentioned separately. Earlier I discussed Fromm's point that success now depends largely on how a person sells himself, on how well he gets his personality across, on how nice a package he is. Social psychologists have explored this phenomenon; they have studied how we go about trying to make ourselves more attractive to people. *Ingratiation is a strategic behavior designed to influence a particular other person concerning the attractiveness of one's personal qualities.*[4] Ingratiating actions are considered "illicit" because they are intended to accomplish something typically not contained in the implicit contract that underlies social interaction.[5] Thus, the ingratiator's task is essentially that of manipulating the feelings and attributions of the target person.

Four major classes of ingratiation tactics have been suggested: other-enhancement (flattering the target person), opinion conformity (agreeing with the target person), rendering favors, and self-presentation (behaving in such a way so as to increase the likelihood of being judged attractive). Of particular interest to us is what happens when these tactics are employed by a high-status person—such as a President of the United States.

Presidents are, of course, not exempt from having to use ingratiation tactics. All leaders who depend heavily on the good will and voluntary cooperation of others in order to lead will do better if they are liked rather than disliked. Unlike the low-status person, when a high-status person, such as a president, makes an ingratiating overture, he does not have to worry much about others suspecting his motives.

There are, however, other concerns. Above all, the president must make himself attractive in a way that does not undermine his respectability and power.[6] To achieve this balance, he would ordinarily wish to avoid the use of opinion conformity, for it is precisely the task of the high-status leader to form independent judgments. There are also problems of self-presentation the high-status person must watch out for. In particular, in his zeal to be liked, he must take care not to compromise his presidential impressiveness. (The use of humor seems to avoid this pitfall.) That leaves other-enchancement and rendering favors as ingratiation tactics generally best suited to presidents. Both tactics have been shown to be effective in situations in which high-status persons seek to make themselves attractive without diminishing what is in fact their most valuable resource—their high status.

Ingratiation is a particularly useful tactic in a political culture long characterized by a tension between liberty and authority, and in a society remarkable for its "unstable pluralism."

Ingratiation softens authority and mitigates, or appears to mitigate, its consequences.

Ingratiation serves as a common denominator in a heterogeneous society that is, however, broadly responsive to the marketing personality.

Ingratiation makes it easier to appear to be all things to all people. Robert Frost was not asking the impossible when he advised John Kennedy to be as much Irishman as Harvard man.[7]

Ingratiation can coax followership at little or no cost.

To understand why this list of political tactics looks the way it does—it is heavily biased toward tactics involving a two-way influence relationship—we must return to the domain in which they are employed. This domain is one in which ideology (especially the egalitarian ethic), politics (multilateral conflicts), and structure (institutional checks and balances) converge to create a situation in which directive leadership is made exceedingly difficult.

We also need to return to the nature of the presidential role which, as we have seen, requires interpersonal skill if discretionary leadership is to be exercised. To accomplish his own ends, therefore, the president—unable very often to command the political elite to "do this" or "do that"—must use one of a variety of political tactics that come under the heading of methods of influence. In short, the above list manifestly reflects that the kind of leadership addressed in this book is one in which "followers" can only rarely be counted on to follow blindly.

To rescue political skill from the realm of the elusive, one task still remains: We must explore what makes it possible for one person but not the next to employ tactics of political skill. In particular, what must a person *be* to exercise political skill in the presidential role?

We have seen that for a president to be effective, a modicum of interpersonal activity is mandatory. One of the most widely used personality variables addresses precisely the predisposition most relevant to such activity: the tendency to extraversion or introversion.*

The fundamental difference between extraverts and introverts is well known. The extravert prefers the outer world of objective events and an active involvement in the environment; the introvert prefers the inner world of subjectivity with an emphasis on reflective and introspective activity.[8] Three further points must be made. First, the presence of extraverted or introverted tendencies in one's behavior is pervasive; it applies to behavior in a wide variety of situations. Second, such tendencies appear in childhood and remain relatively stable throughout the life span. And, third, individual differences ranging along an extraversion–introversion continuum are clearly indentifiable.[9]

Given my central hypothesis that the effective president must lead from within the world of other people, it is important that the behavioral differences between the extravert and the introvert are most apparent in social situations. The introvert is quiet and introspective, and prefers to be with small groups of intimate friends or alone. In contrast, the extravert is sociable and lively, and actively seeks out both the presence of other persons and social activities.

Since there is little argument that sociability is the central aspect of extraversion, the content of sociability has been much studied. For our purposes, the term can be broken down into its two most salient parts: social activity and social facility.

I propose that both are key components of political skill. In particular, I am suggesting that the more extraverted president will have a considerable political advantage over the more introverted one. By expending more energy on social activity, and by being a more facile interpersonal actor, the extraverted president will greatly enhance his opportunity to exercise personal political influence.

In line with what was said earlier about the twentieth century American national character, the assertion that the extravert has a political advantage over his too introverted counterpart makes considerable sense. The more sociable president is able to relate; he is in harmony with a culture popu-

---

*One can probably assume that Riesman's other-directed type is more extraverted than his inner-directed type and, conversely, that his inner-directed type is more introverted. But Riesman is writing about a sociological phenomenon, not a psychological one. In that sense, although related, the dimensions of other and inner-directed, and extraversion and introversion, are different.

lated by marketing personalities. Riesman writes that the other-directed man "possesses a rich store of social skills—skills he needs in order to survive and move about in his social environment; some of these he can deploy in the form of *political skills*. . . . [These skills are] related to his inescapable awareness, lacking in the inner-directed man, that in any situation people are as important as things."[10]

The more extraverted president is also better equipped for transactional leadership. For the process of social exchange to take place at all, a measure of social activity must exist. And for the social exchange to work—that is, for the leader to get his way—he must have at least modest social skills.

All presidents have some minimal ability to work with, and appeal to, others. They could not have become presidents without it. But there are those Chief Executives for whom this ability is merely functional, who derive little or no pleasure from ordinary interpersonal activity, and who regard the interaction they have with most others as means to an end rather than as an end in itself. Of our recent presidents, Richard Nixon and Jimmy Carter fall into this category—both are, in fact, introverts.

There is, in any case, little doubt that the too introverted president is vulnerable in ways that will impinge on his effectiveness as a political leader. These include:

1. A tendency to isolation.
2. Excessive dependency on a few key staff people.
3. Limited contacts, and, as a result, limited success with politically important others.
4. A restricted input into his decision-making process.
5. Restricted ability to dramatize and sell his concerns and to make his presence felt.
6. Limited number of allies at home and abroad who will lend dependable political support.
7. A tendency to extreme sensitivity that will hinder him in his ability to play hardball politics and encourage him to retreat still further from the world of other people.[11]

In sum, the president who is socially inadequate will find himself stymied at every turn by a political culture that makes political leadership difficult at best. Robert Dahl once suggested that "perhaps the most obvious requirement [the professional politician] must have is an unusual toleration for creating and maintaining a great number and variety of personal relationships." Indeed, in *Who Governs,* Dahl put forth the tantalizing hypothesis that "the distinguishing characteristic of the [political] professional is an inordinate capacity for multiplying human relationships without ever becoming deeply involved emotionally."[12]

But if extraversion, or sociability, is critical to political leadership in America, it obviously is not enough. To have directive leadership, leadership must be attempted; to make that attempt the would-be leader must be motivated by the need for power or influence. Indeed, the issue of motivation is particularly salient in a culture that generally scorns politicians, and in which the leader is, in David McClelland's words, "very likely to be attacked by some sub-group as a malicious, power-hungry, status-seeker."[13] Only when we want something badly do we invest our resources (for example, time, energy, prestige, money) trying to get it. Indeed, there is a direct ratio: The more we want to persuade, or influence, or exert power, the more we are willing to risk in the process.

McClelland—a leading student of motivation—has argued that people with high s Power (socialized power) scores are especially well suited for political leadership in America. He contrasts them with those who have a clear need to achieve, for "achievement is a one-man game that need never involve other people,"[14] and also with those who score high in p Power (personal power), who are intent on prevailing over someone else.

McClelland theorizes that leadership has been discredited in this country because social scientists have often used the personal power image to explain how the leader gets others to follow. But in fact the leader high in s Power is influential by "strengthening and inspiriting his audience.... His goal is to make clear which are the goals the group should achieve, and then to create confidence in its members that they can achieve them."[15] Thus, the leader with s Power motivation is able to rely on a subtle and socialized form of influence, in which "followers" feel "like initiators of action rather than pawns."[16]

McClelland is careful to point out that we should not make the mistake of assuming that all leadership positions require high power motivations, or that achievement motivation is irrelevant or unimportant. Nevertheless, for our purposes, the concept of the effective president as high in s Power is useful. The motivation for power will move him to attempt leadership in the first place; and, in its socialized form, it will be especially well suited to a role in which skilled performance depends on social exchange.

Let me now move from personality predispositions to a few key traits that may also be considered requisites for effective presidential leadership. The trait approach to analyzing leadership has long since been abandoned as inadequate. The assumption that all leaders have qualities that make them different from and superior to their followers, and that these qualities are more or less the same in all leaders, has given way to the understanding that what makes a good leader depends on the circumstance. A trait that serves well in one situation, or role, may serve much less well in another.

Although we have moved forward in our understanding of leadership, leadership theorists have had an unfortunate tendency to throw out the baby with the bathwater. To look at the trait studies more carefully is to see that although trait cannot by itself be a sufficient explanation, some traits are important to leadership in most situations. In a recent review of the leadership research,[17] Robert House and Mary Baetz suggest that there are "certain properties of *all* leadership situations that are present to a significant degree and relatively invariant, and that there are likely to be somewhat specific traits required in most, if not all, leadership situations." The authors speculate that because leadership always takes place with respect to others, such social skills as speech fluency, and traits such as personal integrity, cooperativeness, and sociability "are thus prime candidates for the status of leadership traits." Further, since leadership most frequently takes place with respect to specific task objectives, such traits as initiative, energy, and task-relevant ability "are also hypothesized to be associated with leadership."

A 1977 survey of top federal officials would seem to corroborate House and Baetz's emphasis on sociability.[18] Asked about the qualities necessary for effective presidential performance, social and interpersonal skills were most frequently associated with presidential leadership. For example, fully 96 percent of the respondents rated the president's ability to relate to Congress as important. What stands out is the emphasis these bureaucrats also put on what I have labeled the "ability to maneuver from within the world of other people." The quality of the president's relations with members of the political elite was deemed a major determinant of effectiveness by a large majority of at least one group that ought to know.

One last trait deserves to be mentioned, in particular because it has not been mentioned anywhere else; I will dub it "Political intellect." Political intellect is important in at least two ways. First, the president must recognize the necessity for politicking on his own behalf. He must be free of the notion that to wheel and deal to attain political ends is to engage in dirty politics. The successful Chief Executive would likely agree with Henry Fairlie that "politics is the highest art of a civilized people." Moreover, the president must understand that politicking entails an active involvement in social exchange. He must understand that to lead in America is to trade in support.

Second, the president should have a coherent political vision, arising out of strong convictions about the way things ought to be. Only this kind of an intellectual and ideological imperative will motivate the president to lead toward particular political ends.

Having explored what qualities enable the president to employ tactics of political skill, and having discovered that some of these fall into the category of fundamental personality predispositions while others are labeled traits, it remains finally for us to consider whether the skillful use of political tactics is intuitive or learned through apprenticeship and experience.

The answer seems to be both. Personality predispositions are, of course, the core of what one is. It is difficult if not impossible to overcome, by learning, a strong tendency to introversion or a low motivation for power. Similarly, it is difficult to instill, or acquire, during adulthood, certain deeply rooted traits such as high energy. Therefore, it is fair to say that to the extent that the skillful use of political tactics depends on personality predispositions such as extraversion and high power motivation, and on traits as central as, for example, honesty and level of energy and task-relevant talent, political skill is intuitive or inborn. But to the extent that it also invokes traits and behaviors that are more superficial, political skill can be acquired. School can teach technical skills such as speech fluency; life experience instructs on the advantages of interpersonal behaviors such as compromise and cooperation; and professional experiences supply the information and expertise particularly appropriate to advanced leadership roles. In sum, the president who is highly skilled politically is almost certainly the product of both nature and nurture. The would-be president should ideally be a born political operator, and then add further to his or her resources through personal political learning.

5

Presidential Politicking

> Washington is really, when you come right down to it, a city of cocker spaniels. It's a city of people who are more interested in being petted and admired, than in rendering the exercise of power.
>
> *Elliot Richardson*

Because my interest is in directive presidential leadership, I began this book with a discussion of the antiauthority character of the American political culture. Given this character, and the multilateral conflicts and competing institutions of our politics, the president, to be effective in noncrisis situations, must engage skillfully in transactional leadership.

James MacGregor Burns writes that transactional leadership occurs

> when one person takes the initiative in making contact with others for the purpose of an exchange of valued things. . . . Each party to the bargain is conscious of the power resources and attitudes of the other person. Each person recognizes the other as a person. Their purposes are related, at least to the extent that the purposes stand within the bargaining process. . . . But beyond this the relationship does not go. . . .[1]

Although I am in accord with Burns's description of transactional leadership, I believe it is inaccurate to say that the relationship does not endure beyond the actual exchange. For if leader and followers interact over a period of time, the leader's continuing attempts to influence and the followers' responses inevitably evolve into an ongoing relationship; one can quite properly conceive of a leader–follower bond that endures at least so long as the leader tries repeatedly to exert influence. Memory plays a supportive role: If leader and followers remain the same, each successive act of attempted transactional leadership will occur in the context of what has previously transpired.

In order to gain support (followership), the leader must attend to two key factors: *system progress* and *equity*. The first deals with setting goals that may, even if only in a broad sense, be seen to be shared; the second pertains to the followers' sense of being treated fairly. Hollander writes that

44

"where they have a choice, followers require a sufficient feeling of being fairly rewarded" if they are to lend support.[2]

Once a president is in power, the extent to which he is able to exercise leadership in routine situations, on behalf of key policy goals, depends almost entirely on the quality of his interactions with influential members of the political elite. They constitute the followers who respond favorably to attempts at influence.

This is not by any means to discount the public. Because of the impact of the public on the elite, especially in terms of real or imagined electoral pressure, the ability of the president to tap into the themes, ideals, values, fantasies, imagery, symbols, myths, and legends that define the American national character is certainly of critical importance.[3] The greater the president's skill in exploiting the American psyche, and thereby enlisting public support, the greater his leverage with the political elite.

Nevertheless, public prestige is only one component of the political environment and one of several factors that have an impact on how the political elite responds to presidential initiatives. Thus, while the public is in a position to exert political pressure, it is not literally able to decide whether or not to accept the president's influence attempts on a given issue. The political elite, on the other hand, is.

This particular formulation is demonstrated in Figure 2, which portrays presidential leadership as relational and reciprocal, as a two-way influence process between the president and the political elite.

The exchanges that take place between the president and the political elite are, of course, located within the larger environment. The environment impinges on them in important ways, just as the exchanges, in turn, have an impact on it. But because the president sets the agenda, because he initiates the influence process to achieve certain goals, our own immediate interest is in the center and middle circles and what transpires between them.

The arrows in Figure 2 that lead from the president to the political elite represent influence attempts. You will recall that the president's methods may include (1) control over the gains and costs to followers, (2) persuasion, (3) affective control, and (4) control over followers' environment. These methods of influence are generic terms for the specifically *political* tactics that presidents can employ. These were described in Chapter 4 and include consultation, preemption of problems, advance notice, proper timing, use of the cabinet, personal appeals and access, bargaining, arm twisting, services, personal amenities, compromise, detachment, outside support, education, impression management, and ingratiation. In other words, each political tactic may be subsumed under the heading of one of the four methods of influence. Political tactics *are* methods of influence.

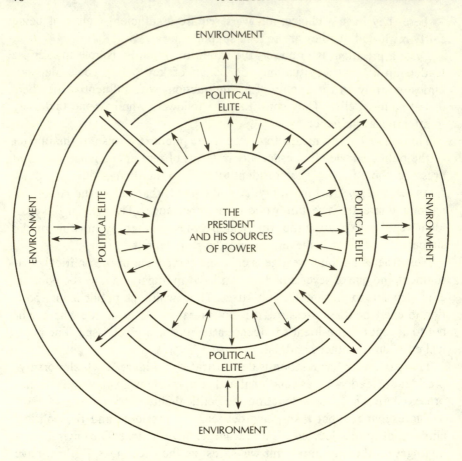

Figure 2. Presidential Leadership: A Transactional Analysis

The arrows leading from the political elite to the president represent the needs, wants, and demands that these actors must have satisfied if the president's influence attempts are to succeed. In particular, they represent what motivates the political elite to "follow the leader." Recall that these motivations include the desire to (1) receive something good or avoid something bad, (2) be similar to an admired person (the president), (3) abide by their values, (4) attain group goals, (5) gain internal satisfaction, and (6) have someone on whom to depend. Figure 2 shows clearly that if the president expects members of the political elite to support him in what he wants, he must supply them with something they want. His ability to do that depends on how skillfully he taps his sources of power, which are depicted in Figure 2 as an integral part of him.

It should be stressed that *all* presidents have similarly large reserves of power sources at their disposal. *Instrumental* sources of power remain fairly constant over time. These are tied to the presidential office, or role, and role changes are typically evolutionary rather than dramatic. *Internalized-authoritative* sources of power vary somewhat more. To the degree that they are allied with the legitimate, or constitutional, authority of the presidential office, they remain the same. But they are also tied to the president's personal ability to demonstrate attributes relevant to the presidential role. Therefore, this source of power varies somewhat according to the president's persona. *Libidinal* sources of power are the most susceptible to change, for they are tied much less to the office than to the man and, quite simply, some presidents have more of this particular source of power than others. For example, simple observation revealed that John Kennedy had more libidinal power—was more ingratiating—than Richard Nixon. Still, even here one could argue that in our political culture the presidency is so exalted a role, so special, that anyone who fills it is endowed with a certain glamour or appeal, especially early on in his administration. Thus, even with regard to libidinal sources of power, there is probably a smaller difference among presidents than one might at first think.

Differences in the objective environment obviously add or subtract from a president's sources of power. For example, a large electoral victory or strong party support in Congress certainly enhance all three sources of power. Situations of high empowerment consequently make political leadership easier. But the question that really interests us is why, given reasonably stable and in any case quite formidable power reserves, do some presidents manage to exert so much more influence than others? I am proposing that these differences can be explained by differences in the level of political skill and will. The *use* a president makes of such sources of power as he has determines his political success. It is one thing to *have* sources of power; it is quite another to have what it takes to draw on them.

If the key to understanding presidential leadership in noncrisis situations is to study presidential interactions with members of the political elite, we need to identify who this elite actually is. Who are these potential "followers" of the president?

Manifestly, they are those whom Neustadt calls "Washingtonians"—members of Congress and of the president's administration, governors, top military personnel, leading politicians in both parties, representatives of private organizations and the news media, foreign diplomats, and the like.[4]

However, Neustadt's definition (as well as his nomenclature) of who constitutes the political elite is somewhat misleading.[5] Not all presidential activity takes place in relation to Washington institutions or personalities and in order to include everyone who constitutes the political elite, we must cast the net further than the shores of the Potomac.[6] Thus, the case studies

in Part II of this book will contain more references to presidential encounters or the lack thereof with Washingtonians than with anyone else, simply
because they occupy most of the president's time. But these case studies
will also include information about members of the political elite from outside Washington, for example, the business community, unions, minority
organizations. Indeed, such interactions are one of the few ways presidents
have of breaking out of their insularity and isolation—if, indeed, that is
what they want to do.

For the purposes of this book, then, followers of the president will be
defined as domestic actors, from within and beyond Washington, from the
public and private sectors, who occupy positions that make it possible for
them to have some direct contact with the president. The following is a
sample of relevant members of the political elite: cabinet members and
White House staff; party leaders; leaders of the House and Senate as well
as members of key congressional committees; leading media correspondents
and columists; labor, business, minority, and interest group leaders; and the
more prominent state and local officials.

The task will be to see how each of the six most recent presidents inter-
acted with these political actors with regard to one key policy goal of that
administration. The quantity and quality of these interactions will be considered indicators of whether the president in question may reasonably be
termed a skilled politician.

"If we define leadership as influence, in turn defined as causality, what
mode of analysis can we use"[7] The task of *proving* that leadership has taken
place, of establishing that "a leader had 'decisive influence' or that a leader's work would not have been done by others" is, as Andrew McFarland
suggests, a formidable one.

> First, we must establish the limits of a person's action in terms of general
> social forces. . . . Second, we "think away" the existence of the particular
> leader, and consider what might have happened if the leader had not
> lived. Third, we compare the more probable "might-have-beens" with
> the actuality in order to assess the magnitude and significance of the
> influence (causality) the leader has exercised on human events.[8]

If the task sounds daunting in the abstract, it is no less so in the particular. With regard to the American presidency, the methodological problems of proving influence loom large: How do we measure the amount of
initial resistance? How can we determine the impact of a president's
attempts to influence, while still controlling for alternative explanations of
the same effects? How do we explain those times a president gets his way
without engaging in any overt influence attempts at all?

The methodological difficulties are compounded because we cannot perform experiments, and we cannot easily compare different presidents under

similar circumstances. (There are not very many presidents, and the circumstances are never exactly the same.) In short, quantitative analyses in this area are well nigh impossible. Moreover, even if the process outlined by McFarland would enable us to establish that the president had decisive influence, it would do so with regard to only one issue at a time. McFarland's method for determining influence requires that each episode must be considered *sui generis.*

The difficulties of measuring presidential influence over even one faction of the political elite—Congress—have been attested to many times and neither subjective nor objective measures have proven very satisfactory. Stephen Wayne writes that the authors of two objective studies "both found very little presidential influence on congressional voting decisions, but neither was willing to conclude that presidents and their staffs could not change votes or affect outcomes. Both, in fact, suggested they could."[9] Wayne finally concludes that "unless and until a closer tie can be established between specific liason activity and congressional voting behavior . . . any administration's operation in particular will remain the subject of considerable speculation and controversy."[10]

An interesting attempt to assess presidential influence in Congress was made recently by George C. Edwards III in his book *Presidential Influence in Congress.* Edwards employs quantitative techniques with the predictable result that his study has certain strengths as well as certain weaknesses. The conclusion, in any case, is unambiguous: Presidential "legislative skills" do "not appear to be a predominant factor in determining presidential support in Congress on most roll call votes and therefore, despite commonly held assumptions, they are not a prominent source of influence."[11]

This is not the place for an extended critique of Edwards's book, but I would argue strongly that the quantitative indicators Edwards uses preclude him from unearthing the rich detail that is often the real story of White House–Congressional interactions.[12] To do what really needs to be done would require that for each president we would have to examine each interaction with each of the 535 legislators. Because this is an impossible task, it is inevitable that our theories will be richer than our evidence.

Indeed, at the end of his book, Edwards himself concedes the point. In order to evaluate the importance of the president's legislative skills,

> we would ideally measure the extent to which presidents exercised these skills on each member of a Congress or on the same members over several Congresses. After controlling for other sources of influence, we would determine whether members of Congress on whom presidential legislative skills were employed provided more support than other members or whether members' support over time fluctuated with the degree to which the president exercised his skills on them.

Unfortunately, we do not have sufficient data on individuals. . . .[13]

What Edwards has given us, then, is some *aggregate* data* and a sugges-tive conclusion. However, it is certainly *not* a full measure of "presidential influence in Congress."[14] Congress is not, essentially, an institution, orga-nization, or cluster of small groups. It is instead a collection of individuals, each with a qualitatively different response to presidential influence attempts or the lack thereof. Only the accumulation of these individual experiences would tell the tale accurately. That data alone would enable us to use the structural and behavioral approaches that McFarland correctly indicates are necessary to "the analysis of leadership, defined as influence."

I have said that the task of measuring presidential influence precisely is almost impossible. But if we take just one domestic policy proposal on which a president has demonstrably staked his reputation for leadership, and if we trace what he did to garner support for this particular proposal, we should be able to form a judgment about the political skills the president demonstrated on at least this issue. To help us understand the components and mechanics of presidential leadership, it may be more revealing to study the president's attempts at influence on a few issues of major importance to him than to measure his success in the aggregate. It is fair to say about most administrations that, apart from major foreign or domestic crises, only a relatively few measures involve the president's personal leadership to a significant degree. There are relatively few political battles dear to each president; it is, therefore, those few that provide a reasonable test of that president's political skills.

In making this point, I might add that I am again taking issue with Edwards, who states that the president does not have a "comprehensive set of priorities" and that, even if he did, we would have no way of knowing them. On the basis of this assumption, Edwards claims that it is reasonable to measure presidential support in the aggregate.

My counterargument is really very simple. I am saying that when the president first takes office, he has relatively few specific policy goals that he (1) feels strongly about, (2) stakes his reputation on by publicly announcing his commitment, and (3) actively tries to gain support for and gain it soon. Thus, even if the president does not have a "comprehensive set of priorities," he ordinarily has, on assuming office, some goals he considers especially important, and ones for which he is willing to take personal risks to have his way. His political activity regarding these goals constitutes a fair test of his political skills.

With this in mind, the following six chapters trace the efforts of John Kennedy, Lyndon Johnson, Richard Nixon, Gerald Ford, Jimmy Carter,

*Edwards uses the *Congressional Quarterly's* Presidential Support Scores.

and Ronald Reagan to push through one policy goal that was of major importance to them. The case studies are of domestic policy proposals, because the domestic universe is more finite—and thus contains fewer variables—than the global one. And the studies are confined to an initiative undertaken during the first year of the president's term because (1) this allows for better comparison (neither John Kennedy nor Gerald Ford served even three years in the White House); (2) the national electorate has recently identified the president's political agenda as generally its own; and (3) the first year, the honeymoon period, is typically the most propitious time for innovative presidential leadership—especially major policy initiations.[15] It has been observed that toward the end of their first year in office presidents start to turn inward, "some sooner than others, the rate depending on personality factors and the ratio of successes to failures." Indeed, an adviser from the Nixon White House went so far as to assert that "Everything depends on what you do in program formulation during the first six or seven months. . . . The White House staff is not hated by the cabinet; there is a period of friendship and cooperation and excitement. . . . You only have a year at most for new initiatives, a time when you can establish some programs as your own, in contrast to what has gone on before."[16]

The six case studies will be John Kennedy and Federal Aid to Education; Lyndon Johnson and the War on Poverty, Richard Nixon and the Family Assistance Plan; Gerald Ford and the Tax Cut; Jimmy Carter and the Energy Package; and Ronald Reagan and the Budget Cuts. These particular cases were selected because they meet the following three criteria: At some point during the president's first year in office they were declared by him to be his most important domestic policy goal; they constituted an issue on which he demonstrably staked his reputation; and they were the beneficiaries of the president's time and attention in the effort to secure early follower support.[17]

We will be looking to compare how *actively* and *skillfully* the six most recent presidents attempted to exert influence on behalf of what they claimed was most important. In terms of Figure 2, we will be placing the executives at the center of the investigation and uncovering, insofar as possible, the frequency and nature of the arrows leading to the political elite with regard to a particular issue. Thus, the interest is in how often the president tried to exert influence; what methods and tactics of influence he used; what movtivated the political elite to accept, or not to accept, the influence attempts; and what sources of power seemed to be the most effective under which circumstances.

Before turning to the case studies, let me state clearly what this analysis will *not* do.

It will offer no proof that influence was decisive in any particular situation, or vis-à-vis any particular member or faction of the political elite. It will show only that influence is an important element in the political process, and that it appears to determine political outcomes some of the time.

This book makes no promise of providing a complete data base, nor of being the "whole story." The case studies are not comprehensive analyses of the objective political situation, nor do they do more than illuminate presidential effectiveness on one particular issue for a limited period. Hence, the focus is on the president's performance early in his administration with regard to only one of several important policy goals; the general context is obscured in favor of the specifics of a single case; followers inevitably receive less attention than the president; there is relatively little discussion of the substance of policy; and the facts are too few to suggest more than preliminary confirmation or disconfirmation of the suggestion that successful directive leadership depends above all on skilled politicking. These case studies are no more than portraits, or even sketches. Like portraits, they are impressions, not literal renderings of the Truth about the subject.

Finally, let me repeat one last time that the book employs the terms influence, leadership, and political skills in a functional sense only. There is no implication that the politically skilled president will use his greater influence to lead us to a better place, merely that he will be better at getting us to go where he wants us to go. There has been some confusion among political scientists studying the presidency about what constitutes "good." Of the criticisms leveled at Richard Neustadt, none have been as serious and enduring as the charge that his book is too preoccupied with power and too little concerned with the question of the end to which that power is used. As Thomas Cronin put it: "Such extraordinary emphasis on means without any clear discussion of ends left the impression that the art of leadership is the art of manipulation."[18]

I wish to leave no such impression. Although I imply no equation between political skill and moral superiority,[19] neither do I believe that the exercise of power is an end in itself. It does matter whether leadership skills are used for good or bad purposes. Indeed, I fully agree that consideration of the moral dimension is imperative if one attempts an examination of leadership with all its possible ramifications.

But this book has the more modest ambition of drawing portraits of presidents as they looked in their politician's garb, at particular moments. The proposition to be examined is that, all things being equal, the president who is motivated and equipped to be politically skilled will prove to be a more effective leader in the American political culture than the one to whom politicking is irrelevant or even distasteful.

II

The Practice of Presidential Leadership

6

John Kennedy and Federal Aid to Education

> Our classrooms contain 2,000,000 more children than they can properly have room for, taught by 90,000 teachers not properly qualified to teach. One-third of our most promising high school graduates are financially unable to continue the development of their talents.
>
> *President Kennedy,*
> *State of the Union message*
> *to Congress, January 30, 1961*

Tom Wicker once observed that during the 1960 campaign John Kennedy stood for nothing if not for federal aid to public schools.[1] And Theodore Sorensen, Kennedy's closest associate other than brother Bobby, called education the subject that "mattered most" to John Kennedy: "Throughout his campaign and through his Presidency, he devoted more time and talks to this single topic than to any other domestic issue."[2] Sorensen wrote that as both senator and president Kennedy addressed countless audiences on the subject, imploring them "to give to the world in which you were reared and educated the broadest possible benefits of that education."[3]

Indeed, as Congressman Frank Thompson, a liberal Democrat from New Jersey who was close to Kennedy, recalled later, as soon as the election was won, John Kennedy turned to education.

> I should mention that one of the major subjects of our Palm Beach dis-cussions* was the Education Bill. . . . I had frequent contact with respect to the education legislation—mostly telephone contact. I saw the President personally relatively few times after he took office. But I talked with him a great deal by phone about the education legislation. He was vitally interested in it. He designated it as the No. 1 priority bill in the Congress. . . .[4]

Immediately after his victory, in keeping with his long articulated com-mitment to federal aid to public schools, Kennedy appointed a task force

*Kennedy spent a good part of the transition period at his family's Palm Beach estate.

on education with Frederick Hovde, president of Purdue University, as chairman. Although the six-member commission contained a divergence of views, it did not go so far as to include spokespersons for the conservative, Southern Democratic, Catholic church, or NAACP positions.[5] It was an important omission, but there is no doubt that by excluding some possible dissidents, the task force's job was simplified. In short order, Hovde's group was able to recommend three major legislative proposals: (1) federal support for the public school system; (2) federal suport for housing and academic facilities for colleges and universities; and (3) federal support to strengthen the National Defense Education Act.

Efforts had been made to get a general aid to education bill through the Congress for almost a hundred years. Each time the arguments for and against had been more or less the same; and each time the players lined up similarly to the way they had before. In particular, the powerfully situated Catholic church could generally be counted on to oppose any aid to education measure that omitted grants to parochial schools, while the public school teaching establishment—and indeed anyone who had anything at all to do with the public school system—was strongly in favor of any bill that would bestow more federal dollars on them.

But if the record on school aid measures was poor, John Kennedy had good reason to think the time might be right for such a three-tiered approach as the one Hovde had proposed. First, for months now Kennedy had made clear that he was staking his professional reputation on such a bill. Second, he entered the White House determined "to get the country moving again," and during those early days there was a profound sense of optimism that the job would get done, at least in those areas deemed most important. Third, there was, after all, nothing so new or startling about Kennedy's education bill; it resembled other similar postwar efforts. Fourth, Kennedy's school bill was one part of a five-part domestic program that he had labeled "top poriority,"[6] and the early indications for at least Senate passage of his most important legislative proposals were considered generally "good."[7] Fifth, a poll by the American Institute for Public Opinion showed that 73 percent of all voters favored some form of "general federal aid to schools." Sixth, the Soviet Union's recent Sputnik triumph had triggered national anxiety about a possible "education gap"—an anxiety that seemed to generate even more public support for an increased federal commitment to schools. And finally, it was encouraging that a school aid bill had passed both Houses of Congress in 1960, and failed only to get a House–Senate conference to resolve the differences.[8]

Yet despite the auspicious signs, other factors boded much less well. Kennedy's margin of victory was narrow. He could scarcely claim a ringing mandate for leadership with a hairline plurality of only 118,000 votes.

Moreover, although the Democrats had a majority in both the House and Senate, the mood in Congress was rather conservative. In fact, several key Democrats were openly hostile to the president's quite liberal program. Finally, even though an education bill had almost passed the year before any new school legislation would inevitably revive old and deeply entrenched passions:

> Whether federal aid should go to segregated schools, to Catholic and other religious schools; whether wealthy states should contribute to the schools of the poorer; whether, if they did, the poorer or the most populous states should have the most aid per child; whether the federal government would follow its investment in education by seeking "control" of local school systems; whether it was not the states' "right" to finance and administer schools; whether the nation could afford vast outlays for this purpose when the budget was out of balance and the national debt rising.[9]

This array of unresolved issues notwithstanding, in 1961 the most ominous sign was the immediate and strongly negative reaction of the Catholic church to the idea of an aid program that did not include grants to parochial schools. Even before Kennedy was inaugurated, the Catholic hierarchy was criticizing the task force's recommendations. In a major address delivered just three days before Kennedy was sworn in as president, Cardinal Spellman of New York served notice: "I cannot believe that Congress would accept the proposals of the task force and use economic compulsion to force parents to relinquish their rights to have religion taught to their children. . . ."[10]

However, the only sign that the White House took Spellman's early warning at all seriously is a memo from Theodore Sorensen to Lee White, Assistant Special Counsel to the President. It is dated January 25.

> Please prepare a memorandum for the President, one page in length, relating to Cardinal Spellman's attack on the school program. Memorandum should compare the Kennedy proposals (check what Spellman said about them); and indicate what aid is going to parochial schools and colleges now constitutionally so as to indicate there is no discrimination.[11]

Whatever information White's memorandum finally included, it obviously did not deter the president. On February 10, reports were leaked to the national press that Kennedy would soon ask Congress to authorize a five-year aid to education program calling for about $900,000,000 in annual grants to states for public schools. *The New York Times* opined that although the proposal faced considerable opposition, mainly from the conservative wings of both parties, it was nevertheless "given a fair chance of favorable action, perhaps in modified form."[12]

On February 20, 1961, only one month to the day after his inauguration, President Kennedy proposed a total package of $5,625,000,000 in federal aid to education from elementary school through college. Key features of the bill were (1) grants to the states for public elementary and secondary schools (to be used to construct school buildings, pay teachers' salaries, or both, at the states' discretion); (2) grants for college scholarships to be awarded on the basis of academic ability and financial need; (3) loans for a new program to aid construction of college academic facilities such as classrooms, laboratories, and libraries; and (4) expansion of an existing program to provide loans to colleges to help build residential housing for students and faculty. Kennedy's message to Congress referred to the proposed program as "modest ... with ambitious goals. ... The sums involved are relatively small when we think in terms of more than 36,000,000 public school children."[13]

But because the bill contained no provisions for parochial schools, the Most Rev. Joseph F. Flannelly, Auxiliary Bishop of the Roman Catholic Archdiocese of New York and Administrator of St. Patrick's Cathedral, responded by urging his flock to register their opposition to Kennedy's proposal, both to their Congressmen and to the president directly.[14]

Between the time of the press leak on February 10, and the formal proposal for aid to education ten days later, it had become apparent that any bill of this nature would face rough weather ahead. Indeed, *The New York Times,* which had said on February 11 that the bill was "given a fair chance of favorable action," prophesied a mere ten days later that although early hearings were scheduled in both the House and Senate, "a long, hard fight was in prospect. The program obviously faced powerful opposition."

In response to the early warning signs, the president made some concessions even before the bill was formally submitted. He asked for far less money than the task force had recommended; and he affirmed that his administration was opposed to withholding funds from segregated schools. This second concession was to appease Southern Democrats who would have fought as a block any bill containing such a restriction.

However, Kennedy had not yielded on the key issues. He had not compromised on federal aid for teacher salaries despite the opposition to such support by House Speaker Sam Rayburn, and he had not changed his position on the most critical issue of all: aid to private schools. When the bill went to Congress, it contained nothing that would even begin to mollify Catholic opposition to any education bill that did not have something in it for parochial schools. As a result, only five days after the bill had been formally submitted, the education editor of *The New York Times* could already observe that "open season" had been declared on President Kennedy's aid to education message.[15]

In his original message on education, Kennedy defended his opposition to aid to private schools by citing "the clear prohibition of the Constitution" against aid to all nonpublic schools. He repeated the point at a news conference in early March. Not even a small olive branch was offered the proponents of aid to parochial schools.

Q. Sir, in view of the criticism that has occurred, could you elaborate on why you have not recommended federal aid to private and parochial elementary and secondary schools?

A. Well, the Constitution clearly prohibits aid to parochial schools. I don't think there's any doubt of that. . . .

Aid to the school is—there isn't any room for debate on that subject. It is prohibited by the Constitution, and the Supreme Court has made that very clear.* And therefore, there would be no possibility of our recommending it.[17]

There were, of course, some religious groups that applauded Kennedy's position. A spokesperson for Protestants and Other Americans United for Separation of Church and State stated: "We congratulate the President for declaring that direct federal aid to church schools at the elementary and secondary levels is unconstitutional."[18] Several Jewish groups also came out in support of the president. But the Catholic church dug in its heels.

Tom Wicker relates that a chance remark by John McCormack, then Democratic Majority Leader in the House, provided the first hint of the storm that was about to break over the Kennedy school bill. McCormack, a Boston Irish Catholic who was close to the church hierarchy but—despite similarities in their backgrounds—no special ally of the president, confided to Frank Thompson that several church leaders were meeting in Washington. Thompson was not only a close friend of Kennedy's, he had also been selected by him to introduce the bill in the House. Wicker writes that it was "in that capacity that Thompson—an outspoken, anti-clerical Catholic, long aware of McCormack's high church connections and not particularly charmed by them—pricked up his ears at the white-haired Bostonian's remarks about a meeting of Catholic leaders."[19] Suspicious, Thompson contacted reporter John D. Morris of *The New York Times* who promptly went to work on the story.

On March 1—the same day as President Kennedy's above-mentioned press conference—Morris filed his report: "The highest United States prelates of the Roman Catholic Church met here today to plan what is expected to be a vigorous fight against President Kennedy's school-aid program."[20]

*The president referred here to *Everson v. Board of Education,* 330 U. S. 1 (1947) in which the Supreme Court ruled it constitutional to use tax funds for transportation of children to and from all nonprofit schools. The court nevertheless emphasized that the constitutionality of such payment rests on the fact that its purpose is public safety, not private education.[16]

The administrative board of the National Catholic Welfare Conference that had assembled on that first day of March consisted of the five United States cardinals and ten bishops and archbishops who headed departments of the Conference. Their intention was clear: to fight any education bill that did not include meeting the educational expenses of Catholics with children in parochial schools. To this end the cardinals, bishops, and archbishops began by drawing up a Catholic position paper that would be aired in church publications, sermons, speeches, and testimony at congressional hearings.

Following the meeting, Archbishop Karl J. Alter, a participant in the proceedings and chairman of the administrative board, released the following statement:

1. The question of whether or not there ought to be Federal aid is a judgment to be based on objective economic facts. . . .
2. In the event that there is Federal aid to education we are deeply convinced that in justice Catholic school children should be given the right to participate. . . .
[3.] In the event that a federal aid program is enacted which excludes children in private schools these children will be victims of discrimatory legislation. There will be no alternative but to oppose such discrimination.[21]

The reaction to the Church hierarchy's statement was mixed. Some expressed shock and dismay that the Catholic church would try to kill the entire school-aid bill unless its demands were met,[22] while others took a more balanced view. James Reston, writing for *The New York Times,* saw the church's strong stand as likely "to hurt both religion and education." He went on to add, however, that by saying "there isn't any room for debate on the subject," President Kennedy "merely envenoms the debate that is now obviously in progress."[23]

On March 8, President Kennedy held another news conference (before the Bay of Pigs invasion, which occurred in April 1961, he met the press almost weekly) and the question of aid to parochial schools occupied almost one-third of the total time. Kennedy repeated his contention that grants to private schools would be unconstitutional, adding that he thought the same rule applied also to "across-the-board" loans. But this time Kennedy distinguished between the different kinds of federal aid: "If the Congress, and Congressmen, wish to address themselves to the problem of loans, which is a separate matter . . . then I am hopeful it would be considered as a separate matter. . . . But I am hopeful that while that consideration is being given, that we will move ahead with the grant program. . . . I definitely believe that we should not tie the two together."[24]

The decision to separate the grant and loan provisions was something of a retreat from the president's earlier position that all forms of aid to private schools were unconstitutional, and that he would, in any case, veto any proposal that distinguished between the two.[25] His step back was almost certainly motivated by the combination of increasing pressure from the Catholic church, and some warning signs from Congress.[26] One of Kennedy's most important allies in the upcoming battle, Rayburn, was continuing to send strong signals that he preferred a school construction bill—that is, one that omitted federal aid for teacher's salaries. There was, moreover, good reason to believe that the church would be relatively uninterested in opposing such a bill. The church was primarily concerned with paying its teachers more money; thus, a simple school construction bill was likely to elicit less church hostility.

Yet, the importance of Kennedy's retreat should not be overstated. The president's commitment to his original bill was reiterated, and his decision to spend so much of his March 8 news conference on aid to schools gave credence to the fact that it remained a priority.

President Kennedy's aid to education bill was routinely referred to the House Committee on Education and Labor, and the Senate Committee on Labor and Public Welfare. On March 8, Senate hearings on Kennedy's proposal opened with Senator Wayne Morse of Oregon presiding, and with most of the education subcommittee members present.* Since only one member of the nine person subcommittee was generally opposed to a substantial school aid program (Senator Barry Goldwater), it seemed likely that the subcommittee would eventually support the administration's recommendations by a large majority. Kennedy tried to ensure Morse's good will by sending him the following personal letter, dated February 21.

> Dear Wayne:
>
> Thank you for introducing the Education Bill in the Senate yesterday. I read with great interest the typically informative and scholarly remarks you addressed to the Senate at the time.
>
> I feel confident that with your leadership in committee and on the floor of the Senate, we will, at long last, be successful in taking the first, but perhaps most important, step towards solution of a grave national problem.
>
> With warm personal regards.
>
> Cordially,
> (signed) John Kennedy[27]

The likelihood of vigorous support from the Senate subcommittee was strong in part at least because of the political style of its chairman. Price

*The education subcommittee consisted of six Democrats and three Republicans.

writes that Morse perceived his role as "quasi-judicial" and regarded himself as

> counsel to the President in regard to the school-aid bill. He was also very conscious of his role as spokesman for the Administration; he even spoke of himself as being "a private" in the ranks of the president's supporters.[28]

It was consequently ironic that during these particular hearings it became unmistakably clear that the president's education bill was arousing unusually fierce opposition.

Morse saw the handwriting on the wall. Even before church leaders brought their resistance to the school aid bill before Congress, he advised them to take the high road, to "say, in effect, to the American people: 'We are willing to agree that we should start with the public school system and, therefore, we are going to urge the passage of this public school law without any amendments.'"[29] But Morse's advice went unheeded. At just the moment that he was offering it, the church was marshaling its forces.

On March 13, five days after the opening of the Senate hearings, Cardinal Spellman released another statement that reiterated his determined opposition to any program of federal aid to education that excluded private and parochial schools on the elementary and secondary levels: "If the Congress decides there should be federal aid, then certainly any legislation should conform to principles of social justice, equal treatment and non-discrimination."[30] One day later, in an appearance before Morse's subcommittee, Monsignor Frederick Hochwalt, director of the Department of Education of the National Catholic Welfare Conference, stated the official church position even more forcefully: "It is unthinkable that this great nation would embark for the first time on a massive program of Federal encouragement to education by leaving out of consideration that dedicated group of parents and educators who have contributed so much to the welfare of this nation."[31]

The church's appearance before the Congress signaled the beginning of an all-out fight. Anyone who had a special interest in education felt called on to take a position. Testimony was heard from officials of the National Education Association (a supposedly powerful interest group), the executive secretary of the Council of Chief State School Officers, the Grand Master of the Masonic Lodge for Puerto Rico, the Baptist Joint Committee on Public Affairs, and the American Jewish Congress. C. Stanley Lowell, an official of Protestants and Other Americans United for Separation of Church and State, stated:

> I should like to call attention to the end result of a program of grants to church schools or loans to church schools. Once the Congress ...

embarks upon such a course, it will find that turning back is extremely difficult.[32]

Dr. Gerald Knoff, of the Division of Christian Education of the National Council of Churches, commented:

> I believe that the general board of the National Council of Churches would observe that any substantial aid to non-public elementary and secondary schools would pose serious dangers to our laws and institutions including our traditional separation of church and state.[33]

And Robert Van Deusen, representing the National Lutheran Council, noted:

> We fear that the availability of low-interest Government loans would encourage the expansion of existing parochial schools systems and the formation of parallel systems by other groups with a consequent erosion of the public school system. . . .[34]

The issue caused antagonisms at every level. When Charles Silver, president of the New York City Board of Education, ventured that the federal government should support both public and private schools, he was chided by the Public Education Association for failing to support "the President of the United States on his proposal for federal aid to public education."[35]

As the storm around the aid to education bill was gathering force, President Kennedy was moved to take some further action. Both he and members of his staff made several efforts both to quiet voices rising in anger, and to stimulate a more active and vociferous support. While Secretary of Health, Education and Welfare Abraham Ribicoff was sent to be the first witness at the Senate hearings—Morse took the opportunity to request "a brief . . . setting forth the position of the administration on the constitutional questions and other legal questions"[36]—the president and his staff were busy sending off letters to solidify support already in place. President Kennedy wrote to thank the National Congress of Parents and Teachers for their support. Theodore Sorensen (Special Counsel to the President) wrote to the Bloomsburg (Pennsylvania) Teachers Association to thank them for theirs. Kenneth O'Donnell (Special Assistant to the President) did the same for the Baptist Joint Committee on Public Affairs, and Ralph Dungan (another Special Assistant to the President) wrote to the National Lutheran Council and to the American Federation of Teachers. Courtesy letters signed by a variety of presidential assistants were also sent out to some "average Americans," while wires in support of the president's message to Congress streamed in from the likes of the Ojai Valley Teachers Association, the Boulder City Classroom Teachers Association, and the Oklahoma Association of School Administrators.[37]

White House mail on the education bill generally went to three catogories of people, two of them representing powerful special interest groups: members of the clergy, teachers or school administrators, and citizens. O'Donnell wrote to Rabbi Marc Tanenbaum of The American Jewish Committee: "Thank you for your letter of April sixth, enclosing the Statement of the American Jewish Committee on Federal Aid to Education. I appreciate your making this available to me—it was thoughtful of you to write." And he wrote the Reverend H. F. Dearing of the First Baptist Church at Kerrvill, Texas: "The President has asked me to write and thank you for your letter of February tenth. He is indeed grateful for your prayers and those of the members of your staff. He appreciates, also, having your commendation of his expressed views on federal aid to public schools."[38] To Dr. Henry P. Van Dusen, President of the Union Theological Seminary, Dungan wrote: "The President has asked me to respond to your letter of recent date calling to his attention the statement which you and your distinguished colleagues have made on the question of federal aid to education. The president greatly appreciates your active support of his position."[39] A few letters went out to Catholics; none, however, so far as I have determined, contained any effort to change a negative attitude toward Kennedy's bill. O'Donnell wrote a warm reply to the Reverend Mark Keohane of St. Bartholomew's Parish in Needham, Massachusetts, after Rev. Keohane separated himself on the school aid issue from the hierarchy of his own Church. "Cardinals Spellman and McIntyre and other Bishops do not bespeak all of us," Keohane had written. "They can only voice their personal opinions."[40] And Kennedy himself wrote to the Reverend John Wright, President General of the National Catholic Education Association. The president's letter carefully avoided explicit reference to the controversy.

> April 3, 1961
>
> Your Excellency:
>
> I was pleased to note the theme of the 58th annual meeting of the National Catholic Educational Association for it highlights the extremely important contribution which private education conducted under religious auspices can make to the nation. You who are in the field of education, I know, are especially aware of the challenges which this nation and indeed the whole of western civilization faces in the next decade. I dare say that never in the more than half century of most productive effort have the members of your association been faced with a more important task of transmitting and applying sound values to modern problems.
>
> Catholic education at every level has served the nation well. I am confident that the dedicated men and women who have served so selflessly

in the past will continue to serve their nation and their Church.

Sincerely,
(signed) John Kennedy[41]

Educators were, on the whole, naturally supportive of the president's aid to education measure. As a consequence, perhaps, the White House paid them only modest attention. Dungan wrote Mr. Ewald Turner, President-elect of the National Education Association, that "The President greatly appreciates the support of . . . the Association in this matter."[42] And he wrote Mr. J. C. Wright of the American Association of School Administrators: "It is reassuring to have you inform us of your belief that a large majority of the American public favors a federal support program for the public schools to alleviate some of the educational deficiencies that exist. The influence which persons in your position bring to bear upon this vital issue will play a large role in helping to achieve the goal of strengthening the American public schools."[43] It was left to Kennedy himself to address Nathan Pusey, the president of his alma mater, Harvard University.

February 27, 1961

Dear Mr. President:

I want to send you a note of thanks for the very persuasive statement you made on behalf of the education program which I recently sent to Congress.

I recognize only too well the reluctance you have to enter public controversies, and I am therefore all the more grateful for the firm and effective support which you have given to the educational legislation now before the Congress. I hope that we can at long last meet with success in this important effort.

With all best wishes.

Sincerely,
(signed) John F. Kennedy[44]

Then there were the exchanges between the White House and the American people. Mr. and Mrs. Raymond Couter of San Francisco wired Kennedy on his inauguration day as follows: "DEAR MR. PRESIDENT: YOUR SUBSIDIZING OF SCHOOLS IS FINE WITH US. WE ARE CATHOLICS AND BELIEVE THAT THESE CATHOLIC SCHOOLS ARE SELF-SUPPORTING. WE WISH YOU ALL THE LUCK IN THE WORLD." On February 3, Dungan wrote back: "Dear Mr. and Mrs. Couter: Thank you for your telegram to the President. It was thoughtful of you to wire and let him have your comments. With the President's gratitude for your good wishes. Sincerely yours."[45]

The president also did a modest amount of face-to-face politicking. On February 28, he met with several representatives from the American Education Association and the American Association of School Administrators. Ribicoff was also present; but the occasion lasted only twenty minutes (from 10 A.M. to 10:20). Every Tuesday morning Kennedy also had a breakfast meeting with legislative leaders. And on March 16, at 5:45 in the afternoon, he had a White House "Coffee Hour" that was attended by over fifty members of Congress.[46]

It was at his early press conferences, however, that John Kennedy made his most heartfelt plea for federal aid to education. Kennedy's performances at these media events were generally excellent—Schlesinger called him "the most skilled presidential practitioner in this medium since Roosevelt"[47]—and here he used the presidency as a "bully pulpit" to try to educate the American people to the virtues of school aid. He also suggested how they might behave during what was turning out to be an unexpectedly (at least to Kennedy) acrimonious debate.

From his press conference of March 15:

Q. Mr. President, your election in November was widely hailed as among other things a victory over religious prejudice. Do you think . . . that the seemingly inflexible stand on the part of some spokesmen for the Catholic hierarchy on the school legislation may provoke more religious prejudice?

A. I am hopeful that it will not. I stated that it is a fact that in recent years when education bills have been sent to the Congress that we have not had this public major encounter. I don't know why that was, but now we do have it. . . .

I am very hopeful that though there may be a difference of opinion on this matter of Federal aid to education, I am hopeful that when the smoke is cleared there will continue to be harmony among the various religious groups of the country. And I am going to do everything that I can to make sure that that harmony exists because it reaches far beyond the question of education and goes in a very difficult time in the life of our country to an important ingredient of our national strength. So that I am confident that the people who are involved outside the Government, and members of Congress and the Administration will attempt to conduct the discussion on this sensitive issue in such a way as to maintain the strength of the country and not divide it.[48]

Kennedy's appeal for both support and reasoned discussion—the latter was widely interpreted as a reminder to the hierarchy of his own church—had little visible impact on those who opposed school aid. But it did seem to hearten his supporters. Immediately after the mid-March press conference, nineteen prominent Protestant and Jewish clergyman and laymen issued a statement urging all groups to work on behalf of an aid to education bill limited to public schools.[49] And *The New York Times* published an editorial calling the president's school aid bill "the most important legislation before Congress—and the most important that is likely to be before Congress for a long time."[50]

Hearings in the General Education Subcommittee of the House Education and Labor Committee began on March 13. The proceedings there went considerably less smoothly than they did on the Senate side. First, Adam Clayton Powell of New York, chairman of the whole House committee, did not display Morse's "quasi-judicial"[51] attitude. The considerably more flamboyant Powell—Price labels him "the controversial Harlem minister-politician"—had just reorganized the subcommittee system. Instead of just one subcommittee to handle education legislation, Powell established three. As Price notes, the "multiplication of subcommittees created some institutional rivalry and complicated the process of setting priorities among the various education proposals."[52] Thus, the General Education Subcommittee, which had direct responsibility for reporting on Kennedy's school aid bill, was operating in a climate of conflict and interpersonal contentiousness rather than—as in the Senate subcommittee—one of compromise and cooperation.[53]

Because Kennedy's bill was similar to the one the Senate had passed (51–34) the year before, because Senate Democrats had lost only two of their sixty-six member majority in the 1960 election, and because the Senate had a reputation for being rather favorably inclined to aid for education,[54] the chances for Senate passage of this bill were generally considered quite good. In contrast, the previous year's House bill was a narrower and less costly version of what Kennedy was proposing in 1961; this time there were twenty fewer House Democrats; and the House was considered to be notably less favorably disposed toward school aid than the Senate. There was every reason to believe, therefore, that the situation in the House would be the more problematic, and that the House would finally determine the fate of Kennedy's bill (and, as both Ellison and Wicker point out, more than a little of his prestige).

The only evidence suggesting that Kennedy fully understood this precarious situation is the considerable effort he made throughout 1961 to keep Chairman Powell happy. On several occasions the White House granted Powell attention, courtesies, and favors that went well beyond what was generally done for Congressmen.[55] For instance:

The President's Appointments Book reveals that Kennedy had a personal interview with Powell as early as February 2.[56]

A warm note to Powell dated February 11, from Walter W. Heller, Chairman of the Council of Economic Advisers, reads: "May I say . . . that we look forward to the very important leadership role that you

will be playing in the critical fields of education and labor. As you
may know, the Federal Government's responsibility in the field of
education has been one of my major concerns. . . . and I now have
every hope that we will be able to achieve some of our objectives
in this field."[57]

A February 16 memo from Lawrence O'Brien (Special Assistant in charge
of Congressional liason) to Henry Wilson (Administrative Assistant to the President) urges him to contact Powell personally and
soon.[58]

A February 22 memo indicates an off-the-record appointment between the
president and Powell scheduled for 9:30 A.M. on February 23.[59] A
second memo, this one from Lee White (Assistant Special Council
to the President) to Larry O'Brien, briefs the president on the current status of the education bill and suggests what might be accomplished in the morning meeting between Kennedy and Powell.

> . . . Powell has been most cooperative to Secretary Ribicoff and his staff.
> Apparently he will ask Congressman Thompson to introduce the ele-
> mentary and secondary education bill and Mrs. Green the higher edu-
> cation bill. In session with Democratic members of Committee, [some
> members] gave Wilbur Cohen* a tough time on why parochial school
> children were omitted. Powell finally said he would relay their views to
> the President when he saw him. The impression is that he will present
> them—not press the position they took. . . .
>
> Although there is some newspaper talk about a Powell Amendment to
> the elementary and secondary bill, apparently there is not commitment
> one way or the other. HEW suggests, if appropriate, the question of
> refraining be put to Powell in the President's meeting with him.†[60]

An article by Paul Duke in the April 4 *Wall Street Journal* notes that
"Powell pays periodic visits to the White House and sprinkles his
conversation with 'Jack told me . . . '" Duke also writes that Secretary of Labor Arthur Goldberg and Ribicoff were both on hand
to pay tribute to Powell at a testimonial dinner.

A memo from Wilson to O'Brien dated July 20 reads: "I arranged the
meeting between Assistant Secretary of State Woodward and Rep.
Powell. Powell's pleased with our attention to it."[61]

The following file note from "Phyllis": "I arranged a special White House
tour for four friends of Cong. Adam Clayton Powell for August
2."[62]

---

*Wilbur Cohen was Assistant Secretary of the Department of Health, Education and
Welfare.
†During the previous Congressional session Powell had proposed an Amendment that
denied federal aid to any schools that were segregated; it was in Kennedy's interest to avoid
a Powell Amendment this time if at all possible.

A memo from Wilson to O'Brien dated November 1 says, "I arranged with Tish for Adam Powell and wife to attend the Munoz Marin dinner. I informed Powell's office."[63]

The General Education Subcommittee hearings proceeded, although much of the House questioning duplicated what had already been covered in the Senate. After listening to seventy-nine witnesses and receiving statements, letters, and resolutions from large numbers of others, the committee held its final hearings on March 29. At about this same time it became clear that the bill President Kennedy had proposed just five weeks earlier, and about which he himself said, "I consider it to be probably the most important piece of domestic legislation,"[64] was in serious trouble.

Although the Catholic church remained perhaps the most significant single player throughout the school aid fight, as the struggle intensified, an array of other players also entered the fray. The lobbying effort was labeled by *The New York Times* as "one of the biggest . . . pro and con, in many years."[65] Among the better known groups that lined up on one or the other side of the school aid controversy were the Chamber of Commerce of the United States, the National Education Association, the American Medical Association, the American Federation of Labor, the Congress of Industrial Organizations, and, of course, the National Catholic Welfare Conference. These groups turned out scores of pamphlets with such titles as "Parents' Rights in Education," and "AFL-CIO Welcomes Kennedy Program for Education." Occasionally, they even produced some very thoughtful analyses. For example, after studying the school aid issue, the American Civil Liberties Union took the position that even loans to private schools would conflict with the provision of the First Amendment that says that "Congress shall make no law respecting an establishment of religion."[66]

Ordinary citizens also made themselves heard. A prototypical concerned American was R. S. MacKenzie who "lives with his ailing wife in a tidily modest white frame duplex on the outskirts of Independence, Mo."

> Lately he has written long, earnest letters to all members of the Senate and House subcommittees considering the Kennedy bill. "I am completely opposed to Federal aid to public schools, and I know of many others who feel just as I do," he has written.[67]

Meanwhile, the brief Senator Morse had requested from the administration on the church–state issue was released on March 28. In general, it buttressed the president's contention that across-the-board loans to sectarian schools would be unconstitutional. It thus provided another opportunity to present the administration view that not only were grants to church-supported schools unconstitutional, but so were across-the-board loans to such schools, also on the grounds that this would violate the First Amendment's mandate on the separation of church and state. Senator Morse then repeated his position that loans (as opposed to grants) to private schools should be handled separately in a measure that could then be given an "early test" of its consitutionality by the Supreme Court.[68] Both he and the president hoped that this might mollify the Catholic hierarchy while at the same time freeing the president's bill for early passage.

I might add here that the relationship between the White House and Morse, while generally smooth, was not altogether free of problems during the spring of 1961. Morse was a prickly sort, independent and proud, and he needed some intermittent attention. A wonderfully revealing episode comes to light in a document that speaks for itself. The memorandum is from Claude Desautels (Special Assistant to the President) to O'Brien, and it is dated April 19, 1961.

> Mrs. Jim Akin visited me today with regard to head count on . . . aid to education. While here, she received an emergency call from Congressman Frank Thompson, with regard to Senator Morse. Apparently Senator Morse is eager to keep a regional post office in Oregon. There had been some talk of transferring it. Morse talked to the President about it some time back and he told Morse that everything being equal, it would more than likely stay in Oregon. It now appears that the Postmaster General asked Morse to come to see him this morning concerning this. Morse was under the impression that they were to discuss the situation. When he got to the office of the Postmaster General, he was informed that the Regional Office was being transferred to Seattle. . . . According to Thompson, Morse is in a complete and utter rage, saying there will be no federal aid to education this year, Oregon has been raped, etc.— Thompson is quite upset. Says that apparently the Post Office mishandled Morse on this—instead of going through the motion of a discussion, they broke it to him as a "fait accompli."[69]

In late April, the administration made an attempt at a compromise on school aid. President Kennedy sent a message to Congress formally requesting extension and expansion of the National Defense Education Act (NDEA). In so doing, he referred to the previously mentioned brief (that Morse had requested) from the Department of Health, Education and Welfare which, although it supported Kennedy's view that across-the-board grants to parochial schools were unconstitutional, did leave room for the proposition that further loans could be made to private schools under the original rationale of the NDEA. Since its passage in 1958, the NDEA had provided loans to public and parochial schools for the purchases of science, mathematics, and foreign language equipment. Thus, by requesting an extension of the NDEA (which was not even due to expire until 1962), and by using careful language, "Kennedy made it plain that, although he could not make the explicit recommendations himself, Congress should consider proposals that would offer loans to non-public schools."[70] This was the president's most dramatic attempt to preserve his integrity on the school-aid bill, while at the same time offer a compromise that would forestall the developing congressional deadlock.

And indeed a brief period of optimism ensued. *The New York Times* ventured that "Sources close to the compromise talks said they believed the Catholic hierarchy would accept the formula as a reasonably satisfactory solution."[71] Moreover, the Catholic church gave its imprimatur when Cardinal Spellman approved a separate bill, introduced by a Manhattan Democrat, that would allow federal funds to be channeled to private schools for the construction of facilities as provided for by the NDEA, and as had been suggested by President Kennedy. The mood of optimism seemed to be justified when, on May 11, 1961, the Senate Labor and Public Welfare committee approved by a vote of 12 to 2 a revised version of the administration bill. The House Education and Labor committee followed suit. The final vote to report the bill out was 18 to 13, with the minority composed of the committee's twelve Republicans plus one Southern Democrat. The revised House bill became item 171 on the calendar; it would remain there until a rule providing for consideration by the full House was granted by the Rules Committee and adopted by the House.[73]

But the bill was no sooner reported out of committee in both Houses of Congress when the mood changed again. What had briefly been a climate of modest hope rapidly deteriorated to one of contentiousness and pessimism. This time the major issue was segregation: should federal funds be allocated to segregated schools? During the Senate floor debate, which lasted from May 16 to May 25, the issue of segregation came to pose a new threat to Kennedy's bill. Two amendments were proposed that vividly illustrate the divisiveness. Senator Strom Thurmond of South Carolina offered an amendment that would flatly prohibit the withholding of funds under the school aid program because of segregation. Senator Prescott Bush of Connecticut, on the other hand, sought to require that funds be granted only to states "proceeding toward full compliance with the constitutional requirement that racial discrimination be ended in public schools."[74]

Although the Senate promptly rejected Thurmond's amendment, a modified version found wider favor. Senate Democratic leader Mike Mansfield told reporters he saw "a great deal of merit"[75] in Georgia Senator Herman Talmadge's more sophisticated proposal, which made no mention of segregation, but would have prevented funds from being withheld from any state education agency that simply "complied with the provisions of this Act."[76] Yet, despite Mansfield's statement (or perhaps because of it), the administration gave no indication that it would back a proviso such as the one Talmadge had proposed. Hubert Humphrey, then the Democratic whip, said he was opposed and that he was certain the administration's attitude at this point was the same. More tellingly, Kennedy's much needed ally in the House, Adam Clayton Powell, reported that he had been telephoned by Secretary Ribicoff and given assurances that the administration would disavow Talmadge's amendment or anything like it.[77]

Powell's role was an important one. In the previous year's school aid fight he had proposed an amendment that would have barred federal aid to segregated schools, and its adoption by the House was a factor in the defeat of the 1960 bill. Now Powell again served notice that he would revive his amendment in the House if the Senate adopted "any such language of any type" as that proposed by Senators Thurmond and Talmadge. "I'll fight them tooth and nail with the Powell amendment, and they won't get any legislation because that will be the end of it over on this side of the Capitol," Powell declared.[78] There was good reason for President Kennedy to try mollifying Powell on this issue, for, despite the Senate furor over segregation, it was by now recognized that the House would put Kennedy's school aid bill to its severest test.

Actually, the push by Southern Senators to guarantee federal funds for segregated schools lost steam rather quickly. The effort provoked a tempest that no one much wanted, and it united a previously fragmented opposition. Liberal Democrats and Republicans joined to ban the likes of even the Talmadge proposal, and Morse predicted that the provision would be defeated. And so it was.

Nevertheless, the administration was still hedging its bets. Although it was quick to reassure Powell that it would disavow the likes of the Thurmond–Talmadge amendment, it was at the same time telling Southern Senators that federal school funds would not be withheld from any state because its schools were segregated. A letter from Ribicoff to that effect was read on the floor of the Senate: "In my opinion, neither the Secretary nor the Commissioner (of Education) would have such authority."[79]

On May 25, the Senate did approve, with only one major amendment*, a bill that provided $2,550,000,000 in school aid. The vote was 49 to 34 with support coming from most non-Southern Democrats, almost half the Southern Democrats, and some liberal Republicans. In a personal "Dear Larry" letter, Morse thanked O'Brien for his help in shepherding the bill through: "The time and consideration you gave to the education bill while it was pending in the Senate were of immeasureable help to us in getting it passed." In response, O'Brien thanked Morse for his contribution: "As I told you over the phone after the Senate action on the aid to education bill,

*The amendment allowed federal funds to be used for operating and maintenance costs as well as construction costs or teacher salaries.

you deserve the credit for its passage. Your gracious note of May 31 assigning me a share of the credit is a characteristically liberal gesture, which I accept with many thanks."[80]

Mike Mansfield opined that "for the first time the prospects of accomplishment [with regard to school aid] are bright,"[81] but *The New York Times* was more guarded. While proclaiming in a front page headline that the aid to education bill had passed the Senate, it noted—also in the headline—that the "House Outlook Is Uncertain."[82]

The religious issue surfaced again in the House, and the issue played itself out in the House Rules Committee. Just four months earlier, the powerful Rules Committee had supposedly been reformed after a dramatic fight between Speaker Sam Rayburn and the elderly Chairman of the Committee, Howard W. Smith. Indeed, it was a fight President Kennedy had played a prominent role in, and which his administration, working together with Rayburn, had ostensibly won. By expanding the size of the Rules Committee, and filling the new slots with "Rayburn Men," the administration was counting on a thin majority to pass its program. But, in Price's words, "such calculations did not take into account the extremely divisive effects of the religious controversy."[83]

During June the battle lines were drawn for the critical Rules fight. The key issue was whether the Catholic members of the Rules Committee would vote to grant a rule on (report on) the public school bill alone. Or would they insist on getting a rule for the NDEA proposals (which would grant loans to parochial schools) first, before turning to the administration's bill? And if they did, how would the other committee members react?

White House strategy seemed uncertain. At first, the administration declared that the president was opposed to anything other than priority consideration for the original public school bill. But by the first week of June there were reports that both Ribicoff and O'Brien were urging that first consideration be given to a proposal that would include federal loans to parochial schools for the construction of science, math, and foreign language buildings as under the NDEA. In the meantime, Sam Rayburn was still insisting that the public school bill come up first; Kennedy himself was said to be staying above the battle. *The New York Times* reported that the question of priority consideration has "apparently not been put to President Kennedy. In the end, it may be settled without White House intervention."[84] As it turned out, this passive approach on the president's part proved costly.

On June 15 it was revealed why the bill was stalled in the Rules Committee. Thomas (Tip) O'Neill, Jr., of Massachusetts and James J. Delaney of New York, both Catholics, both representing districts with heavy Catholic populations, and both Democrats, avowed that they would vote against clearing Kennedy's proposal for consideration by the full House until a second measure, providing aid to private schools, was also ready for the floor.[85] O'Neill and Delaney's position prompted Speaker Rayburn to prophesy privately that the school aid bill was "as dead as slavery."[86]

During the week of June 19 Powell and Rayburn both went public with their gloomy predictions. Powell forecast that unless the White House intervened to mediate between the warring public and private school factions, the education bill would fail to pass. "Someone's got to blow the whistle," he told reporters. When asked whom he meant, Powell replied, "Well, someone beyond the committee and beyond the Congress."[87] And Rayburn, responding to a 9 to 6 vote in the Rules Committee against clearing Kennedy's bill until a parochial school measure was in hand, had the following exchange with reporters:

RAYBURN: I made a statement to the President that the school bill is in trouble—period.
REPORTER: Can you get it out of trouble?
RAYBURN: I don't know. That's why it's in trouble.[88]

The ax finally fell on July 18. The House Rules Committee voted 8 to 7 to table President Kennedy's aid to education bill, as well as two companion measures. As a consequence, said the *Times,* "prospects for House action this session on any of the three bills faded almost to the vanishing point."[89]

The key vote in the Rules Committee was cast by Delaney who, in parting company with O'Neill, still felt that the administration's school aid bill discriminated against parochial schools. Delaney joined with the panel's five Republicans and two conservative Democrats (who opposed federal aid to education on principle) to defeat Kennedy's proposal. On the losing side were the seven Democrats with whom Delaney ordinarily voted to provide a majority for the administration.

What Delaney wanted was a single bill guaranteeing that parochial schools would not be left out of the federal aid package. Essentially, he agreed with Monsignor Hochwalt's reasoning that one measure would pass in the Congress: federal aid as such. A second measure that, in Hochwalt's words, "would provide for our schools"[90] would stand little chance of passage. Thus Delaney felt he had no choice but to withhold support from any bill that did not consider the welfare of parochial schools in tandem with that of public schools.

Larry O'Brien has written that administration officials did in fact exert pressure on Delaney to get him to see things their way. But "nothing could change his mind."

> Had he been bargaining, holding out for some patronage plum, we might have done business, but the only thing he wanted was the one thing Ken-

nedy could not give—federal aid to Catholic schools. Ribicoff and I talked to him many times, to no avail. The President had at least two long, off-the-record talks with him in which he tried desperately to bring Delaney around, but Jim was adamant. He sincerely and deeply believed that he was right and we were wrong, and nothing could persuade him otherwise.[91]

President Kennedy was, of course, very disappointed. When asked at a press conference held one day after the House action how he felt about having his school aid bill torpedoed by the House Rules Committee, he spoke about how this measure was "probably the most important piece of domestic legislation." On the surface, anyway, he refused to give up hope: "I am hopeful that the members of Congress who support this will use those procedures which are available to them under the rules of the House to bring this to a vote and that a majority of the members of the House will support it."[92]

Indeed, Kennedy did make another effort—albeit not a mighty one—to search for a compromise measure that would save at least part of his original program. Powell, for one, kept pushing the president on this. He sent the White House an urgent message warning Kennedy of the unhappy consequences that would ensue if he failed to act on the bill's behalf. Powell's letter was dated July 21.

> My dear Mr. President:
>
> The impasse concerning the education bills reported out from the Committee of which I am the Chairman can be surmounted. During this week I have had extensive conferences with the Democratic Members of my Committee, the authors of the legislation and the chairmen of the subcommittees on education.
>
> I am requesting an opportunity to meet with you briefly as soon as possible to discuss with you the plans at which we have arrived and by which we believe that these bills can be brought before the House and passed during this present session.
>
> The Republican Members of my Committee and the Republican leadership of the House are now united around a project for which they can claim the victory and will result in the loss in this coming election of at least thirty Democratic seats in the House, or enough to give the Republicans control, if their plans are not stopped.
>
> Time is of the essence.
>
> With every good wish.
>
> Sincerely your friend and supporter,
> (signed) Adam C. Powell
> Chairman[93]

But despite Powell's letter, and the president's presumably good intentions, Kennedy still tended to shy away from the center of the action. As a result, the administration made little headway; by early August no mutually acceptable formula had been found. *The New York Times* chided Kennedy for his passivity, for his lack of leadership on the issue: "The President said he was confident that Administration supporters would 'use all their energies to get this bill by' during the present session. This expression of confidence was given two weeks ago, but there has been little apparent evidence of 'energies' calculated to bring victory."[94]

Hubert Humphrey, meanwhile, warned that the Senate would refuse to settle for a "patchwork that would please no one"[95]; and Wayne Morse barred any parliamentary "horse trading" on the issue. "I am not going to support a watered-down politically motivated, legislative horse-trading program on education legislation to be enacted in the dying days of this session," he declared.[96]

Morse's caution notwithstanding, a watered-down version of the president's original bill was precisely what emerged in mid-August as Kennedy's last ditch effort to get an education bill passed during the 1961 congressional session. But the signs were inauspicious for even this weakened measure. There was hard fighting in Congress over a foreign aid bill, and some observers felt that the legislature was in no mood to give "rational consideration" to an emotionally charged issue such as education in the closing weeks of the session. Moreover, Rayburn's support was slow in coming. The Speaker told reporters that he had asked the president for time "to do a little more research" before committing himself. His feeling was that the bill should be set aside until 1962, when religious tensions might abate somewhat.[97]

But Rayburn was a good Democrat and when Kennedy persisted the Speaker agreed to sponsor a compromise measure that would be incorporated into two bills. The plan was to bypass the Rules Committee by invoking a procedural device called "calendar Wednesday," under which a committee chairman could call up bills on Wednesdays without Rules Committee clearance.

Sorensen, however, warned against invoking any unusual procedures. In an August 14, 1961, memorandum to the president he wrote: "Whatever device may be used, there is no real possibility of the bill receiving approval without clearing the House Rules Committee. This means that it must receive the support of either Congressman Delaney or a Republican member." Sorensen went on to recommend that the House Labor Committee Democrats be "asked unofficially" to report out a compromise plan that had been worked out by Ribicoff. Then, "Rayburn, McCormack and Delaney in individual sessions [should] be asked to support the new education bill; and Morse and Humphrey asked not to denounce it. If needed to get Delaney's vote, they will have to be asked to agree to it in conference."[98]

But despite Sorensen's prophetic caution, the administration decided to bypass the Rules Committee. On August 30 Adam Clayton Powell introduced a motion only to *consider* compromise school aid legislation. Powell's motion was defeated without debate. With that defeat, all hope for a 1961 aid to education bill was lost.

The final vote was 242–170. *The New York Times* labeled it "unexpectedly one-sided," and a "stunning defeat for President Kennedy."[99] At a news conference just after the House vote, the president accepted what could no longer be changed. But he added that the ones "who lose today . . . are the schoolchildren who need this assistance. . . . So we will be back next year."[100]

Arthur Schlesinger has written that nothing in the area of domestic policy disappointed President Kennedy more than his repeated failure to get a school aid bill through the Congress.[101] Indeed, during his second State of the Union message the president reiterated his earlier proposal. "I sent to the Congress last year a proposal for Federal aid to public schools construction and teachers' salaries. I believe that bill . . . offered the minimum amount required by our needs . . . and the maximum scope permitted by our Constitution. I, therefore, see no reason to weaken or withdraw the bill; and I urge its passage at this session."[102] But Kennedy's professed dedication was never translated into accomplishment.[103] It would take his successor to transform the dream into law.

The Practice of Leadership

By sending his message on education to Congress just one month after the inauguration, President Kennedy lived up to his campaign promise to put aid to schools at the forefront of his legislative program. Indeed, the act of introducing a school aid bill was important in itself. There is a perceived presidential obligation to see that laws are energetically proposed.[104] But of course directive leadership demands more than formulation and suggestion—it requires mobilization and execution. In fact, it may fairly be claimed that the potential for leadership suffers more when an initiative is taken and then rebuffed than when no initiative is taken at all. Thus, once President Kennedy made education the centerpiece of his legislative program, it would naturally have been to his considerable political advantage to use all the sources of power at his disposal to get the bill passed.

Ostensibly, his task was clear: convince enough members of Congress of the virtues of his school aid proposal. But as we have seen, members of Congress were not the only players. Although they had the actual decision-making power, the way they would exercise that power would depend on pressures emanating from a variety of other sources, especially the Catholic church. Key players then included Cardinal Spellman, Monsignor Hochwalt, and Archbishop Alter, as well as such people as Charles Silver, Ewald Turner and, of course, Abraham Ribicoff, Adam Powell, Wayne Morse, Sam Rayburn, and James Delaney. The extent to which the president would be able to inspire his allies, persuade the undecided, and neutralize his opponents would determine whether or not his bill would get passed.

The record suggests that the Kennedy administration did not fully recognize the controversial nature of the school aid proposal until it was too late. Much has been written about Kennedy's "promise." There was an aura of expectancy, optimism, and even invincibility about the new young president, some of which those closest to the Chief Executive himself undoubtedly came to believe. Liberals especially "looked expectantly to the young president for the leadership that they had been promised, that they believed they had made possible."[105] James MacGregor Burns, commenting in *The New Republic* at the time, evokes for us the myth that was growing even then around Kennedy's persona.

> The Kennedy build-up goes on. The adjectives tumble over one another. He is not only the handsomest, the best dressed, the most articulate and graceful as a gazelle. He is omniscient; he swallows and digests whole books in minutes; his eye seizes instantly on the crucial point of a long memorandum; he confounds experts with his superior knowledge of their field. He is omnipresent; no sleepy staff committee can be sure that he will not telephone—or pop in; every host at a party can hope that he will. He is omnipotent; he personally bosses and spurs the whole shop. . . . He is more than a lion, more than a fox. He's Superman![106]

There is reason to suppose that Kennedy fell victim to his own promise and shining image. Ribicoff reportedly feared from the beginning that Kennedy was overconfident. And indeed the president himself does seem to have played down the possibility that his education bill might provoke a fierce and hardened opposition.

Thus, Kennedy did rather little either before or during the 1961 school aid fight to build coalitions either by stimulating his supporters, or converting or at least neutralizing his opponents. He failed to make sufficient use of political tactics, such as the preemption of problems. He did not ward off the opposition of the Church, or consult early on with Republican leaders. He did not make many personal appeals or grant key figures special access. There is no record of his personal intervention with any of the Church hierarchy, and he did not reach at least one key figure, James J. Delaney, until too late in the game. Nor did he do any arm twisting. If any pressure was ever exerted on Delaney, for example, there is no record of it. Moreover, he did little to suggest he was master of the art of compromise. What he offered was too little and too late. And he never really tried to rally outside support—almost no effort was made to win allies that were not already in place.[107] Conclusively, on this issue, Kennedy made only poor use of any of his sources of power. He was oddly stingy even with regard to tapping his libidinal power, although, as Burns observed, he could be remarkably ingratiating. In short, the urgent rhetoric notwithstanding, the president hung back.

Any exchanges between Kennedy and the Catholic church in particular would obviously be fraught with problems. As the nation's first Catholic president, he felt he could not be seen as violating the separation between church and state and, as one reporter put it, Southern Democrats especially were watching "with hawk-like vigilance for the first sign that the Administration is dominated by the Catholic hierarchy."[108] Indeed, the perceived need for hyper-caution on this score may be partly responsible for his very weak effort to seek a compromise with the church.

But Kennedy's special difficulties with the Catholic hierarchy do not explain why he did not negotiate for a more flexible and dramatic kind of support from the teaching establishment, why he failed to do better than he did with Congress, or why, finally, the situation was allowed to deteriorate so far that toward the end one Western liberal was reduced to saying, "I was willing to die for the education bill. But there's been so much maneuvering and so much controversy that I don't care what happens."[109]

The evidence indicates that Kennedy did little lobbying on behalf of his school aid bill with interest groups representing the educational establishment. There was a very occasional meeting, some exchanges of letters between the White House and key members of the relevant professional associations, but nothing much beyond that. Nor was Ribicoff of special help here. The congressional liaisons complained that the Secretary failed to marshal strong support from either teachers or administrators; some specifically impugned his interpersonal skills. One inter-office memorandum directed to O'Donnell spoke of a Dr. Fuller who was the direct representative of the State School Officers for all States and Territories. "The man has great, immediate direct influence on education in each state. . . . Mr. Fuller has held this post since 1948. With [one exception] he has been on a first-name basis with every Secretary of Health, Education and Welfare. At present, he does not feel that he has this type of relationship with Secretary Ribicoff."[110]

The president's failure to consult with the teaching establishment, to bring them into the policy process, and to persuade teachers and administrators to give their all out support for aid to education proved costly. Throughout, those who should have had a vested interest in supporting the public schools were much less effective on behalf of a bill they professed to support than they might have been, and they resisted any proposal that differed substantially from the one that Kennedy had originally put forth. Thus, one could argue that educators foreclosed the possibility of passage of a compromise bill almost as surely as the Catholic church.

The record of Kennedy's attempts to influence Congress directly on behalf of his legislative program is somewhat confusing. Larry O'Brien writes that precisely because Kennedy was "well aware that he lacked the necessary degree of intimacy" with congressional leaders, he "launched an unprecedented program of presidential activity." O'Brien calculates that Kennedy had about 2,500 separate contacts with members of Congress during his first year in office, exclusive of correspondence.[111] But the nature of these contacts posed another question. It appears that Kennedy used such exchanges more to keep open the lines of communication than to exert direct influence. Several presidential scholars point to Kennedy's distaste for what he perceived as currying favor. For example, Edwards writes that Kennedy's staff "tried to conserve his efforts in personal relations and his involvement in details, knowing that he was impatient with such activities, that he felt uncomfortable with many members of Congress . . . and that he had limited time for and interest in domestic legislation. He was less likely than Johnson to call legislators and ask for their votes."[112]

Paradoxically, Kennedy's need to influence members of Congress personally may have been perceived to have been lessened by the very excellence of his congressional liaison staff. Kennedy ushered in a period in which the liaison staff was more active and assertive than it had ever been before. O'Brien, who coordinated all the liaison work, set the pattern right at the beginning. In that first fight to enlarge the Rules Committee, O'Brien took a head count, appealed to the undecided, and developed a file on each of the representatives and their leanings. The president, in turn, was only too glad to have O'Brien take over a job for which he himself had no appetite. Stephen Wayne reports that the telephone calls Kennedy received from his friends on Capitol Hill during the first weeks of his administration were referred to the congressional liaison office with the query, "Have you taken this up with Larry O'Brien?"[113] Soon enough, the calls came directly to O'Brien, but at a price: Kennedy made less use that he might otherwise have made of the power resources that are *only* at the president's disposal. In other words, precisely *because* of O'Brien's competence, Kennedy made relatively few attempts to exert personal political influence. But because O'Brien was neither Kennedy nor president, he could not achieve the results Kennedy might have achieved.

One could also speculate that Kennedy's distance from the legislature prevented him from having a really good feel for who his most important allies might be. For example, whether it was wise for the president to depend as heavily as he did on Adam Clayton Powell on the school aid issue is surely a debatable question. Might not the Chief Executive have been better off distributing his favors more widely?

But perhaps nothing illustrates Kennedy's relatively weak effort to exert influence on this particular issue as vividly as the handling of James P. Delaney. In retrospect, it is hard to understand why the president allowed this single, previously loyal Democrat, to torpedo his cherished aid to education bill. Why didn't Kennedy recognize that Delaney might prove to be a fatal stumbling block? And if he did anticipate Delaney's recalcitrance, why didn't he try hard to soften that opoosition by coopting him, consulting with him early on, bringing him into the policy-making process, and offering him the personal rewards that he could so effortlessly have dispensed?

Apparently, one did not have to be president to recognize that Delaney would be trouble. Richard Bolling, a Democratic Congressman who was on the all-important Rules Committee along with Delaney, remembers that he in any case "knew way in advance . . . that Delaney was going to vote his conviction."[114] Even if this appraisal were accurate, another question surfaced: Would he vote his conviction with quiet reluctance or in open defiance of his party's leader?

Until the aid to education vote, Delaney had spent "eighteen faithful years in obscurity as one of the Democratic leadership's 'yes' men on the House Rules Committee."[115] But this was an issue of special importance to the Queens Democrat, both as a Catholic and a politician. His district was about 70 percent Catholic; and Delaney had long been on record as being concerned about the ability of local parishes to support their parochial schools. Although Delaney later denied any direct pressure from the church to influence his vote, on this matter he and his pastor, Monsignor Richard B. McHugh, saw eye to eye. Monsignor McHugh was quoted as saying: "It's the principle of the thing. We believe that Catholic children and their parents have a right to share in any government funds for education."[116]

It is impossible to say whether there was anything that Kennedy could have done to change Delaney's vote, although Jim Grant Bolling, who was a Health, Education and Welfare official for congressional liaison, has said that it was "conceivable" that you might have been "able to educate Delaney on this kind of thing."[117] What *is* true is that the president did not try very hard. O'Brien writes that Kennedy and the Congressman had two "off-the-record talks," but there are no indications of well in advance face-to-face meetings, of the promise of a carrot, or the threat of a stick. And there surely is no evidence that Delaney ever paid for his transgression. Wicker writes in this regard: "Here, then, was a President, for all his Irish Mafia, who apparently could be defied with impunity."[118] In other words, Kennedy did not engage Delaney—who was clearly necessary for the passage of the education bill—in a two-way influence relationship. The president failed to understand that the success of his leadership *required* the cooperation of others and so he gave Delaney no motivation to follow. The Queens congressman was shown neither the possible gain in going along with Kennedy, nor the cost in going the other way.

Of course, in our effort to understand how one vote in the Rules Committee slipped through the administration's hands, we must remember that Delaney was only the most obvious candidate to change his vote (or at least he appeared to be the most obvious because he had been a Democratic yes man for so long); the Rules Committee had seven other members who voted no, and any one of them might just possibly have been influenced by Kennedy to switch his vote.

Interestingly, according to Sorensen, Kennedy himself did not blame Delaney or the Catholics, but rather the rest of the Rules Committee.

> Of the three Catholics on the Rules Committee two had voted for it; of the ten Democrats seven had voted for it; but of the five Republicans not one had voted for it, when only one was needed to report it. In short, seven of the eight opponents—five Republicans and two Dixiecrats— had not supported Kennedy's election and were not influenced by Kennedy's wishes. "That's who really killed the bill," he said, "just as they've killed it for fifty years, not the Catholics."[119]

What Kennedy apparently did not question was how it happened that with all the personal and institutional power at *his* disposal, he had not even been able to hold his majority when it really mattered.*

We have seen that with regard to the school aid bill President Kennedy did relatively little to try to influence either the key decision makers themselves, or marshall the special interest groups that might have applied the pressure he did not. He similarly failed to motivate the American public to give him vigorous support. If the president was unwilling to ask members of Congress directly for their vote, his only other option was to go over their heads to the public, which could exert pressure on the members to vote the way he wanted them to.

No one would argue that education is ordinarily considered a hot topic. Nor can one say that going to the people on this subject would have been a political crowd pleaser. One is struck, however, by the fact that only at his press conferences did Kennedy make any attempt at all to educate or mobilize us. The aid to education bill was proposed early in the Kennedy administration; little effort was spent on forging coalitions or constituencies

---

*However, the administration appears to have learned something from this early and bitter experience. In July 1962 on another matter entirely, the following memo was sent by Wilson to Dick Donahue, a Special Assistant to the President: "Jim Atkin tells me there appears to be some question about how Jim Delaney will vote on the Rules Committee if confronted with Medical Care. Perhaps this should be checked out early."[120]

on this, the president's number one priority. There were no trips, for example, to Missouri, a state that, because of its special interest in education, would have provided an excellent forum for at least one good speech on the subject. Nor was much of an effort made to get us to focus on the subject, perhaps by stimulating fresh debate on education. Jerry Murphy of Harvard's Center for Education and Policy Research noted that "Kennedy himself had almost no impact on educational thinking. Most of the well-known critiques of education . . . preceded Kennedy. A new wave of educational writing started in the mid-sixties . . . but this new wave had little or no political catalyst."[121] Furthermore, there was, to quote a contemporary editorial in *Science,* no effort to capitalize fully on the power of the presidency to gain wide attention: "Kennedy has yet to use his position to make a direct appeal to the public for support on specific issues, explaining just what he wants Congress to do and why he thinks the country should be behind him"[122] And finally there was no dramatic gesture, no attention-capturing device that would have drawn the public eye to what he said mattered most. Oscar Glass, writing at the end of the first year of the Kennedy presidency, commented on how the president "chose the path of more reticent action."

> President Kennedy did not call the Congress into joint session to hear his views on the urgency of federal government action for . . . education. That high spectacle was reserved for shooting the moon.[123]

Having made the point that President Kennedy was a less than effective leader with regard to his aid to education proposal, I would like to briefly address other possible explanations for his political failure. First, there is the argument that the public school aid bill failed because it was doomed to fail from the first. Perhaps the religious issue made agreement on school aid simply impossible. However, this does not explain why, after being blocked on school aid, the president never obtained agreement on a minimal academic facilities bill, even one that excluded aid for teachers' pay, thus ensuring that at least something was accomplished.[124] Also, the "lost cause" argument does not fully explain why, on April 11, 1965, President Johnson was able to sign the Elementary and Secondary Education Act into law. To be sure, the circumstances and the context were different, and Kennedy himself may be said to have paved the way for Johnson's success. Nevertheless, Johnson's own description of how the feat was accomplished is politically instructive. One cannot help being struck by the contrast between Kennedy, who imposed a policy, and Johnson, who gathered support along the way.

> As we were hammering out the [aid to education] program, we were also developing a strategy to overcome congressional obstacles. . . . All the centers of power and control within the Congress were consulted. . . .

In addition, a coalition of support was carefully built up among educational institutions and other interested groups, including several former opponents of school aid programs.... Various members of the administration met with Catholic groups....

The bill went to the Congress on January 12, 1965.... The church-state issue erupted in committee soon afterward.... I told Larry O'Brien (and several others) to work out a solution. They met late into the night in Larry O'Brien's office, above mine, and the next morning O'Brien called me and said he thought they had found the answer....

Slowly, in curious ways, opposition melted.... When the bill reached the House floor, I asked for frequent reports and received them by the hour.... Finally, on March 26, by a roll call vote of 263 to 153, the House passed the education bill and sent it to the Senate.... After eleven amendments were beaten down, the measure moved through the Senate with no changes. The vote was 73 to 18.[125]

A second explanation of why the school aid bill ran into trouble rests with Kennedy's men rather than with Kennedy himself. As I indicated, Secretary Ribicoff, for example, was faulted for sins ranging from timidity to frigidity to stupidity.[126] Wilbur Cohen, the Assistant Secretary of Health, Education and Welfare, also had his detractors; Jim Grant Bolling remembers that he had "personality problems." "I think it's conceivable that, say, [Congresswoman] Edith Green* wouldn't let him in the office to talk to her about [the school aid bill]. She didn't like him. I think she felt that he was not frank with her."[127] A problem of coordination also existed among the different persons and agencies. Both Richard and Jim Grant Bolling recall that the congressional liaison people were working in one direction on this issue, and other members of the White House staff—Sorensen especially—in another.[128]

Moreover, Health, Education and Welfare seemed to have had little understanding of the importance of the House Rules Committee. By trying so hard to enlist the support of Education and Labor, the department gave short shrift to the committee that would, in fact, deal the education bill its fatal blow.

But while the above-mentioned problems with Kennedy's staff no doubt hindered his effort on behalf of school legislation, they do not mitigate against the fact that his own effort was not very great. Staff incompetence might be an adequate reason for the failure of an initiative other than one assigned primary importance, but it does not go far toward explaining the lack of success on a bill that was designated by the president himself as his most significant domestic policy proposal.

---

*Congresswoman Green was the Chairperson of the House Subcommittee on Special Education, one of the three education subcommittees of Powell's Education and Labor Committee.

A third explanation for the defeat of the education legislation may be termed contextual. That is, the school bill was defeated in 1961 because of events beyond the president's immediate control. These ranged from his narrow electoral victory, to a generally cautious Congress as well as a reduced number of Democratic seats in the House of Representatives, to the April crisis over the American-sponsored invasion of Cuba (Bay of Pigs). In the fall of 1961 columnist Stewart Alsop commented that for Kennedy, April was "the cruelest month."[129]

Once again, however, to acknowledge that circumstances sapped Kennedy's energies and capacities away from the education bill is not to say that they explain or excuse its failure to pass. My argument is that there was no single circumstance or set of events outside the president's control that fatally doomed Kennedy's attempts to exercise leadership on behalf of aid to schools.

No claim is being made in this chapter that John Kennedy failed during his first year in the White House. Indeed, he had several successes: a minimum wage bill (albeit a much weaker one than originally sought), aid to depressed areas, and a housing bill. What I *am* claiming is that President Kennedy failed to demonstrate effective political leadership in the measure he designated "most important." Why this political failure? Surely Kennedy was motivated to win. Just as surely he possessed a rich store of intellectual and interpersonal skills, ranging from a long memory to a sharp wit—skills that should have made victory on this issue possible. What he did lack, however, was an appreciation of the *politics* of leadership. He failed to exert sufficient influence on those political actors whose support he needed to win. Only weak attempts were made to reward them if they were good, or punish them if they were bad. Because Kennedy did not make following him especially attractive by offering rewards of either a material or psychological nature, few stood to benefit sufficiently from going along with him. Moreover, no cost was incurred for adhering to a position that ran contrary to the president's. Kennedy failed, in short, to draw enough on those instrumental, legal, and libidinal sources of power that would probably have enabled him to have his way on this issue, at least in part. He seemed to prefer playing the statesman instead of politician, a role that better served history's view of him than it did the realities of the American political system, which requires that successful leaders play the parts both of statesman *and* ward politician.

In Chapter 4 I discussed the need for a president to have what I labeled "political intellect." Political intellect was defined as the awareness of the importance of politicking for the attainment of carefully chosen policy goals. On this issue, in any case, President Kennedy did not demonstrate political intellect. He did not recognize the need to apply social skills to political ends. He did not understand the need to wheel and deal with passion for what he believed to be right, and to convey empathy for what his followers felt about their own positions. Finally, he did not seem to know either intuitively or intellectually that politics cannot be played from a distance, nor by proxy when the chips are down. Perhaps more than anything else, it was Kennedy's failure to use politics for his own purpose that spelled the demise of what he himself called his "No. 1 priority bill."

7

Lyndon Johnson and
the War on Poverty

> And this Administration today, here and now, declares
> unconditional war on poverty in America, and I urge this
> Congress and all Americans to join with me in that effort.
> It will not be a short or easy struggle, no single weapon or
> strategy will suffice, but we shall not rest until that war is
> won.
>
> *President Johnson,*
> *State of the Union Message*
> *to Congress, January 8, 1964*

John Kennedy was assassinated on November 22, 1963. On November 23,
President Johnson's first day in the Oval Office, the new president gave the
poverty program a green light.

The concept of a far-reaching poverty program originated during the
Kennedy administration.[1] By June 1963 some of Kennedy's staff, if not the
president himself, were giving consideration to "a possible Kennedy offensive against poverty."[2] But there is also wide agreement that Lyndon Johnson was the first president to focus national interest on a concerted attempt
to end poverty, rather than simply ameliorate its effects.

Walter Heller, Chairman of the Council of Economic Advisers under
both presidents, remembers that during May and June he tried to interest
Kennedy in the idea of a poverty program, but that he had "difficulty getting him on board." Later in the year, in November, just a few days before
the assassination, Heller went back to Kennedy and this time the response
was more forthcoming. Heller quotes Kennedy as saying, "Yes, Walter, I
am definitely going to have something in the line of an attack on poverty
in my program. I don't know what yet. But, yes, keep your boys at work."
Heller adds, however, that although Kennedy seemed to be committed to
doing something, he "did not at that point have a program. There was not
a poverty program at that time."[3]

The contrast between Kennedy's cautious approach and Johnson's
quick—some might say rushed—response is dramatic. Heller relates that

on the very first day of the Johnson administration he introduced the new president to the by now several months old plan for a poverty program. Johnson's response was immediate: "That's my kind of program; I'll find money for it one way or another. If I have to, I'll take money away from things to get money for people."[4]

Johnson himself confirms Heller's recollection. In his autobiography he recalls Heller coming in to see him at 7:40 in the evening and asking if he wanted the Council of Economic Advisers to develop a program to attack poverty.

> The poverty program Heller described was my kind of undertaking. "I'm interested," I responded. "I'm sympathetic. Go ahead. Give it the highest priority. Push ahead full tilt."[5]

There are at least three explanations for Johnson's quick and favorable response to the idea of a poverty program, and for his subsequent commitment to getting the necessary legislation through Congress.

1. To establish continuity in the wake of the trauma of Kennedy's murder. Jack Conway, for a time Deputy Director of the Office of Economic Opportunity, argues that Johnson was understandably anxious to "get off to the right kind of start. He was very conscious of the state of emotion in the country, and he wanted a bridge from the Kennedy Administration to his own and he did not want to drop things that were in the mill."[6]

2. To gain an early and considerable political advantage. James Sundquist writes that the 1964 war on poverty "gave the new President, whose legislative agenda consisted otherwise of left-over Kennedy proposals, a bold and attention-getting proposal on which he could put his personal stamp."[7] Clearly, the president used the poverty program to promote himself as a strong and benevolent leader, and to establish his liberal credentials before the presidential contest in 1964.[8]

3. To lead the nation toward a goal in which he genuinely believed, and to which he could be fully committed. A Kennedy administration holdover said, "The President has a great feeling for this program. It's close to his roots. Where Kennedy may have had only an intellectual appreciation of the need to eradicate poverty, Johnson had a 'gut' reaction to the basic idea."[9] Sundquist adds that the "issue itself was peculiarly suited to the personality of Lyndon Johnson, who could talk feelingly of his first-hand knowledge of poverty in the Texas hills. . . ."[10] Heller also testifies to the raw impulse that underlay the political commitment. When asked if he thought Johnson's positive response to the poverty program reflected a sincere interest in poverty or a desire to gain Heller's support, Heller replied that Johnson's reaction was "so spontaneous and so

immediate . . . that I thought that it was an instinctive and intuitive and uncalculated response."[11] Finally, Doris Kearns, who had long conversations with Lyndon Johnson after he left office, writes that despite the distortions and exaggerations to which Johnson was prone when he spoke of his impoverished past, there were, nonetheless, times of genuine hardship during his childhood. "To Johnson," Kearns observes, "the poor would never be 'the disadvantaged,' an abstract class whose problems must be solved. They were familiar men and women suffering a circumstance he well understood."[12] No wonder, then, that Johnson told Heller to give the poverty program "the highest priority."[13]

The poverty program was hardly the only thing on Johnson's mind during those earliest days of his presidency. He was especially interested in pushing through a tax bill that Kennedy had been working on and to that end he scheduled a private meeting with Senator Eugene McCarthy (who had "some ideas" on the tax bill) as soon as December 3;[14] wrote a personal letter to Harold Geneen, the president of the International Telephone and Telegraph Corporation, stating that "It is my hope your firm opinion (in favor of the bill) will be a persuasive influence in the Congress this year and that the tax bill can be passed";[15] had Secretary of the Treasury Douglas Dillon call Katharine Graham, editor of *The Washington Post,* who "agreed to speak immediately to all her editors to give . . . a hand on the tax bill";[16] and agreed to participate in a one day conference with representatives from the American Bankers Association.[17] Still, the antipoverty effort was his own, the one in which he was personally invested, and for which he could take personal credit. During the month of December, even over Christmas at the LBJ Ranch, aides assembled and discussions continued.

However, a group of Texas cattlemen who were also at the Ranch (to teach the visiting Easterners about the relationship between beef prices and imports) were less than wildly enthusiastic. In fact, they were downright hostile to the idea. They reminded Johnson that this was a middle-class country; that in this great land of ours there was no reason for anyone to be poor; and that jobs were available to all who really wanted them. This opinion was shared by some of the more conservative members of the administration. Rowland Evans and Robert Novak write that "John McCone, the Republican businessman who now headed the Central Intelligence Agency, commented wryly that he had relations who were poor but that the best antidote for them probably was hard work, not a new government program."[18]

At times, Johnson too seemed to have expressed his own second thoughts about what could be achieved. Evans and Novak relate that he hounded

Heller at mealtimes, while sitting on the porch, and while chasing after deer on the ranch in his Lincoln Continental, always demanding to know, "How are you going to spend all this money?" Johnson also considered limiting the poverty program to only nine months.[19]

But if there were any doubts, they must have been fleeting. For by the time the Christmas holiday was over, Johnson demonstrated unequivocal enthusiasm for what he was already claiming as his own creation.[20] Years later, he remembered with some nostaglia the "beginning work on the poverty program" that took place at the LBJ ranch. Walter Heller, Budget Director Kermit Gordon, and presidential assistants Bill Moyers and Jack Valenti worked "at a small kitchen table" while outside the window "white-faced Herefords grazed placidly:"[2]

Even at this early planning stage, Johnson was thinking of the political realities he would have to face down the road. He was the one to insist on enlarging the program into something almost grand in its conception: "Gordon and Heller had been thinking in terms of a pilot venture to be carried out in a limited number of . . . cities. But I urged them to broaden their scope. I was certain that we could not start small and hope to propel a program through the Congress. It had to be big and bold and hit the whole nation with real impact."[22] The president writes that it was he too who pushed for the dramatic slogan "war on poverty." "I wanted to rally the nation, to sound a call to arms which would stir people in the government, in private industry, and on the campuses to lend their talents to a massive effort to eliminate the evil."[23]

At a December press conference President Johnson told reporters that "high" on his "agenda of priority" would be "poverty legislation for the lowest income groups," adding that "any kind of poverty will be a concern of this administration."[24] And in his state of the Union message of January 8, the antipoverty program received what must surely be described as special attention.

The speech was, in fact, a ringing call to arms in a brand new war on poverty—a war to which the president was clearly committed. *The New York Times* observed that although the Chief Executive's "voice was pitched low, his hopes were pitched high. . . . President Johnson acknowledged that the war would not be 'short or easy.' But he did not question that it could be won."[25]

> The richest nation on earth can afford to win [the war on poverty].
>   We cannot afford to lose it. . . .
>   Our aim is not only to relieve the symptom of poverty, but to cure it, and above all, to prevent it.[26]

Johnson's decision to use his first State of the Union message to focus national attention on the antipoverty program had predictable results.

Almost immediately, poverty became newsworthy. The *Nation* wrote about the "rediscovery of poverty," noting that it was "amazing that it took fifteen years to get out from under the incubus of the cold war and to show a decent concern for the victims of industrialism."[28] *Business Week* called the president's State of the Union message "a striking political document" that held out promise to "the deprived, the needy, the aged [and] the unemployed."[29] And *The New York Times* now saw fit to take a close look at poverty in the big city. In a long article titled, "Poverty on the Lower East Side: 6 Live 'Heavy Life' on $1 a Day," the focus was on Marcello Perez who, since he had been laid off from his job, was feeding and clothing himself, his wife, their four children on seven dollars a week and the charity of others.[30]

Johnson may well have anticipated that the time was ripe for the poor to replace Mom and apple pie as America's safest political icons. When the politically less sensitive Senator Barry Goldwater, a leading candidate for the 1964 Republican presidential nomination, criticized the Chief Executive's war on poverty, suggesting instead an inquiry into the question of whether "the attitude or the actions" of the poor had contributed to their plight, the reaction was immediate.[31] Goldwater's opinion that "the mere fact of having little money did not 'entitle' everyone to be permanently maintained by the taxpayer at an average or comfortable standard of living" provoked Abraham Ribicoff, then a Democratic Senator from the state of Connecticut, to declare that he could not share Goldwater's view that "if only the unemployed would have the gumption to go to work, all our welfare problems would be solved."[32] And *The New York Times* placed itself squarely in Johnson's camp on this one with an editorial that suggested that Senator Goldwater's remarks on poverty "must have repelled many of his hearers."[33]

At the time of his State of the Union address, President Johnson had not yet decided how the poverty program would be packaged, or what exactly it would consist of. Responsibility for planning the program gradually shifted from Heller's Council of Economic Advisers to the Bureau of the Budget; what emerged during January was a plan in which a local community action group would act as the coordinating body for an economical yet comprehensive attack on poverty. The new budget would allot the antipoverty program a total of $500 million. As for content, the emphasis was on children and youth, and on services that would help young people develop their capabilities.[34]

Just as John Kennedy had learned in his attempts to get his education program through Congress, Johnson discovered that personal vision does not ensure political success. Mark Gelfand writes that "the Budget Bureau's prescription for a well-ordered, measured war on poverty appeared headed for ready acceptance when it ran into two roadblocks, the Labor Department and the President."[35] Leaders at the Labor Department felt strongly that while improvements in health and education services were desirable, priority should be given to a large-scale employment program. President Johnson agreed—in part at least because the political benefits of job training and creation would be realized far more swiftly than those from community action programs. Stuck also with the very large question of who would administer the new antipoverty program, Johnson decided to go with an independent agency and an independent director.

On February 1, the president announced the appointment of R. Sargent Shriver, as head of the White House task force on the war on poverty. It would be Shriver's task to whip the antipoverty legislation into shape, and thereafter, to help shepherd it through the Congress. Gelfand comments:

> Momentous consequences would flow from Shriver's selection. Although the idea for the various facets of the War on Poverty came from others, it was Shriver who developed the strategy of drafting the legislation . . . as an omnibus package. . . . Finding in Shriver the same passion for getting things done that consumed him, Johnson gave his whole-hearted blessing to what Shriver had wrought.[36]

If indeed Shriver was so important to the success of Johnson's pet program, the question must be posed: How did Johnson come to choose him.[37] Shriver had, by all accounts, done a first-rate job as head of the Peace Corps and under his direction the Peace Corps had come to be regarded in Congress and elsewhere "as one of the outstanding successes of the Kennedy Administration."[38] And, like Johnson, Shriver was a man who thrived on getting things done. Beyond that, however, was the political advantage of the Kennedy connection. Besides directing the Peace Corps under Kennedy, Shriver was married to Eunice Kennedy, the late president's older sister.

The importance of this connection tends to be confirmed because Johnson asked almost all of Kennedy's closest White House aides to remain. Theodore Sorensen, Pierre Salinger, Larry O'Brien, and Kenneth O'Donnell—who all had been with Kennedy since before his election—stayed on into the Johnson Administration. In addition to the very real advantage to be gained by maintaining around him those who had been closest to Kennedy, whose recent slaying had had such a profound emotional impact on the American people, there were political advantages not entirely related to popular appeal. As ineffective as the Kennedy administration had often been in getting legislation passed, these men knew their way around the executive branch, an arena in which Johnson did not have the considerable experience he had had in Congress. Being married to one of Kennedy's sisters, and having administered one of Kennedy's most successful programs, Shriver would bring to Johnson's war on poverty not only a personal link to the keenly felt recent past, but experience in dealing with the executive bureaucracy.

On February 1, President Johnson telephoned Shriver, who had just returned from a world trip. Shriver was asked if he would serve as Johnson's "personal chief of staff in the war against poverty."[39] That afternoon, the two met and Shriver said yes. In a letter of appointment, the president wrote Shriver as follows:

> I am grateful that you have agreed to accept the appointment as my Assistant for purposes of heading our program to eliminate poverty. . . .As my representative, you will direct the activities of all executive departments and agencies involved in the program against poverty. You will also be my representative in presenting to the Congress the Administration's views with respect to necessary legislation. . . .
>
> You will also undertake the coordination and integration of the federal program with the activities of state and local governments and of private persons, including the Foundations, private business and industry, labor unions, and civic groups and organizations. . . .
>
> I shall, of course, consult and work closely with you on this program.
>
> Sincerely,
> (signed) Lyndon B. Johnson[40]

With the appointment of Shriver, the war on poverty went into full gear. One day after he was named to head the poverty program, Shriver met at his Maryland home with Heller, Kermit Gordon, and Adam Yarmolinsky, formerly at the Defense Department and now Shriver's top aide; two days later he called an all-day conference devoted to preliminary planning. Shriver's tactic was to cast a wide net for both people and ideas. The business community, intellectuals, state and local officials, people in private organizations—all were solicited for suggestions on what actually to write into the poverty legislation. By the time Shriver testified on behalf of the Economic Opportunity Act before the Congress, he was able to list 137 people who had contributed to the planning process.

The straightforward purpose of the task force was to address the following question: "How do you fight a war on poverty?" In six weeks the question was answered. The task force had completed both the Special Message on Poverty—to be delivered by the president—and the specifics of the bill that would create by law an Office of Economic Opportunity. Also completed was a congressional presentation, entitled "The War on Poverty," which provided the first systematic explanation of the program, and contained the first budget estimate of $962.5 million.[41]

By all accounts, the early days were heady ones. One participant recalls "the beautiful hysteria of it all"; another remembers those weeks as "chaotic, hectic, unorganized, disorganized, but also historically productive." There was a "constant traffic of people. Government people were in and out of the fifth floor of the Peace Corps building. At one point traffic got so heavy that Shriver said we have to find some more rooms, and we found some on the 12th floor."[42] Johnson himself recalls a time when the "excitement was contagious." The task force "went at it with a fervor and created a ferment unknown since the days of the New Deal."[43]

But what precisely was the president's role during this formative period? How large a part did he play in the actual formulation of the poverty program? The president writes that he "followed closely the work" of the task force,[44] and there is no doubt that he watched over it, played the peacemaker role when absolutely necessary, and gave the task force considerable support and sustenance. But there is also general agreement that with regard to the specifics of the bureaucratic wrangling, Johnson was largely "disinterested and dispassionate." As time went on it became clear that he was "considerably less interested in the content of the program than in his determination to achieve a great national consensus to eradicate poverty. To Johnson, the means were less important than the end."[45] His primary role, in other words, was evangelical; the nuts and bolts work was left to others.

A valuable source for the details of what took place during February and early March is Adam Yarmolinsky, named by Shriver to be the Deputy Director of the War on Poverty Task Force, and generally regarded as the principal author of the actual bill. Yarmolinsky states that Johnson did not play an active role in selecting the task force members, or pay close attention to how it was progressing or what it was doing, nor did he get any more than peripherally involved in the inevitable interdepartmental quarreling among the existing government departments and agencies.

> Well, we reported to him, Shriver and I did, I guess primarily through Moyers, who was the staff man and who was responsible. Occasionally we would get word that this or that aspect of it he had some view on subsequently. But no [he took little direct interest in the Task Force]. . . . I should qualify that. When we had the proposal for legislation in form to present as a proposal, Shriver presented it at a cabinet meeting which I attended as an observer. The President naturally expressed his view and supported certain parts and did not favor other parts that were proposed. . . .[46]

But if Johnson was relatively uninterested in the bureaucratic and legal niceties of the antipoverty program, he was increasingly passionate in his mission to bring it national attention and support.

In his late January Economic Report to the Congress, the president repeated the message: "Americans today enjoy the highest standard of living in the history of mankind. But for nearly a fifth of our fellow citizens, this is a hollow achievement. They often live without hope, below minimum standards of decency."[47] Several weeks later, in a talk to officials of the Internal Revenue Service, he did so again: "President Roosevelt talked with great eloquence about the third of our nation that was ill-housed, ill-fed, ill-clad. . . . By great dedication of selfless men we brought that one-third . . . down to one-fifth. . . . In our budget this year, we will apportion approximately a billion dollars to try to do something to reduce that one-fifth to maybe one-sixth or one-seventh or one-eighth or one-tenth. . . ."[48]

Indeed, Johnson rode herd on the task force only when he was concerned with getting the message to the public. The following memo from Bill Moyers, the president's closest aide, to Yarmolinsky, reveals one way Johnson kept control. The memo is dated February 28.

> I am returning a revised draft of the message you sent me yesterday. It now represents *some* of our thinking and the direction in which we would like to move.
>
> The President particularly thinks that as you work now from this revised draft, there needs to be more logic and less rhetoric in outlining *why* we must wage war on poverty. He wants to appeal to the mind as well as the heart.
>
> He wants to point out . . . how the obligation to help the poor goes beyond even the fundamental moral obligation we have; in other words, eliminating poverty will have what substantial effects on *the total American* economy.
>
> He said he wants the message to be clear and unadorned, factual and compelling. . . .
>
> He also thought the papers could be better organized. The first section. . . . tends to wander. And the section on organizations seems to be out of place and incomplete. . . .
>
> Please have your people work on this over the weekend and have a revised draft ready for us to look at Monday. . . .[49]

At the same time that the task force was preparing the antipoverty legislation, President Johnson also began a letter-writing campaign that was impressive in its size and scope. Almost no segment of the society was left out, and every one of the following letters was signed by the president himself, not by an aide.

Labor. To Charles Luna, President of the Brotherhood of Railroad Trainmen, Johnson wrote: "I wish to thank you for your letter of support . . . [for] the programs this Administration is undertaking against poverty and unemployment. . . . Government policy can influence . . . the economic life of the nation, but the basic decisions regarding jobs, wages, hours and working conditions are in the hands of private individuals in positions of responsibility like yourself. For this reason, your expression of confidence is greatly appreciated."[50] To Mr. Hank Brown of the Texas AFL-CIO, Johnson sent a "Dear Hank" letter which promised to pass on Mr. Brown's "comments on the poverty situation to Secretary [of Labor Willard] Wirtz. I know he'll be interested."[51] And with George Meany, President of the AFL-CIO, who would play a considerable role in getting the antipoverty bill passed, Johnson had the following exchange:

March 6, 1964

My dear Mr. President:

The Executive Council of the AFL-CIO at its recent meeting discussed at great length the war against poverty which your Administration has undertaken. It is a cause to which the AFL-CIO is completely dedicated, as I know you are well aware. Winning this battle requires action on a whole series of fronts, and the Executive Council adopted a detailed statement of our opinion on this matter. Knowing your deep concern with this issue, I wanted you to have a copy of it personally.

I trust the points of view expressed here will be seriously considered by the Administration in drafting its proposals to the Congress. A program that is too narrow, a program that is not based on solving the root causes of poverty in America would, it seems to us, delay rather than accelerate the full impetus of the campaign you have undertaken.

With my warm, personal best wishes, I am

Sincerely yours,
(signed) George Meany

March 12, 1964

Dear George:

When I got your letter of the 6th and the Executive Council's statement on the war against poverty, I immediately called Bill Wirtz and Sargent Shriver and asked them to be sure to give you a full briefing on the situation and to take into serious account the suggestions you and your colleagues have to make.

I have been aware for a long time of the AFL-CIO commitment in this field and your points of view carry, therefore, considerable weight.

I will count on your continued help—as I know you are willing to give it—in the campaign to eliminate poverty in this country.

Sincerely,
(signed) Lyndon B. Johnson[52]

Education. To the Reverend Francis Quinn of Georgetown University, the president sent a note saying that he was "deeply heartened and encouraged to know that the subject of your Third Seminar is Poverty in Plenty. . . . I hope that your discussions will result in constructive contributions to the war against poverty."[53]

State and Local Officials. A wire was sent to Terry Sanford, Governor of North Carolina, congratulating him on his "INITIATIVE IN MOBILIZING FOR AN ATTACK ON POVERTY IN NORTH CAROLINA."[54] To Robert Mallatt, Jr., Mayor of Keene, New Hampshire, Lyndon Johnson wrote that he was "delighted" to learn that Keene had joined the war against poverty.[55]

Religion. The Reverend R. J. Edwin Espy was told that it was a "source of satisfaction to know that the National Council of Churches of Christ in the United States of America welcomes the opportunity to help in this endeavor."[56]

Business. A "Dear Ben" letter to Ben Carpenter, Chairman of the Board of the Southland Life Insurance Company, thanked Carpenter for an advertisement he ran in 59 church newspapers: "I am grateful, my friend, for your devoted contribution to the cause of the war against poverty and misery, ignorance and disease, and the cause of freedom and justice for every citizen. You are a true companion in arms in this war"[57]

Minorities. President Johnson wrote to Philleo Nash, the Commissioner of Indian Affairs, delineating the goals of the war on poverty, and adding: "They are [also] the goals of our Federal programs to assist Indians who are in the front ranks of Americans living under conditions of extreme poverty and hardship."[58]

Antipoverty Volunteers. Milton Ogle, of Pine Mountain, Kentucky, head of the Appalachian Volunteers, was praised by the Chief Executive for his leadership in demonstrating new and creative ways of using volunteers to help relieve conditions of rural poverty."[59]

Legislators. Harrison Williams, Chairman of the Senate Subcommittee on Migratory Labor was thanked for his offer of assistance in connection with the war on poverty. Johnson closed the letter: "I am, of course, aware of the excellent work that your Subcommittee has done and will see to it that the Executive Branch people working on this program keep in touch with you."[60]

The American People. And to Mrs. James E. Ward of East Liverpool, Ohio, President Johnson was consoling: "It was with a note of sorrow, but with a note of pride at the same time, that I read your recent letter. Sorrow for the situation which has befallen you and your husband. Pride because of the strength you have exhibited. . . . I have pledged myself to getting enacted a program that would help people in situations such as yours."[61]

Of course, it was not only the words Johnson wrote that were intended to make the difference. The following memo explains the White House response to opportunities for taking advantage of concrete examples that could say more than a thousand words.[62]

On March 16, President Johnson delivered his formal message on poverty to the Congress. But he made sure to pave the way first. The evening before, the president detailed his domestic plans in a special one-hour television interview that was carried by the three national networks. The relatively informal question-and-answer format—there were three interview-

Bill Moyers — this looks like good idea — any comments? Paul.

U.S. DEPARTMENT OF COMMERCE
AREA REDEVELOPMENT ADMINISTRATION
WASHINGTON, D.C. 20230

February 13, 1964

Paul—Send this over to Sarge

MEMORANDUM

RECEIVED
FEB 1 1 196.

To: Paul Southwick
         The White House

From: Donald W. Stull
         Special Assistant for Public Affairs

Subject: Rug Plant Visit

Out in Anadarko, Oklahoma, is an ARA-assisted carpet mill -- Sequoyah Carpet Mills -- which points up the poverty picture and what can be done about it as vividly as a press agent's dream.

The plant employes 52 production workers -- and only three of these ever have had jobs which lasted more than six months at a time. In other words, 49 of these people, mostly Indians and a few Negroes, are enjoying their first permanent jobs.

A stop-off visit by President Johnson or Sergeant Shriver, chatting with a few of the first-ever workers, would put the poverty picture before the people in heart-wringing terms.

ers, one of whom asked the president how he had succeeded in giving up smoking—provided a relaxed setting in which Johnson might be able to convey his ideas without getting mired in the more legalistic aspects of the antipoverty bill itself. He made his plan sound simple and feasible—the program would work largely through existing government agencies— though at the same time he cautioned against miracles. The president said that his legislation was only "a beginning," the first step toward getting at "the roots and causes of poverty."[63]

The Economic Opportunity Act of 1964 (EOA), as the antipoverty legislation was formally titled, proposed the establishment of an Office of Economic Opportunity (OEO) in the Executive Office of the President. The Director of the Office* would be "provided with coordinating powers with respect to existing federal agency poverty-related programs, and with authority to carry out new programs to attack poverty."[64] The bill contained six titles that, together, constituted a multi-pronged comprehensive package intended to: provide educational opportunities for the underprivileged young; give communities the chance to mobilize their own programs; enable privileged youth to redirect the idealism of the Peace Corps to domestic needs; and assist in the elimination of those factors that reduced farmers and laborers to poverty.[65] The main goals, however, were to help 380,000 underprivileged young people and stimulate local communities throughout the nation into waging antipoverty programs of their own— with federal assistance. The entire program was slated to cost about $962.5 million during its first year—almost 1 percent of the national budget.

Once again, Johnson's antipoverty rhetoric was laced with feeling. In his message to Congress the president said: "What does . . . poverty mean to those who endure it? It means a daily struggle to secure the necessities for even a meager existence. . . . Worst of all, it means hopelessness for the young. . . ."[66]

Many were already convinced. George Meany, for one, hailed the program as a step forward.[67] On the other hand, *The New York Times* was cautious about the proposal's political future. It warned that the president's program "was already under attack in some quarters as an election-year bid for votes," and that therefore it "faced an uncertain fate in Congress." *The New York Times* went on to predict that the passage of the antipoverty bill would depend largely on the persuasiveness of the president and Sargent Shriver.[68]

One day after Johnson delivered his message on poverty to the Congress, legislative hearings began.[69] Clearly, Shriver and the president had their

*In his message to Congress, Johnson stated that he intended to appoint Shriver first Director.

work cut out for them. House Republicans promptly attacked the bill on three grounds: (1) it would give too much power to the director of the OEO; (2) the government already had programs to carry out many of the proposals in the bill; and (3) it was unwise to put all the proposals into a single legislative package covering everything from education to agriculture. The Republicans were clearly not prepared to roll over and play dead on this one, and indeed *The New York Times* was now predicting that the future of the EOA would "undoubtedly" be "long and rocky."[70]

The opposition was led by Peter Frelinghuysen, the ranking Republican on the House Education and Labor Committee. Frelinghuysen contended that there was nothing new in the program. He argued that the Office of Economic Opportunity would merely be yet another layer of bureaucracy, and that interagency cooperation and coordination occurred even now without a "coordinating" office.

Predictions that Johnson's pet program faced a "long and rocky" future in the Congress indicated that to get the EOA passed, the White House would have to pay close attention to legislative strategy. The Johnson White House did. The president assumed primary responsibility for the development of a grand plan that would ensure the program's passage.

One tactic employed immediately was to have one or another member of the cabinet counter Republican efforts to sow discontent with Johnson's proposal. The cabinet took special pains to refute the charge that under the EOA they would would be no more than "doormats," while Shriver would emerge as the "poverty czar." Secretary of Commerce Luther Hodges, commented that "If we as Cabinet officers don't have enough influence, we oughtn't be around." And Secretary of Labor Wirtz added that "There's no master-and-servant relationship in this."[71]

The administration also made it a point throughout the five months to monitor all the House proceedings. It kept close tabs even on its own advocates. Memos tantamount to report cards for those who appeared before the House committee were being sent to Walter Heller by economist Burton Weisbrod. About the appearance of Anthony Celebrezze, Secretary of Health, Education and Welfare, Weisbrod wrote:

> The Secretary was given quite a rough time. I can only conclude that the Republicans were not well prepared for you and Shriver yesterday. . . . Celebrezze did not do well when the questioning became very critical. He reacted unnecessarily defensively, I thought, as if he were expecting to be trapped.

And Wirtz's performance was evaluated as follows:

> Wirtz did an exceptionally fine job. His performance contrasted strongly in quality with that of Secretary Celebrezze. . . .[72]

But perhaps Johnson's most important strategic contribution was to have the bill sponsored in the House by Phil Landrum of Georgia, instead of Adam Clayton Powell. Powell was still Chairman of the House Education and Labor Committee and ordinarily would have been assigned the task of floor leader for the EOA. But Powell was having some special personal and political problems at this time. Hence, after discussions with congressional liaison Larry O'Brien (whose opinion was that on this one they would have to pull a "magnificent rabbit out of a hat"),[73] it was decided that the much more conservative Landrum would be approached. Johnson convinced Landrum to serve as sponsor—and it was also Johnson who in turn persuaded George Meany not to oppose the Georgia Democrat for the job. (Landrum had been persona non grata with labor since his co-sponsorship in 1959 of a bill that many regarded as anti-union.) To short-circuit an angry response from Meany about the selection of Landrum to oversee the poverty bill, Johnson reminded him that "It's the result we're after." And indeed, as the president recalled it later, before the poverty bill was passed "Landrum and Meany were sitting down together for quiet and friendly talks."[74] The selection of Landrum was, in any case, regarded by at least one student of the antipoverty bill (Mark Gelfand) as a stroke of "political genius." Landrum was a "superb parliamentarian with solid ties to conservative southern Democrats whose votes were indispensable for the bill's passage."[75]

By late March it was nevertheless clear to the president that if he wanted the antipoverty bill to pass in-House, politics would not suffice. He would have to make a multi-pronged effort. Johnson again turned his attention to the American public. Hoping for a measure of vigorous support that would give pause to the program's opponents in Congress, he decided to make personal appearances in certain areas where conditions vividly illustrated the plight of the poor.

At an informal news conference held at the LBJ Ranch, the president disclosed his plans: "I want very much to go into some of the poverty areas. . . . and view conditions first hand."[76]

During these weeks, Johnson seemed to become increasingly preoccupied with the subject of poverty in general and—perhaps oddly—less concerned with the specifics of his own antipoverty proposal. It may fairly be said that during April the president metamorphosed from a salesman selling an anti-poverty product to an evangelist fiercely dedicated to solving the problem of poverty. In a speech to editors and broadcasters that was in fact described as "evangelistic,"[77] Johnson urged the American people to foster a "peaceful revolution" in the lives of the poverty-stricken peoples of the world. As he spoke—with great fervor and frequent departures from his prepared text—it seemed the president was moved by poverty abroad, as well as at home.

Oh, how I would like to feel that we could, here in this Rose Garden today, launch a new movement to develop a greater society, a better society in all the world, not only by driving poverty from our midst here at home, [but] by following the Golden Rule ... abroad, saying to these 112 nations, "We are going to do unto you as we would have you do unto us if our positions were reversed."[78]

In a speech given at the late March opening of the World's Fair in New York, the president predicted that visitors to the next great fair would see "an America unwilling to accept public deprivation in the midst of private satisfaction."[79] And one month later he began a five-state tour of just the kind of poverty-stricken area that was slated to benefit most from federal help.

This tour was scheduled so that the president could get a picture of poverty and unemployment. But clearly the visits served two political functions. First, presidential forays inevitably command a great deal of media coverage, and, by leading the television cameras into centers of poverty, the president forced the American people to see what being poor really looked like. (During the early 1960s the poor had been referred to by Michael Harrington as constituting the "other," or invisible, America.) Vivid pictures of grinding poverty, flashed via the magic of television into living rooms all across the country, would certainly prompt new support for any program that promised to alleviate such miserable conditions. Second, the two trips into the heartland of poverty also gave Johnson the opportunity to meet face to face with members of local political elites who would play important roles in getting the Economic Opportunity Act passed and then later in its implementation.

The White House saw these visits as politically important, a fact testified to by the care that went into their planning. Both trips are models of how to maximize a political opportunity. The first tour consisted of stops at South Bend, Indiana; Pittsburgh; Huntington, West Virginia; and two small Kentucky towns, Paintsville and Inez. The following evidence shows how carefully Johnson's interpersonal activity—his politicking—was staged.

Telegrams from Lyndon Johnson to the Governors of West Virginia, Kentucky, Tennessee, Virginia, North Carolina, Georgia, Pennsylvania, and Maryland requesting that they meet with him at the Huntington Airport to discuss matters of common interest.[80]

A memo that outlined who would be with the president when. Two Senators and one Congressman were slated to ride on Air Force One along with the president from Washington to Chicago. Several other Senators and Congressmen were to spend the day with Johnson in Pittsburgh. Another group of legislators from one of these states would stay with him during his swing through West Virginia, and a final trio would remain with the president until he departed Paintsville.[81]

Two lists of persons who can probably best be described as members of South Bend's power elite. One list contained politically useful information. Thus, the publisher of the *South Bend Tribune* was described as "most active in getting the training program started"; the Republican Mayor was characterized as "more and more active and willing to talk to the Federal Government"; and the president of a local bank was revealed as someone who "helped solve the problems of the Credit Union . . . [and who] made things easier for the people who were involved." Others on the lists included the governor of the State, the president and academic vice president of Notre Dame, the Dean of the Cathedral of St. James, the editor of the *Mishawaka Times,* the Co-Chairman of the Manpower Retraining Program, the President of the Local AFL-CIO, the president of Studebaker Local #5, the president of the Chamber of Commerce, the Assistant Superintendent of the South Bend Public Schools, the head of the Northwest Regional Governors Conference, the Chairman of the Democratic Party in South Bend, an official in the Studebaker Corporation, a head of a "group of negro leaders," and one Aloyisius Kromkowski, listed simply as a "leading Polish citizen."[82] All were clearly slated to be tapped as "volunteers" for the war on poverty.

An itinerary for Pittsburgh that accounted for every minute of the president's time, and every person he would come into contact with. There were also brief suggestions on what he might say to whom.[83]

A copy of the president's speech to the League of Women Voters, part of which read "One of the best women I know told me of a social worker who called on a family at meal time. . . . During the meal time she noticed one of the many small children who was not eating. When she asked the child why, the answer was: 'It's not my day to eat.' Our society cannot tolerate that kind of situation."[84]

To all appearances, the president's first trip to dramatize poverty was a great success. He heard what was described as "frenzied cheers" from the crowd,[85] and he reciprocated in kind, driving himself hard—on one day taking time out for no more than a hamburger from early morning until late at night. He insisted that he had come to talk poverty, not politics. But, reported *The New York Times,*

> Somewhere along the way, the roars of the mammoth crowds turned his scheduled poverty tour into a political triumph.

> South Bend mobbed him. Pittsburgh hailed him. And people from
> some of the poorest areas of West Virginia and Kentucky came out of
> the greening hills and coves to tell him their stories of hard luck. . . .[86]

No doubt encouraged by his triumph, the president widened his antipoverty effort and promptly proposed to Congress yet another antipoverty measure, this one to send direct help to the poverty-stricken Appalachian region.

Rather than deflect attention from the Economic Opportunity Act, the president's new request for aid to Appalachia further dramatized the larger problem. Poverty was becoming this president's big issue and indeed the two proposals were being linked. As *The New York Times* said in an editorial just a few days after the president returned from his trip to issue yet another legislative request in the poverty area, "The war against poverty will have to be fought in every urban and rural slum, but Appalachia is a good place to begin."[87]

On May 6 President Johnson went on a second trip to spur his drive on poverty. A staff memo gave suggestions on what he might talk about at the various stops:

1. Cumberland, Maryland. Here the president should discuss unemployment in Appalachia and what could be done about it. (The president was scheduled to visit an unemployment office there.)
2. Athens, Ohio (site of Ohio University). Here he should address the academic community's responsibility and role in the war on poverty.
3. Knoxville, Tennessee. Here he might point to urban renewal problems as well as the retraining factories needed by many cities to attract industry. (The president was scheduled to visit a proposed urban renewal area and then get a briefing by the governor on Tennessee's progress in this area.)
4. North Carolina. This was the place to talk about the rural aspects of the poverty bill. (The president would be seeing "an impoverished farm family"; then the governor would inform him of the rural needs of the state of North Carolina.)
5. Atlanta. The Georgia Legislature was primarily rural and the memo suggests, therefore, that Atlanta would "be an ideal spot for the president to really enlist the rural or southern support for his programs."
6. Gainsville. Here, as in Knoxville, it was suggested that the president point out that local people, if given proper housing, schools, and training programs, would enable the community to attract industry. Then it was proposed that the President "tour an urban renewal area and possibly meet with a Negro or several Negro families on the street. This is the

town that Roosevelt rebuilt in 1936 and is definitely a New Deal type town."[88]

Once again, the attention to political detail was impressive. It seems that people were given the honor of being asked to meet personally with the president either if they were in a good position to help (for example, by giving money or securing the support of others for the EOA), or if they themselves constituted living proof of the need for the Economic Opportunity Act (for example, 27 retrained women blouse factory workers; 150 "selected farmers"; poor—"both white and Negro"). Moreover, if the president was scheduled to bestow the ultimate honor—a few personal words—background material was provided. The report on one of the two young women who sat at the front of the Ohio University auditorium while Johnson gave his speech there, and to whom the president obviously would have to say something, read as follows: "The President presented her with a scholarship check on behalf of the Capital Press Club last year. She is a freshman. . . . Her father is deceased and her mother is unemployed. . . . Thus far she has received two awards . . . totaling $1,150."[89]

Once again Johnson's rhetoric was powerful—"I come here to ask your help in carrying forward the American revolution. . . . This time it is a battle to open the gates of the great society to all who seek to enter"[90]—and once again Johnson's trip to the heartland to dramatize the war on poverty was a great success. The *Times* observed that the president got "an overwhelming reception";[91] *U.S. News & World Report* noted that in one town the outpouring of people was more than double the size of the local population;[92] and a North Carolina Democratic State Committee Official sent the following wire to Johnson aide Cliff Carter.

> . . . JUST WANTED TO REPORT THAT ALL OF US ARE VERY HAPPY WITH THE OUTCOME OF THE PRESIDENTS VISIT YESTERDAY. HIGHY PATROL CAPT. IN CHARGE SAID LARGEST CROWD HE HAS SEEN AT ONE PLACE. . . . THIS VISIT WAS A SHOT IN THE ARM TO PARTY IMAGE IN THIS SECTION.[93]

Meanwhile, the correspondence between the president and the public continued. Indeed, in May it became heavier. No group seems to have been left out. Business executives, state and local officials, veterans, academics, school administrators, social workers, senior citizens, women's clubs, members of the press, minority groups—all were stroked on behalf of the Economic Opportunity Act.

The interest group with whom Lyndon Johnson generated the most correspondence was labor. In one form or another the president was in contact with representatives from all of the following: Retail Clerks Association, United Federation of Postal Clerks, Utility Workers Union of America, United Hatters, Cap and Millinery Workers International Union, United

Auto Workers of America (whose president, Walter Reuther, described himself in a letter to Johnson as one of his "loyal soldiers in the unconditional war against poverty"), International Labor Press Association, Labor—Zionist Organization, United Packinghouse Workers Union, and, of course, the AFL-CIO.[94]

During the spring of 1964, Lyndon Johnson's hammering paid off. Poverty in America was transformed into a pressing national issue. Before Johnson's presidency, America's poor were outside the mainstream of our political life. Six months after he took office, they were, to use Dwight MacDonald's word, "fashionable." By enlisting organizations from the Daughters of the American Revolution to the Socialist Party, by appealing to the people and to their representatives, by personally visiting poverty-stricken regions, by highlighting conditions and reminding members of Congress of their responsibilities to their constituents, by meeting with those in a position to make a difference, by invoking word, deed, and image on behalf of the war on poverty, and finally by promising to help make America the great society that it was surely destined to become—by doing all of this, Lyndon Johnson made the poor fashionable.

The medium, of course, was the media. Seemingly from one month to the next, the nation was "deluged with vivid descriptions of the life of the poor, statistical accounts of their number and characteristics, and details of their geographic location." Even *The Saturday Evening Post* ran a lead article running twelve pages entitled "The Invisible Americans." Poverty was now a subject of public discourse, and by the time the Economic Opportunity Act was brought to a vote in the Congress, it seemed to many Americans to be a matter of the highest national priority.[95]

The first step in making the EOA law—passage by the House Education and Labor Committee—was relatively easy.* Even so, the president took nothing for granted. As the following memo suggests, he kept tabs on everyone. (The memorandum is unsigned but it was probably from Bill Moyers. It was sent the day of the Committee vote.)

Mr. President:

Cong. Carl Albert† called and said:
"The President will probably want this information. I don't want to bother him though, so would you leave a note on his desk or get word to him that the Committee Staff of Education and Labor has completed the final draft of a clean bill for the poverty bill, and that Congressman Landrum dropped it in the hopper about ten minutes ago. . . . The Par-

*The EOA was approved by the House Education and Labor Committee by a 19 to 12 vote along straight party lines. Several changes were made in Johnson's original proposal, but all the essentials were left in tact.
†Albert was the House Democratic Floor Leader.

liamentarian has sent it to the printer and they say they will have 50 copies for the Committee by 9:00 tomorrow morning, and the Committee will meet at 10:00 to report the bill. The only problem we have, and I don't think it's a problem, but the only thing we have to watch for is to be sure that quorum is there because all they'll have to do is to meet and vote the bill out."[96]

But despite smooth sailing through the House Education and Labor Committee, and despite Johnson's unflagging energy as both strategist and publicist, passage of the EOA was still far from certain. Many Republicans and Southern Democrats remained unconvinced. Predictably, Republicans were especially prone to making sharp attacks. At an April press conference Richard Nixon called the war on poverty a "cruel hoax." Two Republican members of the House Education and Labor Committee asserted that the president's poverty campaign was "nothing more than an election year gimmick." New York's Governor Nelson Rockefeller, campaigning for the Republican presidential nomination, labeled the administration's poverty war as a "public relations effort to distract people's attention" from its failure to provide more jobs. And Barry Goldwater continued to maintain that "most people who have no skill, have had no education for the same reason—low intelligence or low ambition."[97]

By mid-May it was evident that the opposition had to be taken seriously. Democratic congressional leaders warned the president that it was questionable whether a Rules Committee majority could be mustered for the poverty bill.

The main stumbling block was Howard W. Smith, the conservative Virginia Democrat who was still the Rules Committee chairman. Although Smith did not, as some had feared, allow the bill to languish—he scheduled hearings on the measure for mid-June—he did not exactly help the proposal either. Smith harped on the racial issue with regard to the antipoverty measure, pointing out that several of its programs demanded racial integration. An exchange between Smith and Landrum, the fellow southern Democrat who was serving as the bill's sponsor, went like this:

SMITH: I assume these job camps will be completely integrated.
LANDRUM: Negroes do not constitute all the poor people in the world. The fact these camps would be integrated is a matter of law over which neither you or I have been able to prevail.

Smith also wondered whether the government could afford such a costly program. "Why not send [these young people] to Harvard?" he asked. Landrum replied: "We might be able to save some youngsters through this program who might make mighty fine students for Harvard."[98]

Smith beat Johnson in a contest of will about when the Rules Committee would finally vote on the antipoverty measure. Johnson wanted to hasten the process and schedule a vote before the Republican National Convention. Smith refused and on June 25 Moyers sent the president the following unequivocal memo.

> MR. PRESIDENT:
>
> Wilson McCarthy* called to say that Judge Smith told Shriver this morning that he would not give Poverty a rule until after the Republican Convention.
> He said that was definite.
> Bill Moyers[99]

Meanwhile the administration was faced with several other important tactical decisions. One major question was whether the bill should be passed by the House before it came up in the Senate, or vice versa. Again there is evidence that Johnson was kept informed, and was in charge, at every crucial decision-making point. On June 26 Larry O'Brien forwarded to the president a memorandum written by Yarmolinsky that "carefully reviewed all aspects of the problem."[100] Yarmolinsky's opinion—which O'Brien concurred with—was that the administration should not press for Senate action until the bill cleared the House: "Even if the Senate Committee could succeed in reporting a bill by the Republican Convention, the risks are too great: To take one example, if the bill were to be on the floor of both Houses simultaneously, there would be less of a chance of correcting crippling amendments."[101] Sargent Shriver made the same point just a few days later in a "Memorandum to the President" that began: "I believe the fastest way to get a Poverty bill out is to put House action ahead of Senate action"[102]

Thus, all three of Johnson's top antipoverty bill aides—Yarmolinsky, O'Brien, and Shriver—were recommending House passage first. But despite their recommendation, the measure went first to the Senate, suggesting that it was Lyndon Johnson who in fact called the shots throughout the congressional maneuvering. It may be presumed that the president's impatience to get the measure passed dictated his strategy, at least in part. Only a month or two remained in this congressional session, and Johnson was determined that the EOA would become law before the November election. Judge Smith, meanwhile, remained uncooperative. Now clearly opposed to the antipoverty program, Smith managed to stretch out the Rules Committee hearings, thereby delaying the required clearance for action by the full House.

The president, never one to pull back from a congressional contest, proceeded to undertake an end run. He circumvented Smith by sidestepping the recommendations of his own aides. By July 6, the bill was reported favorably by the Senate Labor Committee and sent to the Senate floor

*Wilson McCarthy was a Special Assitant for Congressional Affairs.

almost intact. Once again Johnson's impatience seems to have made an impression on all concerned, as shown in the following memo:

> July 1, 1964
>
> Mr. President:
>
> I just talked to Senator Humphrey who just came from a meeting with Lister Hill* and other appropriate Senators. Humphrey says that the full Committee will take up the poverty bill and pass it on Tuesday and the Senate will vote on Wednesday.
>   Humphrey says that's the best he can do.
>
> Bill Moyers[103]

Between the time the bill went to the Senate floor in early July and August 20, the day the Economic Opportunity Act was signed into law, Lyndon Johnson spent an extraordinary amount of energy on the bill's behalf. His final push consisted of intense personal lobbying over a period of six weeks.

A good deal of the interpersonal activity was of course choreographed by Johnson's able and tireless White House staff. He was sent memos on what to say. Before talking to the "*Time-Life* people," for example, he was advised that, "It is of some importance that you discuss the Texas Central Hill Country as a background for your interest in 'The Great Society.' Actually, it is the perfect background for the simple reason that building the 'Great Society' is very similar to the problems that your relatives and neighbors faced and conquered."[104] He was sent memos on whom to see:

> MEMORANDUM FOR THE PRESIDENT
>
> Subject: White House Conference on
>   the War Against Poverty
>
> We propose a two-day White House Conference on the War Against Poverty to be held about August 1.
>   Some 500 leaders would be invited representing Government and voluntary agencies. They would include business, labor, farm, church, student, and university groups. . . .
>   The conference should end in a meeting with you. The action agreed upon would be reported and you would speak. . . .
>
> Sargent Shriver[105]

> July 4, 1964
>
> MEMORANDUM FOR THE PRESIDENT
>
> Sargent Shriver called me the other day. Six of the twelve members of

*Hill sponsored the EOA in the Senate.

the Poverty Advisory Council* have been invited to the Businessmen's
Luncheon on Thursday. He is hopeful that the other six members can
be invited and, after the luncheon, meet with you briefly as a group. Mr.
Shriver feels that such a meeting would be helpful to strengthen the
upcoming poverty legislation this week.
Jack Valenti[107]

And, throughout the six weeks of heightened activity in the Congress, President Johnson continued to receive memos on what exactly was happening
on Capitol Hill. Johnson's singular commitment to the poverty bill is vividly
illustrated in his handwritten reply to one such memorandum, in which he
reminds O'Brien that "this bill means more than any other in our
program."[108]

But if Johnson's White House staff was reponsible for much of the choreography, it is still true that the president's own political performance was
remarkable for its tenacity and passion. And indeed the president's efforts
paid off. On July 23 the antipoverty bill passed the Senate—after nearly
ten hours of "often bitter debate"[109]—by a vote of 62 to 33. Liberal Republicans joined with 52 Democrats to vote for the EOA; conservative Democrats, most of them Southerners, joined with 22 Republicans to vote against
the measure.

The administration's revised strategy—sending the EOA through the
Senate first—had worked. The larger than expected Senate victory gave
the bill a certain momentum and on July 28 it narrowly cleared the House
Rules Committee. The 8 to 7 vote there paved the way for action by the
full House, although Democratic leaders were still predicting a "hard fight"
ahead. House Republicans, contending that the measure was "phony," a
"sloppy piece of work," and little more than an election year bid for votes,
formed an almost solid opposition bloc and accordingly promised an all-out
floor fight. The administration was thus in the position of having to secure
some support from conservative Southern Democrats—a prospect not
enhanced by the manner in which Judge Smith announced the bill's clearing through his committee: "This crazy bill was reported out of committee,
and I don't care if you say I called it that."[110]

Hence began the period of the most intense lobbying of all. With Republican ranks closing against the bill, the administration focused its attention
on Southern Democrats who now seemed to offer Johnson's measure per-

*The White House had also compiled a longer list of businessmen who constituted the
"Business Leadership Advisory Council" of the Economic Opportunity Program. Members
of the Council included the presidents of the New York Stock Exchange, Detroit Edison,
Douglas Aircraft, Utah Mining and Construction, Pittsburgh Chemical Co., Parker Pen
Co., Morton Salt Co., Hotel Corporation of America, and the Mechanics and Farmers
Bank. A list of blue-chip Mayors was organized for a similar lobbying purpose; it included
the mayors of New York, Boston, Chicago, Philadelphia, Los Angeles, St. Louis, Nashville,
Denver, Tampa, and Atlanta.[106]

MEMORANDUM

THE WHITE HOUSE
WASHINGTON

July 9, 1964

MEMORANDUM TO THE PRESIDENT

FROM: Larry O'Brien

Judge Smith has notified the members of the
Rules Committee that the Social Security bill
will be taken up in Committee Tuesday, July 21,
and hearings will continue on the Poverty bill
starting Wednesday, July 22. I have talked to
Speaker McCormack and Tip O'Neill - both are
clear that it will probably be necessary to invoke
the 7-day rule on Poverty.

[handwritten note]

haps its only chance of gaining House approval.[111] The growing signs that
the bill might be in serious trouble—one House leader was quoted as saying
"It's close, mighty close. I'm not a bit comfortable about it"[112]—propelled
President Johnson into high gear. Using lists of doubtfuls, he made personal
contact. Eric Goldman* writes:

*Goldman was a Special Consultant to the President between February 1964 and September 1966.

LBJ's phone went into high digit, to bring Democrats back into the fold and to pick off detachable Republicans. Most of his arm twisting was the usual effort to add an affirmative vote, but in a case where the representative clearly would not support the bill, the forcible suggestion was made that he "take a walk"—find himself inextricably busy some place other than the House chamber at the time of the vote. President Johnson relentlessly pressured congressmen and relentlessly pressured other people to pressure congressmen. He went after not only the usual allies of such legislation but publishers, industrialists and bankers. . . . Lyndon Johnson threw everything he had into the fight, including the White House photography room. Doubtful congressmen suddenly found that they were cordially welcome at the White House for a joint photograph with the President, along with a few words on how sensible it would be to vote for EOA.[113]

In addition to Johnson's strenuous interpersonal effort, he used another political tactic: compromise. Apparently fearing that without compromise on his part the EOA would indeed go down to defeat, Johnson, with seemingly little hesitation, met his oppoinents halfway or more on several key points. Some of these measures were matters of policy, such as the elimination of two rural programs, the requirement of a loyalty oath from all enrollees in the Job Corps, and a governors' veto over antipoverty projects in their states. But one compromise was a matter not of policy but of personnel, and it was the most controversial of all. To this day, it leaves many with a bad taste.

For all the lobbying and compromising, by early August the fate of the EOA still remained in doubt. Southern Democrats were holding out in dangerous numbers. The question was: What could Johnson offer them without compromising the essentials of the antipoverty bill? The answer was Adam Yarmolinsky.

Since the task force on poverty had been established, Yarmolinsky had played a central role—first in the formulation of the EOA, and later in the attempt to get it passed. Accordingly, it was widely assumed that as Shriver's number two man, he could expect a top level job in the Office of Economic Opportunity once it was formally established. But Yarmolinsky was, in the words of Eric Goldman, "one of those occasional Washington figures who are custom-tailored to raise the darkest suspicions of Southern Congressmen. He was from New York City, a Harvard graduate, short, dark, Jewish, militantly liberal, brilliant and quite aware that he was brilliant."[114] Moreover, Yarmolinsky was especially associated with federal efforts to foster desegregation; while at the Defense Department he had helped set up a commission to investigate racial discrimination in the Armed Forces. Thus, it is perhaps not altogether surprising that as the contest between Johnson and the Southern Democrats came down to the wire, it was Yarmolinsky who was the last pawn.

On August 6, in the office of the House Speaker John McCormack, a meeting was arranged between conservative North Carolina Democrats* and Shriver. In short order the demand was made: The Congressmen would vote "no" on the antipoverty bill unless they had absolute assurance that Yarmolinsky would be excluded from any part in administering the new program. Shriver tried to dodge. All matters of executive personnel were uncertain, he said, and in any case they were up to the president. Then telephone the president, the Congressmen demanded, which Shriver did. A few minutes later he returned from the phone to report that "The President had no objection to my saying that if I were appointed [as Director of the OEO] I would not recommend Yarmolinsky." The next day Phil Landrum pronounced sentence on Yarmolinsky by telling the House that he had it on the "highest authority" that "this gentleman will have absolutely nothing to do with the program."[115]

Johnson never publicly acknowledged the trade-off. He omitted reference to it in his autobiography, and at a press conference 48 hours after the meeting in McCormack's office the following exchange took place:

Q. Mr. President, I want to ask a question about Adam Yarmolinsky. . . . He had been with the Department of Defense—
JOHNSON: He still is.
Q. I thought he had been working . . . on the poverty bill.
JOHNSON: No, your thoughts are wrong. . . . He is still with the Department of Defense.
Q. I was also asked to ask you, sir, if he was going back to the Pentagon, but you say he is still there.
JOHNSON: He never left.[116]

On August 8 Johnson's antipoverty bill passed the House by a larger margin than anyone had expected: the final vote was 226–184. The Senate had only to give its final backing to the amended measure before Johnson could sign the EOA into law. This last step was accomplished on August 11, in what the *Times* labeled "a strangely quiet climax to what had been one of the most partisan political battles waged in Congress in recent years."[117] A summary of the EOA as finally passed by the United States Senate reads as follows:

> The Economic Opportunity Act of 1964 would establish an Office of Economic Opportunity in the Executive Office of the President. The OEO would be headed by a Director who would have a planning and coordinating staff responsible for coordinating the poverty-related programs of all Government agencies. Within the OEO, separate staffs would operate a Jobs Corps, a program for Volunteers In Service to America (VISTA), a Community Action Program, and special pro-

*Evans and Novak claim that South Carolinians were also present.

grams for migrant workers. In addition, the OEO would distribute funds to existing agencies to operate other programs authorized under the bill. . . ."[118]

Reaction to Johnson's legislative triumph was mixed—even among those who had supported his antipoverty efforts. *The New York Times* lamented that the antipoverty bill had been "deprived . . . of much of the force it should have as the first step in a noble crusade." In particular, the newspaper decried the loyalty oath requirement and the "Administration's supine sacrifice" of Adam Yarmolinsky.[119] Other allies of Johnson were simply grateful that the bill had passed. Carl Albert reportedly told the president, "I really can't figure out . . . how in the world we ever got this through."[120]

The president himself was gratified, to say the least. He smiled and "beamed happily" at the signing ceremony, at which he made sure to use and then hand out as souvenirs a total of 72 pens. "The days of the dole in our country are numbered," he said on that occasion.[121] And in his autobiography he wrote of that week, "It just couldn't have been more encouraging or rewarding."[122]

The Practice of Leadership

There were, of course, problems in the implementation of the Economic Opportunity Act, problems that emerged even during Johnson's own presidency.[123] But if we pose only the question most central to this book—was the president able to get what he wanted when he wanted it?—the answer quite simply is yes. With regard to the first volley in the war on poverty, Johnson accomplished what he set out to; by the time of the 1964 presidential election, the EOA was law.

To grasp the full dimension of Johnson's leadership on this issue, we must go back to the beginning. Lyndon Johnson started the antipoverty effort almost from scratch and almost alone. As previously noted, some interest in the problems of the poor existed during the Kennedy administration. But Kennedy himself could scarcely be described as especially concerned; as with most of those with political influence, his consciousness had yet to be raised. When Lyndon Johnson took office on Nobember 23, 1963, poverty simply was not seen as a pressing national issue. The concept of an antipoverty bill, unlike the aid to education bill that was discussed in the last chapter, was essentially new.

Therefore, the president had to exercise leadership in three distinct areas. First, he had to develop a public policy that addressed itself to poverty in America. Then he had to create a climate in which the poor would no longer be invisible to those with political power. And, finally, Johnson had to convince key members of the political elite that the legislation he proposed would effectively attack the problem as they now perceived it.

In step one of the president's task, the key players were the individuals who actually wrote the antipoverty bill that was proposed to Congress in March. Heller, Gordon, Yarmolinsky, and Shriver—all were at various stages and in various ways pushed by the president to give form and content to what was, in the beginning, little more than a vague notion. We have seen that the president had little interest in the details of what they were doing. On the other hand, he had a great deal of interest in seeing that they did it.

Johnson's position vis-à-vis those who drafted the antipoverty legislation was straightforward. He was their superior, their boss. He did not have to persuade or convince them to do his bidding. They did so or they were out. Still, the evidence suggests that those who worked on the antipoverty bill were doing more than just taking orders. They willingly and even eagerly followed the leader who had assigned them a task they genuinely believed in.

In fact, Johnson's posture concerning both the early, informal group and the task force on poverty was unusually felicitous. He seemed to strike the right balance between granting leeway and maintaining control. In order to get what he wanted, and get it quickly, Johnson provided the members of his antipoverty team with several benefits: a job that they were ideologically as well as politically motivated to complete, a high sense of personal efficacy, and his own personal encouragement and support.

The precise nature of Johnson's involvement with the development of the EOA during early 1964 still remains unclear. Gelfand observed only recently that certain key decisions along the way that are not documented could only have been made by the president. In addition, "a large gap in primary sources exists in relation to Shriver's role."[124]

However, we can say that Johnson succeeded in carrying out step one of his leadership task. He assembled and directed a task force that gave form and substance to what was known in the beginning only as an attack on poverty. Moreover, he did so in short order. Although we now know that a slower drafting process might have precluded problems of implementation that arose later, Johnson was faced with several frankly short-term goals. We may recall that these included—perhaps above all—his desire to put forth early on a "bold and attention-getting proposal on which he could put his personal stamp." And it was important to him that his credentials as a strong and benevolent leader be established in time for the November election. Thus, the president did not have much time in which to formulate a public policy out of what was, initially, little more than an amorphous idea.

Step two of Johnson's task was to make poverty a "hot topic." The only environment in which any antipoverty bill would stand a chance of congressional passage was one in which the following perceptions were widely shared: (1) the problems of the poor were acute; and (2) remedial action was a moral and political imperative.

Lyndon Johnson's success in this can hardly be questioned. Almost singlehandedly he educated us to the plight of the poor and thereby created a climate receptive to his proposed war on poverty.

Although Johnson has not generally been described as a great orator, his speeches on America's poor nevertheless constituted highly effective propaganda. The language was dramatic; the rhetoric appeared to be deeply felt; and the appeals from any number of different pulpits* were frequent and unabashed. Lyndon Johnson never missed a chance to display his commitment to what he argued was a just and noble cause. The following excerpt from an address at the convention of the Amalgamated Clothing Workers of America conveys Johnson's characteristic tone on the subject.

> The march of progress in America has left 30 million hungry, aimless, forgotten refugees in its wake, and I saw many of them in the Appalachian states this week. . . .
>
> But poverty stalks not only in the hills and valleys of Appalachia. It is here today. It is here in this city on all sides of the track right around where you live. It is the widow around the corner barely surviving on a pension of $70 a month. It is the teen-ager down the block unprepared by schooling and unwanted by an employer. It is the retired factory worker sick of body and tired of soul depending on charity for his miserly medical needs.
>
> I am here today to prophesy and to predict and to tell you that we are going to do something. This Administration has declared unconditional war on poverty, and I have come here this morning to ask all of you to enlist as volunteers.[126]

But Johnson's speech making was only one of several devices he used in his role as pitchman. There were the staged visits to poverty-stricken regions; the countless meetings with black and white, rich and poor, business and labor, urban and rural, public and private, right and left—almost every single interest group was approached; and finally there were the mails, letters signed by the President of the United States thanking people all across the land for support already given or requesting what was not yet firmly in hand.

*Johnson was especially concerned with his performances on television. Careful memos were prepared evaluating them. With regard to a televised press conference at the height of the poverty bill fight, Paul Southwick wrote Bill Moyers that the president's "prepared statements in the beginning were deadly," but that his performance "in the give-and-take later in the conference was excellent."[125]

Indeed Johnson's success in getting America to focus on poverty, in making it a national issue, cannot be questioned. But while we have considered his methods of influence, we have not yet asked why the public at large accepted his influence attempts. What motivated the American people to fall into line behind this pied piper of the poverty program?

It would seem that Americans followed Johnson on this one for three reasons. First, in the wake of the death of John Kennedy, there was a national yearning to heal the wound. One way of doing that was by legitimizing the leadership of the man the dead president himself had chosen to stand by as a possible successor. Johnson enlisted the support of many Americans who wanted to see him succeed not so much for his own sake as for the sake of the country he now led.

Second, Lyndon Johnson repeatedly appealed to our own better instincts. Over and over again, the president implied that it was no less than our duty as decent human beings to support him on the EOA. Thus, another reason for following the president on the antipoverty bill was that it gave the American people a political opportunity to abide by what many of them perceived to be their most deeply held values.

Finally, I would suggest that Johnson succeeded in creating a climate hospitable to the war on poverty because he adroitly linked the alleviation of the plight of the poor to an improvement in the quality of life for us all. By the spring of 1964 the president was beginning to think in terms of a "great society." Thus, when Johnson spoke of an Economic Opportunity Act that would, for example, educate the underprivileged young and retrain the unemployed, he was talking not only of bettering the lives of those who would benefit directly, but of improving the lives of the rest of us as well. If the least among us profited from the great society, so too would we all gain.

Having developed a public policy on poverty and then succeeding in making the plight of the poor a stain on America's conscience, Lyndon Johnson now faced his third and final challenge: to persuade key members of the political elite—especially members of Congress—to follow him by passing the Economic Opportunity Act.

The relative speed and ease with which Johnson moved the antipoverty bill through the legislative process are deceiving. The EOA's passage in both houses of Congress in little more than five months suggests that it was a routine measure, whose success was almost assured. As we have seen, it was not. First, the legislation was highly innovative and was a significant departure both ideologically and substantively from what had been before. Second, the Congress that Johnson inherited had not been overly responsive in the past. According to the *Congressional Quarterly Almanac,* Kennedy had secured passage of only 27 percent of his legislative proposals in 1963.

Thus, Gelfand is correct to make a special point of the fact that "the anti-poverty program found a smooth and quick route through the legislative morass, something no domestic reform proposal had seen since the glory days of the New Deal." He adds: "By all accounts Lyndon Johnson is credited with this success."[127]

Johnson was by nature a political animal. He thrived on a schedule packed with the kinds of interpersonal activities that constitute the essence of politicking. That became apparent immediately after he succeeded to the presidency. One month after Johnson took office, articles appeared that talked about how "astounded" news reporters were by his hectic pace: "His discussions with Negro leaders, top businessmen and labor executives and key members of both Houses came one upon another. . . ."[128] And three months after that, president watchers were no less impressed—both by Lyndon Johnson's level of activity and by his drive to establish contact with anyone and everyone who might make a political difference: "Cyclonic activity is the hallmark of the Johnson style. . . . If Kennedy's instinct on confronting a problem was to analyze it, Johnson's is to be in touch with the man who knows the answer."[129]

As Kearns notes, the unprecedented number of meetings with public leaders that occurred during the first ninety days of the Johnson presidency served a variety of purposes. Most important, they provided the president with information about each person with whom he would have to deal, especially "their feelings and attitudes toward him. In the immediate presence of another man, Johnson felt utterly confident of his ability to judge what that man really wanted."[130]

It is not surprising, therefore, that close interpersonal contact constituted much of Johnson's intense lobbying on behalf of what he wanted. Nor is it surprising that the impact of Johnson's personal attention, whether by phone or in person, was considerable. Stephen Wayne writes that "Johnson had a very effective telephone manner. He tended to be disarmingly informal and ultimately persuasive. In describing his own telephone tactics, Johnson wrote: 'When I made these phone calls, I had no set script. Sometimes I would ask: "What do you think of this bill?" Or: "Say, Congressman, I haven't seen you around in a while, just wondering how you've been."'"[131] And, as Walter Heller recalls, the president was no less effective in person.

> People just [left] singing paeans of praise for Lyndon Johnson; it didn't matter which group it was.
> I thought he'd come a cropper when he came up against the university presidents. But he'd speak for, typically, ten minutes from his notes, and then he'd put his notes aside and lean over that lectern and talk to those

people as if he was having a personal man-to-man conversation with every person in the room. . . .

He has a mastery of men in this respect. It was just a marvelous thing to behold.[132]

When Johnson wanted something badly enough, certain key persons who stood in his way were subjected to a full course of the "Johnson treatment." The "Johnson treatment" was the president's highly personal, intense, sometimes quite overwhelming effort to win friends and immediately enlist their support (in this case, members of Congress who could serve as swing votes for the EOA). Ordinarily, the treatment was not applied to anyone who had indicated either strong support or strong opposition to a given proposal. Rather, Johnson worked on those who might yet be persuaded to follow and then convince others to do the same.

Johnson's more than twenty years in Congress had provided him with a rich store of information about its processes and personnel. Such information was freely used in the Johnson treatment. But it is hard to say whether it was this rich experiential learning, or an intuitive sense of how to get someone to go along, that best explains his political effectiveness. It was probably a combination of both. For a good part of his career Lyndon Johnson had a sixth sense about how to exercise leadership in America. He understood that leadership usually involves a two-way influence relationship, that to lead the leader must somehow obtain the willing cooperation of others. "Give a man a good reason for voting with you," he would say, "and he'll try. Try to force it down his throat and he'll gag. A man can take a little bourbon without getting drunk, but if you hold his mouth open and pour in a quart, he'll get sick on you."[133]

To get the EOA passed, Johnson used three different methods of influence: control over the gains and costs to his followers, persuasion, and control over his followers' environment. In turn, people became followers for reasons ranging from the desire to receive a reward or avoid punishment (who among us wouldn't prefer an invitation to dinner at the White House to an order to "take a walk"?) to the wish to express their own best instincts. (Jack Valenti writes that the classic Johnson approach was to "create a mood and feeling within the legislator that the best interests of the nation . . . would be served if a particular law was passed."[134])

Johnson was too clever to depend only on one or two political tactics. His bag of tricks was large. To persuade key members of the political elite to go along, Johnson did each of the following: he *educated* and *aroused* us about poverty in America; he gave the political elite *advance notice* that he would submit an antipoverty measure; he *timed* his policy initiative for the recovery period immediately following Kennedy's death; he *preempted problems* by, among other actics, bringing a wide range of people and groups into the policy-making process and making skillful and extensive use of his White House staff; he arranged for his *cabinet to testify* on the bill's behalf; he made countless *personal appeals*—in person, on the phone, on television, and by mail; he provided *services* and *personal amenities* to those who were deserving or might yet be; he *arm twisted* as he deemed it necessary; he *compromised* on matters of policy and personnel; he generated strong *outside support* (testimony to his sure knowledge that one way to a Congressman's heart is over his head through his constituency); and last, but by no means last, he *impressed* his followers with his own sure sense of command and control.

A close look at Lyndon Johnson's persona helps us get a still better feel for why he was so effective in interpersonal situations. For example, for all his pushing and shoving, he had generally high esteem for his followers, especially for members of Congress who had long been colleagues. He understood them as individuals; and he understood their collective wish for attention and respect. Valenti writes that one of his first instructions from Johnson went like this: "I want you to understand one thing more than anything else I will tell you. The most important people you will talk to are senators and congressmen. You treat them as if they were president. Answer their calls immediately. Give them respect. They deserve it. Remember senators and congressmen, they are your most important clients. Be responsive to them."[135]

Moreover, Johnson's bullying of others was made more palatable by his own fierce devotion to the cause. Many people worked many hours to get the EOA passed, but no one worked harder than the president himself. Carl Albert pointed to this zeal when he spoke of the president's general leadership style.

> President Johnson's intensity of interest was such that he not only sent all of these [bills] up, but he never rested from the time one was passed until you started another. He would never rest on his laurels, or let us rest on ours. He would insist and urge us to go with the next bill just as fast as we could. He had his staff, himself personally, working with not only the leadership, but with committees—everybody that had something to do with them. I'm sure that in all the history of Congress there has never been so much presidential activity in pushing legislation and in successfully not only proposing, but disposing of legislation as we were able to do with his leadership. . . .[136]

Finally, there was something about Lyndon Johnson that can best be described as vaguely menacing. Johnson appeared larger than life—not just a big man physically, though of course he was that too. Rather it was the way he used his body along with his power.[137] Johnson leaned into people; he touched them, he held them in place until his last point was driven home.

He made it clear that he was very keen indeed on getting what he wanted. If that meant, in Goldman's words, a "forcible suggestion," then so be it. If it meant the sacrifice of a man's career, well, that was too bad. LBJ's former press secretary, George Reedy, captures this well. Reedy writes: "By sheer size alone, [Johnson] would dominate any landscape. And no one could avoid the feeling of an elemental force at work when in his presence. One did not know whether he was an earthquake, a volcano, or a hurricane but one knew he possesed the force of all three combined and that whatever it was, it might go off at any moment."[138]

In Part I of this book I wrote that presidents have three sources of power: instrumental, authoritative, and libidinal. My argument was that the differences among the presidents in terms of these power resources are fewer than one might think. Therefore, what must interest us in terms of explaining why some lead more effectively than others is the will and skill with which these resources are tapped.

Here too Johnson excelled. Because he was highly motivated to get others to follow, he drew heavily on his own personal resources, as well as on those of the presidential office. Each of the three sources of power was freely used by Lyndon Johnson to draft the Economic Opportunity Act and then to get it passed. We can theorize that Johnson was, in David McClelland's terminology, high in the need for power. Whether he had the need to prevail over others (p Power), or the more democratic impulse to simply get others to go along (s Power), is not important here.[139] What is important is that we understand that without Johnson's fierce determination, legislation such as the EOA would never have seen the light of day.

Johnson's extraversion was also critical to successful passage of the EOA. Actually, Johnson's sociability, indeed his fear of being alone, was so extreme that it was, at times, dysfunctional. Kearns writes that Johnson "could not bear to be by himself, not for an evening or for an hour. Always there were people, in his office, at his house, in the swimming pool, even in the bathroom."[140] But measured by what was required to pass the antipoverty bill, Johnson had a personality predisposition that, to understate it, came in handy. It seems clear that if Lyndon Johnson is to be credited with the successful passage of the EOA, that aspect of his behavior to which most of the credit must go is the quantity and quality of his interpersonal activity.

John Kenneth Galbraith describes the man's genius with people:

> The Johnson method played on the natural preference of people to say yes when asked by the president personally, especially if the request is in strong and urgent language with the presidential chair and face moved up very close. By agreeing, you could ingratiate yourself while believing that you were rendering a public service. Johnson reinforced

his requests with appeals to vanity—the support of the individual being asked was always decisive—and, if it seemed useful, to plead for sympathy or resort to something close to tears. Fear, if it was invoked, was the result of the individual's hearing, along with Johnson's inspired scatology, how ineffable, stupid, or absurd were those who had refused to see the light and go along.[141]

Finally, it should be pointed out that Johnson had a high degree of what I have called political intellect. He understood, as well as any president, the need to politick on behalf of what really mattered. Johnson simply did not subscribe to the notion that wheeling and dealing was dirty politics, that horse trading was tacky, or that coalition building, buttonholing and arm twisting were beneath the dignity of the nation's Chief Executive. He recognized that to exercise directive leadership in the American political culture was, necessarily, to play politics. It was a game Lyndon Johnson played gladly, even if, from time to time, his hands got somewhat soiled.

Despite the problems that ensued once the Office of Economic Opportunity was in place, Johnson's efforts on behalf of the antipoverty bill during his first nine months in office provided at least two clear benefits. The president profited from having proved that he was a "can do" leader. And America profited from a heightened awareness of its poor. Beginning with President Johnson's declaration of a war on poverty, magazines, newspapers, and television made common knowledge what only a few had known for some time—our nation had too many poorly housed, badly educated, underemployed, desperate, and unhappy people.[142]

Let me finally make explicit what has been implicit for most of this chapter. With regard to the passing of the Economic Opportunity Act, Lyndon Johnson was the very model of a political president. He demonstrated a gut feel for leadership as social exhange. "I knew from the start," the president once said, that "all relations of power rest on one thing, a contract between the leader and the followers such that the followers believe it is in their interest to follow the leader. No man can compel another—except at knifepoint—to do what he does not want to do."[143]

8

Richard Nixon and
the Family Assistance Plan

> We cannot simply ignore the failures of welfare, or expect
> them to go away. . . . And that is why tonight I therefore
> propose that we abolish the present welfare system and that
> we adopt in its place a new family assistance system. . . . The
> new family assistance system I propose . . . rests essentially
> on these three principles: equality of treatment across the
> nation, a work requirement and a work incentive. . . . What
> I am proposing is that the Federal Government build a foun-
> dation under the income of every American family with
> dependent children that cannot care for itself—and wher-
> ever in America that family may live.
>
> *President Nixon,*
> *televised speech to the nation,*
> *delivered August 8, 1969*

When Richard Nixon took office in January 1969, he was preoccupied with
the war in Vietnam. The politics of Southwest Asia had dominated the
politics of the 1968 presidential campaign, as indeed they continued to
dominate American politics during Nixon's first term in office. Moreover,
Nixon's own interests lay more in foreign than domestic policy. Thus, the
objective situation coincided with the president's personal preferences to
produce an initial term in which there was a particular emphasis on foreign
instead of domestic politics.

It was not that Nixon failed to initiate—on the contrary. During his first
year in office he sent over forty domestic proposals to Congress, including
a tax reform package, a message on electoral reform, and a slew of proposals on crime, pornography, and drug control. Furthermore, the president
did battle with Congress over his nominations of Clement Haynsworth and
Harrold Carswell to the Supreme Court. But in all this activity, perhaps
only one domestic policy proposal constituted a major effort on Richard
Nixon's part to lead the American people to new ground: welfare reform.

In 1968 the problem of welfare in America was perceived to be massive
and it had been exacerbated in the recent past by its numbers alone. In

1940, 2 percent of American children were on welfare; from 1940 to 1962 the proportion had doubled; in the next eight years it had doubled again; and by 1972 it reached 11 percent. The movement of mothers onto welfare rolls in the 1960s reflected both the growth in the pool of eligible persons and a change in attitude that made getting welfare much less stigmatizing than it had previously been.[1]

But the problems were more than just the swelling of the welfare rolls. They also included state-to-state differences between welfare benefits that created a pattern of migration of the poor; state residency requirements that acted harshly on many families; a dollar-for-dollar forfeiture that made it almost impossible for people to go off welfare (and encouraged welfare cheating); rules that treated families without fathers more leniently than those with nonearning fathers or fathers who earned only little (thus creating an incentive for fathers to leave home); and a large professional establishment that had perhaps a vested interest in perpetuating a welfare system guaranteed to supply them with a large clientele.

Therefore, when Nixon took office in January 1969, he had essentially three choices regarding what he had described as the "welfare mess": he could ignore it, even though during his campaign he had promised not to; he could tinker with machinery that was already in place, even though he had maintained that the machinery itself should be replaced; or he could propose a radical departure from the status quo. After eight months of dickering, the president chose the last approach. In August 1969, Nixon proposed the Family Assistance Plan (FAP), which would provide every American family with a guaranteed minimum income but would, at the same time, stress workfare instead of welfare.

The story of the FAP, however, finally bears little resemblance to the tales told in the previous two chapters. For although President Nixon referred to the FAP repeatedly as his "highest domestic priority,"[2] his support for his own welfare reform proposal was so sporadic that he gave many the impression that he never really cared very much whether or not the legislation was passed. In contrast to his predecessors, this president—his rhetoric notwithstanding—appeared at times to be either an ambivalent or unconcerned sponsor. This, then, is the uneven saga of a bill that never had either an especially proud or especially pushy parent.

Dan Rather and Gary Paul Gates write that during the 1968 campaign the "welfare mess" had been one of Nixon's favorite targets. He would tell well-dressed crowds at suburban shopping centers that "The time has come to get people off the welfare rolls and onto payrolls."[3] But, as Daniel P. Moynihan's detailed chronology points out, only toward the end of the campaign did Nixon talk at any length about the problem, and then only in rather vague generalizations that no one could actually argue with. In a radio address on October 28, the Republican nominee for President of the United States laid out the following two proposals. First, Nixon declared, the government must help those unable to help themselves—"the poor, the disabled, the aged and the sick"—in a way that "preserves the dignity of the individual and the integrity of the family." And, second, the government should "offer the opportunity and incentive for those who can to move off welfare rolls onto private payrolls."[4]

Not surprisingly, these two broad statements of goal engendered little resistance, if for no other reason than that there was bipartisan agreement that the welfare system did seem to be out of control.

Accordingly, when Nixon became president he had a mandate to do *something* about the welfare problem, but at the same time he had no clear idea of what that might be. As Rather and Gates write, "he did not come into office with a concrete plan or coherent policy. All he knew for certain was what he did not want."[5]

This uncertainty seemed confirmed when it took the administration eight months to submit to Congress the reform bill Nixon himself had called his highest domestic priority. There were indeed other reasons for what might be considered a critical delay in submitting the FAP, including the unusual complexity of the welfare issue, as well as the strong disagreements among members of the administration about what to do. But the Rather/Gates explanation for why it took the president so long to construct a policy may well be the best—when he came into office Nixon had given little hard thought to what a welfare reform proposal might actually look like.

Since Nixon's first executive act was to establish the Urban Affairs Council, some recognition of this lack of forethought may have existed. This Council was charged with assisting the president in the development of a national urban policy. Nixon told its members that he was interested in judicious yet bold change, and that the time to initiate such change was sooner rather than later. Unaware, no doubt, that his welfare reform proposal would have a gestation period of eight months, the president stressed the importance of getting into position quickly. "The 'magic time' to change policies, he said on January 23, and to take the political 'heat' for doing so, would be the first few months of the Administration. The nation, he felt, recognized the need for change. 'We don't,' he added, 'want the record written that we were too cautious.'"[6]

The administration's first task was to collect information. Presidential aides were told to conduct a "thorough investigation" of the "New York welfare mess,"* and to draw up a memorandum explaining why, although

---

*This request was actually made several days before the inauguration.

male unemployment was on the decline, the number of new welfare cases was on the rise. The president also wanted to know whether there had "been a change in the social acceptability of welfare. Were people less reluctant to get on and stay on?"[7]

There was a problem, however. To each of Nixon's questions, no clear answer surfaced. Moynihan describes this period:

> The president now was getting more and better information about the problem of welfare than any of his predecessors.... [However] it remained the case that no one could fully explain why the welfare rolls were soaring. Nor did anyone suppose there was an easy way to reverse this trend....[8]

Thus, the perfectly reasonable attempt to gain a better understanding of the welfare rolls did little to point Richard Nixon in the right direction. On February 12, after the third meeting of the Urban Affairs Council, during which New York's Governor Nelson Rockefeller gave a detailed analysis of the state and local fiscal crisis, the president was able to utter nothing much more substantive than "We have got to indicate we are going to do new things in welfare."[9]

Yet to assume that Nixon was a blank slate on welfare is misleading. For even though he said rather little on the subject of welfare during his campaign, and once in the White House he said even less (Moynihan writes that early on "the president had no view; at least none he disclosed"[10]), the act of appointing Moynihan as Executive Secretary of the Urban Affairs Council* surely hinted at a position. Moynihan had a well-established reputation as an expert on welfare, one who had firm ideas on what should be done about the welfare problem.

Moynihan's position on welfare reform had long been clear: The poor would have to be put on some kind of an income maintenance program, either through a guaranteed income or by receiving support payments for families with dependent children. It sounded simple: to eliminate poverty, give the poor some money. But, in fact, such ideas were rather radical. The establishment of a guaranteed income would clearly constitute a sharp break with previous practice. Indeed, only months before Nixon proposed the FAP, two highly respected political scientists had prophesied: "Income by right is not politically feasible in the near future. The President will not support it and Congress would not pass it if he did."[11]

As Moynihan tells it, the Family Assistance Plan that Nixon proposed in a televised address to the nation on August 8, 1969, strongly resembled the Family Security System (FSS) presented to the Urban Affairs Council

---

*In November 1969 Moynihan was elevated to cabinet rank. From then on he was Nixon's adviser on urban affairs, and he no longer served as Executive Secretary of the Urban Affairs Council.

Committee on Welfare twenty weeks earlier.[12] Robert Finch, Nixon's Secretary of Health, Education and Welfare, had proposed a straightforward negative income tax limited to families with dependent children. Each family of four was to be guaranteed a basic income of $1,500 per year (although, in the plan that finally emerged, the combined cash and food stamp payment to a family of four came to approximately $2,460). Like Moynihan, Finch believed that if you give poor people cash, and in such a way so as to distribute payments equally throughout all the states, both inequities and red tape would be reduced. Thus, although having the government dole out cash was a radical idea, it was felt that by cloaking it in the garb of a reduced governmental role once the money was distributed, it might just win support from both sides of the political spectrum.

But what was to Finch and Moynihan a relatively straightforward solution was to others on the president's team—especially Arthur Burns, serving as Counsellor to the President with special responsibility for program development—a prospective nightmare. Concerned that such an extreme departure from past practice would bring along with it a host of unanticipated consequences,* men such as Burns faced an ideological issue: they had not joined the Nixon administration to preside over a program that flew in the face of their long-standing convictions that the government should play only a minimum role in the lives of private persons, and that welfare costs especially should not be permitted to further strain the federal budget.

But to Burns's astonishment, the president was receptive to Finch's ideas.[13] At the very least, Nixon did not reject FSS out of hand. Moynihan has commented that what surprised him was the manner in which Nixon involved himself. "You will never understand what happened," Moynihan said, "if you do not know that Richard Nixon was raised as a poor boy in a depression. In meeting after meeting he would say, 'Look, don't tell me what it is to be poor. I've been poor and it is no good.'"[14] Nixon slowly came to accept at least the basics of the Finch proposal as a desirable and realistic answer to the welfare mess. It remained now to rework FSS so that it would be palatable to the basically conservative mindset of the Nixon administration.

As the debate between administration conservatives (led by Burns) and liberals (led by Moynihan) took on a more strident tone, it became clear to the president that a mediator was needed, someone who would keep the essentials of FSS reasonably intact, yet make the concessions necessary to overcome the most virulent objections of someone like Burns. For this task,

*Conservatives learned that Family Assistance might more than double the existing number of welfare recipients, and they feared that the FAP might exacerbate rather than alleviate the problem of doling out a national income payment in a nation that had wide divergences in income and living standards among the states.

Nixon chose Secretary of Labor George P. Shultz (later Ronald Reagan's Secretary of State).

Shultz's major contribution was to incorporate into the FSS a work incentive. The idea of rewarding the working poor—that is, of making the welfare check at least to some degree dependent on a demonstrated adherence to the work ethic—made it possible for the president to at least partially reconcile his radical solution to the welfare problem with the traditionally conservative Republican ideology.* (Ironically, the workfare component of FSS proposed to nearly double the initial cost of the proposal.)

For all the tinkering, by late spring the president still had "nothing *specific* to propose. There was no message to Congress, no bill."[16] Finally, in late June, Nixon took the bull by the horns. He assigned John Ehrlichman the job of integrating the ideas of Shultz and Burns—who were talking not work incentives but work requirements—into the original Finch/Moynihan proposal. Ehrlichman was to develop three documents: a presidential address announcing the specifics of a new welfare reform program, a message to Congress proposing it, and a draft bill incorporating the measure.

Insofar as possible, Ehrlichman did what he was asked, but the climate for FSS within the administration did not improve much. Nixon became increasingly convinced, but most of those around him took a strong stand against what would shortly be renamed the Family Assistance Plan even as it was on the verge of being announced. Spiro Agnew, for example, objected to the content of the bill; he also predicted that it would cause trouble: "It will not be a political winner. . . . After months of heated oratory, suitably whipped to a froth by the liberal press, the issue will be Nixon's niggardly ideas against the progressive proposals of the Democrats [who will inevitably advocate spending more]."[17]

Moynihan recalls that on August 6 the last of countless planning meetings on the FAP took place: "The president summoned the Cabinet to Camp David, where, in Laurel Cottage, his decision to propose a guaranteed income was set forth to the discomfort, even the dismay, of most of those present."[18]

The Camp David encounter was somewhat peculiar in that several cabinet members seemed bent on opposing a decision that clearly had already been made. Moreover, the president apparently took some pleasure in the fact that he was acting *against* the wishes of a majority of his cabinet. Evans and Novak relate that just after the Camp David session the presi-

---

*The concept of a guaranteed income with a built-in work incentive was first advanced by economist Milton Friedman in 1964. The "negative income tax," as it came to be known, proposed to sustain work by providing some payments *above* the level of income guarantees.[15]

dent reminded an aid of a famous story about Lincoln. When opposed by his entire cabinet on the Emancipation Proclamation, Lincoln declared, "The ayes are one, the nays are nine; the ayes have it."[19]

Two days after the Camp David meeting, the president went on television to announce the details of his legislative program. His speech contained four different proposals,* but the Family Assistance Plan was at the core. Nixon's hope was that the American people would appreciate that (1) at last the federal government was proposing a viable solution to the welfare mess; (2) the initial cost of the proposal would be so high only because it would allow many of the working poor who had not been on the welfare rolls to participate in the benefits; and (3) the FAP would encourage many welfare regulars to enter the work force because they would no longer be subject to a dollar-for-dollar forfeiture of welfare benefits.

Richard Nixon announced his radical solution to the welfare problem by wrapping it in conservative rhetoric. The emphasis in his televised address was on "workfare" rather than welfare.[20]

> In the final analysis, we cannot talk our way out of poverty; we cannot legislate our way out of poverty; but this nation can work its way out of poverty. What America needs now is not more welfare but more "workfare." . . . For those in the welfare system today, or struggling to fight their way out of poverty, these measures offer a way to independence through the dignity of work. . . .
> This new system establishes a direct link between the Government's willingness to help the needy, and the willingness of the needy to help themselves. . . . [21]

The initial response to Nixon's proposal was overwhelmingly positive; both Democrats and Republicans applauded the FAP. The reaction of Wilbur Cohen, who had served under both Kennedy and Johnson, was one of "delight." The head of the National Urban League, Whitney Young, Jr., said that the FAP was the "first recognition that welfare is a national problem, demanding income guarantees by the federal government." The Senate Majority Leader, Democrat Mike Mansfield, observed that the president had made "some very interesting suggestions." The Senate Minority Whip, Republican Hugh Scott, thought "most people" would support the welfare plan. House Republican leader Gerald Ford opined that Nixon's welfare reform proposal represented "the true spirit of America."[22] And Wilbur Mills, Chairman of the House Ways and Means Committee, which was scheduled to take the first vote on family assistance, indicated he was

---

*The first measure that Nixon proposed was a complete reform of the present welfare system (the FAP); the second was a comprehensive new job training and placement program; the third a revamping of the Office of Economic Opportunity; and the fourth a start of revenue sharing.

open minded about the proposal, and indeed that he was enthusiastic about those parts of the FAP that provided for work incentives.[23]

The press followed suit. The liberal *New Republic* crowed that "It must have been quite a scene, the Camp David cabinet meeting at which President Nixon informed the Neanderthal men that he had accepted and would assert creeping socialism, the principle of the federal government guaranteeing a minimal income to all disadvantaged Americans."[24] The conservative *National Review* was at least open minded: "[Several important questions] need to be . . . responsibly discussed and pondered in the massive public congressional debate sure to come over this sweeping program that is undoubtedly the major domestic proposal of the first Nixon administration."[25] And the establishment was no less than effusive. James Reston, writing for *The New York Times:* "Nixon has taken a great step forward. . . . He had repudiated his own party's record on social policy . . . and this tells us something both about the President and the country."[26] The public was also well disposed. An initial Gallup poll on FAP found that, by a margin greater than three to one, favorable opinions about FAP (65 percent) outweighed unfavorable ones (20 percent).[27]

Several days after the original announcement, President Nixon sent the details of Family Assistance to Capitol Hill. Congress was given a list of the following "firsts" for America: All dependent families with children would be assured of minimum standard payments based on uniform and single eligibility standards; the more than two million families who make up the "working poor" would be helped toward self-sufficiency; training and work opportunities would be given to millions of families who would otherwise be locked into the welfare system; the federal government would make a strong contribution toward relieving the financial burden of welfare payments from state governments; and, finally, every dependent family in America would be encouraged by government policy to stay together.[28]

As soon as the details of the FAP were spelled out, the National Council on Hunger and Malnutrition charged that Family Assistance would reduce the purchasing power of the poor in 44 states by cutting off the receipt of food stamps. And Mitchell Ginsberg, New York City's Human Resources Administrator, said that the idea that many mothers who head welfare families should be required to seek jobs or training was a "major mistake." Such a requirement would be "impossible to administer," Ginsberg declared. "More important, it's unnecessary."[29]

The fact that the FAP came under fire so soon after it was introduced— especially from the left, which might have been expected to be more sympathetic—hinted at what was to come. Early attacks focused not only on the program itself, but also on the president. It was suggested that perhaps the Family Assistance Plan was just a way for him to get headlines, or make a pitch for a broader constituency. Observers such as Evans and Novak concluded that such charges were false, but that "there were grounds for making [them]. Through the rest of 1969, Nixon was so preoccupied with foreign policy that he seemed to have forgotten this hothouse project."[30]

It was true that once the president had delivered his televised address on the FAP in early August and submitted his proposal to Congress, he promptly left Washington for a month in California. Almost nothing was heard from the White House about the FAP for two long months after the original August 8 message. (There was one exception. During a speech to the nation's governors on September 1, Nixon did briefly remind his audience that he had "proposed the first major reform of welfare in the history of welfare."[31])

Finally, in mid-October, the FAP surfaced again. In what amounted to a belated State of the Union message, Nixon sent Congress his complete legislative agenda—which naturally included his proposal for welfare reform. The president faced a daunting task: leading a legislature in which both houses were controlled by the opposition party. The Republicans had only 43 seats in the Senate and 192 in the House.

Nixon took a moderate tack. He called on the Democratic Congress to enter into a "working relationship" with the White House so that together they might enact a legislative program that would meet "the needs of a nation in distress." Mike Mansfield responded in kind by describing the president's message as "restrained, understanding, in good taste and in good form." And Hugh Scott said that Nixon was acting "in a spirit of cooperation with Congress and a desire to work together with the Democratic leadership."[32]

The principal part of the president's legislative package dealt with "reforms." But by now, welfare reform was only one among *many* reforms, and indeed it came second on the list—after "reform of the draft" and before "reform of the tax code," "revenue reform," "postal reform," "manpower reform," "social security reform," "reform of the grant-in-aid system," "electoral reform," "D.C. Government reform," "O.E.O. reform," and "reform of foreign aid."

To be sure, to listen to Nixon was still to hear him selling the FAP:

> The family assistance system . . . provides incentives for families to stay together. It provides economic rewards for men and women on welfare who enter training programs and search out jobs. It provides a floor under income that assures the minimum necessary for food and clothing and shelter.[33]

But convincing rhetoric such as this was no more than very occasional; moreover, little action backed up the words. The president was making hardly any face-to-face effort to win broad support from members of the political elite for family assistance. Having initiated the FAP, Nixon seemed to think that he had completed his work.

But with or without the president to move things along personally, once he proposes, Congress must dispose. Wilbur Mills announced that the House Ways and Means Committee would hold joint hearings on Social Security and welfare reform to begin on October 15. Less than one month later the hearings were over. Administration witnesses—especially Finch and Shultz—did well enough, but there is little evidence that the hearings themselves, or anyone testifying at them, made much impact. The press largely ignored the proceedings, and Moynihan concluded that his cherished plan was being slighted.

> It was not clear who in the Congress was listening. . . . The subject [of Family Assistance] simply had not impressed itself. . . . The hearings on FAP had taken place in a general atmosphere of dissatisfaction with, or indifference to, the president's proposal.[34]

It is surprising that the House hearings on welfare reform went quite unnoticed, perhaps especially because just as they were taking place, a blue-ribbon presidential commission released its long awaited report on the same subject. The President's Commission on Income Maintenance Programs (which had actually been formed by Lyndon Johnson) concluded that there was a need for a universal income supplement based solely on need. Although an important difference existed between the Commission's report and the FAP with regard to the work requirement—the Commission challenged the notion that work was the answer to poverty—there were nevertheless strong parallels between the two approaches with regard to the initial amount of aid.[35] In other words, the Commission's report lent added credence to Nixon's welfare reform proposal.

Naturally enough, the administration used the report as confirmation of the Family Assistance Plan. President Nixon, who was under no formal obligation to receive the report, was described by Ben Heineman, the head of the Commission, as being "extremely gracious," and Daniel Moynihan was quoted as saying the Commission's recommendations were "remarkably compatible" with the administration's plans.[36]

For their part, Commission members were inclined to link their report to the FAP in order to increase their chances of being heard. In a cover letter to the report addressed to President Nixon, Heineman wrote:

> We feel that the Family Assistance Program that you proposed to Congress earlier this year represents a major step forward towards meeting the needs that we have documented. We are pleased to note that the basic structure of the Family Assistance Program is similar to that of the program we have proposed. . . . [37]

Yet in spite of the congressional hearings, and in spite of the Commission's report, the truth was that because of the president's low level of political activity, for most of 1969, the FAP remained almost invisible. In December President Nixon seemed to regain a modest interest in his own bill. He urged the White House Conference on Food, Nutrition and Health to support three administration proposals, one of which was the FAP. Observing that his welfare reform measure was considered by many the "most important piece of domestic legislation proposed in the past 50 years," the president reminded his audience that, "The needs of the poor range far beyond food. . . . And they need these [other] resources in a program framework that builds incentives for self support and stability. Let the reform of the bankrupt welfare system be the next great cause of those who come together here today."[38]

The December initiative was followed up in January by Secretary Finch, who flatly accused Congress of trying to scuttle the FAP. In a speech before the National Press Club, he attributed the lack of national debate on welfare reform primarily to confused hearings by the House Ways and Means Committee: "This revolutionary proposal is being threatened with death by invisibility at the hands of a Congress apparently too preoccupied with other matters even to offer alternative proposals of its own."[39]

Nixon also spoke on behalf of the FAP in January—quite vigorously, in fact. But his statement was short. In his first State of the Union message to Congress, the president said that he did not intend to "go through a detailed listing of what I have proposed or will propose." Then he added that he would, however, like to mention three areas of "urgent priorities." And "mention" them is all he did. The following constitutes his entire declaration on the FAP.

> First, we cannot delay longer in accomplishing a total reform of our welfare system. When a system penalizes work, breaks up homes, robs recipients of dignity, there is no alternative to abolishing that system and adopting in its place the program of incomes support, job training and work incentives which I recommended to the Congress last year.[40]

Despite the president's renewed profession of interest in his own proposal, the impression of a lack of real concern was still lent credence by the president's behavior. When the White House Conference on Food, Nutrition and Health issued a recommendation calling for a $5,500 minimum income for every family of four, President Nixon said at a news conference that he could not "give really sympathetic consideration" to the idea because it would cost too much. He failed, as he had failed with the Heineman Commission's report, to exploit the parallel concerns. Moreover, the president's attention seemed to be diverted now from what he had recently claimed was so important. When Nixon entered his second year in the White House his emphasis shifted somewhat from a few key proposals to what administration officials referred to rather vaguely as "the quality of life."[41]

Still, to many of those who troubled to review the first twelve months of the Nixon presidency, the FAP remained the administration's most significant domestic policy proposal. The *New Republic* called it "the most substantial welfare reform proposal in the nation's history."[42] The *National Review* referred to family assistance as "a step in the right direction; perhaps as big a step as is politically feasible."[43] And *The New York Times* pointed out that "probably the shrewdest job of political preemption was the way the Administration took the welfare issue away from the Democrats. . . ."[44] In sum, Nixon's original initiative, the *idea* behind the FAP, was still finding favor.

But if the positive press response to family assistance remained intact, the situation in Congress was less clear than it had been earlier when it seemed the Democratic legislature would be hard pressed to reject welfare reform. The administration had three main concerns: first, that a band-aid bill would emerge from Wilbur Mill's Committee rather than one that incorporated the basic reforms advocated by Nixon; second, that the expected support from Northern Democrats—which was sorely needed if the FAP stood a chance of passage—was suspiciously slow in coming; and, third, that, as Finch had already complained, organized labor was, at best, wavering on the welfare package. As the chief lobbyist for the AFL-CIO put it, "For most of the working poor, the simple solution for poverty is that employers should be required to pay decent wages."[45]

Although a congressional study issued in January (prepared by the professional staff of the House Ways and Means Committee) warned that the FAP might break up poor working families, put some college students on welfare, and indirectly finance the purchase of color television sets,[46] President Nixon nevertheless did push gingerly on. In his February Budget Message to Congress, the president finally returned again to the Family Assistance Plan.

> For the Family Assistance Program, I have included outlays of 500 million in this budget for 1971. . . . We intend to make every effort now and after the Congress has acted to initiate the high priority program on a responsible and workable basis.[47]

By reaffirming his commitment to the FAP in his Budget Message to Congress, President Nixon signaled the beginning of what amounted to his first real, if cautious, campaign to push the proposed bill through the legislature. In fact, Spring 1970 turned out to be the high point of the fortunes of the Family Assistance Plan—relatively speaking. The administration called the FAP an integral part of Nixon's plan for a "new America" in which more emphasis would be placed on the environment and human resources, and less on defense, space, and foreign aid. A top White House official was quoted as saying, "The emphasis now is on problems at home. These are the new priorities."[48]

The increased White House activity was almost certainly motivated by political realities. After months of sporadic hearings, laboring over the proposals, and listening to witnesses, the House Ways and Means Committee was now finally looking to make a recommendation on the FAP one way or the other. Yet there was still no reading on the outcome. As *The New York Times* observed, the situation was so complex that almost no one was predicting the final result.[49]

But the uncertain outcome of the Ways and Means vote was not the only thing prodding the Nixon administration: The FAP also had the Democrats to contend with. In mid-February Senator Fred Harris proposed a more liberal alternative to Nixon's welfare reform bill, one that increased the minimum annual income without employment from $1,600 a year (for a family of four) to $3,600 a year, and that also federalized the entire welfare system.* (Family Assistance, as its name suggests, would be available only to families.)

It was impossible to tell whether the increased activity surrounding the issue of welfare reform would hurt or help the Nixon proposal. Some reports had the Nixon administration fearful that the Ways and Means Committee would drop the FAP in favor of a Democratic alternative.[50] Others had the White House encouraged by the renewed activity on the theory that it would oblige Chairman Mills to advocate assistance for the working poor.[51]

In any case, Nixon lobbied harder than at any time since the preceding August. Plans were made to add a full-time professional to the White House congressional liason team with the specific job of promoting the Family Assistance Plan in Ways and Means and then, if necessary, elsewhere in Congress. Moreover, Moynihan, who all along had served not only as architect, but as salesman—for example, in November he told a Jewish group that the nation was in position to achieve "one of the most extraordinary social revolutions in the history of liberal society"[52]—was chosen to head a seven-man team sent to Capitol Hill to confer with House Democrats. (Other administration officials met with leading House members as well.) In addition, Nixon issued another public plea. Speaking again to the nation's governors, he urged them to put pressure on Congress to approve

*In January, Senator George McGovern also offered a poverty plan, but it was not, strictly speaking, an alternative to the FAP. McGovern proposed a $50 to $65 monthly allowance for each child, regardless of the family's income level.

several of his programs, among them the FAP. Saying that he believed there was now a 50–50 chance of approval, President Nixon declared that if the governors lined up behind welfare reform, the prospects would be "more than 50 percent."[53]

The administration's late winter push paid off. From early March on, an amended version of the FAP proceeded to clear every House hurdle with little trouble.[54] On March 5, the Family Assistance Plan was overwhelmingly approved by the House Ways and Means Committee. Moreover, Mills, once regarded as a certain opponent, announced that he would personally co-sponsor the measure and would probably also serve as floor manager.* *The New York Times* labeled the Committee vote as "probably the most significant Congressional victory the Nixon Administration has won in its 14 months in office,"[55] and the White House appeared jubilant. Acting almost as if it had received final passage, administration officials held a briefing on the bill, and President Nixon issued a statement hailing the Committee move.

> ... It is often said that nothing in this world is as powerful as an idea whose time has come. In my view, the Family Assistance Program is an idea whose time has come—and the welcome action of the Ways and Means Committee confirms that judgment. Not every Congress has the opportunity to enact a fundamental reform of our basic institutions. The 91st Congress now has that historical opportunity.[56]

Soon after clearance by Ways and Means, the House Rules Committee voted to send the FAP to the floor. Shortly after that, the full House approved the Family Assistance Plan by a vote of 243 to 155.[57] President Nixon hailed the decision as "a battle won in a crusade for reform that we cannot afford to lose," adding that he hoped that the Senate would act "with the same responsiveness and the same responsibility" as the House to achieve reform for "the poor and the helpless—and the taxpayer."[58]

Almost as soon as the FAP was submitted to the Senate Finance Committee, the crossfire between the administration and Congress began. Both liberals and conservatives found something in the Family Assistance Plan to criticize. The committee chairman, Louisiana Democrat Russell Long, started off by challenging the testimony of the administration's lead-off witness, Secretary Finch. Long suggested that the FAP would encourage people to accept welfare rather than a job. Other committee Democrats argued that the program did not provide enough money for the poor it would help, and did not help enough people in the first place. Meanwhile, the ranking

---

*Credit for converting Mills from agnostic to believer went to a team of administration officials headed by Shultz.

Republican on the committee maintained that the administration was underestimating the cost of the welfare bill by one billion dollars.

Despite these early signs of trouble in the Senate, it was still generally believed that the FAP would pass the Finance Committee in a form not too different from that approved by the House.[59] Moynihan writes, "In part the surge of optimism was due to the view, widely held, that the Senate was more 'liberal' than the House. If the FAP could pass by a large margin in the House, it would surely pass the Senate: everybody—anybody—knew this, and for those who did not, journalists explained."[60]

Simply stated, the sunny outlook was misleading. Moynihan admits that the administration "was not sufficiently aware of the danger. . . . The altogether different mood of the Senate Committee [from Ways and Means] was not sensed."[61] This unwarranted optimism may have been partly responsible for the bill's fate in the Senate.

Only two days after the Finance Committee hearings started, they were over. The Committee flatly refused to work on the proposal that had been presented, and requested instead that the Nixon administration integrate the FAP with a series of other, already existing federal programs for the poor.[62]

The administration tried to minimize the damage. Finch announced that a revised proposal would be "ready within a matter of a few days,"[63] and he promised that Nixon would assign the job of reworking family assistance to his top experts, including Ehrlichman, Shultz, Moynihan, Budget Director Robert Mayo, and himself.

But it was clear that the FAP had quickly become a very big headache. Even if the White House had been able to develop a new program that passed the Finance Committee, and then the whole Senate, that measure would have had to go back to the House again for its approval. And House leaders were saying that they would certainly not accept any welfare reform bill that materially increased the cost of the program as it was now designed.

Nixon's continuing reticence regarding the FAP naturally put an extra burden on other administration officials, especially Moynihan. However, Moynihan had at least two major liabilities. First, he was disliked by blacks whose support was deemed essential if the FAP was to become law. This distrust dated back to the 1960s, when Moynihan published a highly controversial report on the breakdown of the black family; but it flared anew at the precise moment when the FAP was most in need of help. In March, some of Moynihan's private memos to Nixon were leaked to the press. One of them (written in January) contained the following sentence: "The time may have come when the issue of race could benefit from a period of 'benign neglect'." Blacks were furious and a group of civil rights leaders subsequently charged that Moynihan's suggested policy of "benign neglect" was "symptomatic of a calculated, aggressive and systematic" Nixon administration effort to "wipe out" two decades of civil rights gains.[64]

Moynihan's second problem was a reputed lack of administrative skills. It has been said that for all his cleverness and originality, Moynihan was less capable when it came to organization and detail. Rather and Gates write that it did "not take Nixon long to become aware of Moynihan's tendency to 'wing it,' to make do with generalities, when hard, specific facts were needed to back up a point. His early draft on welfare reform was shot through with technical deficiencies."[65] Thus, Moynihan's problems with the black community made him less persuasive than he might otherwise have been as a pitchman for the FAP, while his deficiencies as an administrator made him less than fully convincing within the administration itself.

It took President Nixon a full five weeks after the abortive end of the Finance Committee hearing to reenter the scene. He presented an outline for a revised FAP that was, however, "the same welfare program, but now supported by a series of promises to smooth the notches out of Medicaid, food stamps and public housing assistance through an ingenious series of revisions in those programs that Congress might—or might not—enact [the] next year."[66] But Nixon did seem anxious to quell recurring reports that the administration had lost its enthusiasm for family assistance. He took the occasion to issue another one of his statements of full support: "Let there be no mistake about this Administration's total commitment to passage of this legislative milestone this year."[67]

With the submission of the revised FAP, there was once again a flurry of optimism; and once again it lasted no more than several days. By June 22, *U.S. News and World Report* was stating in no uncertain terms that, despite the revisions in the Family Assistance Plan, the "outlook in Congress is dim."[68]

A few administration officials attempted something of a rescue mission. Moynihan warned the Urban Coalition Action Council that "If we do not get family assistance in this Congress, I do not see how we will get it in this decade."[69] Several other Nixon aides explored ways of bypassing the Senate Finance Committee in order to get the bill considered by the full Senate, but the president had once again chosen to distance himself from the main event. During these critical weeks he was 3,000 miles away from the action and, apparently, unaware of just what was, or was not, happening. *The New York Times* reported as follows:

> Administration officials are planning to inform the President of the seriousness of the welfare bill situation when he returns from the California

White House. . . . They will urge him to take a personal hand with Republican members of the Finance Committee.[70]

To the mild encouragement of the administration, Senator Long announced on July 9 that the Finance Committee would resume hearings on welfare reform within several weeks. In fact, the announcement inspired another burst of White House activity on behalf of the FAP. In mid-July President Nixon left what he called the White House "isolation booth" to seek the support of governors of Appalachian states for, among other things, the bottled up welfare reform bill. Moreover, as soon as the Finance Committee hearings resumed, the administration sent its new, articulate Secretary of Health, Education and Welfare to testify for the FAP. Even critics praised Elliot Richardson's presentation as informed and forthright.

Still, there was a feeling even as the Senate hearings started again that the FAP might be doomed. Moynihan writes that by July 1970 "there simply was no prospect of any but the faintest support for Family Assistance from the Republican members of the Senate Finance Committee."[71] And when asked at a news conference how he assessed the prospects of the FAP getting through the Senate, President Nixon's response was rather weak: "I would probably know more about that after I see what happens in a meeting with some of the Senators today. I put the chances as fair. I expect to meet with our legislative leaders in the morning and may have more to report on that later."[72]

During August the welfare reform issue, instead of becoming clearer and less complicated, became muddier, more complex, and more contentious. The furor and uncertainty propelled President Nixon to act more forcefully on behalf of the FAP than at any time during the past 12 months. First, the administration took the highly unusual step of ordering a public opinion poll to determine voter support for welfare reform. The survey report concluded that at least several features of the FAP had "extraordinarily strong support."[73] Second, Nixon began to lobby for Republican votes by meeting at least once with minority members of the Finance Committee. Third, the president offered a generous compromise to Senator Abraham Ribicoff, now a leading Democrat on the Finance Committee, by agreeing to allow for a year of field tests for the FAP before it went into full operation. Fourth, in his statement announcing the compromise, Nixon elected again to praise the welfare reform bill as "the most important piece of domestic legislation of the past 35 years." Fifth, presidential aides were sounding properly alarmist. When asked by a reporter to account for the note of "doom" in his voice at a late August press briefing on the FAP, Moynihan replied that it was "five minutes to midnight"; Finch (now counselor to the president) added that "This has been a long and arduous piece of work and we don't want to see it go down the drain." Even Nixon let it be known that he was concerned that the FAP was "slipping out of our hands."[74] Finally, the Chief Executive made a somewhat more strenuous effort with regard to selling his product. He invited six members of the Finance Committee, and their wives, to attend a State Dinner in San Diego for the president of Mexico. Moynihan recounts what happened when President Nixon conferred with his Senate guests as they sat around the cabinet table at San Clemente.

> FAP, he said, was a "controversial move, an unpredictable program." Anyone looking at it might well throw up his hands and conclude there were "too many risks." He no less than any other. "What convinced me," he said, "to take the risks was what was [now] going on in New York City. It was an unanswerable argument for doing something. . . ." He ended with an appeal as likely as any to influence these six senators. . . . "I am for Family Assistance because while . . . it is a possible disaster, what we have now is a certain disaster. . . . The future . . . lies with the men in this room."[75]

But if Moynihan and other Nixon assistants remembered that the president "really laid it on the line" in San Clemente, insisting that he wanted the FAP out and soon, that was not the reported recollection of at least two of the Senators present. Columnist John Osborne wrote at the time that these two recalled that "they and their colleagues did most of the talking, that Mr. Nixon 'just listened, mostly' and that all of them left the President with a feeling that, sure, he wanted the bill enacted, but not badly enough to make them sorry if it wasn't reported out and passed."[76] This actually sounds like a fair summary of Nixon's position: He wanted the bill, most of the time, but not that much.

By mid-September President Nixon had pretty much done all the personal lobbying he was going to do. Other than the occasion at San Clemente, he made only a meager or even nonexistent effort—even with members of the Finance Committee. Senator J. William Fulbright does "not recall any effort of the President to lobby for the bill."[77] Senator Albert Gore does "not have the faintest indication as to President Nixon's lobbying efforts to get the Family Assistance Plan through Congress in 1970."[78] Senator Fred Harris was "never" contacted in any way by the president.[79] Senator Jack Miller was a member of the party invited to San Clemente; otherwise he recalls that "President Nixon never lobbied personally on any matter before the committee—at least as far as I was concerned."[80] Senator Paul Fannin remembers that Nixon did "lobby enthusiastically" at San Clemente, but *only* at San Clemente.[81] And Senator Carl Curtis— who, Moynihan writes, was "appalled by the FAP initiative"[82]—states flatly that President Nixon "did not personally lobby on behalf of the FAP."[83]

On September 23, the Senate Finance Committee concluded its hearings on welfare reform, and on October 8, the Committee voted the FAP down by a 14 to 1 vote. All six Republicans came out against the bill, joining an opposition composed of conservatives who objected to the very idea of a guaranteed income and liberals who felt that such income guarantees as the FAP provided were inadequate. Once again the administration agreed to rework the plan and resubmit it for Finance Committee approval.[84]

In late October and November, the Nixon administration made a last-ditch effort. For the first time in many months the president took his case for welfare reform to the American people. On a campaign swing around the country on behalf of Republican candidates in the upcoming midterm election, he remarked on the FAP at nearly every stop.

> Every American wants to be sure that anyone who needs assistance and who cannot care for himself receives assistance. . . . America is able now to look at a program in which we can provide for every family that needs a floor of dignity on which to stand in terms of its income.[85]

Just after the election, President Nixon reassembled the original family assistance team at the White House to try one last time to get the FAP through the Senate before the close of the 91st Congress. Moynihan writes that a "systematic and sustained effort followed." He quotes approvingly from the *National Journal*: "The Administration has devoted more man-power and manhours to the Family Assistance Plan . . . than to any other single piece of domestic legislation it has proposed." And he notes that during these final weeks the president talked to congressional leaders, "and was available for other chores. Once again morale rose."[86]

It was for naught. A revision was proposed but no sooner was it offered than it was turned back. *The New York Times* quoted Senator Fred Harris—the FAP's lone Finance Committee supporter in the October vote—as saying that "every Administration change has made the bill worse. If its bad features can't be eliminated, I think it ought to be killed, and we should start all over."[87]

On November 20, the final vote of the Senate Finance Committee took place: The decision was 10 to 6 against attaching a revised version of the FAP to a pending Social Security bill. Elliot Richardson called the nay vote "extremely unfortunate." Richard Nixon, said his press secretary, was, "of course, disappointed."[88]

As far as this congressional session was concerned, the FAP now had only a few last gasps left. Richardson and Ribicoff were the chief architects of a compromise measure—the administration had gone so far as to accept seven out of ten changes proposed by Ribicoff—that was offered as a floor amendment to the Social Security bill. But the omnibus bill that finally emerged was more confusing than edifying (the *Washington Post* called it a "Godzilla-like monster"), and in short order the Senate Finance Committee's chief Republican critic of welfare reform, Senator John J. Williams of Delaware, had created a parliamentary situation that insured that the FAP would not come to a Senate vote before adjournment. President Nixon might have at least tried to forestall Williams's well-known animosity toward the measure but, as Williams recounts, he did not.

> I do not recall the President personally lobbying for the bill; in fact, it was the reverse. Some of the other committee members and I arranged at least two appointments with the President at which time we pointed out to him why we felt the bill should be defeated or recalled by the Administration. During the interviews the President, very properly, presented his views and at the same time listened attentively to ours, the result being that neither succeeded in persuading the other.[89]

December 1970 saw a major congressional logjam with the Senate still stuck on several key bills including the financing of a supersonic transport plane, Cambodian aid, trade quotas—and welfare reform. But, mysteriously, December also brought out in Richard Nixon the impulse to make what has to be considered his most vivid plea for the passage of the Family Assistance Plan. The president chose to write his own speech for the White House Conference on Children; Moynihan notes that "at long last he determined to say in public what he had been saying all along in private."

> ... I remember back in the Depression years of the nineteen thirties, how deeply I felt about the plight of those people my own age who used to come into my father's store when they couldn't pay the bill because their fathers were out of work, and how this seemed to separate them from the others in the school. None of us had any money in those days, but those in families where there were no jobs, where there was nothing but the little relief then offered, suffered from more than simply going without. They suffered a hurt to their pride that many carried with them for the rest of their lives.
>
> I also remember that my older brother had tuberculosis for five years. The hospital and doctor bills were more than we could afford. In the five years before he died, my mother never brought a new dress. We were poor by today's standards. I suppose we were poor even by Depression standards. But the wonder of it was that we did not know we were poor. Somehow my mother and father with their love, with their pride, their courage and their self-sacrifice were able to create a spirit of self-respect in our family so that we had no sense of being inferior to others who had more than we had.
>
> Today's welfare child is not so fortunate.
>
> His family may have enough to get by on. They may even have more, in a material sense, than many of us did in those Depression years. But

no matter how much pride and courage his parents have, he knows they are poor—and he can feel that soul-stifling, patronizing attitude that follows the dole.

Perhaps he watches while a case-worker—himself trapped in a system that wastes, on policing, talents that could be used for helping—while this case-worker is forced by the system to poke around in the child's apartment, checking on how the money is spent or whether his mother might be hiding his father in the closet. This sort of indignity is hard enough on the mother—enough of a blow to her pride and self-respect— but think what it must mean to a sensitive child. . . .

Our task is not only to lift people out of poverty, but from the standpoint of the child to erase the stigma of welfare and illegitimacy and apartness—to restore pride and dignity and self-respect.

I do not contend that our Family Assistance Plan is perfect. In this confused and complex and intensely human area, no perfect program is possible—and certainly none is possible that will please everybody. But it is a good program, and a program immensely better than what we have now, and vastly important to the future of this country and especially to the neediest of our children. For the Senate to adjourn without enacting this measure would be a tragedy of missed opportunity for America and particularly for the children of America. . . .

Columnist Mary McGrory—no friend of Richard Nixon's—wrote of this appeal that it was "magnificent." She commented that "bureaucratic and parliamentary failures would have meant little, if the President's true mind would have been known. . . . The speech was splendid—and too late."[90]

After a five-day Christmas recess, the legislature returned to Washington to finish its work. Since the Constitution sets January 3 as the expiration date of Congress, the Senate had only a very few days left to accept the welfare reform proposal. But the FAP compromise that was agreed on by the administration and Senate liberals never even got to a vote: The Social Security bill was sent back to the Senate Finance Committee, stripped of its welfare reform amendment.

Nixon's press secretary insisted that the president still had a "very real hope the Congress will move on the urgent legislation" before January 3; but at the same time Ronald Ziegler admitted that the president had "pretty well concluded that he would resubmit much of the unfinished legislation" when the new Congress convened. It was Ribicoff who called a spade a spade. He decried the Senate's decision to set aside the Family Assistance Plan as "a tragic end to a noble cause."[91]

But, like the proverbial cat, the FAP had many lives. In January 1971, Nixon did resubmit the bill, once again calling it his number one domestic priority. Over the next year and a half the earlier drama repeated itself, although this time around the president's involvement was even more erratic and half-hearted, and this time around there was less suspense and less fanfare. Nevertheless, as Rather and Gates observe, "like a terminal cancer patient, welfare reform was allowed to linger on without hope or purpose." In September 1972 Nixon's highest domestic priority was "put to sleep once and for all."[92]

The Practice of Leadership

In 1972, a psychohistorian, Bruce Mazlish, wrote of Richard Nixon that, "He has, I believe, a real sympathy for the poor and deprived, as long as they are not being coddled or made 'self-indulgent,' and he sincerely backs the Family Assistance Plan."[93] Yet the fitful nature of Nixon's performance suggests that the clarity and depth of his commitment to the FAP were less than fully convincing. Many of those who watched Nixon during his first years in office were never persuaded that what he called his highest domestic priority was ever really a priority at all.

I have said that the will to lead is essential to successful leadership. In the two preceding chapters, the premise was not tested. Kennedy was manifestly determined to get congressional approval for aid to education, and Johnson for the antipoverty act. But the matter is less simple in the case of Richard Nixon and the Family Assistance Plan. It is clear—and we will explore this further—that he did not display great political skill in this instance. But if Nixon was not honestly motivated to get the FAP passed, what appeared to be poor politicking may in fact have been premediated passivity. In any event, President Nixon's erratic performance on family assistance—especially the convincing rhetoric punctuated by weeks of silence and inaction—raises real questions about how much and even whether he wanted his welfare reform plan to succeed.

Unfortunately, we are unlikely ever to get certain answers. All we have is circumstantial evidence, and some of that is contradictory. It is certainly true that Richard Nixon did not *have* to propose anything like family assistance. It was a radical and complex piece of legislation,[94] and previous presidents had successfully managed to steer clear of the issue. Moynihan pointed out that Nixon's "was the first Presidential message on welfare in history. All previous President's were afraid of it and tucked the subject under Social Security."[95] Why then did he do it? Why, after eight months in the White House, did President Nixon elect to complicate his life by proposing the Family Assistance Plan?

First, we might reasonably take the president at his word. He may have initiated the FAP because he genuinely believed it was "a good program, and a program immensely better than what we have now." A second reason the president might have proposed a welfare reform plan was that he was growing increasingly sensitive to the view that he was, in John Osborne's words, "a domestic laggard."[96] Given the pressure to do *something* in the domestic sector, there was a certain logic to the choice of a welfare reform bill: Everyone agreed that the existing patchquilt system was deplorable, and many felt that it was up to the federal government to do something about it. Finally, Nixon may have proposed the FAP because it was consistent with his self-image. Garry Wills has written eloquently about "Nixon Agonistes: The Last Liberal."[97] Here I will point out only that there clearly was some part of Richard Nixon that saw himself as a reformer. Why else take on Moynihan, a liberal Democrat, and a member (at the subcabinet level) of both the Kennedy and Johnson administrations, and put him so close by? Moynihan was, in the pointed words of William Safire, an "oddity" in the Nixon administration, "a concession Nixon made to his own facet of anti-establishment imagination."[98]*

A well-known story has Moynihan telling the president early in his administration that he had before him a golden opportunity to become a modern Disraeli. Late one afternoon, the story goes, the Executive Secretary of the Urban Affairs Council recalled for his boss that when the conservative Disraeli was Prime Minister of Britain he utterly confounded his opponents by "advocating a series of social reforms which they, as Liberals, were honorbound to support. In this way, Disraeli broadened his political base, increased his power, and established the tradition of Tory Reform—the art of clothing liberal policies in conservative dress."[99] Safire writes that Nixon was "delighted with the Disraeli comparison," which spoke to that part of the president that was a "progressive politician, willing and even eager to surprise with liberal ideas."[100]

But to look closer at why Nixon chose to make the FAP the centerpiece of his legislative package is to see that each of these three reasons is somewhat weak. The first is made suspect by his behavior; where was the action to back up the words? If Nixon was so convinced that the FAP was a good and important program, why, after classifying it as his top domestic priority, did he behave in the weeks and months that followed as if it were anything but that. "During this time, he almost never brought the subject up himself, and when others did, his general attitude seemed to be one of pious indifference: he acted as if he couldn't care less."[101] This confused Democrats accustomed to the ways of Lyndon Johnson, who fought hard to get what he *really* wanted (as opposed to what he said he wanted), and it clearly "encouraged those Republicans who didn't like the bill, anyway, to

---

*Whether or not Nixon was well served by having put the FAP in Moynihan's lap is an open question. On the one hand, the Democratic Moynihan should have had better luck in getting liberals to accept the plan since its success could then be attributed to a Democrat's advocacy as well as to Nixon's sponsorship. But, on the other hand, Moynihan's working for the Nixon administration itself cost him credibility and respect within the liberal community.

think they could line up against it without incurring much in the way of presidential displeasure."[102]

The second reason Nixon may have had for proposing family assistance—the need to undertake a major new initiative in the domestic sector—smacks of a proposal by default. The plan was conceived only after Nixon came into office, and it was finally announced only after many months of uncertainty and internal dissension. Osborne wrote about how events unfolded after that; once again the chief symptom was passivity.

> Nothing infuriates Mr. Nixon's people more than the suggestion that his good faith in this matter needs to be demonstrated. . . . Mr. Nixon has in fact supported Family Assistance, but with nothing like the vigor that he applied in his fights for the ABM, for his rejected Supreme Court nominations, and against amendments that would have restricted his freedom to end or prolong the Vietnam war as he chooses. . . . Mr. Nixon's personal "sell" for Family Assistance has been so soft that some of the legislators who want to enact his program leave his presence wondering whether he wants it as much as they do.[103]

I am not suggesting that President Nixon was wholly insincere, but instead that he was less than a fervent believer in his own cause. There is a big difference between thinking that something might be worth trying and being convinced that it is a national imperative. We should also remind ourselves of where the president's real interests lay—in foreign policy. He entered the White House preoccupied with Southeast Asia; if anything, that preoccupation intensified during his first term in office. Moreover, on April 30, 1970, the second of the three day Finance Committee hearings, the president announced the United States' incursion into Cambodia. As Moynihan admits in his chronology of the Family Assistance Plan, once that happened, "there was little time for anything else. . . . Cambodia broke the administration's stride."[104]

Finally, an underlying weakness is present in the argument that Nixon proposed the FAP because it appealed to the part of him that wanted to be a modern Disraeli. As I indicated, there is some truth to that view. The very number of reforms proposed by Nixon during his first two years in office suggests that the image he had of himself as a moderate reformer was not unappealing, or, for that matter, inaccurate. Nevertheless, there was something about it that did not ring true. (Wills once wrote that Nixon was "the least 'authentic' man alive."[105]) The "new Nixon," the reformer, did not fit comfortably alongside our image of the old Nixon, the beetle-browed conservative for whom priority number one was rooting out America's "reds" rather than doling out cash to America's poor. There was, at the least, a disjuncture between past and present that cast doubt on the integrity of the newfound impulse to reform.

Thus, Nixon must be distinguished from his two predecessors in the questionable conviction he brought to the task. Unlike earlier chapters, this one deals with a case in which there is some uncertainty about motivation. As Osborne suggests, when Nixon really wanted something badly enough, when his vision was unencumbered and his attitude unambivalent, he was able to politick with at least some vigor. Just possibly, Nixon's failure to get the FAP through the legislature was really not a failure of ability. Maybe, as far as he was concerned, the bill's demise was just as well. We will never know for certain, but in any case the issue of political skill must be seen in a somewhat different light. As I have already suggested, President Nixon's poor political skill in this case can be labeled "poor" *only* if one assumes that he was genuinely and significantly motivated to see family assistance become law.

For the remainder of this discussion, I will take the man at his word. I will assume that President Nixon would much rather have had the Congress approve the FAP in 1970 than vote it down. Thus, I will turn now to the question of Nixon's ability to successfully politick on his own behalf.

I have already implied that the welfare reform measure should have been drafted more quickly. Nixon ought not to have tolerated the in-fighting, especially between Moynihan and Burns, that resulted in several months' delay in writing the bill; nor should he have been so quiet on the subject. Both gave the impression that the FAP did not matter very much.

Another mistake was made during those early months: The president seemed not to recognize that members of his own team were among the key players in the political game. It was one thing to condone dissension while the Family Assistance Plan was still in the planning stage; it was quite another to continue to tolerate it once the decision was made to go ahead and go public. By all accounts, the August 1969 meeting in Laurel Cottage at Camp David was the last of a string of lost opportunities to rally the side. Moving against the fervent advice of the majority, Nixon did not appear to understand that members of his cabinet constituted a potential cadre of much needed allies if the FAP fight was to be won. His failure to recognize that simple fact meant that throughout the campaign for the FAP, the president's troops were in disarray, and hard core loyalists small in number.

Although we may eventually find more than we expect regarding Richard Nixon's private efforts on behalf of family assistance, we can speak with absolute certainty about his meager effort to win public support. How could he convey commitment and conviction if, for many weeks and even months at a time, he was simply silent on the matter? Nixon's reticence on family assistance is the more notable because of the promising response when the plan was first announced. There was enough initial enthusiasm to create a momentum on which another leader, a more vigorous one, could easily have capitalized.

But Nixon failed to seize the day. In contrast to Johnson, he never even tried to create a climate hospitable to his highest domestic priority. Instead of following up on his own proposal and milking early interest, the president left for a month to vacation in the California sun. At the very least, it was bad timing.

Still more damaging, perhaps, was the way in which President Nixon finally returned to the FAP. Instead of emphasizing the importance of this domestic priority, the measure got lost in a sea of other proposed reforms, ranging from "reform of the draft" (which actually took precedence over welfare reform) to "D.C. government reform." In other words, the message was unchanged; even though on occasion the president insisted that family assistance was of primary importance, he did not behave as if he really meant what he said.

The president's failure to present an altogether honest picture of family assistance was another reason that energetic public support—that is, the kind of support that translates into pressure on legislators—was lacking. Although Nixon's utterances, such as they were, naturally favored the FAP, they were not designed to create—Disraeli-like—a base of support within the enemy camp. In particular, he repeatedly emphasized the bill's work requirements and incentives, and deemphasized its provision for a guaranteed income. The president played up those parts of family assistance the old Nixon would have been comfortable with, and played down those that the old Nixon would have despised. Since these latter provisions lay at the heart of the program, one can say fairly that the president never really enlightened us about his very own proposal. Instead of providing us with a vision of how the government might help those whom Elliot Richardson once called the "casualties of the free enterprise system," all we got was Nixon's notion of a stern corrective. Osborne writes of the manner in which the president addressed the welfare reform issue during his preelection campaigning in the autumn of 1970.

> His campaign audiences would never have known from what he said about it that its great social virtue . . . lies in its promise of a guaranteed minimum income, underwritten by the federal government for every American family. . . . Instead he reverted to his 1968 campaign line, placing his major emphasis upon the requirement that adult recipients who can work or be trained for work will have to work or get off welfare.[106]

Nixon also failed to capitalize on political opportunities, opportunities that might have brought the FAP strong additional backing. For example, when the White House Conference on Food, Nutrition and Health proposed a minimum income of $5,500 for every family of four, the president could easily have picked up on this as "a goal toward which his own plan would make the first contribution."[107] Instead, he chose to reject out of hand a recommendation that, in fact, closely resembled his own. In sum, especially in the early months, Nixon seemed content to have merely proposed. He apparently thought that whether the FAP passed or not was out of his hands.

Having lost the time between August 1969 and the beginning of 1970, the White House then began to play a somewhat more active role—even though Nixon himself continued to stay in the background. It is impossible to determine how much of a difference this increased effort actually made; probably not a great deal. With the president himself still removed from the process, only a team of administration officials could at least partially account for the success of the FAP in the House of Representatives.

That success was nevertheless remarkable, as Warren Weaver Jr.'s summary article for *The New York Times* suggests. The headline was "Revolution in Welfare from an Unlikely Source." The House was described as subscribing "decisively to a doctrine that was radical even revolutionary." Weaver called this "an astonishing development," and went on to say that "for the first time in its history, Congress has endorsed the startling notion that there should be some sort of floor under human misery and that it is up to the Federal Government to lay down that floor."[108] However, what is especially noteworthy for our discussion is that nowhere in his article does Weaver attribute this "astonishing development," even in small measure, to the political skill of Richard Nixon. Instead, Weaver argues that the House bought the FAP because (1) 103 Republicans were convinced of the disastrous state of the existing welfare system, and on this major political issue they felt themselves obliged to display a measure of party loyalty; and (2) 140 Democrats could scarcely turn their backs on legislation they had long sought simply because it came to the floor under the aegis of Richard Nixon. Thus, although the Family Assistance Plan achieved an early success, the president's role seems to have been incidental. The House passed the FAP without Nixon's having to personally draw on his instrumental, authoritative, or libidinal sources of power.*

Although up to that point the president could get away with being relatively passive, the crunch was on as soon as Family Assistance reached the Senate Finance Committee. If the FAP was to make it through both Houses of Congress, Nixon had no choice but to assume a more active role.

*There is a theory that Wilbur Mills's newfound enthusiasm for the FAP explained the bill's success in the House. Those who expand on this theory claim that Mills supported the measure only because he knew full well that in its existing form it would never become law.

At this stage the president's leadership was most inept. There were two basic problems. First, the White House failed to recognize before the fact that the Finance Committee might prove to be a serious stumbling block. Nixon and his men were blissfully, if inexplicably, unaware of the staunch resistance. In fact, that resistance, even among members of his own party, was so strong, and so close to the surface that it would halt the first round of hearings a mere two days after they had begun. More specifically, the president's failure to try, in advance, to soften the positions of at least the two key opponents of the measure, Chairman Long and John Williams, was a costly mistake.* Long and Williams would prove to be durable and clever foes whose persistent opposition played an essential role in the bill's failure to pass. Moreover, the White House also failed to see to it that the support of Wallace Bennett of Utah, the Finance Committee's only Republican supporter of family assistance, was any more than lukewarm. Consequently, there was no preparation for what the Finance Committee held in store; once the members' opposition was unleashed, the momentum gained by family assistance in the House was promptly lost and never regained.

The second problem, actually a concomitant of the first, was the president's very low level of political activity. There is no evidence that Nixon successfully influenced—or even tried to—members of the political elite—the Congress, labor, business, the press, or the relevant professional organizations or community action groups. For instance, we have no record of his approaching an interest group such as the National Welfare Rights Organization (NWRO), a welfare client group that would play an increasingly active role in attacking family assistance. Once the NWRO had concluded that any welfare bill that could pass Congress would impose new constraints on some benefits already in place, and might contravene some of the rights NWRO claimed for its welfare mothers, its slogan became "Zap FAP." But despite NWRO's high visibility and the considerable political activity of its membership, there is no evidence that the president ever made the slightest overture in its direction. Indeed, Nixon did precious little to win over any of the opposition, budge any of the undecided, or rally those troops already in line.

During the late summer and fall the president did bring himself to employ a few political tactics—vis-à-vis members of Congress at least—to try to get family assistance through the Finance Committee. In the effort to persuade key Senators, Nixon compromised; he offered a few personal amenities (for example, the invitation to San Clemente); he met with mem-

*During the original hearings, Williams was the Finance Committee's most vocal opponent of the FAP. Later on, as we saw, his parliamentary maneuvering was largely responsible for the defeat of the compromise measure co-sponsored by the administration and Senate liberals.

bers of Congress to make personal appeals; he made good use of a new member of his cabinet (Richardson); and he even made something of an attempt to win public support. But the use of these tactics was not only belated, it was generally ineffective. Only the compromise with Senate liberals was a powerful weapon that brought results. As for the rest, they were feeble efforts that accomplished little. The personal amenities appear to have been carefully rationed; the meetings with Senators were few and far between; little use was made of the cabinet largely because so few members supported family assistance; and the attempt to win public support was as confusing as it was half-hearted.

Moreover, an array of political tactics lay totally unused by the president, both vis-à-vis Republicans and the majority Democrats. Nixon never really tried to preempt problems, give advance notice, make judicious use of careful timing, render services, "twist arms," or, as we have seen, ingratiate. He himself did not—except on a very few occasions—try to persuade; nor did he attempt to control the gains and costs to potential followers on the basis of whether they did or did not support the FAP. In short, his target audience was small—a few Senators at best—and his repertoire of political tactics narrow.

I am arguing in this book that an important quality of presidential leadership is the ability to engage other persons in two-way influence relationships. I believe that executive leadership is frequently a relational process that depends as much on gaining the cooperation of followers as it does on the task-related expertise of the leader. To get that cooperation, the president must trade benefits; to get something, he has to give something.

Nixon has always been an unusually private person. This was clearly evident in his relationship to the Congress, as both Stephen Wayne and George Edwards note:

> Unlike Johnson, [Nixon] did not enjoy personal interaction. . . . He preferred to work alone and off paper. . . . He saw only a few close associates on a regular basis.[109]
> President Nixon reportedly did not feel that he should have to lobby for his programs. He saw himself more as an administrator and executive decision maker and not as a power broker pushing to get his bills through Congress. He usually called only members of Congress whom he knew and then mainly for small talk. . . . Calls to the president from members of Congress were carefully screened, and 90 percent never got through to Nixon. . . . Occasionally the White House asked a department or agency to call a legislator concerning some specific legislation. The president rarely made such requests himself. . . .[110]

Elsewhere, I have described Nixon in some detail as an introvert, not only in his relations with Congress, but more generally.[111] With regard to his behavior in the world of people, I pointed out that although Nixon has

always been *in* the world of people—through family and friends, through
political associates, through his tie to the American body politic that did,
after all, twice elect him president—he has never been *of* it. One of the
most remarkable aspects of this remarkable man is that in a life that is so
well populated by all manner of persons, he has managed to be so alone.
What emerges is a picture of a man who did not behave much differently
with regard to the Family Assistance Plan from the way he might have in
any other circumstance. He was, quite simply, disinclined to reach out.
Thus, although there is some doubt about how motivated the president was
to see the FAP become law, there is no doubt that it was in any case difficult
for him to do the extensive personal politicking that would have made such
an outcome possible.

Throughout the years, several observers have attempted to explain why
the president did not lobby harder for his highest domestic priority by questioning the nature and degree of his commitment. Perhaps Nixon was
"working both sides: if the bill passed, fine; if it failed, he could claim that
he tried, blame Congress for the welfare mess, and not antagonize his conservative supporters by trying too hard."[112]

Or perhaps all his energies were sapped by the crisis in Southeast Asia.
Recalling an urgent request that the president step in forcefully on behalf
of the FAP, Moynihan comments: "This asked something different of the
president: his time, rather than simply his support. It was one thing to let
his advisers work up [something] and send it to Congress with his approval.
It was another for him personally to begin lobbying for a welfare bill in the
midst of his first great military-diplomatic-political crisis, especially as he
would be asking precisely those senators he could count on for support in
Vietnam to change their minds about FAP."[113]

Finally, there is the proposition that Nixon in fact *did* work reasonably
hard to push through family assistance, and that any suggestion to the contrary grows largely out of an unfair stylistic comparison to his predecessor.
Whereas Johnson was a large man with larger than life solutions—an "all-
out war on poverty"—Nixon was by nature more restrained. According to
this argument, the difference should not be construed as a lack of will on
President Nixon's part; it merely reflected another leadership style. In the
words of one Nixon aide, "The Johnson Administration was too bombastic,
too much of a grind, addicted to extravagant claims, too breathless.
[President Nixon] wanted to give the country a cooling off period."[114]

I would suggest that there is some truth to all these theories. The political
situation was certainly complicated enough: a Republican president who
had won the election only by a plurality of 43.4 percent, proposing a liberal
bill to a Democratic Congress at a moment of extreme political polarization; and a circumstance in which Senate Democrats were reluctant to

credit Nixon with so promising a reform, and Senate Republicans were either indifferent or downright hostile. At the same time Nixon was not under any real pressure from his own crowd to force laws through Congress. As Joseph Kraft pointed out at the time, the president could "claim it as an achievement that he has come up with only one new major program—family assistance—and passed none."[115]

It was also true that from the start the political and military situation in Southeast Asia took a heavy toll on the president. Moreover, the drain on his time and energy became even greater after the White House decision to expand the war into Cambodia. Crises seemed to multiply and escalate, at home now as well as abroad. The May 1970 killings of four Kent State University students, two protesting the Cambodian decision and two bystanders, symbolized the chaos. It was *not,* in fact, a good time for domestic political initiatives.

Finally, it is clearly correct to say that although Nixon's leadership style differed from Lyndon Johnson's, this does not necessarily imply that family assistance was an orphan. To be a distant father is not to abjure the responsibilities of parenthood altogether.

But because this bill in particular was so new and different, such a radical break from the past, there is no gainsaying the truth that it required a strong and committed president to lead it through the political process. Even with such guidance, it is not at all clear that the FAP would have emerged intact; without it, there was no chance. A few of President Nixon's advisers were well ahead of him on this one—Finch and Moynihan first among them. But their enthusiasm and motivation could not make up for a president who lacked the skill and, to some extent, the will to press the cause.

John Osborne wrote of President Nixon only ten months after he took office that he "isolates himself to an extraordinary and increasing extent from all except a very few chosen advisers."[116] Considering that Osborn was writing this at just about the time the Family Assistance Plan needed Nixon most, it was an inauspicious sign. But it revealed much. For the truth is that for all that has been said of Richard Nixon as the consummate politician, he was not what is commonly referred to as a "political animal." President Nixon almost certainly did prefer for the FAP to pass. But he was not naturally equipped to shepherd his pathbreaking proposal for family assistance through to the end of what promised from the very beginning to be a rough political journey.[117]

9

Gerald Ford and the Tax Cut

> This country needs an immediate Federal income tax cut of
> $16 billion. Twelve billion dollars or three-fourths of the
> total of this cut should go to the individual taxpayers in the
> form of a cash rebate amounting to 12 per cent of their 1974
> tax payments—up to a $1,000 rebate. If Congress acts by
> April first, you will get your first check for half the rebate
> in May and the rest by September.
>
> *President Ford,*
> *televised speech delivered to*
> *the nation, January 13, 1975*

In December 1973 Gerald R. Ford became the first person to be sworn in
as Vice President of the United States without an electoral mandate. It was
the start of a hectic nine months. By April 1974 the Watergate crisis was
escalating so fast that the odds were—as Ford recalled them—"50–50"
that President Nixon would have to step down;[1] and by August, in the East
Room of the White House, Ford was being sworn in as president—also
without the benefit of an electoral mandate.

The most important task that Ford faced as Chief Executive was to salve
the wound inflicted by Watergate. For America it was, as the title of Ford's
autobiography quite properly suggests, "a time to heal." Thus, during his
first three months in office, President Ford's time and energy were sapped
by the overriding issue of Nixon's pardon: first the decision to do it, then
the need to defend it.

But it was unlikely that Ford would be content only to play nursemaid
to a nation on the mend. Although he was new to the executive role, he was
by no means new to Washington politics. Gerald Ford had been a member
of the House of Representatives for twenty-five years, serving almost nine
of them as House Minority Leader. He manifestly evinced a certain ideology, clear policy preferences, and a political style. It should, therefore,
not have come as a surprise when only weeks after he took office, President
Ford seized the initiative. He announced that America's number one problem was its failing economy, and that his first priority as president would
be to find a solution.

156

Gerald Ford had the misfortune to assume the presidency under extremely difficult circumstances: He lacked an electoral mandate; he had little more than two years left before the next presidential election; and he faced a basically hostile Congress (in 1975 the Republicans had only 37 seats in the Senate and 144 in the House). Moreover, the country was faced with an entirely new phenomenon—what came to be called "stagflation." For the first time since economists started advising presidents on a regular basis, the choice was not simply Keynesian—between higher deficits to stimulate the economy at the price of new inflation, or lower deficits to rein in inflation at the price of creating greater recession. What simultaneous inflation and recession meant was that, in theory at least, President Ford was in a situation in which orthodox economics required the diametrically opposed solutions of a tax increase to stem inflation on the one hand, and a tax cut to stimulate the economy on the other.

Ford's initial and, in retrospect, too hasty response was to argue that one of the two ills was clearly more devastating than the other. Declaring that in fact inflation was the most dangerous symptom of our ailing economy, the president lost little time in announcing his plan for a tax surcharge. Almost immediately, however, Ford was forced to acknowledge that his initiative for this tax increase had not only been extremely unpopular politically, but possibly ill advised. In December the president backed down; and in mid-January, bowing to political and economic pressures, he made what his own press secretary, in an attempt at some jocularity under difficult circumstances, described as a "179 degree turn." Just a few days before his first State of the Union speech, President Ford recommended to the Congress an immediate, if modest, tax *cut*.

What Ford had offered in his economic message in October was, as *Time* commented, "pretty much more of the same from the Nixon years."[2] However, the January proposal for a tax cut constituted the new president's first major policy break with his predecessor and represented Ford's most significant attempt to exert genuine leadership during the early months of his short presidency.

Having made his "ungainly twist" from supporting a tax increase to proposing a tax reduction, Ford fought hard for the timing and size of his proposed legislation. But his agitated response to the outcome of that fight suggests that perhaps his longstanding distaste for the idea of a "quickie quick-fix" tax cut may have colored his reaction to what was at least a partial victory.

What Nixon was especially bad at—winning friends—Ford was especially good at. He liked people and they liked him. Ford was proud of saying he didn't have a "single enemy" in the House, and when he went to

Capitol Hill for the first time as president to address his former colleagues, they interrupted him with applause 32 times.[3]

Ford was a natural extravert. In his autobiography he makes a point of saying that from the first, he sought an "open" administration.[4] Former colleagues were told "My office door has always been open, and that is how it is going to be at the White House."[5] He was true to his word. During his first two weeks in the White House the new president invited visitors ranging from George Meany to the Congressional Black Caucus. And many of those he could not see, he telephoned. White House phone logs show that on August 16 the president called Senate Majority Leader Mike Mansfield to congratulate him on his new record of serving longer than any previous Majority or Minority Leader; on August 20 he phoned Representatives John Rhodes and William Harsha to thank them for their "great work" in reducing funds for mass transit; on August 24 he called Senator Harrison Williams to congratulate him on his marriage; on September 9 he phoned Senator Henry Bellmon to express his concern about the Senator's walking pneumonia; and on September 30 he made no less than nineteen calls to drum up support for his decision to appear before the Hungate Committee.[6]* In early November an attempt was made to expand still further the "Presidential Telephone Program." An inter-office memo read in part: "We want to focus attention on the Presidential Telephone Call Recommendation Program. . . . Presidential telephone calls provide an excellent opportunity to increase the President's exposure and identify the President with unique and worthwhile events and programs."[7]

But Ford could not live off good will alone. Faced with a long list of "pressing policy issues" that covered everything from agriculture appropriations to cargo preference to safe drinking to Rhodesian chrome to privacy legislation,[8] the president decided right at the start to give his best effort to the ailing economy.

It seemed a sound idea. Galloping inflation, concomitant with rising unemployment and a possible recession, indicated the economy was in trouble; one sympathetic economist was quoted as saying bluntly that Ford had inherited "a disaster."[9] And so during his early months in the White House, President Ford spent "more time discussing the economy than almost anything else."[10] In fact, the topic of his first major address as president— delivered only three days after taking office—was what to do about the nation's economic problems.

But other than seconding a proposal already made by Mansfield for a "summit meeting" of labor, industry, and government officials to devise a

---

*Representative William Hungate was chairman of the House Judiciary Committee's Subcommittee on Criminal Justice. On September 30 Ford agreed to appear personally before the subcommittee to answer questions about his pardon of Richard Nixon.

bipartisan approach to economic stability, on his first big occasion Ford had little to say that was new. As one reporter put it, this presidential speech resembled nothing so much as "a little straight talk among friends."[11]

In late August the president became more specific. "Public Enemy Number One," Ford proclaimed, was inflation. He elaborated slightly at a press conference: "If we take care of inflation and get our economy back on the road to a healthy future, I think most of our other problems will be solved."[12]

Ford had ample reason to be confident of his diagnosis. In a memorandum to him written only days after he became president, Assistant to the President Alexander Haig summarized the policy views of the president's top economic advisers. Haig noted that although they differed on the recommended treatment, there was no disagreement about what constituted the disease. Haig's memo read: "All agree that inflation is the prime problem with forecasts ranging from $6\frac{1}{2}$ to 10 percent."[13] Understandably, the new president accepted this expert and unanimous judgment without question.

Plans were made to precede the planned economic summit with a series of White House Conferences on inflation. In keeping with Ford's promise to have an open administration, the White House made an impressive attempt to keep key members of the political elite—both in and out of government—in touch and informed. For example, in late August President Ford met with eighteen prominent economists. The purpose of the meeting was, "For the President to discuss the state of the economy and his personal desire for a thorough review of where we are currently and an exploration of new policy initiatives."[14]

During those early weeks of the Ford administration both liberals and conservatives seemed to back Ford's emphasis on licking inflation. Ford wrote to the standard bearer of the conservative wing of the Republican Party, Senator Barry Goldwater, as follows:

September 7, 1974

Dear Barry,

... I want you to know that your remarks concerning the priority problem, inflation and the economy, are extremely encouraging to me. We are in agreement. . . .

Barry, in setting the priority of a battle to control inflation and stabilize the economy, I moved into the first phase by calling these conferences. . . . It means a great deal to me to know that my valued and respected friend will be marching with me to achieve these goals for our great and beloved country.

With warmest personal regards.

Sincerely,
(signed) "Jerry Ford"
Gerald R. Ford[15]

A lengthy article on inflation written for *The New York Times* by economist John Kenneth Galbraith, points up the confusion of the time. Historically, between inflation and recession it was inflation that better served the little man at the expense of the rich folks by reducing the debtor's real burden and the creditor's real asset. The monetarists believed that inflation was so pernicious that it warranted even the severe treatment of inflicting a little recession on the country. But now the ultra-liberal Galbraith was taking the position that inflation generally took from "the old, weak and small" and gave to "the big, organized and fast on their feet." Further, Galbraith warned the president that unless he solved the problem of inflation, he would almost surely "be another in our extending list of Presidential basket cases."[16]

Clearly enouraged by what appeared to be broad support, on October 8 President Ford delivered his major economic address before a joint session of the Congress. He urged a "new mobilization" against inflation and proposed a broad, basically conservative program ranging from a reduction in oil imports to a one-year tax increase for corporations as well as many private citizens. The one-year tax increase for individuals would apply to married couples with incomes in excess of $15,000, and to single persons with incomes in excess of $7,500[17]* In short, to cut consumer spending, Ford was proposing a tax increase for most individuals above a bare middle-income level. He called his tax initiative the "acid test" of his administration's determination to whip inflation.

Right from the start, prospects for passing the acid test were poor. The main problem was that almost no one liked the idea of a tax increase—not the public, the press, nor the Congress. Key members of the House and Senate hailed the spirit behind Ford's efforts, but took exception to the specifics, especially the proposal for an income tax surcharge which, it may be added, was made right on the eve of an election. As Senator Hugh Scott dryly noted. "There [is] a reluctance to share the President's enthusiasm for sacrifice."[18]

Thus, Richard Schweiker, a Pennsylvania Republican then running for reelection to the Senate, called it "a travesty" to impose a tax surcharge on families earning $15,000 a year. A Republican conservative on the tax-writing House Ways and Means Committee, Joel Broyhill of Virginia, insisted that he would refuse to "sit still any longer for efforts to get more

*In 1984 dollars these figures would be roughly double.

tax blood out of the so-called middle earners." And one Midwestern Republican Representative who was facing an uphill fight for re-election frankly wondered who would fight for the tax increase. "That's the President's program," he said. "It's not mine."[19]

The American people also responded negatively. By a margin of two to one they expressed their opposition in various polls to the president's surtax. Moreover, much of the press was positively hostile. *The Wall Street Journal* called Ford's proposals "neither surprising nor bold,"[20] and *The New York Times* judged the "overall impact of Mr. Ford's speech [to be] weak, flaccid and generally disappointing."[21] Indeed, only five days after Ford had proposed the tax increase, the *Times* predicted that the measure "was likely to be revised if it is adopted at all."[22]

From the onset, then, Ford was forced to go on the defensive. At a news conference a mere two days after his congressional address, Ford promised that his surtax would be in place only one year, and calculated that for a family of four with a gross income of $20,000, the extra tax would amount to only $42, or "12 cents a day."[23] The president also had his staff send out several fact sheets. For example, Secretary of the Treasury William Simon composed a letter to be sent to every member of Congress that began "There has been a great deal of misunderstanding about how the President's individual surtax proposal would work. I am writing to see if I can clear it up."[24] Finally, the president hit on the idea of getting the public involved through a voluntary anti-inflation campaign. The name of the campaign was "Whip Inflation Now," and its gimmicky symbol a button stamped with the acronym "WIN." In his autobiography, Ford provides the rationale: "Once you had 213 million Americans recognizing that inflation was a problem . . . positive results would have to follow."[25]

But while in public Ford appeared convinced of the virtue of his tax plan—at least through early November—in private he was being warned, almost from the start, that his proposal was in for a very rough time. A memorandum to the president from his Assistant for Public Liaison, William Baroody, Jr., dated October 10—only two days after Ford's speech to the Congress—warned that the surtax "was in serious trouble."

> With the surtax in serious trouble on the Hill and very unpopular politically, the likelihood is that the Congress will pass a bill which spends more and raises less than you have proposed. An inflationary bill would have to be vetoed, which would put us back where we are today. It would be a serious and damaging blow to public confidence and to an already soft economy.[26]

But the surtax poposal presented the president with much more than just a political problem: Objective economic indicators showed that the country was definitely sliding into a recession. Unemployment was projected to rise from 5.8 to 7 percent; there was a reported 2.9 percent (annualized) decline in the Gross National Product; and on October 29 the index of leading indicators reported the largest decline in any single month in twenty-three years.[27]

Around mid-November, the president began to back down. The record indicates that by then Ford had already separated himself from his top economic advisers on the matter of tax policy. Although the Executive Committee of the Economic Policy Board was still hoping that Congress would give "the highest priority to acting this year on the inflation package,"[28] and urging the president to "stand firm" on his proposals ("If we dilute our own proposals at the outset, we just undercut our own bargaining position"[29]), Ford himself was facing facts. On November 12 the president's press secretary, Ron Nessen, let it be known that his boss was prepared to be flexible. Nessen said that President Ford "is not wedded to the 5 percent surtax. He is wedded to a surtax or some other method of raising the money for his program."[30] On November 16 Ford said in an interview that he would accept "a modification or a change" in his surtax proposal. "I would," the president indicated, "as long as they don't abandon the concept. In other words . . . the revenue."[31]

Ford's statements were the first signs of what would amount to a *complete reversal* of administration policy. The president recognized that even as his economic advisers suggested that he stand firm, conditions were changing so rapidly that what had formerly been a slim chance for passage of his unpopular tax proposal had now become no chance at all.

In particular, two things had changed. The first was the composition of Congress. The November election determined that the new legislature would be overwhelmingly Democratic—the Democrats gained 43 more seats in the House—and therefore even less likely than it had been before to leave Ford's anti-inflation program intact. A telling memo to the president from Secretary Simon addressed the altered political situation.

> I conferred Monday with Chairman Mills (of the Ways and Means Committee) concerning tax legislation. His attitude appears to have shifted greatly since my telephone call to him in Arkansas last week, when he was more receptive about moving ahead with your tax proposals. I concluded that since his return to Washington, he has been under great pressure from Democrats to put over major tax legislation until next year when the new and more liberal Congress can deal with it. . . .[32]

The second factor that changed was the economy. It was deteriorating with surprising rapidity, even since the president's October 8 speech. A memo to Ford from Alan Greenspan, Chairman of the Council of Economic Advisers, read in part: "Although recent developments have not altered our basic outlook for the economy during 1975 they have caused our estimates of economic conditions during the first half of next year to slip toward the bottom end of the range of possibilities that appeared plausible earlier."[33] Thus, although some of Ford's advisers, including Simon and Greenspan, were still recommending that he hold firm to his October 8 proposals, the Chief Executive himself—who had by now announced that he would run for president in 1976—was ready to seriously consider changing course. From his point of view, the costs of consistency were clearly starting to outweigh the benefits.

On November 29 there was a report in *The New York Times* that Ford now believed the recession required as much attention as inflation, and that several economic policy makers "were starting to think seriously about the possibility of a tax cut in 1975." A tax cut would increase disposable income and thereby stimulate spending, production, and employment.

In December the administration decided definitely to change course. A series of meetings occasioned by the quarterly review of the Economic Policy Board provided the forum for discussions. On December 18 Ford met with his Labor Management Committee. On December 19 he had a lengthy meeting with 29 nongovernment economists from which emerged a "strong consensus favoring a tax cut."[34] And on December 21 the Economic Policy Board itself decided to accept what was "probably inevitable: the restimulation of the economy through tax reductions."[35] The Board recommended that the individual tax cut be "tailored to respond to Congressional concern over the effects of inflation on low-income taxpayers."[36]

Late on the afternoon of December 21, the president met with the Economic Policy Board Executive Committee for almost two and a half hours. Among the issues presented for Ford's consideration were the size, duration, form, and distribution of a tax cut. Roger Porter writes: "The President asked a number of clarifying questions, then ... he asked different members of the Executive Committee for their individual comments and asked what would happen if he did nothing on taxes. ... Near the end of the discussion the President ... declared ... that he supported the notion of a tax cut. ... He said that his mind was 'pretty well made up.'"[37] Ford indicated that he wanted the discussion to continue at Vail, Colorado, over the Christmas holidays; he also stressed the need for confidentiality.

Between the meeting in Washington and the meeting only five days later in Vail, the pressure on Ford to propose a tax cut continued to increase. A former member of the Federal Reserve Board proposed a 10 percent reduction in Federal income taxes due the next April. The Congressional Joint Economic Committee unanimously recommended an "immediate" tax reduction to check the recession. Walter Heller, Chairman of the Council of Economic Advisers under Kennedy and Johnson, recommended a tax cut of at least $15 billion. The new chairman of the House Ways and Means

Committee, Al Ullman, said that his panel would move quickly to approve a "sizable" tax cut. And *The New York Times* opined that a "major" tax cut was necessary "to overcome that unplanned and undesirable buildup of fiscal drag."[38] Moreover, the president was being warned by his own staff that he had to reach a decision soon. In a December 26 memorandum to him from Counselor to the President Jack Marsh, Ford was told that it was "essential that pending economic program decisions be made this weekend" lest it be necessary to request a delay in the submission of the budget to Congress. The senior staff view was that "it would be desirable to avoid such a request."[39]

By the time the president and his advisers had gathered at Vail, Ford was plainly ready to break with his past. The minutes of the Executive Committee meeting of December 30 acknowledged what was already an accomplished fact: "The surtax proposal has been dropped."[40]

Through early January President Ford played his cards close to the vest; the dramatic change in fiscal policy would be announced only at his convenience. Ford's concern with style and form was understandable for, in truth, he was in an extremely embarrassing position. On economic policy, the administration was perceived to be making a complete "about-face."[41] Before Ford had said a single public word about his *new* economic policy, his *old* economic plans were said to "rank among the most quickly eaten Presidential words of recent history," and his Administration was accused of being "in the midst of performing an ungainly twist" away from what had been proposed only three short months ago.[42] Moreover, a Harris poll takn in December had indicated that an overwhelming "86 percent of Americans surveyed had no confidence in the ability of the President to manage the economy."[43]

It was decided that the State of the Union message would be the appropriate occasion on which to reveal the administration's new tax package.[44] Months earlier, Baroody had written Ford about what this particular address would mean to him: "Your State of the Union message will mark a formal end to the transition period and the beginning of what will be seen by the public and by history as the Ford Administration."[45] Precisely because the occasion was such an important one, and because the White House was in such an awkward position on economic policy, there was considerable concern about leaked information. William Seidman, the president's old friend who was now serving as his Assistant for Economic Affairs, made it a point to "avoid economic interviews until after the State of the Union."[46] And Nessen advised the president as follows:

Mr. President:

You might want to remind your economic advisers not to discuss publicly the proposals which have been reviewed at this meeting.

You might want to remind them that your State of the Union speech will have maximum impact if your program has an element of surprise. You might want to say that if all your proposals have been discussed publicly before the speech, then the speech will appear to contain nothing new and you will lose the impact of a totally new program for dealing with economic problems.

Ron Nessen[47]

But for whatever reason, the attempt at confidentiality did not work. On January 4, still concerned, Seidman, Nessen, and Frank Zarb (the Director of the Energy Resource Council) proposed an alternative: "The considerable and generally accurate leaks about the contents of your planned economic and energy programs are damaging the planned impact of your proposals. We feel that you should reevaluate your plans to announce the economic and energy proposals in the State of the Union speech and consider making at least some announcement before then in order to prevent a complete loss of impact."[48]

By early January many people did in fact know that Ford was about to propose an economic program considerably different from the one he had put forth on October 8. Nessen's unenviable task was to smooth the way. In December Ford had told an audience of business executives that he did not intend to make any "180 degree turn" in economic policy. When he was reminded of that statement in January the president's press secretary joked, "Well, it could be 179 degrees."[49]

A major decision still had to be made on what form the tax cut should take. During the first ten days of the month, Ford had at least three separate meetings with the Executive Committee of the Economic Policy Board.[50] The Committee had final responsibility for all issues of timing and content, not only for the State of the Union address, but also for both "pre" and "post-State of the Union activities."[51] At the meeting of January 8 it was decided that the Committee would recommend to the president a "total temporary tax refund [of] $15.9 billion."[52] And at the meeting of January 10 the president agreed that he would recommend among other items, a temporary, one-year, across-the-board 10 percent reduction in individual income taxes.

Despite Ford's carefully mapped out plan to reveal his new tax package only in the State of the Union speech, he outlined the measure on nationwide television 48 hours in advance of his formal address to the Congress. Circumstances were now such that Ford felt obliged to upstage himself. As

Seidman, Nessen, and Zarb had cautioned, there was a real danger that unless he did, he would be beaten at his own game by Congressional Democrats. Speaker of the House Carl Albert declared on the very morning of Ford's televised speech that he expected the House to act within 60 days on legislation to cut federal taxes on low and middle income families by somewhere between $10 and $20 billion.

Consequently, Ford felt pressed on January 13 when he went on television from the White House Library to announce what *The New York Times* referred to in a full-page headline story as "a drastic turn in his economic policies."[53] He proposed to enact before April 1 a $16 billion income tax cut that would include a rebate to individuals of up to $1,000.*

The president's reviews were good, at least with regard to his performance. His attempt to pass over Congress and appeal directly to the people was enhanced by the warm, informal setting—a fire glowing in a fireplace, shelves of books—and by the fact that this time around Ford had done his homework.

> President Ford did not sit down at a desk and read with the Presidential flag on one side of him and a picture of Abraham Lincoln or his family on the other.
> When he started he was standing up, against a background of bookshelves. Then he sat down at a desk in the library. All the while he was reading steadily.
> The President had obviously been rehearsed. When he said that America had to be turned around, his hand moved in a circular motion. When he spoke of a "three front campaign" he held up three fingers. . . .[54]

Ford's official State of the Union speech, however, delivered two days later, was less well received. First, the president's tone was gloomy. "The state of the Union is not good," Ford declared. "Millions of Americans are out of work, recession and inflation are eroding the money of millions more." Second, since Ford had been forced to reveal his hand two days earlier, by the time of the State of the Union speech, the opposition had already started to solidify. Thus, whereas the reaction to Ford's television speech was good, the reaction to his State of the Union talk was, at best, mixed. Conservatives were upset about projected high budget deficits, while liberals felt strongly that the $16 billion rebate of taxes on 1974 income was not enough to bring the nation out of its rapidly deepening recession.

Plainly, President Ford had his work cut out for him. If he was not to be humiliated a second time, he would have to move quickly to get his tax proposal through Congress. But whether the political center in Congress

---

*On this same occasion the president also called for higher taxes on natural gas and oil, and proposed several other measures relating to the economy and energy.

was large and tractable enough to be induced to support the president on this issue was an open question. The early signs were that the 94th Congress—overwhelmingly Democratic, young, and liberal in character— would be uncommonly partisan and inclined to quarrel with the White House.[55] Moreover, the president had been put in an awkward position, both ideologically and politically. As vice president, Ford had opposed any "quickie quick-fix tax cut." And in a magazine interview just a few days before Nixon's resignation, he had urged Nixon to submit to Congress "an honest-to-goodness balanced budget."[56] Thus, the Ford who was compelled by events to initiate legislation that would have been almost unthinkable just a few months earlier was now at odds even with his own past.

During the two weeks just before and after the presentation of his new tax proposal, President Ford was extremely active politically. He initiated contact with different factions of the political elite both to explain his new tax plan and to expound its virtues. Reasonably enough, Ford's most energetic sales pitch was to Congress. Throughout January, Ford himself and, at his encouragement, his staff, attempted insofar as possible to bring key members of the House and Senate into the decision-making process.

On January 4 a memo was sent by Jack Marsh to Max Friedersdorf, Assistant to the President for Legislative Affairs, on the issue of involving Democratic congressional leaders in the economic program. "Bill Seidman is quite anxious to get these inputs and we should also talk about how we get inputs from the Senate."[59]

In early January the president issued a request to Republican congressional leaders for their input into the State of the Union address. Senate Republican Leader Hugh Scott responded that both he and the House Republican Leader, John Rhodes, "would be delighted to meet with you personally to present our views, if you so desire." Scott added that he supported the president on a tax cut: "It seems to me that an immediate tax cut is one good way to increase savings and increase productivity through higher demand."[58]

On January 10 the president invited Al Ullman to the White House. The purpose of the discussion was to "advise Representative Ullman of the President's decisions on the economy and energy." Ford's aides supplied him with several "Talking Points"* that included:

1. Al, I have reached a number of decisions regarding recommendations for the economy and energy.

---

*"Talking Points" are key points condensed by staff into pithy phrases which are then typed on a sheet of paper that the president can refer to quickly and easily, either on the phone, or when talking face to face.

2. These will be submitted to the new Congress soon and I wanted to share them with you.
3. Basically, my economic decisions involve recommendations for a tax cut and no new spending requests. . . .
4. I would like your support and would appreciate your reaction and suggestions.[59]

A memorandum to Friedersdorf confirmed that the president approved Friedersdorf's plan to have him brief congressional leaders of both parties on the content of the State of the Union message immediately prior to its delivery.[60] Friedersdorf had other suggestions for the president as well. He recommended that Seidman and Zarb talk personally to Representative James Wright (designated chairman of a committee to coordinate Democratic economic/energy policy by the House), Representative Tom Foley (chairman of the Democratic Study Group, Representative Philip Burton (chairman of the Democratic Caucus), Representative Richard Bolling ("for consultation purposes"), and three other key House Republicans. Moreover, Friedersdorf reminded Ford of Ford's upcoming meeting with Mike Mansfield, and he recommended that the president also meet with Senator Scott, and the Chair of the Senate Finance Committee, Russell Long. Finally, Friedersdorf suggested that Seidman and Zarb get together with Senator Hubert Humphrey (chairman of the Joint Economic Committee) and Senators Robert Griffin and John Tower ("for consultation purposes").[61]

On January 11 the president met with the Senate and House Minority Leaders. He advised Scott and Rhodes "of Presidential decisions regarding the economy and energy, and [then sought] their reactions and recommendations." At the end of the meeting, Ford told his guests, "We will push for prompt consideration and enactment. I will need your strong support, if possible."[62]

On January 13 the president met privately with Russell Long. Once again, the purpose was first to brief the Senator, then enlist his support. Ford's final Talking Point: "I know you will give my proposals all possible consideration, and I'm sure we can work together on a sound program for the nation's economic and energy needs."[63]

On January 14 and 15 two large meetings were held. On January 14, the president and fourteen of his advisers met with nineteen Republican leaders from the Houe and Senate. On January 15 there was a breakfast meeting with Ford, six presidential advisers, and twelve bipartisan leaders from the House and Senate.[64]

On January 20 the president's staff replied carefully and courteously to a letter of concern from the Congressional Black Caucus. Immediately following the State of the Union message, the Black Caucus had sent the president a letter expressing its "disappointment in major aspects of your economic proposals." Black Representatives were upset that the Ford administration was "preoccupied with current symptoms of economic unrest, rather [than] with the basic systemic causes which have brought about this period of continuing economic dislocation." In particular, the Black Caucus recommended that the president consider major tax reforms, a minimum of one million public service jobs, and increases in benefit levels. The letter from the Black Caucus was signed personally by seventeen members of the House of Representatives. The White House response assured the Black Caucus that its letter would be "called to the President's attention without delay. In addition, copies will be shared with his energy and economic policy advisers."[65]

But if the president and his staff directed their most strenuous political activity toward Congress, members of the legislature were by no means the only focus of White House attention. The president sent Alan Greenspan a letter saying that he looked forward to the Council's "cooperation and assistance as we work to meet the challenges of 1975."[66] He took time to have lunch with seven executives from *The New York Times*.[67] And he participated in an East Room briefing that was a follow-up to the State of the Union address for presidential appointees, "particularly those of subcabinet level who are spokesmen for the Administration." The purpose of the briefing was to "provide these men and women who will be speaking out in various forums throughout the country with a broad and firsthand understanding of the Administration's programs and policies."[68] Also as a follow-up briefing to the State of the Union address, the president took part in a White House meeting of state and local leaders. Included were "governors, state legislators, mayors and county officials and their representatives . . . where the official was unable to attend."[69] Furthermore, the president agreed to a request from New York and New England governors to have "at least 30 minutes" with him in yet another follow-up to the State of the Union message.[70] And finally, Ford sent letters to several well-placed members of the general public who had taken the trouble to write to the White House. In response to a letter of support from Tim Roudebush, County Chairman of the Johnson County (Kansas) Republican Central Committee, President Ford wrote:

> Thanks so much for your good comments following my State of the Union address. . . .

I know the program I have offered will work. I look to people like you across the country for support and cooperation in implementing it and setting America in a new direction of stability and progress.[71]

President Ford encouraged his team to support the cause in whatever way possible, and they responded accordingly. All assistant secretaries and their chief public affairs officers were supplied with a "State of the Union briefing package." In turn, they were asked to "relate their speeches where possible to the President's proposals."[72] In addition, the Executive Committee of the Economic Policy Board occupied itself with developing an "understandable summary statement of the economic proposals announced in the State of the Union Message for distribution to departments, agencies, Congress, and interested citizens."[73] Finally, several of President Ford's top advisers appeared on television to urge prompt congressional approval of the president's program: William Simon on NBC's "Meet the Press"; Interior Secretary Rogers C. B. Morton on ABC's "Issues and Answers"; and Frank Zarb on CBS's "Face the Nation."[74]

Whatever the political problems that eventually interfered with President Ford's tax cut proposal, they clearly did not stem from an initial failure to try to influence others to go along. At least at the early stage, a solid administration effort to sell the president's product existed. Yet despite this effort, there were signs that Ford might get other than exactly what he wanted. Ways and Means, with the concurrence of the president, decided to work on the proposed tax cut before turning to anything else, but even this early attention did not prevent criticism of "Too Little, Too Late."[75] Columnist Tom Wicker, among many others, made the argument: "The two major deficiences of the antirecession tax cut . . . are, first, that the $12 billion personal income tax rebate does not provide enough stimulus, particularly on a one-shot basis limited entirely to 1974 taxes. Second, when that $12 billion is further subdivided into May and August payments, it becomes both too little and too late."[76] Similar concern was expressed by Democrats and even a good many Republicans that President Ford's plan for tax rebates would provide "too little stimulus, [would be] too slow acting, and [would] fail to get enough purchasing power into the pockets of low and middle income families."[77]

Given these objections, the Democratic Congress was expected to put together its own tax package, one that would contain a tax cut considerably more radical than the president could easily support. (Ullman had already proposed an alternative measure that differed substantially from the president's.) At the same time, the president was expected to persist in his warning that more government spending, or greater tax cuts than the ones he proposed, would lead to dangerously large federal deficits and, soon thereafter, to renewed and greater inflation.[78] What had either been missed or ignored by those favoring alternative plans was that *as early as late January* President Ford was hinting that he might be willing to accept a tax compromise. *The New York Times* report on this remarkable development read as follows:

> Meeting with a small group of reporters in ... the White House ... , Mr. Ford said he would accept some changes in the details of his program to reduce taxes this year.
>
> "There is room for flexibility," the President said.
>
> In fact, his answers suggested that he was resigned to having the House Ways and Means Committee introduce a tax bill that differed substantially from his own plan. . . .
>
> Noting that Representative Al Ullman ... had also come up with a tax proposal, the President said it appeared Congress would pass its own program "whether we agree or not."
>
> Although he did not say so, Mr. Ford's answers left the impression that he would not veto a tax-cut bill that differed from his proposals. . . . [79]

Still, President Ford continued to champion his own tax cut plan. He even made several "sales" trips that were deemed, by White House staff anyway, to be successful. Nessen sent Rumsfeld a memo saying he had received "a large number of letters from editors, publishers, and broadcast executives [that were] overwhelmingly favorable. The Press Secretary went on to "urge the continuation of these out-of-town selling trips . . . OOPS . . . explanatory trips."[80]

But it was clear, probably as soon as early February, that although the president would get a tax bill from Congress, he would get more of a bill than he had bargained for. On February 3, Doug Bennett, a Special Assistant for Legislative affairs, sent Friedersdorf a memo warning that the "tax bill Al Ullman introduced last Tuesday could be the cornerstone of diffusing the President's plan."[81] And on February 6, Ullman's Ways and Means committee gave all but final approval to a tax cut bill that totaled over $20 billion compared to the $16 billion that Ford wanted.*

Although the final House vote was to cut taxes even more—the figure was now $21.3 billion—the president was still reported as ready to accept the House tax plan. By compromising, Ford apparently hoped at least to get the fast action he wanted. Indeed, this hope may explain why the White House was reported to be showing "no signs of alarm" over rumors that the Senate would pass an even bigger tax cut than the House.[83]

Ford's main strategy during February and early March—that is, after he should have recognized that Congress would go considerably further

---

*There were other differences as well. A detailed comparison between the Administration Tax Rebate Proposal and the Ways and Means Bill was drawn up by White House staff and is available at the Ford Library.[82]

than he wanted with regard to the size of a tax cut—was to remain focused on the issue of speed. All else was sacrificed to trying to get the tax cut through the Congress as quickly as possible. Ford's thinking seemed to be that any delays would make it more likely that his original proposal would be tampered with even further; that they would reduce his chances of getting credit for whatever tax reduction finally did emerge; and that they would prevent the fiscal cure from working in time for the 1976 presidential election—when Ford would be the Republican candidate.

Ford employed two tactics. First he harangued Congress to move faster. The president said that it was "unconsionable" that the House had delayed action on the tax cut by one week, and that it was "unbelievable" that the Senate was so slow in scheduling its own hearings on the matter. Nessen claimed the president felt "about as strongly about this delay in Congress as he has about anything since taking office last August."[84] At a news conference President Ford reiterated the point. When asked about reports that he believed that Congress might not act on a tax cut until June, the president replied:

> [The process] could conceivably take until June. I think that is very ill-advised and extremely serious. We had hoped that Congress would act by the middle of March at the latest and they could have if they had taken the simple specific tax reductions that I recommended.
> . . . We need a stimulant now and I hope the Congress will realize the urgency of the need for action and I trust that now that they have been reminded of their slowness that they will expedite the process.[85]

The second tactic Ford employed was to offer compromise in exchange for quick action. This willingness manifested itself on several occasions: The president made it quite clear that he would agree to a tax reduction measure that looked rather different from the one he had proposed; he signaled his readiness to meet the Democrats half way on key aspects of his energy proposal,[86] and he complied with demands made by key members of Congress regarding specific points of the legislation of special interest to them. In particular, President Ford went out of his way to mollify Senator Long. The tax cut bill that the House approved also provided for repeal of the controversial, fifty-year-old oil depletion allowance. Senator Long strongly opposed such a repeal, and he promptly phoned the White House to see if he and the president might not be able to agree on a strategy that would be in both their interests. Specifically, Long told the White House that he thought he could win the fight to keep the oil depreciation measure out of the tax bill, "but that he needs help." Long suggested to a White House aide that "the President state that he is opposed to removal of the oil depletion allowance . . . and . . . indicate that [he] favors consideration of the two measures—tax cut and oil depletion—separately." Ford, who had no interest at all in having the oil depletion issue complicate or delay his tax cut proposal, responded to Long's second suggestion with the handwritten comment that it "sounds desirable."[87]

Just as Ford was ahead of his economic advisors in recognizing the need to abandon the tax increase proposal of October 8, he was ahead of them this time. While the president was busy signaling his willingness to compromise, members of his administration were still recommending that he stand firm. William Simon's position was that Ford should continue to insist that Congress "accept our original formula," and "urge that they do more for middle-income persons."[88] In fact, when Simon testified before the Senate Finance Committee, his denunciation of the version just passed by the House of Representatives was so strong that it could not help contrasting sharply with the earlier impression that the president basically found the House bill acceptable, despite some reservations. (Simon's strongest complaint was that the House bill failed to provide enough relief for groups who buy big ticket items such as automobiles and appliances.[89])

Ford lost no time in disassociating his position from that of Simon's, which he apparently saw as counterproductive in the task of trying to persuade Congress to act quickly. At a press conference he backed the Treasury Secretary's view that "the House version of the [tax] bill was too limited," but nevertheless implied once again that he would accept the House measure: "I believe that the program we have as it appears to be moving through the Congress is at this stage of the game moving in the right direction. The big problem is not the size of tax reduction, but the slowness with which the Congress is acting on it. . . . What we need is speed."[90]

Considerable evidence exists that Ford's conciliatory words were matched by his behavior. In his zeal to get a tax cut quickly, the president continued to engage in a rather high level of political activity, especially vis-à-vis Congress. On March 4 Ford received a memo that Representative Barber Conable had called. Conable wanted the president "to know how much appreciated is the heavy round of consultation you have been having and continue to have with the Republican leadership. He said he believes that relations between the White House and the minority leadership in the House have never been better."[91] On March 7 President Ford sent Senator Long a "Dear Russell" letter expressing his pleasure over the fact that the Finance Committee had tentatively gone along with Long's suggestion to consider the oil-depletion issue separately from the pending tax bill.

> . . . It is my hope that the Congress will produce a tax relief bill which provides an effective one-time stimulus to the economy. I also hope that this can be done quickly, certainly before the Easter recess. The decision of the Finance Committee to deal with the depletion issue at a later date is a significant step toward achieving these goals.

With warm regards.[92]

And on March 12 the president called Representative Bob Michel, who had just been elected Republican Whip, to tell him what a great job he was doing on behalf of the administration's program.[93]

But Ford was not all sweet talk. He continued to put pressure on Congress to act quickly by enlisting outside support. On March 14 he told a group of newspaper executives assembled in the East Room that "In many ways, the President and the American people now wait for the Congress to catch up with us."[94]

Yet, still in a posture of compromise, Ford met for ninety minutes on March 18 in the White House Cabinet Room with eighteen Republican Congressional leaders to "discuss legislative issues." Talking Points one, two, and three read as follows:

1. With the Congressional recess approaching for the Senate this week, and the House next week, there are several important bills before the Congress.
2. Most important, of course, is the income tax cut bill. The House has passed a $21.3 billion cut, and the Senate will consider a $29.2 billion cut this week.
3. Both of these are in excess of our recommendations, but hopefully, if the Senate acts, the amount can be reduced and a bill presented for my signature which can be signed.[95]

All this politicking may have been effective because the Finance Committee reached a decision by mid-March. The Committee reported a bill; but the bill they reported did ask for a tax cut of $29.2 billion—over $13 billion more Ford had requested!

The president's reaction to this huge disparity remained muted. During the eight critical days that elapsed between the action by the Finance Committee and the action by the full Senate. Ford was passive. Although a question-and-answer sheet prepared for him suggested he complain that he was "very disappointed" by the size of the proposed Senate cut, warn that $29 billion is "playing with dynamite," and hedge when asked if he would sign such a bill,[96] President Ford did not really use this critical week to try to whittle down the figure the Finance Committee had proposed. In fact, both his appointment book and telephone files show that during the all-important third week of March, the president was less politically active than he had been earlier and would be later.

He certainly had reason enough to be worried. White House aides informed him that the whole Senate was inclined to go along with the recommendation of the Finance Committee, and that Senators were "getting increasingly restless and particularly sensitive to White House criticism for delaying the bill."[97] Accordingly, Nessen at least became freshly concerned about offending Senators' sensibilities on the tax issue; on March 22 he sent the following letter to Majority Leader Mansfield:

> Dear Senator Mansfield:
>
> I hope you took my remarks this week about the congressional progress on a tax cut with the same good spirit in which I took your reply on the Senate floor.
>
> You know, of course, the high esteem President Ford has for you personally and for the Congress of the United States and I certainly share his view on this.
>
> Like all my statements, my remarks about Congress and the tax cut were meant to reflect the President's own view and I certainly intend no personal insult to you or the Congress.
>
> I am sure that this exchange has had no effect on our friendship and good relations.
>
> Sincerely,
> Ron Nessen
> Press Secretary to the President[98]

To all appearances, the Senate did give President Ford what he most wanted—speed. On March 22 one week after the bill was reported, by a solid margin of 60 to 29, the entire Senate voted to pass the $29.2 billion tax cut. The measure was now slated to go to a joint House–Senate conference committee to work out a compromise between the higher figure passed by the Senate and the lower one passed by the House. That left Ford one last chance to obtain a bill closer to what he wanted. He had to persuade the conference committee to pass a tax cut measure nearer $16 billion than $29 billion.

Led by William Simon, Ford's economic advisers recommended a tough approach. They told the president they had reached consensus on the recommendation that he "make it clear that [the] Senate bill is unacceptable and would be vetoed."[99] Caspar Weinberger, the Secretary of Health, Education and Welfare, also "strongly recommended that unequivocal veto signals" be given about certain portions of the tax bill, telling the president that if those veto signals were given, "obviously the bill should be vetoed if it arrives with any of these features." Weinberger concluded that such an action would not end the possibility of a tax cut: "There is ample sentiment for a tax cut in the Congress, and if a veto is sustained . . . the Congress will not dare let the matter rest there."[100]

Prodded by his advisers to resist surrender, the president did, in fact, finally signal that he might well veto a tax bill that so totally rejected his position. Nessen appeared on "Face the Nation" to announce that Ford had "not ruled out a veto."[101] Another White House aide let it be known that if the Congress thought "this bill [was] veto proof, they better think again."[102] And the president himself sent some of his former congressional colleagues identical long letters stating that the Senate bill was "unacceptable." Part of Ford's letter read:

> I am writing you while the Conference Committee is considering the . . . tax cut which I urged last January to stimulate the economy. Although I am most anxious to sign a bill along the lines I have proposed, I am now concerned that Congress is trying to do too much in the legislation the Conferees are considering, thereby providing an economic stimulus far beyond that which is needed.
>   The Conferees and the Members should understand that I will be unable to accept a bill so encumbered with extraneous amendments and of such deficit-increasing magnitude as to nullify the intended effect of a one-time stimulant. . . .
>   I urge the conferees basically to accept the House bill with minor revisions. . . . [103]

Ford's pressure tactics worked to some extent. The bill that was finally approved by the Congress on March 26 did reduce the Senate figure to $22.8 billion. But it is also clear that Ford was far from happy about signing a measure that not only called for a much greater tax reduction than he wanted, but also had other provisions he found undesirable. Although Ullman insisted that the president "should be overjoyed that we brought him a $22.8 billion package," and although Long maintained that if the president vetoed this bill "that means he didn't want a tax bill in the first place," Ford was not convinced. At the time Nessen revealed only that the president had "serious concern" about the measure; but the record shows that the White House really did give genuine thought to a veto.[104]

In his autobiography, Ford writes that the decision whether to veto the tax cut bill or "swallow my pride and sign it into law" was one of "the most difficult . . . I ever had to make."[105] It is easy to see why. His political future and the nation's economic fortune were at stake, but it was not at all clear whether signing or not signing served or disserved each objective. Moreover, the pressure on Ford from all sides to go each way was so evenly divided that he really was a man caught in the middle.

March 27 and 28 were devoted to making the decision. Ford solicited and received the advice of many of the most influential members of Congress. There were actually two questions the president sought to to have answered: Should he veto the bill? And, if he did, would that veto be sustained?

On March 27 Friedersdorf sent the president a memo containing both his own opinion that "sustaining the veto would be close and could be lost," and the more objective observation that there was "strong disagreement on our ability to sustain [a veto] with Republicans fairly confident and Democrats doubtful." Friedersdorf also sent along a sample of the congressional reaction: Joe Waggonner felt that "If vetoed, Demo Caucus will work hard to override. Thinks a second bill would not be much different—probably worse. . . .Long's and Ullman's reaction would be adverse. Long would carry a grudge into a second conference and on other matters he would be handling in the future." Phil Landrum was also concerned that "a second bill would be worse. Demos would try to put President in a hole with a $30+ B bill. Afraid if reopened, rebate, social security and housing provisions would get worse. . . . Does not think veto can be sustained." Dan Rostenkowski opined that the president "would make a terrible mistake by vetoing the bill. . . . If vetoed, Congress will say he didn't compromise, didn't want partnership, President wants it all his way."[106]

A member of his staff also sent the president a list of how various senators would decide. For example, Bob Dole would "vote to override a veto." Barry Goldwater would vote to sustain. ("His press releases against the tax bill have been very favorably received in Arizona.") John McClellan would vote to sustain but would not "presume to advise the President" on what he should do. Strom Thurmond recommended a veto "and, of course, will vote to sustain." Charles Percy advised the president "to sign," and Ted Stevens was "traveling in Alaska."[107]

And finally Friedersdorf sent President Ford a memorandum that contained analyses and opinions by certain key individuals in the House. For example, Minority Whip Bob Michel felt that "there is an excellent chance that your veto could be sustained in the House." Congressman Barber Conable—whom Ford describes in his book as "a personal friend whose political judgment was very astute"[108]—said that he "personally would like to see you veto the bill, but would not be upset whatever you do." And Minority Leader John Rhodes said that it was his belief that a veto "could be sustained."[109]

On March 28, the pressure on Ford became even more intense. It was becoming clear, as Senator Robert Griffin had warned, that a veto would "present a public relations problem in view of [Ford's] campaign for a tax cut as soon as possible."[110] On the other hand, the attitude of fiscal conservatives, who were getting increasingly worried about huge federal deficits, was becomming more rigid. Senator Mark Hatfield wrote the president a personal letter urging him to veto: "The deficit in the bill will haunt us in the years ahead as a hidden tax."[111] And Barber Conable, who, it was reported only 24 hours earlier, "would not be upset" whatever the president

did, was now apparently operating on a much shorter fuse. Seidman sent
Ford the following memo:

> Barber Conable called at three o'clock to say that the Republicans who
> voted against the tax bill would be very upset if it is not vetoed. He
> includes himself in that group.
>
> He recognizes that you did not make a commitment but that all felt
> that they were doing what you would like to see them do. He believes
> that failure to veto would have a very bad effect on Republican morale
> in terms of fighting spending programs in the future.[112]

As Congress was split, so were Ford's advisers. Some strenuously urged
him to sign, and others to do the opposite. Simon prodded the president to
veto the bill on the grounds that the size of the cut would "send the federal
budget deficit soaring out of sight," and that certain provisions of the bill
were "hastily conceived, ill advised and counterproductive."[113] Weinberger
encouraged the president to veto, stating that there were several provisions
"of particular concern to HEW. I find none of them welcome, and two of
them extremely undesirable."[114] Meanwhile, Burns, Greenspan, and other
expert advisers were convinced that the president would invite fewer problems if he signed the bill than if he vetoed it. Ford quoted them as saying,
"You'll give the economy a shot in the arm when it's needed most, and
besides, you can't please the right wing anyway."[115]

Press opinion was also divided. Nessen sent the president a compilation
of editorial views on whether he should sign or veto the bill: Nine papers
had come out in favor of signing, two in favor of a veto, and three had no
definite position yet, but were "leaning toward veto."[116] Ford's press secretary took the opportunity to cast his own vote as well. Understandably,
given his job, what he worried about was the president's image. Nessen
urged the president to sign: "A veto now could raise doubts about the consistency of your economic policy and could be interpreted as stubbornness
on your part. . . . To veto this bill, and especially to be overriden, would
damage [your image] as a forceful leader in the areas of the economy and
energy."[117]

Ford delayed making the agonizingly difficult decision until the last
moment. In fact, on March 28 the White House drafted a statement from
the president to the House of Representatives that began: "I am returning
H.R. 2166 without my approval."[118] But, finally, the president obviously
concluded that the benefits of signing the tax cut bill outweighed the costs.
On Saturday March 30, President Gerald Ford did reluctantly sign into
law the $22.8 billion tax cut bill that he had been handed by the Congress.
Even as he announced his decision on nationwide radio and television, his
reservations came through loud and clear.

As President . . . I cannot under the Constitution accept part of this bill and reject the rest. It comes before me on a take it or leave it basis. Congress has gone home. I believe my veto would eventually be sustained but I am by no means sure that this Congress would send me a better bill—it might even be worse. . . .

I have, therefore, decided to sign this bill so that its economic benefits can begin to work.

I do this despite the serious drawbacks in the bill. . . .

[But] I am drawing the line right here. . . . I will resist every attempt by the Congress to add another dollar to this deficit by new spending programs. . . .[119]

In the end, Ford got his tax cut, and he got it on time. But he somehow felt betrayed. Forced to accept what Congress handed him on a "take it or leave it" basis, the president obtained scant pleasure from signing into law a measure that, in his eyes, distorted his original proposal.

The Practice of Leadership

President Ford's first major break with his predecessor was his January 1975 tax cut proposal. Ford got a new tax law before April 1, yet even years after leaving the White House he still remembered the decision to sign the bill as "one of the most difficult" he ever had to make. Thus the question arises: Who here was leading whom?

My own position is that President Ford did in fact achieve what he said he wanted. But much of the time what he said he wanted did not reflect everything he was thinking and feeling. Therefore, when Congress handed him a tax cut bill that went considerably further than what he had proposed, he felt frustrated and impotent instead of the least bit gratified.

Taking into account Ford's October through March history on tax policy—rather than just the period January through March—helps us to understand better why the president was vexed by what could have been interpreted by him as at least a partial victory. It may be recalled that until the economic indicators turned sharply downward, Ford wanted nothing to do with what he had earlier referred to as a quick-fix tax cut. What he had pushed for was a tax surcharge.

Some unfortunate twists and turns of the tax policy saga resulted from the troubling new condition called "stagflation." Still others resulted from the extraordinary circumstances under which President Ford came into office. In particular, since he was appointed instead of elected he had special problems in the area of impression management. Ford never had the benefit of an extended national electoral campaign in which to demonstrate that he was presidential timber. It was assumed, therefore, that in the White House he would be the same as he was in Congress.

Ford had never been described as having much style or flair. It was said of him that he had managed for nearly 25 congressional years "to project like an upstate Michigan stump."[120] He was also the man about whom Lyndon Johnson once said—apparently for all the world to hear—"There's nothing wrong with Jerry Ford except he played football too long without his helmet."[121] The image problem, however, was one of substance as well as style. In particular, the question was whether Ford was capable of exercising the strong leadership expected of the nation's president. His reputation in Congress was as a manager, not as an authentic leader. The truth was that "not one major bill [had] ever come out of Congress under Jerry Ford's name or aegis."[122]

Moreover, Ford was known to actually eschew the role of power player. His strength in the House, the reason he was elected Minority Leader in the first place, resulted precisely because he had no apparent need for power, nor any visible affection for power games. The following comparisons, by two fellow Republicans, between Ford and Melvin Laird, a competitor in the mid-1960's for the position of House Leader, make the point:

> Laird has some characteristics which make him better suited for the conference chairman than Ford. He's not afraid to step on people's toes, to push people. Ford was too good-natured, too affable.
>
> Laird was more controversial. He's more dynamic. He's got more leadership. At the same time, he's irritated and antagonized some people, made enemies along the line. Ford has not. . . . There were fewer people mad at Ford and some people who were quite opposed to Laird.[123]

Robert Peabody, author of *Leadership in Congress,* sums it up this way: "The forthright and likeable Ford was respected by his colleagues. Yet some of them felt he lacked initiative and had failed to exploit the potential of the Republican Conference."[124]

Once he became Minority Leader, Ford continued to play the consummate nice guy. One Congressman recalled that, "He rode us with a very loose rein"[125]—which fits right in with the pride and pleasure Ford took in the idea that he did not have "a single enemy" in the House. And it befits the president who, on learning that his predecessor had kept an "enemies list," commented, "Anybody who can't keep his enemies in his head has too many enemies."[126]

With regard to power politics, Ford's reputation—given added credence by his controversial decision to pardon Nixon—was as someone who preferred to keep the peace rather than wage war. One journalist observed that he had a very keen head for people, "but unlike some other people-dealing politicians, he always used that head to keep track, never to keep score."[127] In David McClelland's terminology, Ford plainly had a high need for affiliation (to be with and liked by people) and a relatively low need for power. Unlike Lyndon Johnson, for example, Gerald Ford apparently was not bent on dominating or, for that matter, leading.

What subsequent effect might this reputation for being perhaps too affable have had on Ford's presidency? According to Richard Neustadt, the impact would have been at best mixed. Neustadt's clear implication is that nice guys are not necessarily going to finish first.

> A President who values power ... has every reason for concern with the residual impressions of tenacity and skill accumulating in the minds of Washingtonians-at-large. His bargaining advantages in seeking what he wants are heightened or diminished by what others think of him. ... [128]

With regard to his January proposal for a tax cut, President Ford had at least two major problems of impression management right from the start. He was a very well-known quantity, and what was known about him was not especially conducive to his exerting a strong presidential role. Ford was not—Johnson's wicked comment notwithstanding—seen as stupid or ineffectual. But neither was he regarded as especially likely to grow in the nation's highest office.

Another difficulty was that only three months before Ford went to Congress to plead for a tax cut, he had gone before that same body to plead for a tax surcharge. Inevitably, the January tax initiative was played out in the context of the failed tax proposal that had come just before.

The fiasco of the surcharge hurt the president politically in several ways. Above all, there was the humiliation of the "about-face." It is one thing to have a proposal turned back; it is quite another to be compelled immediately thereafter to draft a second bill that appears to be in direct contradiction to the first. By the same token, it is one thing to have a measure go down to defeat after a good fight; it is more damaging to have it be stillborn.

Ford had gone on record in October as saying that "Public Enemy Number One" was inflation. What did it say about his ability to diagnose what ails us when, only a month later, he avowed that the recession now required as much attention as inflation? Of course, Ford was only responding initially—if too hastily—to what his "expert" advisers told him. Moreover, the economy had subsequently deteriorated further than anyone expected. But those things mattered hardly at all to a nation keeping close watch on its new president, but not too much watch on a confusing and troubled economic picture. All that 86 percent of Americans cared about when they said they lacked confidence in Ford's ability to manage the economy was that the man in charge did not seem to know what he was doing.

But if Ford turned in a weak performance on tax policy in the fall of 1974, his performance in the winter of 1975 was somewhat better. He made every effort to keep his finger on just exactly what was happening. Porter writes of Ford's "involvement in making a large number of detailed decisions on the specifics of the [tax] proposals. From the outset, the president was willing to invest a great deal of time, never suggesting that any specific decision was nonpresidential."[129] Furthermore, although he may have upstaged his own State of the Union speech by first delivering what William Safire called his "prime-time television pitch,"[130] he did nevertheless manage during the second week in January to focus national attention on the tax issue and to make his particular tax proposal the starting point of any discussion on future tax policy. Finally, Ford understood a good deal better than his predecessor had that he was primarily responsible for convincing Congress of the need for a tax reduction of a particular size that could be enacted soon. Indeed, to begin with at least, size and speed were the president's two main points of emphasis.

The president continued to be in good form for most of January, drawing with considerable agility on skills he had developed in Congress. In fact, he positively shone when engaging in low pressure forms of interpersonal activity—with Democrats and Republicans alike. The contrast to President Nixon was especially striking. One Nixon holdover noted at the time that, "Ford sees everyone in sight."[131] Another observer commented that he was "willing to call, see, and keep in contact with many members of Congress."[132]

Of course, Ford skillfully employed an array of other political tactics as well, some of which were no doubt new to his repertoire. The president tried to preempt problems by soliciting input before the tax cut bill was formally submitted. He gave former colleagues advance notice of what was being planned. He sent members of his administration out into the field to spread the word. He enlisted outside help in trying to prod Congress to act quickly. And he made personal appeals and provided broad access not only to members of Congress, but also to members of the press and a wide range of state and local officials. Finally, President Ford also demonstrated a willingness to compromise that was used in part to very good effect.

But there was a problem here. The president almost certainly did not *need* to pull out all the stops to get a tax reduction measure reasonably soon. The Democrats had already made it quite clear that they intended to enact such legislation as rapidly as they could. It could reasonably be argued that when Ford harangued Congress to move quickly, he was only gilding the lily.

There was, however, one real bone of contention between the White House and Capitol Hill: size. Ford wanted a relatively small tax cut. He was highly wary of further increasing the federal deficit. Clearly, size was the issue to which he should have applied whatever leadership skills he could muster. Unfortunately, it was also the issue that suggested that although Ford was skilled at making the kind of low key personal appeal that stood him in good stead in Congress, he was much less skilled when called upon to act the role of forceful and determined leader. Put simply, on the matter of size, Ford waffled.

Although in January the president had said that it was important that the tax cut be limited in size, it was not a point on which he appeared to be holding firm, or got us to focus on, or on which he tried very hard to mobilize Congress or the American people. Throughout the three-month period under study, he said little about the issue of size, certainly when compared to how much he said on the issue of speed. In fact, in February he was reportedly calm about the possibility that the Senate would propose a tax cut even greater than that proposed by the House; during the critical third week in March between the Finance Committee vote and the action by the full Senate, he was inexplicably silent; as late as early March he was still saying that "The big problem is not the size of the tax reduction but the slowness with which Congress is acting on it"; and three weeks before he was handed a bill by the Congress he was still referring to size as "not a big problem."

Moreover, by indicating only a scant two weeks after his State of the Union address that he was willing to accept changes in his tax cut proposal, the president gave away his hand even before the game was fully underway. As we have seen, the willingness to compromise is generally a useful political tactic. But it also must be employed in just the right way and at just the right moment. Ford's premature gesture of compromise was more than a signal. In effect, he had telegraphed that the size of the tax cut was negotiable.

This president in particular could ill afford the mistake of indicating a willingness to compromise too early. In him, more perhaps than with a leader with a reputation for being less nice and more forceful, a premature willingness to compromise could too easily be construed as a reluctance to engage in two-way influence relationships with his gloves off. Indeed, President Ford's failure to indicate in no uncertain terms that size mattered a great deal to him appears to have been interpreted by those who should have been playing the part of followers as a sign that defiance on this issue would be almost cost-free. Considering that he had little leverage anyway with a Congress that was overwhelmingly Democratic, this was a costly mistake.

Essentially, Ford may be said to have failed on two counts: he neglected to communicate clearly and forcefully just exactly what it was he wanted; and he was less than adroit when it came to backing up his political tactics with evidence of instrumental and authoritative sources of power. Ford's liberal use of political tactics seemed to produce smaller and fewer results than they should have. For example, although Ford was accessible, it is not clear that his accessibility produced very much in the way of results. In particular, his "Talking Points" were almost invariably bland; members of the House and Senate were never clearly told what they might gain by moving closer to the president's position. Ford asked nicely for their support, but it seems he was unfamiliar with the benefits of bestowing the great reward, or making the extravagant gesture—either of which would have garnered him more support than merely being a good fellow did.

Concomitantly, Ford never gave his would-be followers the impression that they had much of anything to lose by lining up against him. As I suggested, he showed no proclivity for arm twisting, or, for that matter, for doing anything that was likely to incur the wrath or even displeasure of another. Ford's main source of power was libidinal. His affective relations were excellent and we can assume that all manner of people would have gone along wih the man if everything else had been equal. But everything else was not equal.

Only after the fact did President Ford finally make a primary issue out of what had all along seemed only a secondary one.* But by then it was too late. He could have vetoed the tax bill, of course. Indeed, by the end of March 28 the consensus among his advisers was that a veto could be sustained.[134] But he decided against a veto, in part, no doubt, to take some credit for the cut, and in part out of the well-justified fear that the next tax measure might be, so far as he was concerned, even worse.

Perhaps Ford's uneven performance on the matter of size can be attributed to his strong preference in any event for a quick cut. He certainly did push for speed whenever he reasonably could; or perhaps he simply did not have it in him to hang tough on this issue. Or perhaps it was that neither he nor key members of his administration really believed that he would finally be handed a tax reduction measure that so far exceeded his original request. What is clear is that most of the leverage Ford may have had on this issue was lost as a result of what others interpreted as relative unconcern and a lack of strong resolve. Had the president been more clear and unyielding about what it was he was after, and had he fought with greater tenacity and muscle, it is likely that he would have gotten at least a little more than half a loaf.

---

*Size was not Ford's only objection to the tax measure—but manifestly his biggest problem was the projected "Total Revenue Loss."[133]

10

Jimmy Carter
and the Energy Package

> Our decision about energy will test the charater of the
> American people and the ability of the President and the
> Congress to govern this nation. This difficult effort will be
> the "moral equivalent of war"—except that we will be unit-
> ing our efforts to build and not to destroy.
>
> *President Carter,*
> *televised address to the nation,*
> *April 18, 1977*

The American dream of an endless supply of low-cost energy came to a sudden, shocking end in 1973. No longer producing enough oil to meet our own energy needs, we had been importing about six million gallons of oil per day, with one-third coming from Arab countries. When these countries, angered by our support of Israel in the Middle East war, cut off oil ship-ments to the United States, they brought on the sobering realization that our dependency on others for fuel amounted to no less than a dependency on them for our national welfare and security.

As a result, President Nixon described the energy shortage as the most serious the nation faced since World War II, and President Ford wrangled with Congress over his programs geared to energy self-sufficiency. Thus, Jimmy Carter's energy package did not come out of the blue, nor did it address a problem perceived to be unimportant. Instead, it emerged from a situation in which considerable efforts had already been made to convince the American people that an "energy crisis" existed and that it was of major national concern.

To detail the intricacies and complexities of Jimmy Carter's energy plan would require a volume in itself. As we will see, even those professionally involved had a tough time understanding just exactly what was happening. The main difficulty is that the energy package—instead of being a single bill—was actually a pastiche of many bills, and each focused on something different. For example, one section of the legislation dealt with higher gas-oline taxes, another with the price of natural gas, and still another with the increased use of nuclear power. Moreover, in a few cases an item that seemed important in the beginning—for instance, penalties for cars with above-average gasoline consumption—was unimportant in the end; the issue of natural gas prices, which received less attention at the start, eventually became the issue that dominated all else.

This chapter will make no attempt to convey the details of President Carter's energy plan, nor will it minutely chronicle its tortuous year and a half journey through both houses of Congress. Rather, it will focus on what amounted to an on-the-job political training program for the president. At first, Jimmy Carter thought all he had to do was show the way. It took time and failure for him to discover that pointing others in a certain direction was not enough and that to get others to walk along that path would entail personally leading the way. This chapter chronicles how one executive learned about the political presidency the hard way.

President Carter spent more time on energy policy than on any other domestic issue.[1] In his autobiography he writes that "there was never a moment when I did not consider the creation of a national energy policy equal in importance to any other goal we had."[2] At the same time, his memories of the attempt to bring about energy reform are clearly unhappy ones. He wrote in his book that "In looking back on the moral equivalent of war against energy waste and excessive vulnerability . . . I see nothing exhilarating or pleasant. It was a bruising fight, and no final clear-cut victory could be photographed and hung on the wall for our grandchildren to admire."[3]

President Carter chose to enter into this "bitter four-year struggle,"[4] as he termed it, at the very start of his presidency. In fact, he set himself a deadline. Although energy was one of the most complicated domestic problems, and Carter was brand new to the presidential office and even to Washington, he decided that within three months of his inauguration his administration would have a completed energy package to present to the Congress. By his own testimony, Carter moved with "exceeding haste,"[5] but at the time he clearly believed he had a mandate for change that would signal an end to automatic and perpetual growth in America and reverse the ever-increasing expectations of the post World War II generations.

Ten days after Jimmy Carter became president he warned the country that it would face a "permanent, very serious energy shortage" that would require a national energy policy based on strict conservation measures. Conservation, he said, would be the major component of a "comprehensive, national energy policy" that he would send to the Congress no later than April 20.[6] A few days later, during the president's first "fireside chat," there was further confirmation that energy would be a major concern of the Carter administration. Seated in a red velvet chair set near a fireplace in the White House library, and dressed informally in a beige cardigan and navy blue trousers, President Carter spoke somberly of the need to take the energy problem seriously. The nation was warned that the energy shortage in this country was permanent, and there was "no way we can solve it quickly."[7]

Having made that pronouncement, Carter now chose to remove the issue from public debate. During February and March he had his energy legislation drafted in almost total secrecy by James Schlesinger, formerly Secretary of Defense and now Carter's nominee to serve as the first head of a newly constituted Department of Energy. Even before Carter had moved into the Oval Office, Schlesinger had quietly begun work on a national energy plan. Thus, it was not surprising that after Carter became president, he still preferred to rely on Schlesinger and his team, and to let them work almost exclusively on their own.

Meanwhile, everyone else—including the political elite—received only bits and pieces of information. In late February it was revealed that the administration was considering broad and perhaps even mandatory controls on the use of energy; but still the president and his associates confined themselves to talking in generalities, with only sketchy references to specifics. When asked about the details of his energy program at a news conference, Carter would say only that "I do not know how to answer your questions about the specifics of the proposal."[8] On February 22 he told a bipartisan group of congressional leaders that he had just about completed the outline of his energy policy, but that he would only reveal its contents in a major speech, not scheduled until mid-April. Carter said this was his most important piece of domestic legislation and that he needed congressional cooperation, but—to the general consternation of his audience—he refused to divulge exactly what it was he would need cooperation on.[9]

Even members of the administration were kept in the dark. In late March, Jack Watson, the president's cabinet secretary, complained that the president's chief economic advisers hardly knew anything. "What in effect is happening is that the substance of the energy plan is being put together independent of economic impact and analysis. And that can be devastating. Some of these people want to negotiate with Schlesinger before the plans go to the president, before anything is blocked in."[10]

More significant was the growing displeasure of members of Congress. When Carter met with Democratic leaders on April 5, Senate Majority leader Robert Byrd asked him outright if any Senators at all were being included in the discussions on energy policy. A contentious discussion ensued in which party leaders complained that neither experts nor those who had already worked on energy-related matters such as air pollution were being consulted.

But if he failed to do some early congressional bridge building, Carter did not neglect his role as educator. He recognized the continuing need to instruct the public on energy, and soon after his fireside chat he appeared at a series of public forums both in the White House and around the country to stress the importance of his upcoming legislation. The most publicized of these was a visit to Charleston, West Virginia, in which President Carter participated in a meeting on energy problems with state and local officials as well as other interested parties ranging from coal and power company heads to conservationists. His appearance in West Virginia got high marks. John Osborne of *The New Republic* wrote that the president's "greatest service in Charleston was his rejection of the myth, started with Richard Nixon . . . and sustained with waning conviction by Gerald Ford, that the US can and should make itself independent of foreign energy sources."[11]

Carter's own inclination to fight the good fight on energy was given strong support by several other prominent members of the fourth estate. For example, Tom Wicker wrote that "The energy crisis is not going to go away . . . [Nor is it] going to be solved by gimmickry or swift technological breakthroughs." Wicker added that the long hard winter just past gave Carter a new opportunity to make his case, implying that he would be a fool not to do so with the utmost vigor.[12] Conservative columnist George Will struck the same chord. In a column titled "Hit Us Hard, Please, Mr. Carter," Will noted approvingly that the new president appeared "prepared to *govern*. He knows popularity is capital that cannot be banked forever. After hearing Carter on energy, the nation may feel that someone big has hit it hard with something heavy."[13]

As Schlesinger's plan evolved, Carter writes "its controversial nature and its inevitable complexity became increasingly apparent." After reading the first draft, the presendent sent Schlesinger a critical note: "I am not satisfied with your approach. It is extremely complicated. . . . Even perfect equity can't be sold if Americans can't understand it."[14] But simplicity proved to be unattainable. Carter himself came to believe that "the subject was too complicated to express simply." He recalls that as the time approached for his proposal to go to Capitol Hill, he was "shocked to learn" that its various pieces might have to be considered by "as many as seventeen committees and subcommittees in the House of Representatives."[15]

Carter had good reason to be worried about the Congress—even so early in his administration—for he would have almost no honeymoon with it. This was in spite of the fact that both Houses of Congress were controlled by middle of the road Democrats: In 1977 there were 22 Democrats in the House and 62 in the Senate.*

Part of Carter's problem was that he came into office as an outsider and chose to remain one. Here was a president who had all along made a distinction between himself and "the insiders," and who did not shy from that distinction after assuming the presidency. Naturally, his anti-Washington stance did not especially endear him to those who had long been part of the local establishment, nor did the day-to-day results of that posturing prove politically useful.

A month into President Carter's term he had invoked the ire of a good many legislators by proposing to kill off nearly a score of politically dear regional water resource projects; the Speaker of the House had warned that "the problem with the people around Carter is that they spend so much of their time running against Washington they don't know they are now part of Washington;" and the president himself had managed to personally alienate members of Congress with his visible distaste for "the kind of stroking that old settlers on the Hill regard as their due."[16] Furthermore, Carter's first breakfast meetings with Democratic congressional leaders were reported to be embarrassingly stiff; and a presidential aide had avowed that his boss did not want to be "big pals" with the denizens of Capitol Hill. Even Charles Kirbo, the president's close friend and adviser from Georgia, concluded early on that if Carter was to avoid being frustrated by Congress, he would have to appeal to the public for support. In a *Washington Post* interview, Kirbo predicted that that his old friend would have a "continuing problem" with the Hill—a judgment that Carter, at his second White House press conference, felt obliged to dismiss as "just a private citizen's opinions."[17]

An article that ran in *The New York Times* on April 15 only five days before the president was to submit his energy package, confirmed the early tensions. The headline: "Energy Plan Faces Bitter Struggle and Uncertain Future in Congress."

> President Carter's energy program is likely to lead to one of the most bitter battles in decades, according to influential members of Congress. . . .
> They foresaw a situation in which a President could well be rebuffed by a Congress controlled by his own party.[18]

On April 18, two days before addressing a joint session of Congress on energy, the president went on television to deliver what he described as "an unpleasant talk." Bluntly warning that unless the nation changed its

*The last time an overwhelmingly Democratic Congress had coincided with a Democratic president was after the 1964 election.

"wasteful" use of fuels it would begin to run short of energy supplies in the 1980s, Carter announced that he would call for higher prices, higher taxes, and an end to unlimited increases in energy consumption. Speaking in a "soft, even tone without histrionics and nearly without gesture or expression of emotion," President Carter called for sacrifice.

> We do have a choice about how we will spend the next few years. Each American uses the energy equivalent of 60 barrels of oil per person each year. Ours is the most wasteful nation on earth. We waste more energy than we import. . . .
> I am sure each of you will find something you don't like about the specifics of our proposal. It will demand that we make sacrifices and changes in every life. To some degree the sacrifices will be painful. . . . It will lead to some higher costs, and to some greater inconvenience for everyone.[19]

"Our decision about energy," the president went on, "will test the character of the American people and the ability of the president and the Congress to govern this nation. This difficult effort will be the 'moral equivalent of war.'" This last phrase was borrowed from William James; for better and worse, it immediately came to symbolize the president's campaign to push the energy package through the Congress.

In his televised address to the nation, the president sounded, according to at least one commentator, "like Winston Churchill on the eve of the Battle of Britain."[22] The alternative to his energy policy, he warned, may well be national catastrophe. But on April 20, standing before Congress, he was distinctly less apocalyptic. He now suggested that the best part of his program was that it would protect jobs and the environment.[23] This much milder assessment was given further credence at a press conference. "By increasing the costs of energy and returning the proceeds to all Americans we can save energy, save money, and continue to have a healthy economy," the president announced. As a consequence, the *Washington Post* ran a front page headline that read "Energy Plan Now Pictured as Consumer Boom";[24] Ralph Nader opined that the president was like a "sheep in wolf's clothing"; and Russell Baker could not resist pointing out that the acronym for Carter's "Moral Equivalent of War" was MEOW.[25]

In addition to the declining level of passion, questions were raised about White House competence. Having predicted in an administration "fact sheet" that the energy program would have a "small but generally positive impact" on the nation's economy, the White House promptly reversed itself. The administration declared now that the proposed program was expected to have "no significant effect on economic growth."[26]

Despite Carter's desire to keep the program simple, the legislation he submitted was both complex and controversial. The following highlights are only some from the energy program he proposed to a joint session of Congress on April 20, 1977: new gasoline taxes; excise taxes on certain domestically produced crude oils; graduated penalties for cars with above-average gasoline consumption; an increase in the price of newly discovered natural gas; and increased use of nuclear power.[20] Given this list, with several items bound to be unpopular, it was little wonder that House Speaker Tip O'Neill prophesied that the president's energy proposals would trigger "the toughest fight this Congress has ever had."[21]

In the event, President Carter did succeed in putting energy on the front burner. Early on the press was given to writing about Carter's "tough talk on energy,"[27] and there were several thoughtful pieces on how our resolve on energy would test the national will.[28] Although no one was very happy about the need for a national energy program, there seemed to be relief, certainly in some quarters, that the president was willing to tackle this exceedingly difficult issue and to do "what had to be done."[29] One news weekly likened Carter to an "evangelist, preaching to a nation living in energy sin."[30] Another called his campaign to alert the nation to the energy crisis a "one-week blitz . . ., the most intensive effort by a U.S. President, in or out of wartime, to rally the nation behind a common cause."[31]

But if there was widespread agreement that Carter had, at least initially, been leader-like in his call to all Americans to sacrifice for the commonwealth, little agreement existed on anything else. Above all, there was no consensus on what was likely to happen next. *Newsweek* proclaimed that "Congress seemed ready to act on the entire package—with the likelihood that nearly all of it will be law by the end of the year."[32] By contrast, *U.S. News & World Report* predicted that Carter's program might not "be put to a vote for more than a year—or until the next energy crisis hits the country."[33]

The latter analysis proved closer to the mark. Special interest groups were marshaling their forces; lawmakers were dividing along regional, party, and ideological lines; and Americans across the land were insisting that they would find it difficult if not impossible to cut back on their own energy-consuming habits. The response of a Portland, Oregon, bookkeeper and secretary was typical. Her driving, she maintained, was out of necessity. "My reasons aren't going to change just because it costs me a nickel a gallon more to get there."[34] And few, it seemed, would be untouched by passage of the proposed legislation. Motorists, homeowners, low-income familes, public utilities, auto manufacturers, oil and gas producers, coal producers, and industry would all be affected by one part or another of Carter's bill.[35]

Moreover, the congressional task was nearly overwhelming. Majority Leader Robert Byrd warned the president that, in order to handle the energy legislation, the Senate would have to stop all other work; it was believed that implementing this program would take at least twenty-five separate pieces of legislation.[36]

However, in spite of the daunting prospects, President Carter was still insisting he would stand firm. In an interview in early May, he declared that he would be satisfied with no less than the entire energy package, and that he had received support for that position from the leadership in both the House and Senate. And he had a date in mind: "Bob Byrd has told me that his goal was to complete passage on the entire package prior to the first of October. And the Speaker has told me that he intends to beat that deadline." When told by the interviewer that passing the energy program was no doubt "going to be a very long and hard struggle," the president interrupted, "It's one I don't intend to lose."[37]

But once the dust had settled on President Carter's whirlwind performance in April, energy politics wound down fast. The president himself fell almost silent on the issue, and the energy package was left without White House guidance to find its own way down the long and convoluted corridors of Congress.

In the House of Representatives, Carter had a powerful and reliable ally, Speaker O'Neill. In order to resolve conflicting regional interests, O'Neill took the unusual and imaginative step of appointing a special Ad Hoc Committee on Energy. The Ad Hoc Committee would pave the administration's way by combining into a single package the decisions of the different committees before they went to the floor for debate and a final vote.[38] Representative Thomas Ashley—known among his colleagues in the House as a good "harmonizer"—was chosen by O'Neill to chair the forty-person committee.

The situation in the Senate was more complicated, however. There the energy package was divided into five different bills, each to be considered separately. The key committees were Energy and Natural Resources, headed by Henry Jackson, and (again) Finance, chaired by Russell Long. With characteristic understatement, Carter wrote in his autobiography, "Since both of these men were strong-willed and jealous of their own legislative prerogatives, some personal conflict was inevitable."[39] On the Republican side, meanwhile, it was predicted that Minority Leader Howard Baker would be a "significant adversary" of the president.[40]

The chief architect of the energy bill, Schlesinger, made his first appearance before the Congress in early May. The session did not bode well for the administration. Schlesinger encountered what The New York Times labeled "skepticism and resistance from Republicans and Democrats."[41] The opposition was primarily to the president's price and tax proposals that would make energy more expensive to use. In addition, there were charges that the administration was not providing sufficient incentives to encourage the development of new energy supplies. Moreover, although Senator Jackson led off with a statement praising President Carter's effort to provide leadership on energy, he nonetheless went on to remind the administration that his panel had already been "deeply involved in energy policy for many years," and would expect "convincing answers" to a broad range of questions.[42]

Carter's response to these early signs of resistance was to say little. When he did speak up, what he said bore scant resemblance to the passionate commitment evinced before. It was reported that during a one-hour meeting between the president and the Ad Hoc Energy Committee, the president had retreated from his "Churchillian summons" of a month earlier. Representative John Anderson described the scene: "He said that until a month ago, he honestly felt that some substantial sacrifices were required on the part of the American people. He said that now he had changed his mind and the sacrifices would not be substantial."[43]. The White House also dropped its insistence that the Secretary of Energy be given the sole power to set prices paid to producers of natural gas and crude oil, and it signaled Senator Byrd—who had taken a neutral position on the energy package—that it fully expected changes in the proposed energy legislation. This willingness to acknowledge that the administration anticipated that Congress would provide alternative proposals could be construed as yet another sign that the president was prepared to be flexible.[44]

The single indication during May that there was still urgency to what had been so vividly referred to as the moral equivalent of war came not from the president but from one of Schlesinger's aides, who tried to orchestrate a campaign to sell the energy program to the American people. The campaign was to include Hollywood stars in radio and television commercials, cabinet officers giving speeches, and the formation of a speakers' bureau to answer requests for information. John Denver, Johnny Carson, Dinah Shore, Pearl Bailey, and the Captain and Tennile were all signed up; one commercial already getting air time showed singer John Denver walking through a sylvan glen and telling the audience, "The difference you make makes all the difference."[45]

President Carter's shift in behavior—he was zealous, passive, and withdrawn by turns—proved costly. Even before the end of May, *The New York Times* accused the Chief Executive of flagging too fast. "There is nothing on the President's own agenda of greater importance . . . than the energy crisis. On April 18, Mr. Carter solemnly summoned the nation to an age of sacrifice. By May 4, he was telling members of Congress that he had changed his mind; the sacrifices would not be that substantial."[46] *The Nation* went even further: "A great silence has fallen over the 'energy crisis' which the President proclaimed in such urgent tones just seven weeks ago. . . . The utter lack of a sense of urgency will suggest to Americans that the President's Energy Week was just another grandstand play, a media hype, something to remind people that the President is still here."[47] And *Newsweek* asked somewhat bemusedly, "What ever happened to Jimmy Carter's energy program?"[48]

Probably in response to questions about the depth of his commitment, the president decided to reenter the fray. Angered especially by the clout of lobbyists—his diary entry for June 9 reads: "The influence of the special interest lobbies is almost unbelievable, particularly from the automobile and oil industries"[49]—he appealed again to the American people. Speaking to the Magazine Publishers Association, the president declared that "Unless the American public can be aroused to help me and others who believe that this is extremely important . . . I'm afraid we are not going to have an adequate program when it's over. Unless the American people speak up, the special interests are going to prevail."[50] But as journalist Haynes Johnson observed, "Why or how they were supposed to speak up when he wasn't was an unanswered question."[51]

At a mid-June press conference, the president warned again of impending doom. His scenario was a populist one: the people against the special interests.

> I am deeply concerned about the inordinate influence of the lobbyists and representatives of the oil companies and the automobile manufacturers. I've never criticized the Congress as a whole. . . . It's important that the American people be aroused to the fact that unless they are deeply involved in helping the Congress and me to come up with a substantive, comprehensive, fair and adequate energy policy that the special interests groups will prevail. . . . I don't say that everything we've proposed has to be passed just as though we put it forward, but I think cumulatively if we don't take strong and active action the economic and political consequences will be catastrophic.[52]

Of course, what Carter had actually encountered was little more than politics as usual. *Naturally* lobbyists were trying to maximize their impact on the formulation of energy policy by packing the committee meeting rooms to overflowing, deluging staff and legislators with position papers, and buttonholing influential people.[53] But by all accounts, several measures, such as the proposals for a standby gasoline tax and rebates for fuel-efficient cars, were falling without any push from the industry.[54] For example, the demise of the gas tax was considered more than anything else a victory for people who commute by car. (Word had it, nevertheless, that the killing of the tax made the president "furious."[55])

What was remarkable, in fact, was not that Carter's energy package was encountering congressional roadblocks, but rather that it was faring as well as it was. Given the complexity of the proposals and their potential to shake up so many different constituencies, the energy bill was making reasonably good progress. Indeed, by the end of June the House Ways and Means Committee had approved a bill that killed the rebate and gas tax, but sanctioned Carter's tax on gas-guzzling cars as well as tax credits for home insulation and solar energy, a tax to push industries and utilities away from oil and gas toward coal, and a major tax on oil that would raise the price of energy for everyone. Al Ullman, chairman of the committee, made it clear that he was satisfied; he suggested that the president should be too: "The plan that emerges is not only a more practical design for energy savings but also carries a better guarantee for enactment."[56]

Nevertheless, Carter's position vis-à-vis Congress remained almost completely adversarial. Upset at one point by two House committees that he felt had gutted his energy package, the president telephoned Speaker O'Neill to ask whether he should go on television to denounce his congressional opponents. O'Neill's advice was to relax; nothing that had happened came as a surprise to the House leadership, nor did the Speaker think the damage would be permanent.

The president was also getting nervous about the timetable. Chairman Ashley of the Ad Hoc Energy Committee had cautioned that there was a "real possibility" that the legislation might not meet the leadership schedule and reach the floor before the August recess. "There may be slippage," Ashley warned. "It's well within the realm of possibility."[57]

His growing concern motivated the president to take further action. Carter ordered the preparation of a standby gasoline rationing plan, to be imposed in the event of an emergency such as another foreign embargo. He met with forty of the nation's governors for two days of discussions on energy matters.[58] And he made his first really optimistic statement on the subject of energy since April. Suddenly pronouncing himself "very pleased" with the progress of his energy package on Capitol Hill, the president added benignly that "If we should not get 100 percent of our program this year, we'll be back next year."[59]

But several weeks later, President Carter reverted, sounding both gloomy and punitive. Even though the energy bill was still moving along rather well—the Rules Committee had just cleared it for consideration by the full House—Carter chose that moment to chide the public, the same "American people" that until now were supposed to have been his most likely allies against the greedy energy lobbies and balky Congress. The president asserted that the American public was "not paying attention" to energy problems. He predicted that a series of crises would have to occur before

Americans decided to "quit wasting so much fuel." And he suggested that if his voluntary plan proved insufficient, he might be forced to take harsher measures: "I am concerned that the public has not responded well, and I think voluntary compliance is probably not adequate at all."[60]

Still, the energy bill continued to move along, largely because of O'Neill's adroitness. On August 1 the Speaker volunteered to reporters that the president's program was doing "very well," and journalists started to detect signs that the program would emerge from the House "virtually intact." At O'Neill's urging, the president finally made a personal pitch: Four White House lobbyists were dispatched to the House, and Carter released a statement that set forth in detail what he wanted the House to do. He added that he was deeply appreciative of the efforts of the House leadership "in moving the National Energy Plan forward for consideration by the full House in record time."[61] The president also sent a two-page message to every member of the House—praising those who "put their shoulder to the grindstone" for his plan. Finally, Carter made a number of personal phone calls, including a key one to a Pennsylvania Democrat that was said to have won him three or four more votes in favor of his proposal to keep price controls on natural gas.[62]

On August 5 the House did approve, by a margin somewhat narrower than predicted—244 to 177—an energy bill that closely resembled the one originally submitted by the president the preceding April. The principal casualty was the standby gas tax increase. But the centerpiece of Carter's program, a massive tax on most domestic oil, remained intact. President Carter was described as being "positively ebullient." He proposed a party for key House members, and he placed an emotional and well-deserved thank you call to Speaker O'Neill. (One reporter wrote that Jimmy Carter's Energy Crusade has been "transformed into Tip O'Neill's Party Caucus."[63]) "I'm ever grateful to you," said Carter. "Jeez, Mr. President, you're bringing tears to my eyes," replied the Speaker.[64]

O'Neill would be missed. It was widely agreed that it was largely due to his efforts that the energy package passed in the House and that the president had no such clever and loyal ally in the Senate. As one White House aide summarized the situation after the House victory: "Well, we're two-fifths of the way along, but I have to say, it's the easy two-fifths."[65]*

Although once the energy package moved to the Senate it was generally understood that it would be on less certain terrain, President Carter remained quiet for most of the rest of the summer and well into fall. He returned, in short, to what seemed to be his preferred mode: Having pro-

*The next two-fifths was the vote on the Senate floor, and the reference to the last fifth was to the work that would be done in the House–Senate conference committee.

posed, he behaved as if the legislature would indeed, and without much help from him, dispose.

The future of the energy bill in the Senate depended in good part on the attitude of Russell Long. Long's Finance Committee would consider all the tax aspects of the president's program, including the gas guzzler tax and a heavy tax on domestically produced oil and gasoline. But Long hailed from the nation's second most important oil and gas producing state, which meant that several of Carter's past provisions would clearly be anathema to Long's powerful constituents. In fact, the Senator had already labeled Carter's plan "an unmitigated disaster on the production side."[66]

The position of Henry Jackson's Energy Committee was equally unclear. Although the Committee had endorsed nearly all the items in the president's conservation program, it was deadlocked on the important question of deregulation of natural gas prices: nine were opposed, nine in favor.

Yet despite the widely shared feeling that the White House would have some problems in the Senate, there was nonetheless optimism that in the end the president would prevail. Both Senator Long and Speaker O'Neill considered it possible that the Senate might pass the energy package before October 1, and even those who were more cautious expected final passage no later than Thanksgiving.[67] As Schlesinger's legislative aide put it, "I think we have a good chance of keeping up this momentum."[68]

From the American people, however, there was an ominous lack of support. The overriding conclusion drawn from a *New York Times*/CBS poll was that "too few people believe the nation's energy problems are serious enough—and even fewer understand them well enough—to provide broad support for the Administration's energy program."[69] The findings were significant, for the survey also suggested that the public's willingness to shift priorities for the sake of energy depended on how convinced they were of the imperative to do so.

Carter had no choice now but to turn to the senators themselves. His main hope for congressional approval before the end of the year lay in his own willingness and ability to influence enough legislators on the bill's behalf. It was not a task the president took to naturally, and by mid-September the situation looked grim. Although no formal votes had yet been cast, the Energy Committee had set aside the president's request for federal authority to restructure utility rates; the Finance Committee let it be known that it was planning to substantially modify the proposed new tax on domestic oil; and the Senate as a whole seemed ill disposed to the administration's plan to tax industry for the use of oil and natural gas as a means of forcing conversion to coal. Indeed, a few weeks later the Finance Committee actually did vote down another of Carter's most cherished proposals—the "gas guzzler" tax on inefficient automobiles. Moreover, the Committee indicated that it would support the proposed tax on domestic oil only if the administration would agree to plow the tax receipts into mass transit and other public services. Finally, supporters of the administration's plan to continue natural gas price regulation failed to kill a deregulation measure on the floor. In short, Carter's entire energy plan seemed to be disintegrating. By the end of the month the survival of any of its major provisions was in question.

Clearly alarmed now by the speed with which the Senate had taken an unfavorable stance, and more educated about the importance of politicking in Washington, President Carter stepped up his political activity. First he appeared in the White House briefing room to deliver a televised statement. The president summoned the Senate to "act responsibly" and "reject narrow, special interest attacks on all segments of the national energy plan." As in the past, he attacked the oil and gas industries, reminding the Senate that the "House has faced this lobbying pressure and has acted both wisely and courageously."[70] And in spite of the growing evidence that the Senate was preparing to approve the deregulation of natural gas prices—a move strongly opposed by the White House—the president did not now repeat a threat made a week earlier that if he was handed an energy bill that contained price deregulation, he would veto it.

Carter also began to make it a point to maintain somewhat closer ties to the Senate leadership. Not that he always liked what he heard. When the president asked Byrd at the end of September how quickly the Senate could be expected to pass the energy bill, Byrd replied ominously: "The Senate is a place of shifting moods."[71]

October 1977 proved to be the cruelest month. In the Senate, as in the White House, energy hung over everything, "dominating the discussions and debates, private and public; dividing the Democratic majorities; pitting regional interest against regional interest, Northeast vs. Sunbelt; arraying special interest against special interest, consumer groups vs. the oil companies; and attracting an army of powerful lobbyists to the legislative process."[72] Through it all, despite Carter's revived efforts, hopes for the energy package continued to diminish.

The situation became exacerbated when congressional liberals, intent on staving off a floor vote on the deregulation of gas prices, started the Senate's first filibuster in thirteen years. The filibuster produced "days of endless amendments, midnight roll calls and tortuous parliamentary maneuvers that left Senators exhausted and short-tempered."[73] It also produced a very angry Russell Long. An impassioned advocate of deregulation, Long was incensed at the filibuster tactic and lost no time warning those who would cross him: "I am willing to play by any rule book anyone wants to hand me. If the other guy is going to be a poor loser, I'm going to be a poor loser."[74] Meanwhile other Senators were getting angry at Long. Senator Abraham Ribicoff termed the president's bill "a shambles," and assailed Long's plan for avoiding antagonisms by sending only a skeleton plan from his committee to the floor: "A bare bones bill could cause a lot of resentment on the floor. One hundred members of the Senate might not be very happy to have a few members write an energy program in conference."[75]

Although the filibuster had been started by supporters of the administration's position on natural gas prices, the president had little interest in prolonging a tactic that was paralyzing the Senate and exhausting its members. But rather than give the liberals an honorable way out—as Carter had agreed to do in a telephone call with Arkansas Democrat, Senator Dale Bumpers—Byrd *and* Vice President Mondale moved without warning to kill the filibuster.[76] Feeling double-crossed, administration supporters were enraged. Senator James Abourezk of South Dakota was so mad that he called the president a liar. "Why did the Vice President come up here to make these rulings? Why did that happen? I have been told . . . that all goverments lie. . . . There is one thing I never thought would happen, and that is that Jimmy Carter would lie."[77] As a result of all the unpleasantness *The New Republic* concluded that Mondale's "presiding over the dismantling of a filibuster conducted by allies of the administration . . . assured that nothing resembling a Carter energy bill [would] ever emerge from that chamber."[78]

A very worried President Carter was compelled finally to depend almost wholly on the politicking he disdained. He delayed some of his other legislative proposals until the energy bill was in better shape. He ordered an all-out White House campaign to muster still flagging public support. And he made another personal appeal, this time in an opening statement at the start of a mid October press conference.

> The package that was presented to the Congress in April is fair. It's well balanced. It assures that the American people are not robbed. It also insures that the oil companies get enough incentive to insure adequate exploration and production. . . .
>
> I cannot overemphasize the importance of this question for the present and future security of our country. . . .
>
> Energy is the most important domestic issue that we will face while I'm in office. And I attribute the highest possible importance to it in my own Administration.[79]

Before the end of the month Carter also made it a point, for the first time in a long while, to go back in person to the people.

During a six-state trip across the country, the president repeatedly reminded audiences that the acceptance of the energy package "by the American people and the Congress is a test of our strength and our national will." He warned that although his program was "bitter medicine," it was not as bitter "as the catastrophe that will follow" without its application.[80] Finally, the president once again reiterated his attack on the oil companies. "The oil companies want more and unless we stand firm, they may get it," he said, "and if they do, it will come out of our pockets."[81] In sum, on his tour Carter seized every chance he could find to hammer home the argument that nothing less than the future of this nation rested on the fate of his energy legislation. He also put his prestige on the line. At one point he declared: "I have equated the energy policy legislation with either success or failure of my first year in office as a leader of our country in domestic affairs."[82]

In addition, the president ordered members of his cabinet to make themselves heard. Mostly they wedged their appeals into long-scheduled speeches on other subjects. Appearing on "Meet the Press," Secretary of State Cyrus Vance stood a question on its head in order to insert a plug for the energy program. Asked whether the president planned to visit Saudi Arabia during his forthcoming trip abroad, Vance fairly pounced. "Well, let me say that the oil situation is a critical one. Oil is one of the most pressing problems that faces the whole world because of the impact that any oil-price increase could have on the economies of the world."[83] Attorney General Griffin Bell managed to shoehorn an energy pitch into a speech to the National Security Traders Association. At a commissioning of a new nuclear-powered aircraft carrier, Defense Secretary Harold Brown found a way to deplore the fact that the nation "relies on overseas sources for half the oil we consume." On a swing out West, Secretary of Health, Education and Welfare Joseph Califano argued that the poor would suffer most if the Senate failed to approve Carter's plan to rebate a tax on crude oil to consumers. Interior Secretary Cecil Andrus told a conference of coal producers that coal was America's "ace in the hole that will win us the energy game in the years immediately ahead." Agriculture Secretary Bob Bergland suggested to rural audiences that they use solar power to heat their houses. Walter Mondale put in a pitch on the "Today" show. And James Schlesinger, continuing in his role as most active pitchman—though sales were hardly his forte—tried to mollify consumer groups who feared the administration would compomise too much with the Senate.[84]

President Carter eventually went so far as to break some of his own past habits. For the first time in his administration, be became engaged in some measurable interpersonal activity. Senator Abourezk, who had recently been so angry at the White House, noted with relief that the president "was talking now, really talking, and that's good and I'm glad." Senator Howard Metzenbaum, who, like Abourezk, had been stunned when Mondale participated in quashing the filibuster, commented that "we're on the right track now." And Senator Edward Kennedy emerged from his conference with the president assaulting the oil companies and talking about "rip-offs" and "boondoggles" at the expense of America's consumers.[85] Even Senator Long came out of a one-hour White House meeting sounding more flexible and sanguine than before. "I think it's possible to work out a bill the President will sign," Long told reporters after his meeting with Carter.[86]

Nevertheless, the pace continued slow. Even the least controversial of the five measures—the energy conservation bill—required endless hours of deliberation. Still, after the filibuster fiasco, the president was reported to be standing firm. There would be "no deals," the White House insisted; one House member quoted Carter as saying "I don't plan on giving ground."[87]

On October 31 the president received a modest reward for his efforts. The Senate finally passed an energy tax bill by a vote of 52 to 35. But there were two small problems. First, the tax bill passed by the Senate bore only a passing resemblance to the one the president had originally proposed; and, second, the House–Senate conference committees that had been appointed to resolve congressional differences on the entire energy package were evenly divided on some of the most controversial issues. Therefore, the Senate's action on one part of the proposal meant rather little. Carter was still far from having a measure on his desk that he could comfortably sign— which meant he was far from achieving the goal he himself had insisted would determine the success or failure of his first year in office.

As a result, President Carter reluctantly signaled his willingness to postpone a long-planned 25,000 mile journey to nine countries on four continents in eleven days. That was not a trivial decision. It was embarrassing for Carter to cancel a series of foreign visits less than three weeks before his scheduled departure. But he was clearly worried about the prospect of suffering a major political defeat while abroad on what was to be primarily a ceremonial tour. As Press Secretary Jody Powell put it, the energy legislation remained the administration's highest immediate priority. And the president was determined that neither the trip nor any other plans would be allowed "to interfere with that goal."[88]

During the last weeks of 1977 Carter also worked on improving his relations with Congress. Apparently he succeeded, at least to an extent. John Brademas, then a Democratic congressman, noticed that there was "a gradual metamorphosis. At first there was a reserve; everyone was taking each other's measure. Now [our] meetings are very pointed, very frank. . . . [The president] is learning that the left hand washes the right and they both wash the face."[89] Carter liked to make sure that his new and improved relationship with Congress and his harder lobbying was not being overlooked. Asked at a news conference whether he was meeting personally with members of the House–Senate conference committee, Carter used the opportunity to make a point of his changed ways. "Yes, as a matter of fact," he noted, "tomorrow I have another meeting scheduled with the House chairman, Congressman Staggers. I have met with him previously and with Senator Long. Senator Jackson and I had a long meeting Sunday afternoon and I've met with Senator Byrd Saturday afternoon for a couple of hours. I meet with the House and Senate leadership weekly at breakfast. And in the past I've called in the entire sub-committees that relate to particular aspects of the energy package."[90]

The president also went on television yet again to appeal for public support. It was the third time in ten months that he had used the national networks on behalf of energy. In general, his speech had a familiar sound: Although on the one hand he tried to sound nonadversarial—"This is not a contest of strength between the President and the Congress"—on the other he served notice that he would sign an energy bill only if it met what he called his basic criteria for equity and effectiveness.

Most remarkable of all, the White House also made a stab at improving relations with key interest groups. James Schlesinger was dispatched to take on 3,000 antagonistic oil executives at the annual meeting of the American Petroleum Institute. The Energy Secretary told his audience that despite their belief that "all the folks up in Washington have it in for the industry," the administration's National Energy Plan was "a major step forward" that was "intended to be balanced" by "national concepts of equity." Not surprisingly, Schlesinger made little impact. The applause was perfunctory and many oilmen walked out during his presentation.[91]

Schlesinger played a difficult role during the tension-filled final weeks of 1977: front man for the administration. During the course of an hour-long news conference on November 21, the Energy Secretary made the informal suggestion that the administration might now be willing to make major compromises on energy just to get a bill signed before the end of the year. The president himself had previously given no indication that he would compromise nearly as much as Schlesinger suggested—which almost certainly means that Schlesinger had been instructed to float a trial balloon. In any case, Carter's supporters were highly irked by what they took to be his premature public showing of his hand on key issues. Chairman Ashley of the Ad Hoc Committee on Energy suggested that the administration "shut up"; Representative Toby Moffett, a staunch protector of consumer interests, said that Schlesinger had been tactically and strategically "stupid"; and a Republican opponent of Carter's plan, Senator Ted Stevens, complained that Schlesinger's remarks might make reaching an agreement "impossible."[92]

As a consequence, the White House moved quickly to disassociate itself from Schlesinger's remarks. The president's men stated unequivocally that

Carter had no intention of staging a retreat on energy, adding that he might well veto rather than sign any bill that seriously undermined his original proposals. "Anyone who believes the President will sign a bad bill is seriously mistaken," Jody Powell insisted; "no bill may be better than a bad bill." The White House was particularly serious about reassuring its supporters that the president would continue to work through them rather than attempt to reach an agreement on his own with Senator Long.

The administration did succeed in calming the storm of protest. Two days after Schlesinger's original statement, Ashley said that he had been given assurances that "as agreed, initiatives on compromise will come from the House conferees." And Moffett claimed that Schlesinger had assured him in a lengthy telephone call that the administration would stand firm. Moreover, he said that Carter had told him some weeks earlier that he did not "have to have a bill."[93]

But the brouhaha over Schlesinger's remarks was yet another indication that despite much more active politicking by the White House, the energy bill was still a source of confrontation rather than cooperation. In fact, positions were hardening. At a November 30 news conference the president restated his now uncompromising support for his friends. Carter maintained that he had never had "any conversation" with Senator Long that would either "encourage" or "require" that he change his position from what it was last April, and he reiterated that he had no "inclination to modify that position any time soon." The president further contended that if any of his basic principles were violated, he "would not sign the bill."[94]

In mid-December the White House was finally forced to concede—albeit indirectly—that there would be no energy legislation during this congressional session. A White House press secretary admitted that Speaker O'Neill's open pessimism about getting an energy bill before the end of the year was "certainly" a reflection of the obvious.[95] But the president could not at the time bring himself to publicly acknowledge that what was to have been the centerpiece of the first year of his presidency had failed to materialize.[96] Only years later, when writing his autobiography, was Carter able to admit that, as of December 1977, the "moral equivalent of war" was lost.

> It was one of my few major disappointments of the year, but it was serious, because everyone realized the bills were our most important legislation. *Congressional Quarterly* wrote, "The first session of the 95th Congress could be said to have had two agendas: energy and everything else." On all other domestic issues, I had done extremely well, but on energy I still had a long way to go. . . .[97]

As far as President Carter's energy legislation was concerned, January 1978 began on an upbeat note. Senator Jackson, who had been a key figure in the impasse over natural gas pricing, agreed to begin a new effort to break the deadlock; Schlesinger predicted that Congress would approve an energy bill by no later than early March; and Tip O'Neill was even more optimistic. He prophesied that it would be on the "President's desk by the middle of February."[98]

The big push came from Carter himself. At a mid-January press conference the president promised that this year his energy legislation would again be "the first order of business—the first priority." He declared that because he was now prepared to compromise, a bill that "will be acceptable to me and to the country . . . will come very early in the session."[99] The same message was reiterated in the president's first State of the Union address. Speaking before a joint session of Congress on January 19, Carter stated that on energy legislation both he and the Congress had "failed the American people. Almost five years after the oil embargo dramatized the problem for us all, we still do not have a national energy program. Not much longer can we tolerate this stalemate."[100]

The specifics of the agenda were somewhat different now. The big energy tax section, the most substantive and controversial piece of Carter's program, had been put aside in the fall until the issue of natural gas pricing could be settled. But by the following spring, when the House–Senate conferees got around to rehashing that question,* the energy tax was already in a gravely weakened condition. By March it was felt that it had "virtually no chance of enactment unless President Carter somehow can turn Congress around with a compelling argument as to the tax's necessity."[102] Thus, from then on, until the energy package was finally passed months later, the pivotal issue was whether and how to deregulate price controls on natural gas.

Despite the optimism in early 1978, the president's political difficulties were by no means at an end. Too many of the legislators on either side were still refusing to budge from their earlier positions. Once again Carter reached out for public support. But, happily for him, this time he combined his public appeal with two private ones. As he indicated in his autobiography, in addition to "going directly to the public" he also chose at this time "to increase [his] efforts to explain our policies to the major economic and political leaders outside Washington."[103] Carter writes that during 1978 he frequently brought to the White House "groups of leaders from business, labor, agriculture, finance, transportation, the elderly, international trade, local and state government, the news media, consumer affairs, electric utilities, mining and the oil and gas industries for briefings and appeals. . . .

---

*In May, Schlesinger told a luncheon gathering that he understood "now what Hell is. Hell is endless and eternal sessions of the natural gas conference."[101]

Slowly we won more of them over, and they joined with us in appealing to Congress to act. Our efforts continued month after month."[104]*

The other tactic Carter now tried was compromise. In fact, what he proposed amounted to an important reversal of previous policy as well as of his own vow not to make any major concessions. Until 1978, the administration had been on record as firmly *against* the deregulation of gas prices. The original energy package called for the maintenance of controls indefinitely, and during 1977 the White House repeatedly denounced the idea of deregulation as a multi-billion-dollar "ripoff" of consumers. But Mondale's participation in the breaking of the filibuster, and Schlesinger's previously mentioned trial balloon were, in retrospect at least, early signs that the administration might eventually accept some kind of a deregulation compromise. In the first months of 1978, this position became more or less official. By taking part in the Senate negotiations on natural gas pricing policy, Schlesinger conceded President Carter's willingness to go along with a middle-of-the-road approach—a phaseout of price controls coupled with an extension of price ceilings.[105]

But by now what was still being labeled as the president's most important domestic priority—the energy package as a whole—was being crowded off the agenda. The early optimism and array of new tactics notwithstanding, the vitality that accompanied the first mention of a "moral equivalent of war" was lost. Boredom was setting in. And instead of a politically desirable energy shortage, in 1978 there were surpluses: There was an abundance of natural gas; oil imports, at least from the Organization of Petroleum Exporting Countries (OPEC), were down; and coal production was up. Moreover, rapidly increasing energy prices gave way to stability and even some decline. In sum, on the first anniversary of the moral equivalent of war, circumstances were working against President Carter's coutinuing—although reduced—effort to get the energy package through the Congress.

But if the nation had lost *its* enthusiasm for a war on energy wastefulness, Carter himself clearly had not. From now on he would link America's lack of an energy policy to other major policy problems, both foreign and domestic. For example, during a speech in April to the American Society of Newspaper Editors, Carter tied both rising inflation and the falling dollar to America's failure to have a national energy plan. Announcing the speech, Jody Powell said that "You really can't talk about one of these

*A perfect example of the complicated alliances on energy was the position of the National Association for the Advancement of Colored People. Citing the argument that blacks needed jobs that, in turn, demanded an expanding economy and greater energy supplies, the usually liberal NAACP joined industry and the Chamber of Commerce in supporting decontrol of natural gas prices.

problems without talking about the others." And as House Majority Leader James Wright reported on emerging from a White House breakfast meeting, "The President believes . . . that our failure to achieve a solution to the energy problem is the one thing that is, more than anything else, causing the drop in the value of the dollar."[106] Finally, President Carter went even so far as to try to sell the energy bill on the grounds of national security. Although the connection may not have been an unreasonable one, by mid-1978 the energy legislation was increasingly being sold by the president as the necessary precursor to almost every other item on his domestic and foreign agenda.[107]

There was some progress. During July the Senate passed a measure that would force most electric utilities and industries to shift from oil and natural gas to coal, the nation's most abundant fuel. But although the approval vote was surprisingly large, no one assumed the energy package was home free. In fact, it was generally agreed that the main sticking point—still the natural gas bill—was not likely to be resolved any time soon.

President Carter had originally staked his reputation on getting an energy package through the Congress within a few months. Almost a year and a half later, still no energy bill emerged. As a result, the president's image was becoming badly tarnished. In August, *The New Republic* editorialized: "The administration has a remarkable record. Almost everything it proposes turns to ashes. . . . The list of wrecks is impressive. The energy program has spent 15 months being launched and is still in danger of going under."[108]

By late summer the congressional conferees had produced a natural gas bill that they considered—as did the administration at this point—a fair compromise: The price of most natural gas would be increased immediately by 15 percent, and then continue to rise each year until controls ended in 1985. Propelled into action now by the increasingly public expression of doubts about his ability to exercise any kind of effective political leadership, President Carter finally pulled out all the stops. Cutting short a vacation in the Grand Tetons, he returned to Washington to take charge. His personal politicking on behalf of energy at long last reached fever pitch in early September and stayed there for the next month and a half.

First, the president lined up Robert Byrd who previously had been of little help. Now, in what seemed to be something of a change of heart, Byrd referred to the energy legislation as "the axis on which our image turns."[109] According to Carter's autobiography, by this time Byrd attached "such importance to the passage of this legislation that he told each senator he considered it a direct test of his success or failure as the Senate Majority Leader."[110] Next, the White House enlisted the help of bartenders, bankers and bakers, farmers, mayors, and pipefitters, steel, automobile and textile executives, and any other stray bodies who might agree to say something nice about the bill—or at least to shut up if they had nothing nice to say. To make the pitch, the White House lined up Mondale, Schlesinger, public relations expert Gerald Rafshoon, assistants to the president Hamilton Jordan and Stuart Eizenstat, and administration troubleshooter Robert Strauss. "If you ever listened to Bob Strauss, you know how personally appealing he can be," said the vice president of the Chrysler corporation. The administration also brought in Anne Wexler, a veteran political campaigner who took on the task of working with special interest groups. Over 1,000 corporate leaders were invited to the White House for briefings, including many chief executive officers of the Fortune 500. As Wexler put it, "We don't just bring them in and send them away";[111] follow-up checks were made of each person who attended the sessions to find out their reactions to the energy proposals and to ask what additional information they might like. Finally, by this time, the administration had learned how to coordinate its activities. At 8:30 every morning, the White House lobbying teams met in the East Wing office of Carter's congressional liaison aide, Frank Moore. There they plotted strategy for the day and then fanned out to appeal to anyone who could help. The pitch was by now a familiar one: America needs the energy bill to stop the decline of the dollar and convince foreign nations that the U. S. can put its own house in order.[112]*

Moreover, for the first time really, President Carter himself was right in the middle of the action. He told a group of eleven governors that the energy bill simply had to pass. "The entire world," he said, "is looking at our Government to see whether we have the national will to deal with this difficult challenge. If this legislation is not enacted, it will have a devastating effect on our national image, the value of the dollar, our balance of trade, and inflation."[114] He made calls from Camp David. When he phoned Nebraska's Democratic Senator Ed Zorinsky to wish him a speedy recovery from a hernia operation, the president made sure to add before hanging up, "Keep your mind open on the energy bill." [115] He also resorted now to the kind of horse trading that he had previously deplored. For instance, James McClure, an Idaho Republican, was promised White House support for a $1.5 billion appropriation for the development of a breeder reactor—the research would be done in Idaho—if only McClure would agree to sign the conference report in favor of the gas price compromise.

By outhustling the opposition for the first time since the energy war was launched, the Carter White House finally got the natural gas component of the energy package through the Senate. An opponent, Senator Metzenbaum, groused that the bill was pushed through because of the admin-

*The Democratic National Committee also mailed public relations packets on the program and made more than 1,500 phone calls to organize grass roots lobbying.[113]

istration's "Herculean lobbying effort." Complained Metzenbaum, "They lined up the Business Roundtable and General Motors. They made it a patriotic issue to vote for the bill. The Administration put anything on the table to get votes. They really turned out the troops. How could any of us combat that kind of power?"[116] As one unofficial political adviser to the administration put it, "It was the kind of reaching out . . . they have needed from the beginning. They really have done the job."[117]

The natural gas vote started the president on a modest roll that received a considerable boost from the successful Middle East summit meeting at Camp David. Carter's highly effective third party intervention between Menachem Begin and Anwar Sadat visibly enhanced both his self-confidence and prestige. Thus, it was a relatively propitious moment for the final push on energy.

The president rose to the occasion. He urged 150 businessmen seated in the East Room to "add your voices to mine and others in asking the House of Representatives to pass" the entire energy package. He then asked each of those present to contact 25 or 30 members of the House, adding that he had talked to that many himself that day alone.[118] During a nationally televised news conference the president once again pointed to the energy package as "the single most important vote that will be cast by members of Congress this year," and he reiterated that its passage would be vital to the restoration of confidence in the American dollar.[119] Carter also placed a twenty-five minute conference call to 15 governors who had previously supported his energy legislation to ask for their help in lobbying Congress; and he telephoned 20 congressmen with the same appeal.

The end was frantic. (Carter described it as a "nightmare."[120]) House opponents of the natural gas bill tried to separate it from the rest of the package, figuring that it would be vulnerable to attack if isolated. The White House, on the other hand, insisted on lumping all five conference reports together "calculating that a majority could be rounded up to swallow a legislative mixture of the bitter and the sweet dressed up as a national energy policy."[121] The final showdown resulted in a victory for Carter. The decision to bundle all five bills into a single package passed the House by a margin of one vote—cast by Republican Congressman Tom Evans, who broke party ranks after a private Oval Office meeting with the president. (Later, the Congressman referred to his decision as "the single most difficult vote I have cast since coming to Congress."[122] Carter naturally had nothing but praise for Evans. In his autobiography he called him "an extremely courageous man—and one who kept his word."[123])

The compromise five-part National Energy Plan was passed by Congress at daybreak on Sunday morning October 15, 1978, after one of the longest legislative battles in years. Three weeks after that—one year, six months and 19 days after President Carter sent the energy package to Capitol Hill—he signed the National Energy Act into law. Its major provisions included: gradual deregulation of newly discovered natural gas by 1985 and price increases in the interim; a mild energy tax bill; a requirement that most electrical power plants burn coal; a demand that state regulatory agencies consider new rate structures for utilities that promote conservation; and a series of general conservation measures. Compared to the president's original proposal, the Congress put less emphasis on forced conservation and more on providing incentives to expand fuel production.

The National Energy Act was hailed by the president as vital to the "economic health and well-being and, indeed, even the national security of our country."[124] Still, Carter was honest enough to admit that in the moral equivalent of war, he had won only half the battle. He declared that he had "not given up on his original proposal."

At the same time, however, the president was clearly tired, and acutely aware of the toll the fight over energy had taken: "As was pointed out this morning in the signing ceremony, this is one of the most difficult legislative tasks that the Congress has ever undertaken possibly in the history of our country. It's complicated. It's contentious. It's very difficult to understand. It has international implications. And politically, I don't think anyone could win from it. It was not something that's politically attractive."[125]

The Practice of Leadership

There are certain times when the problems of leadership in America are exacerbated. Jimmy Carter entered the White House at just such a moment. In particular, the war in Southeast Asia and the Watergate crisis had left a legacy of doubt, distrust, anger, and frustration that would take longer than Jerry Ford's interregnum to overcome. A by-product of these crises—which many saw as the necessary results of abuses of presidential power—was a growing congressional assertiveness, especially in the Senate.[126]

This assertiveness was reflected in two ways. First, there was diminished deference to the president by individual members of Congress—as evidenced in this case by Senators Russell Long and Henry Jackson. Although both were Democrats, neither was moved to push for the energy package just because the Chief Executive recommended it. Each had been around a long time, far longer than the president, and was tougher and more skilled as adversary and ally than the Carter administration had anticipated.

Second, members of Congress were less willing now to bow even to their own institutional leadership. For example, throughout most of the period covered in this chapter, Robert Byrd would probably have been unable to influence his peers on behalf of the president's energy bill, even if he had wanted to.

But even if we accept the proposition that the late 1970s were unusually hard years for presidential leadership, the main argument of this book is that whatever the objective circumstance, there are certain things presidents can do to ease their own way. The question I am concerned with is: How well did Jimmy Carter manage to overcome what was in some ways a difficult situation? (In other ways, of course, particularly the Democratic majority in Congress, the president was in fact in a strong position.)

As we have seen, on energy at least, the answer is not very well. Because the president was neither an intuitive politican nor an experienced one (at least not in Washington politics), it took him many months to learn the ropes. (As one aide put it later, "We just didn't know what was on the stove."[127]) This cost him lost time, but more important, it left a bad taste in the mouths of too many people who were personally offended by his hostility to Washington politics and his lack of sophistication about the role such politics played in fueling the policy process.

Carter's problems with energy began with his faulty political planning.[128] Mistakes were made well before the president declared the moral equivalent of war. James Fallows, in a widely regarded critical assessment of Carter for *Atlantic,* wrote:

> Pleading urgency, Schlesinger obtained Carter's permission to work in total secrecy.... For some matters, this approach made sense; there were technical answers to questions as how much solar energy could be produced. But the major decisions about energy were political, not technical.... If Carter himself had no clear predisposition on these questions, then any rush project should have been directed not by technicians but by politicians, who could balance the different interests, argue over deals, see just where the compromises must be made.[129]

President Carter's failure to recognize the need for political as well as substantive planning proved to be especially costly on an item such as energy, which suffered two major political liabilities. First, energy was an inordinately complicated subject, and the energy legislation itself reflected that. As Senator Ribicoff declared at one point, "It's a Rube Goldberg scheme the people don't understand and neither do members of Congress."[130] Second, energy conservation lacked a built-in constituency. No coalitions of any significance backed the comprehensive energy package. It was too liberal for conservatives and too conservative for liberals; what the Northeast liked, the Southwest disliked; and if it pleased consumers, it was certain to displease business and industry. Precisely because so many different groups were offended by one item or another of Carter's proposed energy legislation was it imperative to have at least some political groundwork.

But Congress was left out of the planning process almost completely. Energy executives were excluded altogether. Even members of the president's own administration were kept in the dark: The Secretary of Transportation was not consulted even though his Department's policies were intimately tied to energy; the Office of Management and Budget was sought out only after the basic energy plan had been drafted; the Assistant Secretary of the Treasury for tax policy was brought into the process only at those points when his expertise was needed; and it was late March before the Treasury Secretary and the chairman of the Council of Economic Advisers heard even "snippets" of Carter's energy plans.[131]

The president failed, in sum, to employ two elemental political tactics: preemption of problems and advance notice. His deficiency in this regard, his insistence that Schlesinger and his aides be allowed to function "as if they were a self-contained unit and their task as hush-hush as the Manhattan Project,"[132] ended up costing him dearly. For instead of walking into the joint session of Congress in April 1977 with a band of well-disposed allies, and with some of the important others at least neutralized, he came in alone and vitually unarmed. His failure to co-opt, in advance, any segment at all of the political elite inevitably meant that in fighting the energy war, Carter would be under-staffed and ill-equipped.

Although the president at least tried to instruct the American people on the dangers posed by the energy crisis, here too he failed to do as well as he had hoped. He *had* succeeded in focusing early attention on the issue. Yet in July 1977, three months after the moral equivalent of war had been declared, a prominent pollster told a Senate committee that "Our conclusion is that the public is not yet clear in its thinking on the problem. . . . The people are caught up in a confusing kind of double-think, a state of mind we associate with a problem that is only half thought through."[133] Put another way, if the Congress was looking "for clear signals from the public on a national energy program, it might as well forget it."[134]

One of the problems was that Carter's appearances on both television and in person catered perhaps too much to the image he had of himself as a populist president. At his first fireside chat, he wore a beige cardigan to tell us that the energy crisis in this country was permanent and that there was absolutely no way we could solve it quickly. The virtues of plainness were also supposed to manifest themselves in the content of his speeches. Fallows, who was a speechwriter for Carter, recalls that while he was working on that same fireside chat, he received a lecture from the president: "I should not use words such as 'cynical,' because average people wouldn't understand them."[135]

The difficulty was that there was an ill fit between Carter the common man and Carter the preachy moralist who tried to lead on the strength of his authoritative sources of power. Although the president was uncomfortable being called a "born again" Christian, he did come across as someone who thought he had seen the one true light. He seemed to think he could lead simply by "being correct." Thus, he failed, so far as energy was concerned, to generate any excitement, to mobilize us on behalf of what he had proposed. Mainly, he gave the impression that we really *ought* to grant him his superior knowledge and good intentions, whereupon we really *ought* to go along and, indeed, pressure our representatives into doing the same.

Thus, there was a boringly moralistic quality to Carter's approach, and a joyless one as well. We were chided for being "the most wasteful nation on earth"; we were warned of impending "painful sacrifices"; we were threatened with the "catastrophe" that would ensue if we did not swallow the president's "bitter medicine"; and we were told that we were being tested: should we fail to pass the national energy plan, we would fail as well a "test of our strength and our national will."

Moreover, President Carter was too quick to lose patience and too prone to withdraw. This was a cold and distancing father-leader who offered us no palpable gratification of any kind for consenting to follow. The president's notion of pride in sacrifice, in the hair-shirt virtue of lowered expectations, was simply not convincing or sufficient in this particular situation. By 1977 the energy "crisis" had lost some of its edge. It seemed vague rather than immediate; and the doomsday of which we were constantly being warned appeared very far in the future.

Carter's failure to educate as well and as quickly as he would have liked may also have had something to do with the fact that early on his administration was tarnished by the scandal that surrounded his old friend, now Budget Director, Bert Lance. By the summer of 1977 Lance was caught in the middle of an inquiry concerning the propriety, if not the legality of his banking practices;[136] before he left Washington in late September, the entire affair cost the president dearly. In Richard Neustadt's words, it "played hob with his professional reputation, and cast doubt on the affinity he claimed to have with voters."[137] "Lancegate" coincided in any case with a precipitous administration slide in the public opinion polls. According to Gallup, 42 percent of the public strongly approved of Carter's performance in March, 1977, but only 24 percent did so in October.

But if Carter impressed us as being vaguely ineffectual, the primary reason was the strong and widely prevailing doubt, expressed very early, about his capacity as a political leader. The general feeling was that he and his team, the "Georgia Mafia," were all too new to Washington, and, as a group, too inexperienced in federal politics. It was a worry the energy saga did little to relieve. For the energy package, more than any other single issue, uncovered the president's strking distaste for Washington politics. His refusal to politick on his own behalf, coupled with his inconsistencies and uncertainties, led within short order to the genuinely damaging suspicion that what Carter had called his highest priority "was just another grandstand play, a media hype, something to remind people that the President is still here." Moreover, President Carter's own insistence on equating his success as president with his ability to have an energy program in place within months—an ability he manifestly did not have—only served to underscore the appearance of both personal and professional weakness.

For much of 1977 and 1978 a key question was how this president could lead these people on this issue. Carter was not an immediate success as a political leader; neither the public nor the political elite was much inclined to follow; and the issue itself, energy, was friendless at best. What then might President Carter have done to help both himself and his National Energy Plan?

Two moments presented special opportunities and unfortunately for him, Carter took advantage of neither. The first came during the summer of 1977 when it was clear that the locus of action on energy would now shift from the House to the Senate. It would have been the perfect moment for heavy White House lobbying among members of the upper chamber. But after his success in the House—which, in any event, was widely credited to the political skill of Speaker O'Neill[138]—the president took a parallel success the Senate too much for granted. Although, as we have seen, Carter was grateful to O'Neill, he appeared nevertheless to underestimate the extent to which the Speaker deserved credit for the House victory. One can only assume that if the president had recognized this, he would have understood that either he himself, or a Senate surrogate, would be needed for equally successful Senate action. Instead, President Carter failed again to do any substantial political groundwork. No significant attempt was made to build coalitions or soften up senators who would inevitably play a key role in determining the fate of the energy package. But if White House lobbying was both late and lame, oil and gas interests, meanwhile, took advantage of the opportunity to organize. As one senior White House official admitted after the fact, "We were all kind of happy and patting ourselves on the back for what we did in the House and they were getting their act together."[139] Later, Carter himself conceded the point: "I think that in retrospect it would have helped had I had more meetings with members of the Senate."[140] Indeed, during this time the battle lines on energy were drawn.

Carter's second big opportunity arose during the final weeks of 1977. By then the administration was doing much better; effective politicking was taking place. But the president failed to consider all the consequences of his own actions. Having staked his reputation on getting an energy bill out before the end of the year, he really should have thought long and hard about what he was willing to concede to obtain that goal. After some early vacillating, President Carter decided to hang tough, to stick with his policy of "no bill is better than a bad bill." But as things turned out, only a few months later he ended up compromising anyway on both taxes and the decontrol of natural gas prices. Had he made the same concessions a little earlier, he might have gotten the same bill in 1977 that he signed in 1978, and at a much lower cost to both his person and his presidency.

Carter backed off from compromise in 1977 because of the strenuous objections of some of his supporters (several had just recovered from their rage over the filibuster fiasco). But if these same people had been brought into the policy-making process at an early stage, and if Carter had personally engaged them in some form of social exchange, he might have won enough support from them for an early compromise of some sort. Of course, even without such support, the president could have considered making prompt concessions. For although some administration supporters, such as Ashley, were relatively becalmed by 1978, others, such as Moffett, were as incensed then as they had been earlier. (In March, Moffett moved toward an open break with the administration by suggesting that the House should avoid at all costs making further concessions on natural gas and energy taxes.) What, then, did Carter gain that was of any durable value by giving in in December 1977 to the liberal hard-liners? Had he followed through on his early signals of a willingness to compromise, he could have claimed the same energy "victory" that he claimed a year later—and saved face and considerable grief along with it.[141]

President Carter's failure to seize either of these two opportunities meant that he was thrown back again on his own personal resources. Here, of course, he was weakest. During the first eight months or so of 1977, on the matter of energy in any case, President Carter displayed a failure to understand either intuitively or intellectually that the energy program would have to be approved by a great many different people—in and out of government—whose wants, needs, and wishes would finally have to be taken into account. His inability to recognize the deep concerns and divisions that his energy package had provoked meant that for many months he continued to ignore them at his own peril.

Washington is a city of informal networks, each available to any president who wishes to use them.[142] Had this president been inclined to do so, he might have compensated at least in part for his poor planning, his intermittent wavering (especially his retreat and withdrawal after the initial Churchillian summons), and some of his subsequent tactical errors. But

Carter was both naive about and adverse to politicking;[143] it was said he didn't even know how to "schmooze."[144] Although he was motivated to achieve, initiate, and implement, he was neither extraverted enough to naturally politick on his own behalf, nor experienced enough, early on anyway, to be intellectually convinced of the need to do so. Thus, although President Carter could be remarkably charming in face-to-face encounters,[145] he was disinclined to do much encountering and loathe to use interpersonal activity as a means to an end. The problem was compounded because Carter was a newcomer to Washington; there was no reservoir of old ties or good will to draw on. As Jody Powell put it years later, "Nobody was going to carry his water out of personal loyalty."[146]

In fact, it often seemed as if Carter actually disdained politics and politicians. Sometimes, especially in the beginning, he was downright short-tempered, petty, and even mean-spirited. His labeling of an early congressional recess as "what they call a district work period" was not much appreciated. Nor was his reputation enhanced when in a meeting with a Senate subcommittee he said that deregulation of natural gas prices would be "obscene and immoral," or when, on losing that committee vote, he was publicly outraged—a display of temper that seems especially injudicious in light of subsequent history.[147]

Carter's hostility was by no means directed only at Congress. A month into his administration, he expressed anger and surprise when the Executive Editor of the *Washington Post,* Ben Bradlee, refused to delay publishing a story that the president had asked him not to. And later, when a cabinet member complained about an inaccuracy in *The New York Times,* Carter suggested issuing a press release to attack and correct the item, and urged that the Washington press corps be bypassed in favor of the Sunday television interview shows. But, in fact, television fared little better. According to Secretary Califano, Carter began a January 1978 cabinet meeting by commenting on his extensive foreign trip, covered, the president said sarcastically, "by our foremost diplomatic reporter, Barbara Walters."[148]

But on the matter of energy, the president's strongest hostility was directed against the special interest groups, lobbyists who, from his vantage point, were no more than greedy interlopers on what should have been his preserve. Such anger might have been productive if all the lobbying had emanated from only a small segment of private industry, specifically the oil and gas companies. But the private sector had many different players in this particular game, players ranging from the home-building industry, to the trucking industry, to Dow Chemical. Moreover, the lobbyists were by no means confined only to those from business and industry. Labor unions, public interest organizations, and environmental institutions were among the many groups that spoke for or against different pieces of the energy package.[149] But at least the first time around, the president rarely made a personal appeal to any of these groups to forge alliances or gain their support in the moral equivalent of war.

Still, it was vis-à-vis Congress that the president's distaste for politicking proved most costly. This distaste became evident early in the Carter presidency, even before the energy bill was introduced, and it triggered a contest of will between the executive and the legislature that deprived Carter of much of the post-election momentum that he might otherwise have enjoyed. For example, the president's hasty and insensitive decision to cancel thirty-two water projects that Congress had already approved set the stage for an unnecessarily difficult first year.[150] Although there may have been considerable merit in what he was trying to do, the way it was handled was quite damaging to him on a variety of other issues that may have been equally or even more important.[151]

The problem was that Carter's cutting back on the water projects went to the core of what politicians see as their public duty, and it left many senators in no mood to oblige the president.[152] Among those senators from the affected states was Russell Long, who spoke about this in the spring of 1977:

> Nobody's asked to trade anything. Nobody talks in those terms. But I know this much: If you have unhappy troops up here they are a lot harder to lead than happy troops. It's not the way to look at it to ask whether the President is going to trade one thing for another. . . . But the effective Presidents have had a way of remembering who is helping them with their problems. Lyndon Johnson believed if you're going to help them, help them in spades. So far, that hasn't been established in the Carter Administration. When a President calls and asks someone for help with his problem, the question is how is it going to be when the phone call is at the other end? After a while, a senator will say, 'If you can't do this and you can't do that, just what is it you have in mind that would be good for my state?' The hell of it is, the logic is to vote against him and find out.[153]

Carter not only refused to play the political game himself for the better part of 1977, he also failed to make sure that others played—and played well—in his stead. The White House congressional relations staff was ineffective for much of the year, and by October the liaison team headed by Frank Moore was under heavy fire.* "The Georgia Mafia has a complete lack of understanding of Congress and the way it operates," said one congressional aide. "This isn't ignorance, it's arrogance. They don't really like Congress."[155] Said another Washingtonian, "They don't seem to understand the mechanics of the art, and when they do figure out where to apply

---

*Frank Moore had once lobbied the Georgia legislature for Carter. Fallows wrote of Moore that he "had barely laid eyes upon the Capitol before Election Day."[154]

the pressure, it is usually too late."[156] To make matters worse, the administration's lobbyists were accused of not understanding the very energy program they were supposed to be selling.[157]

Of course, the president's team was simply a reflection of the man in charge. As one congressman who was with the president at a White House state dinner observed, "He . . . has a withdrawn way about him that is vaguely troubling. . . . When the dinner came to a close, he walked out without showing the camaraderie that one learns to expect from political types. He just doesn't have the traditional politician's need for the warm kind of personal bond you feel with people you work with a lot."[158]

In fact, Carter seemed to despise the notion of leadership as social exchange. Fallows wrote that Carter's "skin crawled at the thought of the time-consuming consultations and persuasion that might be required to bring a legislator around. He did not know how congressmen talked, worked, and thought, how to pressure them without being a bully or flatter them without seeming a fool."[159] After the president had been in office six months, his own press secretary said of him: "It's the damndest thing. . . . He went all over the country for two years asking everybody he saw to vote for him for President, but he doesn't like to call up a Congressman and ask for his support on a bill."[160]

Neither amenities nor trading were part of Carter's natural leadership style. He raised hackles by sending senators unsigned photos for their offices and identical "personal" letters, by failing to make simple courtesy calls, by not administering niceties (he sold the presidential yacht, a frequent scene of productive entertaining), and by neglecting small talk.[161] And he freely admitted his reluctance to trade. As late as August 1978, he said that "horse trading and compromising and so forth have always been very difficult for me to do. I just don't feel at ease with it."[162]

Thus, Carter's original conception of presidential leadership demonstrated an almost complete lack of understanding of our antiauthority political culture. For many months, Carter failed to recognize that in order for him to get something—even as president—he would have to give something; he failed to realize that routine political leadership in America involves many different two-way influence relationships. As a result, for most of 1977 methods of influence were not employed; an array of political tactics lay unused; and sources of power remained untapped. It was not that this president lacked social skills; it was that during his first year in office, even regarding his highest domestic priority, he had neither the natural inclination to use them, nor the awareness that he would have to if he was to enjoy any measure of success. In fact, even later in his presidency, in 1978, when it began to be clear to him that politicking was important, he seemed to see it as helpful rather than vital. Small wonder that the

Congressional Quarterly reported in the fall of 1978 that there was "near unanimity in Congress that Carter and his staff had blundered repeatedly in pushing their proposals."[163]

But although he was hardly a changed man, President Carter did in fact behave differently in fall 1978 than he had during the preceding eighteen months. Indeed, although it took time for the effects to be felt, a process of learning and change had already begun to take place as early as summer 1977, when Carter and his staff began to recognize that the congressional liaison effort had to involve intimate contact with the members of Congress, and be much more sensitive to the needs of the individual legislators.[164] Thus, the size of the liaison staff was increased and its operations were improved. But the big change was in President Carter himself. His handling of the energy package in 1978 was superior in every way to his performance the year earlier. Above all, he had learned from his bitter experience that a hands-off approach would get him nowhere.

In 1978 the president continued his attempts to educate the public; he also turned his full attention to the political elite. By no means did he become a master at sweet talking, nor did it ever become second nature for him to "wheel and deal." However, he did learn to use his staff—enhanced now by some savvy newcomers—to better effect; he did do some coalition building; he did do some horse trading; he did remain consistent about what he was and was not willing to negotiate about; he did compromise; he did vastly increase the number of his personal appeals and make himself more accessible; he did put a massive effort—especially in the late summer and early fall of 1978—into drumming up outside support, for example, from the business community; and finally, in part by capitalizing on his triumph of diplomacy at Camp David, he did manage to convey the impression of competence and command.

Once Jimmy Carter began to see the link between politicking and leadership, he learned to reward people for being good. They got invitations to the White House, for example, or phone calls; sometimes they were even promised a breeder reactor. He also learned to harness our shared values and interests for his own personal political benefit. By alluding constantly to the connection between his energy bill and both a healthy economy and national security, it became almost unpatriotic to go against the man. Finally, he learned to draw on his own competence. By tapping into the momentum of Camp David, President Carter enabled members of the political elite to conceive of themselves as going along with someone who had respectable political credentials, and who now had at least one major success under his belt.

Jimmy Carter campaigned on and even used the anti-political mood of the country in 1976. Why then were we so surprised and angry when he tried to govern in the same anti-politics style?[165] The fact is that campaign posturing is one thing, and governing another. Ironically, it was precisely because the president failed at the start—out of inclination and inexperience—to think through the tactical ties between policy and politics[166] that he failed his own test for presidential leadership. Moreover, the damage done in the first year—nowhere more blatantly in evidence than with regard to the moral equivalent of war—carried right over into the rest of his presidency, and indeed on to Election Day, 1980.

The problem with Jimmy Carter was that he is, to return to David Riesman's apt phrase, an inner-directed man. He did his presidential duty as he saw fit, and he failed, therefore, to use the opinions and feelings of others for guidance in the matter of goals. His need was to achieve, but unlike the need for power, "achievement is a one-man game that need never involve other people." Politics, however, is a two-person game—which brings us to the answer to the question posed in the Preface of this book: Jimmy Carter was a political failure not because he was stupid, lazy, cowardly, or immoral. He was a political failure because, especially in the initial and very critical months, he was very much a failed politician.

11

Ronald Reagan
and the Budget Cuts

I am asking that you join me in reducing direct Federal
spending by $41.4 billion in fiscal year 1982. . . . Spending
by government must be limited to those functions which are
the proper province of Government. We can no longer afford
things simply because we think of them. Next year we can
reduce the budget . . . without harm to Government's legitimate purposes or to our responsibility to all who need our
benevolence.

President Reagan,
State of the Union address,
February 18, 1981

Witnesses to the "Reagan Revolution" should not have been surprised by
what they saw. This was a revolution whose leader was doing nothing other
than what he said he would do.[1]

Reagan's candidacy represented the culmination of almost fifteen years
of politicking across the land, almost all of it on behalf of a broadly articulated philosophy that included social views rooted in traditional American
values, and political and economic ideas grounded primarily in resentments
against big government and high taxes. Thus, Reaganomics—described by
Reagan biographer Lou Cannon as a "nonword which embraced President
Reagan's simultaneous attempts to balance the federal budget, increase
defense spending, and slash income taxes"[2]—was rooted in Reaganism.
And Reaganism is a set of conservative attitudes whose fundamentals may
be captured in three adjectives: radical, simple, and optimistic.[3]

In 1980, the times finally caught up with the man. Americans were sick
and tired of high inflation, high interest rates, high taxes, and high unemployment, and they eagerly scanned the political field for someone who held
out the promise of redemption from economic distress. Reagan was ready
and in place. For many years he had been promulgating general solutions;
during the 1980 campaign he was identifying himself with a specific cure-
all called supply-side economics.

220

Supply-side economics holds that those workers, entrepreneurs, and investors who supply goods and services must be adequately rewarded by receiving sufficient disposable income, profit on innovation, and reward for risk. Government can do its part primarily by reducing taxes—a solution thought feasible only if simultaneously government reduced spending.* Thus, candidate Reagan marched through the 1980 campaign carrying two banners: budget cuts and tax cuts.

This chapter focuses on Ronald Reagan's effort to reduce federal spending. Such a plan would, at the least, have to "run the gantlet of the 'iron triangles,' interlocking government and private interests that work to protect and expand their favorite federal programs."[4] Middle-level bureaucrats, members of interested congressional panels, and lobbyists for the beneficiaries of government programs are only some of the large stumbling blocks that face any aspiring budget cutter.[5]

These prospective opponents almost certainly account for candidate Reagan's vague responses when called on to explain how his spending cuts would be achieved. Rather than enumerating exactly which programs would suffer, he spoke only of the need to trim excesses. In his August 1980 acceptance speech at the Republican National Convention, Reagan declared: that "our government should go on a diet."[6] Similarly, in a campaign address delivered in Chicago on September 9 that served as a blueprint for his subsequent economic policies, Reagan avoided any mention of specific cuts in actual government services.

> Waste, extravagance, abuse and outright fraud in federal agencies and programs must be stopped. . . . This does not require altering or taking back necessary entitlements already granted to the American people. . . . This strategy *does* require restraining the congressional desire to "add on" to every old program and to create new programs funded by deficits.[7]

As a campaign tactic, the device of stressing the ends and avoiding the means worked well—as did the candidate's more general strategy of focusing national attention on the economy. Reagan won more than 90 percent of the electoral vote, and Republicans were slated to control the Senate for the first time since 1954.†

Understandably, the president-elect regarded the outcome as a mandate for his economic policies. Ronald Reagan's quite remarkable electoral vic-

---

*The cost of cutting taxes without cutting spending would be, of course, still higher federal budget deficits. Until recently it was assumed that higher deficits would inevitably create greater inflation. The growing deficits and simultaneous relative deflation of the early 1980s was an unexpected phenomenon.

†The Republicans had 53 Senate seats and 192 seats in the House; Republican control of the Senate was occurring for the first time in the political lives of nearly all members of Congress.

tory gave him the right and, as he seemed to see it, even the duty, to take the ball and run with it.

President Reagan's assault on federal spending has been described as possibly "the most carefully planned invasion since the Allied troops flooded ashore on the beaches of Normandy.[8] Clearly, Reagan and his team had their work cut out for them. Just before the election, *Business Week* concluded that if he were elected, Reagan would "find it difficult, if not impossible, to accomplish his promised spending cuts";[9] some weeks later, just after the election, the magazine still opined that "almost any budget cut Reagan would make will be politically tough."[10] The problem was, of course, that now the president had to get down to specifics. Extant programs—many of which bestowed important benefits—would have to be cut down or perhaps eliminated.

President Reagan's chief economic strategist was David Stockman, a young man who had acquired an encyclopedic knowledge of budget matters while working as an aide to Congressman John Anderson and serving two terms of his own as a Republican representative from Michigan. More than anyone else, Office of Management and Budget Director Stockman was the brains behind the operation to reduce federal spending. As Laurence Barrett put it in his chronicle of Reagan in the White House, "Stockman in the beginning would be everything: formulator of policy, administrator, advocate before congressional committees and the press. He would extract Reaganomics from Reaganism."[11]

The details of President Reagan's budget proposal were worked out by such men as Stockman, Murray Weidenbaum (about to become chairman of the Council of Economic Advisers), and Donald Regan, the new Secretary of the Treasury. By February, Stockman and company had produced a document that identified $41.4 billion dollars in projected savings from the federal budget for fiscal year 1982. Naturally, a few administration officials had reservations about some of the assumptions that underlay the proposed budget (for example, that inflation could be halved); still others wondered whether Stockman's handiwork would be politically feasible. On the whole, however, the naysayers were muted in their response. Taking their cue from their leader, most of Reagan's team exuded optimism and self-confidence. Later, Stockman would recall that a "pioneering mode" had come over the group, a sense that whatever the obstacles were, they would be overcome.[12]

In fact, the planning of Reagan's invasion was taking place on several different levels. Edwin Meese III, counselor to the president, recruited the foot soldiers and saw to it that presidential appointees continued throughout the early months to function as loyalists dedicated to the pursuit of presidential objectives. Anyone given a cabinet job had to demonstrate a commitment to Reagan's "economic philosophy"; tolerate being assigned some deputies with closer ties to Meese and the White House than to the secretary under whom they served; and take part in economic briefings with Reagan prior to the inauguration in order to get used to working with him before working with their own teams. Meese explained that all these steps were taken to make sure that cabinet officers did not develop "a departmental stand as opposed to an administration-wide stand. We wanted our Cabinet Secretaries to have both the knowledge and the resolve to resist the protectionist attitudes of their departments."[13]

The president assumed personal responsibility for two further tasks. The first was to generate a strong team spirit among members of his own administration. During the nine full cabinet meetings held during the first month of the Reagan presidency, the president was observed by a member of his staff to be "very comfortable with himself." Moreover, the staff member added, "he has a very clear vision of where he wants to go."[14] As a result, cabinet meetings were said to be rather informal and free-wheeling discussions during which participants were encouraged to voice their opinions. Reportedly, the president liked to poll his cabinet by "going around the table and asking them for their views." Meese was quoted as saying that "We want our Cabinet members to express themselves vociferously."[15] Thus, the combination of Meese's preparatory work and Reagan's directed yet open style ensured that by the time the president was ready to make his formal proposals, his team would be alongside, ready to do battle for him.

Ronald Reagan's second task during this planning period was priming key members of the political elite who were not connected to his administration. Almost immediately, even before moving into the White House, Reagan made an effort to win important friends. The president-elect and his wife threw a party for fifty of the top names in Washington's cultural and civic hierarchy; they went to dinner at the home of conservative columnist George Will; and they attended a party given by Katharine Graham, the liberal publisher of the *Washington Post* and *Newsweek* (other guests included such opponents of Reaganism as Vernon Jordan, then head of the National Urban League, and Lane Kirkland, president of the AFL-CIO). President-elect Reagan also played host to Edward Kennedy, and met with Chief Justice Warren Burger, Speaker of the House Tip O'Neill, and the top Republican leadership on Capitol Hill.[16] In addition, Reagan had a separate congressional transition Liaison Office whose staff was making courtesy calls well before Inauguration Day. It was reported that the president-elect was so eager to do the same that he had to be "lassoed" to "keep him off the Hill."[17]

After Reagan was sworn into office, the pace accelerated. By the time he had been in office three weeks he had met with 60 senators and House members, sometimes in large groups, but more often in intimate meetings with one or two lawmakers at a time.[18] He made it a special point to greet key leaders in the House and Senate, and even had Speaker O'Neill over for two private White House dinners. Additionally, the congressional liaison staff, operating under the direction of Max Friedersdorf, "began making visits to Capitol Hill, serving members of Congress, and observing amenities immediately after the inauguration. Phone calls from members of Congress were returned promptly (usually within four hours), and all correspondence was to be acknowledged."[19]

The overriding spirit during these early weeks and months continued to be one of optimism and exuberant self-confidence. I have noted Stockman's feeling of being in a "pioneering mode." This theme was to be replayed constantly. For example, Deputy Treasury Secretary R. T. McNamara asserted that the president's radical budget cuts *"will* happen."[20] But the greatest optimist—his wife called him the "eternal optimist"—was the president himself. It was a quality that would be commented on by almost all who watched the Reagan presidency. Barrett writes that Reagan's "own good fortune in navigating the squalls of life brought him to harbor at the White House with an unsinkable belief in happy landings and happy endings."[21] Cannon strikes the same chord: " 'Life is just one grand sweet song,' Reagan had written as a high school senior in 1928. . . . More than half a century later, this pervasive optimism was driving the economic decisions of his administration."[22] Still others recall the incoming administration's remarkable confidence that in the initial economic recovery program announced in February, 1981, it had discovered the guiding principles of successful economic management."[23]

By early February, then, President Reagan had his economic proposals in place; he had a thoroughly loyal team; he had made some friends; and he resonated the conviction that *his* economic policy in particular would work. One final ingredient propelled the "Reaganauts," as they were sometimes called, into immediate action: their conviction that victory would depend in good part on a fast start. One in-house document stated flatly that "The public sense of urgency requires that the President immediately undertake to steer a new course. . . . The momentum of presidential activity. . . . emphasizes the sense of urgency and provides the basis for the President's leadership opportunity."[24]. Thus whatever could be put on hold would be. Ronald Reagan was prepared to concentrate on putting into practice those theories of economics and politics that he had been espousing for years.

By the first week of February, the administration's effort to sell Reaganomics was in full swing. Stockman's Office of Management and Budget was distributing heavy, loose-leaf briefing books to Republican members of the Congressional Budget Committees, and preliminary lists summarizing its contents were being circulated all around Capitol Hill. These suggestions for spending reductions were tentative, vague, and incomplete. Nevertheless, they provided members of Congress with some indication of what was coming, and with opportunity for participation and consultation.

Meanwhile, President Reagan was preparing to take his case to the people. A televised address on the economy, scheduled for 9 P.M. on February 5, would constitute his first major test as a public persuader. His closest ally in Congress, Senator Paul Laxalt, declared that this television appearance would constitute "the kickoff for his second campaign in two years, the first to win the Presidency and the second to sell his program to the people and through them, to Congress. . . . He's going to be playing the role of educator."[25]

The president's performance that evening was described as "vintage" Reagan, "spoken in easy cadences and relaxed delivery, studded with frowning candor, smiling promises and homey statistics."[26] He was careful to keep his message blunt and simple: "The federal budget is out of control." To get us out of the "worst economic mess since the Great Depression," we need a new approach to tame inflation. Once again, the president was vague about specifics. And, once again, he employed what had by now become his standard technique. Like candidate-Reagan, President Reagan combined premonitions of gloom and doom if we did *not* do what he said with rosy promises of a better future if we *did*. Finally, the president sounded more conciliatory than challenging, and more compassionate than polemical: "Let us work together. . . with sensitive understanding of those who must be protected."[27]

Of course, not everyone liked what they heard. *The New York Times* complained that President Reagan never really described the "pain and sacrifice" that any budget surgery would entail, thereby preserving "his avuncular image and also the impression that some vast, voracious, distant monster called The Government had only to be disciplined. . . before growth and stability would be everyone's reward."[28] In addition, several economists contended that the president had misused key economic statistics, while others were simply skeptical that the president could do what he said he would. Moreover, more than a few members of Congress became anxious about the prospect that some of their favorite programs—whether foreign aid, synthetic fuel, or energy assistance for low income people— would be the ones to be axed.

On the whole, however, President Reagan was widely praised for his performance. A leader of the opposition, Speaker O'Neill, gave him a rave review. "He comes across beautifully," observed the Speaker. "He's running high right now."[29]

Well aware of the generally favorable climate, the administration continued its considerable efforts to ensure public support for the president's economic policies. For example, one day after the president's television address, special briefings were held at the Kennedy Center in Washington for Reagan supporters, many of whom had been heavy contributors to his presidential campaign. In turn, about 500 of them met in private sessions to plan a grass-roots drive to put public pressure on Congress to approve the president's economic program.* Moreover, the administration demonstrated at least some sensitivity to the increasing fears about what exactly the proposed cutbacks would mean. For instance, the president personally assured a group of county executives and state legislators that proposed cuts in aid to local governments would be softened by easing restrictions governing the use of such aid. Reagan also met separately with 18 members of the Congressional Black Caucus and 30 leaders of farm organizations, telling them in soothing tones that the administration planned to spread the pain of spending reductions equitably. Most important, the White House let it be known that the president planned to spare, at least for fiscal year 1982, seven basic social programs: Social Security's Old Age and Survivors Insurance, Medicare, Veterans Administration services, Supplemental Security Income that served the disabled and elderly poor, the school lunch and breakfast program, Head Start, and the Summer Youth Jobs Program. Thus was the concept of what Stockman called a "social safety net" introduced. The administration was promising to maintain those social programs that protected the "truly needy."

With all these exemptions, however, not that much was left to ax.† Hence, it became fairly obvious that programs such as legal services for the poor, the black lung trust fund, solar subsidies, job programs, mass transit, national endowments for the arts and humanities, dairy subsidies, and guaranteed student loans constituted some of the likely targets.[30] As a consequence, certain groups—labor unions, educational, environmental, and consumer groups as well as local officials and minority organizations—started to protest slashes they now recognized would inevitably affect them.[31]

In response to the growing anxiety, the White House continued to mount what was described as "the biggest public relations campaign in memory

---

*At first, the group had the active cooperation of top level White House aides. Later, after suffering some criticism over these White House ties, the group disbanded.
†The president was still planning to recommend increases in defense spending.

... replete with briefing sessions for influential legislators, businessmen and news media representatives, television appearances by Cabinet officers and economic aides and masses of data to augment the President's own message."[32] An appearance by Vice President Bush at a New York City Republican Lincoln Day Dinner was typical. "A new beginning has been made," he declared. "If it takes weeks, if it takes months, if it takes years, we're going to break down those unneeded empires-within-empires. . . . The muscle, bone and marrow of essential government programs aren't the target of President Reagan's program. He's after the fat."[33] The president's own continuing participation in the campaign to sell his economic policies was also characteristic. On the eve of his State of the Union message, President Reagan met with aides to discuss plans for the upcoming lobbying drive. He also took the time to make yet another personal appeal for support. In his usual can-do fashion, he told leaders of conservative organizations that he refused to be "anything but optimistic about what's going to happen."[34]

Reagan's first State of the Union speech, delivered on February 18, focused almost entirely on Reaganomics. The president proposed an increase in defense spending along with budget and tax cuts. It was a radical program, based loosely on supply-side tax ideology that proposed to "free the capitalist system from the dead hand of government through income tax reduction,"[35] and on predictions that included the halving of inflation, 13 million new jobs by 1986, and an overall growth rate of 4 to 5 percent a year. Democrats and Republicans agreed that the president aimed to do no less than bring about a watershed shift in economic thinking, and that as a result he was confronting Congress with a set of decisions on domestic policy "that were of probably greater magnitude than any since the New Deal period."[36]

But considerable confusion still existed about exactly who and what would be hardest hit. Some felt that since President Reagan's budget revisions combined a reduced rate of growth in federal spending with a large boost in defense spending and a continued increase in the portion of the budget devoted to income transfer programs aimed at the poor, the hardest hit federal endeavors would be those "outside those two categories—from Amtrak to the National Endowment for the Arts and Humanities."[37] Others presumed that the most drastic aspect of Reagan's proposals involved "consolidating and trimming back on the vast array of programs in the education, health and social welfare areas," especially those that grew out of Lyndon Johnson's war on poverty.[38]

What everybody did seem to agree on was that the policies Reagan had proposed did indeed constitute a "revolution." No one much argued that

the president was trying to launch the nation on a "dramatic and unex-
plored course that (would) reverse decades-old policies in Washington."[39]

The reaction to Reagan's State of the Union speech was similar to the
reaction to his television address of two weeks earlier. Liberals were generally unhappy. Economist Robert Lekachman wrote in *TheNation* that

> No one can say with complete certainty that this voyage into uncharted
> economic waters will end on the rocks, but one thing should be clear....
> The benefits of [Reaganomics] will accrue quickly and massively to
> stockholders, corporate executives and other affluent types. The costs
> will afflict the poor, the unemployed, the young, the female and the
> black....[40]

And a broad coalition of labor unions, civil rights groups, and social welfare
organizations promised to fight the president's program with an alternative
one of their own "that would meet the nation's economic needs with fair-
ness and equity."[41]

Yet the president himself seemed to be even more confident than he was
before. One day after his State of the Union speech, he was reported to be
"elated" with its reception.[42]

The president's optimism was justified. A *Washington Post*/ABC News
poll taken 24 to 48 hours after his talk showed better than 2–1 support for
his program.[43] Furthermore, Ronald Reagan was getting remarkably high
marks for his performance. Many praised the president as the most adept
communicator in the Oval Office since Franklin Roosevelt.[44] His high rate
of activity also worked to his advantage. In little more than four weeks he
had delivered two prime-time television addresses, held one news conference, met informally with reporters, and sat down repeatedly with members
of Congress, state and local officials, farmers, blacks, union leaders, and
others. The net result was a widespread impression—especially perhaps
among members of the press—that the president was doing a good job. As
one White House correspondent put it in early March, "So far, there's been
a lot of kissy journalism."[45]

There were, in addition to President Reagan's perceived competence, at
least two other explanations for his continued honeymoon with the press.
First, as we have seen, the administration had a magnificently orchestrated
and ongoing public relations campaign. Before Reagan's speech to Congress, reporters had been given extensive briefings and hefty press packets.
The day after the address, the president met with about 125 newspaper and
broadcast editors to further explain his economic program.

Second, Ronald Reagan was well liked personally. In part, this was
because the austere and relatively humorless Jimmy Carter was an easy act
to follow. And in part it was because Ronald Reagan, a lifelong performer,
had his act down pat. An account in *The New York Times* told of how the

president "mowed down the other speakers in the competition for laughs" at a February dinner at the Washington Press Club with his "dazzling series of one-liners."[46]

President Reagan understood that his abundant skill as a communicator could profitably be used to his own political advantage. Observed Cannon, "Reagan may feel that there is a liberal cast to the press, but he also feels he will do better if he communicates with reporters than if he does not."[47] In sum, after two months in office, the president had good reason to exude his typical self-confidence. As one journalist saw it, "The Chief is way ahead on points. He's controlled the dialogue with ease. No one's laid a glove on him."[48]

As the weeks passed, the Reagan administration became increasingly convinced that delays in the budget process would reduce the administration's chances of capitalizing on the mandate of the election and on the momentum the president had been able to generate since his inauguration. Friedersdorf was perfectly blunt about this. "The President has a lot of political momentum going for him," he argued. "The climate for dramatic action is better now than at any time I can recall."[49] Senate Majority Leader Howard Baker concurred. "It is my intention to move these budget cuts in less than a month," he declared. "Every day that this is delayed makes it more difficult to pass."[50]

Perhaps the most immediate result of the Reagan juggernaut was to intimidate the Democrats. For the story of Reagan's successes during his first nine months in office is also the story of a generally emasculated and disorganized opposition. The Democrats lacked a leader. Jimmy Carter had vanished into the Georgia countryside; Robert Byrd, who was not, as we saw in the previous chapter, a strong leader even as head of the majority party, was even less consequential now that Senate Democrats were in the minority; and Tip O'Neill seemed to be out of his element as leader of an obstructionist opposition. Moreover, of the fifty-seat advantage that O'Neill ostensibly had in the House, three dozen or more were conservative Democrats who were not likely to align themselves with a liberal Democratic opposition against such typically conservative issues as tax and spending cuts.

The desultory nature of the collective Democratic response to the Reagan offensive was evident almost immediately. In mid-February a *New York Times* editorial titled "Where are the Democrats?" decried the fact that no one seemed to be "articulating general social values .... Senate Democrats, in the minority, act increasingly like freelancers. Democratic House members seem interested mainly in protecting one ox or another."[51]

Perhaps in partial response to such broadsides, the Democrats made a brief stir. O'Neill, who just happened to be getting on well with the president on a personal level, nevertheless served notice that the Democrats would not allow Republicans to "tear asunder the programs we've built over the years." And in Washington, a liberal, largely Democratic coalition of trade unions, civil rights groups, and social welfare organizations developed plans for a joint lobbying effort against any reductions in spending on welfare, food stamps, child nutrition, and medical aid for the poor.[52]

But on the whole, the opposition had little direction or substance. The Democrats' unusually passive attitude was especially apparent in their response to the president's State of the Union speech. Although party leaders made vague promises about plans to seek changes in Reagan's tax cut proposal, all they could muster regarding the budget cuts was the charge that they seemed tilted toward the rich at the expense of the poor. At the same time, the Democrats took pains to praise President Reagan's "initiative," and let it be known that they considered that there was "much in the President's program that most of us can enthusiastically embrace."[53]

In this hospitable climate the White House announced that Stockman, Regan, and Weidenbaum, who had previously been the main promoters of the president's new economic policies, would now be joined by other members of Reagan's cabinet, who were scheduled as a follow-up to the State of the Union message, to hold news conferences every day for a week. The administration encouraged television coverage and asked that each of the secretaries always be quoted by name.

Straight through the first week of March, the president kept a brisk pace. When he learned in late February about what was being termed a "miscalculation" in the projected growth of government spending, he decided simply to request $3 to 6 billion more in additional budget cuts. Stockman announced that "Budget saving options sufficient to hold the line were presented to and approved by the President today. We are back on track."[54] When Reagan addressed 4,000 mayors at a conference of the National League of Cities, he said that he understood that they, and others who faced reduced federal aid, had a "legitimate concern." He went on to add, however, that he was "finding it increasingly difficult not to call some of them 'selfish interest groups.'" [55] And at a session with reporters, Reagan declared that he was about to replace a temporary hiring freeze with "new permanent ceilings" on federal jobs.

The informal half-hour press sessions that Reagan held throughout this period brought out his naturally ingratiating manner. His style usually involved deflecting hostile questions with humor. When a longtime Texas newswoman asked Reagan if his rule for dissident Republicans was "off will go their heads," he cocked his head, paused for effect, and said, "How can you say that about a sweet fellow like me?" In response to a reminder of his bellicose reputation among critics, the president feigned amazement and cracked, "I've been here more than six weeks now and haven't fired a shot."[56]

Finally, throughout these weeks, President Reagan continued to use the presidency as a "bully-pulpit." He told Walter Cronkite of CBS News about the 100,000 letters and telegrams he had received, most in support of his program.[57] And at a news conference, the president took the opportunity both to sell Reaganomics and to present himself as compassionate and caring.

> Q. I don't understand how the nation's poor are going to survive this almost across-the-board cut in social programs. Can you explain this. . . .
> A. Yes, I think I can. We're not cutting into the muscle of a program where it is going to require taking aid away from those people that must have it. . . . I speak with some confidence of this because this is very much what we did in California with our welfare reforms. . . . Some 350,000 people in that one state disappeared from the welfare rolls. We never had a single case of anyone suddenly appearing and saying, "I am destitute. I've been cut off welfare". . . . They just disappeared as the spotlight began to be turned on—possibly out of recognition that they were going to be caught—and the rolls just shrank. And it's this theory that is behind what we're doing. Our safety net of programs—the seven programs we spoke of—is intact.[58]

Nevertheless, resistance to Reagan's budget increased. A growing number of legislators from the Northeast and midwest complained that the South and Southwest would benefit from the president's proposed budget cuts at their expense. Democratic members of the House Ways and Means committee worried that there was a "tremendous lack of information about the social as well as fiscal impact" of the cuts.[59] A national coalition of 157 groups representing unions, civil rights groups, religious organizations, and social welfare agencies declared that such budget reductions as the president proposed "could wreak great damage to the fabric of this nation."[60] The National Association for the Advancement of Colored People organized a campaign involving 1,700 branches around the country to lobby against the White House plan to cut spending on social programs. And Lane Kirkland appeared before a generally hostile House Budget Committee to declare that in his opinion the president's economic package was "unfair and shortsighted" and "based on an untested theory, unrealistic projections, and questionable logic." Kirkland added: "The Reagan budget constitutes the most costly roll of the dice ever proposed for this nation by economic policy makers. On the lines are the living standards of millions of working Americans, the unemployed and the poor."[61]

Still, the opposition was not making much noticeable headway. Members of the Senate Committee on Labor and Human Resources spared some of the items on the president's "hit list" such as fuel assistance to the poor and benefits to victims of black lung disease. But they backed most of the other proposed reductions. Moreover, the House Conservative Democratic Forum, composed of those three dozen or so conservative Democrats whose votes could give the Republicans a working majority in the House, asked President Reagan to push for still another $11 billion in cuts. (The president's reply: "You've made my day."[62]).

Meanwhile, Reagan appeared more determined than ever. At the Rose Garden ceremony to sign the formal budget proposal, he warned that he might have to cut the budget still further. "These cuts are not necessarily the last ones," he cautioned. "If more cuts are needed to keep within our spending ceilings, I will not hesitate to propose them."[63]

The spending plan President Reagan sent Congress on March 10 sought to reverse the pattern of increased spending for social programs that had typified federal budget setting for the past two decades. Job programs authorized by the Comprehensive Employment and Training Act (CETA), economic development subsidies intended to promote construction, arts and humanities outlays, unemployment benefits, medicaid, student aid, and other government programs were scheduled to be pared down or axed altogether. Even those programs whose constituences included important business interests were slated to be cut. Transportation, for example, would get fewer federal dollars to contract for highway, airport, and mass transit construction.[64]

From the time the president's budget bill was formally submitted to Congress to the end of March, its progress was steady, if perhaps slightly erratic. The Republicans were solidly behind the measure. The Democrats, meanwhile, continued to have difficulty reaching consensus on exactly which position to take. Neither support nor opposition made them comfortable; consequently, there was a little of each. As their own consultant, pollster Peter Hart, put it, their message so far had been "confusing." They were advised to speak with greater "force and clarity."[65]

Representative Jim Wright, the House majority leader, finally responded to rank-and-file Democrats who had complained that none of the party leaders wanted "to be first out of the box to criticize the President."[66] Wright sent a nine-page analysis to each of 242 House Democrats stating that the president's package "imposes a grossly unfair burden on those least able to carry that burden." An accompanying letter suggested that his analysis serve as the basis of any public comments about the Reagan economic package. O'Neill, on the other hand, was being remarkably cooperative with the administration. Claiming that he was trying to bring all factions of his party "under the tent," the Speaker consented to accelerate consideration of the budget for fiscal 1982, and to adopt a timetable that would call for final action on the budget by mid-July and final action on a tax cut bill immediately thereafter.[67] Since the generally accepted view was that delays would help opponents of the budget cuts, it was clear that by relinquishing control of the legislative schedule, O'Neill had given away one of his strongest cards. (Later, one of his advisers sought to explain the Speaker's decision; "What the Democrats did . . . was to recognize the cataclysmic nature of the 1980 election results. The American public wanted this new President to be given a chance to try out his programs. We weren't going to come across as being obstructionists."[68])

But the oddest display of Democratic confusion was still to come. On the morning of March 19, members of the Democratic minority of the Senate Budget Committee complained that they were being enlisted in a "forced march" that would result in a budget that would "wreak unbelievable havoc" on the poor. But later that same day, these very Democrats unanimously voted out the Republican package, which called for budget cuts even deeper than those recommended by the president. Swayed, it seemed, by real or imagined pressure from their constituents, they caved in, later arguing that such leverage as they did have would best be saved for the issue of spending priorities.* Budget Committee member Senator Daniel Moynihan complained that his committee had "undone 30 years of social legislation in three days,"[69] but during an evening meeting when some key votes were taken he was in New York City at a United Nations dinner party.[70]

As Americans started to worry more about the form the cuts would take, President Reagan's public support waned somewhat.[71] But the president's aides professed to be unconcerned and unsurprised, promising instead that the administration would be undeterred. Although Senate Republicans decided to postpone debates on emotional issues such as abortion and school prayer until the budget cuts were through the Congress, the "Reagan cannonball" continued to barrel ahead.[72]

President Reagan told a group of legislators invited to lunch at the White House that bureaucrats who criticized his budget cuts were "more worried about losing their position than they [were] about the people they represent."[73] He questioned the accuracy of a Congressional Budget Office analysis that countered the administration's projected spending estimates for fiscal 1982.[74] He told the Conservative Political Action Conference that government could once again be made responsive to the people, "but only by cutting its size and scope."[75] And either explicitly or implicitly he gave Budget Director Stockman the leeway to make his most sweeping statement yet about what citizens should legitimately expect from their govern-

*The Democrats also intended to try to restore some funds for social programs after the measure reached the Senate floor.

ment. Said Stockman, "I don't believe that there is any entitlement, any basic rights to legal services or any other kinds of services."[76]

Then, on March 30, President Reagan was shot by John Hinckley.

At least one pollster concluded that the event increased the public's respect and admiration for Reagan's personal qualities.[77] Indeed, the president's grace under pressure is beyond refute.[78] "Honey, I forgot to duck," he told his wife after she had rushed to his side just after the shooting. "Please tell me you're Republicans," he quipped to the doctors preparing him for surgery. "All in all I'd rather be in Philadelphia," he wrote on a notepad in the recovery room, when he could not yet speak.[79]

But above all, the American people were grateful that Ronald Reagan would survive. There was an almost tangible feeling of relief that he would not die, that he would thereby spare the United States yet another terrible trauma. Thus, the period of Reagan's recovery turned out to be more of a holding pattern than anything else.

There was one notable exception. An April 9 vote in the Senate Budget Committee dealt the White House an unanticipated blow by withholding final approval of the draft budget for fiscal 1982. Although the setback was viewed as probably temporary, the administration was concerned that any loss in momentum might cause real problems for Reaganomics further down the line. As a result, just as soon as he was able, President Reagan re-entered the fray.

At his first White House meeting after he was shot, the president ordered his staff to repudiate any reports that he would be willing to compromise on his proposed tax cuts. The administration also let it be known that it was again preparing to push as hard as it could for the budget cuts. Immediate plans included: inviting 900 editors and broadcasters to Washington for a series of economic briefings, an intensive speaking schedule for Vice President Bush, more public appearances by cabinet members, and lobbying the three Republican Senators who had voted with Democrats in the Senate Budget Committee to reject the draft budget. The president's special interest in the three Republican dissidents—who were objecting to the proposed spending cuts on the grounds that they would still result in too large a federal deficit—was evidenced the next day at his next meeting on economic strategy. There he ordered budget officials to furnish the three senators with additional information on the proposed budget. (Within days, the dissidents fell into line.)

Thus began a two week period during which President Reagan mounted yet another major personal campaign to lead the nation on economic policy. Clearly concerned that progress had slowed during his recovery, Reagan sought to ensure that whatever had been lost while he was incapacitated would quickly be regained. He telephoned several legislators; met with his main speech writer to begin drafting messages to Congress; laid plans to deliver the commencement address at the University of Notre Dame; started implementing his strategy of dividing the opposition by backing a budget plan advanced by conservative Democrats; and played host to eight governors, including seven Republicans and one conservative Democrat.[80]

Soon President Reagan came around to making his grand gesture. The White House announced that the president's first extensive appearance in public since the attempt on his life would consist of a personal appeal before Congress on behalf of his budget proposals. His deputy press secretary said that the speech had been scheduled because Reagan felt that it was "particularly important that he outline his views as his program moves forward in the legislative process."[81]

The announcement of Reagan's speech—which would be sure to elicit further sympathy for him coming so soon after the shooting—drove the fear of God into his opponents, at least for the moment. On the day before his talk, congressional Democrats admitted that they had serious doubts that they could defeat the proposed budget. Admitted Speaker O'Neill in what was described as a dispirited tone, "Support the President—that's the concern out there—and Congress can read that. I've been in politics a long time, and I know when to fight and when not to fight."[82]

Not every House Democrat was gratified by O'Neill's acquiescence. One complained that he had received a 15-minute telephone call from President Reagan, but had yet to get one from a Democratic leader. "That's a symptom of the Democrats' problem around here," the representative claimed. "The White House really has its act together," while "we've been reeling" since the November elections.[83]

By all accounts, the president's April 28 speech before Congress on behalf of his economic plan was formidable politics. As Reagan entered the packed chamber, his audience broke into thunderous applause. He responded with a great smile, a thumbs-up sign, and a typically optimistic, patriotic talk—delivered in a voice still hoarse. With the consummate skill that was his trademark when talking from a prepared text, the president made a smooth transition from the general to the specific: "Now, let's talk about getting spending and inflation under control. . . . "[84]

Reagan's speech had two main goals. The first was the more general one of rekindling the spirit of hope and cooperation he felt characterized the first months of his presidency. In this, the president succeeded admirably. Journalists wrote of a second honeymoon, and there was general consensus that it would be even more difficult to buck the president now than before. As one White House aide put it, "Normally, you have the idea that a new President has an open window for just so long and it shuts very quickly in terms of public interest and support. But the shooting incident and the way the President handled it . . . has reopened the window and given him a second opportunity."[85]

Reagan's second goal was narrower. He sought to win support for the Gramm-Latta bill, a so-called "compromise" budget measure now before the Congress that, although nominally bipartisan, actually bore an exceedingly strong resemblance to the president's original budget proposal. In fact, House Democrats—led by chairman of the House Budget Committee Jim Jones—had generated an alternative budget bill that would also have given the president 75 percent of what he asked. But the Democratic alternative had already come under attack by Stockman who charged that the Democrats were "changing their words but still singing the same old tune" of more taxes and spending, and by Treasury Secretary Regan who called the alternative "well-intentioned but inadequate."[86] Instead, the White House decided to throw its weight behind the Gramm-Latta bill, which was officially co-sponsored in the House by Texas Democrat Phil Gramm and Ohio Republican Delbert Latta. Gramm, dissatisfied with the Democratic budget proposal, let it be known that he was willing to cooperate with the administration. The administration was responsive; it had only to convince some Republicans who were leery of working on so important an issue with a Democrat. (At one point Vice President Bush telephoned the wavering Latta and explained that the president, still convalescing, was counting on his cooperation.[87]). Once the Republicans were persuaded, the White House had in hand a congressional measure that reflected Reagan's thinking and also bore a bipartisan imprint.

President Reagan took the occasion of his April 28 speech to make his position crystal clear. He told Congress that he backed Gramm-Latta 150 percent, and would not even hear of a compromise. In fact, the very notion of compromise was anathema to the administration at this point. Reagan was on a roll; he felt that even a hint of a willingness to make concessions would not only damage his changes for a good budget bill, but for his three-year tax cut proposal as well. Declared the president:

> The House will soon be choosing between two different versions, or measures, to deal with the economy. One is the measure offered by the [Democrats]. The other is a bipartisan measure—a substitute introduced by Congressmen [Gramm and Latta].
> On behalf of the Administration, let me say that we embrace and fully support that bipartisan substitute. It will achieve all the essential aims
> . . . .
> At the same time, however, I must state our opposition to the [alternative] measure [which] quite simply falls far short of the essential actions that we must take.[88]

Reagan's appearance before the Congress was a great success. According to *Time,* on only a few previous occasions had any President "enjoyed such a shouting, clapping, emotional reception from the assembled lawmakers."[89] Said one Republican congressman, reflecting the general view, "The President drove a velvet steamroller through the Congress. He cleared the way for his supporters to carry his program on the floor, and even though he flattened his opponents, he did it in such a way that it was almost painless."[90]

Round 1 of the budget battle was scheduled for May 7, when the House would vote on a general spending plan. (That vote was only the first step in a complicated process by which Congress approves federal budgets. Appropriations committees would subsequently have to decide on specifics in line with the broad spending goals established in early May.) A first round victory was important to Reagan. It would maintain the recent momentum and, by establishing Reaganomics as a winner in Congress, it would provide an important psychological boost both to the rest of the budget process and to the tax cut measure that lay just ahead.

Accordingly, President Reagan did what he could to win convincingly. Although still on a restricted schedule while recovering from his bullet wound, Reagan nevertheless held small, informal meetings in his office with 60 lawmakers, mostly with conservative Democrats and moderate Republicans regarded as "swing" votes. His approach with the Democrats was easygoing; he almost never asked directly for their support. Generally he just sat and listened, answered some questions, and had his aides give away free concert tickets for the President's box at Kennedy Center.[91]

Wavering Republicans were also invited over for one-on-one talks. More often than not, the tactic worked. For example, New York Republicans Guy Molinari and Gregory Carman had been counted in the uncommitted column. But after President Reagan told them that this budget resolution was only the start of the process, and that there would be ample opportunity later on to make adjustments, both men pledged their support.[92] Similarly, Republican Matthew Rinaldo from Union, New Jersey, went to Washington to tell the president that he was concerned about administration proposals to cut spending for mass transit, education, and health and social services. When Rinaldo expressed fears that workers being laid off in his district were too old to find jobs, Reagan quipped, "What do you mean? I got one at 70." When Rinaldo told him that he headed a subcommittee on aging, the president joked, "Well, I have to have a private talk with you. I have a few problems on my own." Rinaldo reported that the president never asked for his vote directly. "It was a very, very soft sell in an extremely gentlemanly manner." Reagan told Rinaldo that all he was asking for was a vote "on a broad parameter, the spending target. There will be plenty of time to make adjustments on the individual programs. and I'll work with you." By the time Rinaldo left the White House, he had in hand a pair of presidential cufflinks, and Reagan had Rinaldo's vote.[93]

But the administration was also capable of taking a tougher tack, especially vis-à-vis Republican lawmakers. Some were warned that a vote against the president's budget could cost Reagan's support in the 1982 elections; others were simply threatened with a cutoff of tickets for White House tours.[94]

As a result of all the White House lobbying, most political analysts expected the president to prevail. But the president himself insisted that he was still "running scared." "You know me," he said, "I run scared all the time."[95]

Running scared paid off. A coalition of House Republicans and conservative Democrats gave President Reagan a victory by adopting a budget that was intended to sharply curtail the growth of federal spending. Gramm-Latta beat back the Democratic alternative by a vote of 253–176. Reagan declared that he was "extremely grateful" for the "resounding victory," while both Democrats and Republicans agreed that the president was setting a new course for the nation. "The consequences of today's vote will cast a very long shadow," said House Majority Leader Wright. "The issue is not one of figures, but philosophy," said House minority leader Robert Michel.[96] The press, meanwhile, was increasingly in awe of the president's political skills. The *National Review* commented that Reagan was a "master of timing and symbolism."[97] *The New Republic* grudgingly admitted that "Reagan knows where the votes are."[98] And *The New York Times* editorialized that there was "no minimizing the President's political accomplishment. It was a lesson for the rest of us in leadership—and how not to generalize too quickly about the weakness of the modern Presidency."[99]

Once the Republican-controlled Senate had also passed a budget endorsed by the president, the general budget goals for fiscal 1982 had to be translated into specifics: $38 billion had to be cut from extant federal programs. As Jim Jones put it, "The time for fun and games is over."[100]

Sixteen House and 13 Senate committees had until mid-June to draft legislation cutting programs in their jurisdictions. According to the plan, these proposals were then to be packaged into a single bill that would be sent to the floor by the House and Senate Budget Committees. To accomplish the all-important procedural details as smoothly as possible, the administration had—at Stockman's urging—exploited a little-used and little-known provision of the 1974 Budget Act called "reconciliation." That act had created a budget committee in each house and imposed a timetable calling for two budget resolutions each year. In an effort to put teeth into the second budget resolution, to be adopted by September 15, the lawmakers created the reconciliation procedure. If appropriations committees voted more money than the Budget Committee deemed wise, the second resolution could demand changes in outlays. Using recommendations from the other committees, the Budget Committee would prepare an omnibus reconciliation bill changing laws as necessary to prevent overspending.

This year, however, Gramm-Latta had applied reconciliation instructions to the first budget resolution, the one of May 7. If the committees failed to make the necessary cuts, the Budget Committee would do the work for them. Similarly, if the committees approved spending plans that exceeded the budget ceilings, the legislation would not leave Capitol Hill. Thus, Congress could impose fiscal discipline before special interest groups could divide and possibly conquer the committees.[101]

But implementing reconciliation instructions would be harder to accomplish than legislating them. Congress's willingness to abide by its own budget would still have to be tested. It had waived its own rules in the past, and it could do so again.

The administration faced two main problems. Although the Republicans held 44 percent of the seats in the House, Speaker O'Neill had allowed them only 40 percent of the seats on the Budget Committee, 34 percent of the seats on the tax-writing Ways and Means Committee, and 31 percent of the seats on the Rules Committee. The result, according to the ranking Republican on Ways and Means, was that key decisions were in the hands of "people more interested in protecting programs than in fiscal policy."[102] The second problem was that because House Democrats were in the majority, they controlled all the Committees. And because they controlled the committees, they would surely try on occasion to circumvent the spirit if not the letter of the first budget resolution.

For example, by cutting a proposed expenditure of its own, one House subcommittee made it possible for another House subcommittee to approve a shift in spending priorities established in the Reagan budget by allocating a billion and a half dollars extra for social programs that aid the poor. Said the Democrat who headed the Public Assistance Subcommittee, "We are not committed to taking inhuman and irresponsible positions, just because Gramm-Latta says so."[103]

Thus, in spite of the reconciliation instructions that would at least force Congress to consider the budget whole (instead of on a program-by-program basis), the president still had his work cut out for him. House Democrats were continuing their debate on whether to take a strong stand against the White House by resisting the repeal or modification of such popular programs as child nutrition, job training, and student loans. And a monitoring of the work of House committees by Stockman's Office of Management and Budget had concluded that "the Democratic-controlled committees were systematically deviating from the ceilings set by the First Budget Resolution." As Stockman calculated it, these deviations meant that savings would actually amount to only one-quarter of what had been projected when Gramm-Latta was approved in May—an alteration that clearly would further imperil the administration's already shaky deficit strategy.[104]

The Democrats' growing resistance did not go unnoticed by administration supporters already unnerved by tampering that would save less than originally envisioned. In fact, Phil Gramm was reported to be joining Republicans in considering whether to co-sponsor a new measure that would eliminate what he considered the phony aspects of the budget cuts.

It was roughly at this point that Ronald Reagan redoubled his efforts. Both in public and behind the scenes he demonstrated once again his powerful will to win and his unrestrained approach to going after what he wanted.

Typically, he started this phase of his campaign by turning again to the American people. Atypically, he attacked Congress, in particular, Speaker O'Neill. President Reagan began his news conference by reading an opening statement appealing for passage of the budget.

> There is now clear danger of Congressional backsliding and a return to spending as usual. Some House committees have reported spending cuts they know can't be made; closing, for example, one-third of the nation's post offices. . . .
> This practice is unconscionable. . . . I urge the House leaders to revise the committee work so that it honestly and responsibly achieves the original spending goals. But if that proves impossible, let me be clear: My Administration will have no other choice than to support the proposal of a number of Representatives in the House to offer a budget substitute on the floor that matches the resolution they voted for in May.

During his response to a last-minute question, the president launched into an uncharacteristically emotional self-defense, and into an attack on the Speaker.

Q. Tip O'Neill says you don't understand about the working people, that you have just a bunch of wealthy and selfish advisers.
A. . . . He said that Tip O'Neill has said that I don't know anything about the working man. I'm trying to find out something about his boyhood because we didn't live on the wrong side of the railroad tracks, but we lived so close to them we could hear the whistle real loud. And I know very much about the working group. I grew up on poverty and got what education I got all by myself and so forth and I think it is sheer demagoguery to pretend that this economic program which we've submitted is not aimed at helping the great cross-section of people in this country. . . . [105]

According to a White House official, the president's tone had changed because he was being warned that "a lot of games [were] being played up there [on Capitol Hill] with the reconciliation budget."[106] Whatever the reason, the Democrats' reaction was to close ranks and fight back. The personal assaults on their collective behavior as being "unconscionable" and on their leader as guilty of "demagoguery" finally galvanized the opposition.

The Democrats were heard from immediately after the news conference. Wright said that "There has never been an Administration that has demanded to dictate so completely to the Congress. . . . I don't know what it will take to satisfy them. We elected Mr. Reagan as President. We did not coronate Mr. Stockman as king."[107] Richard Bolling, the chairman of the House Rules Committee, used even stronger language: "This is an incipient tyranny," he declared. "A popular President is attempting to tyrannize a whole Congress, a whole people." Most significant, conservative Democrats who had previously been allies of the Republicans in the battle of the budget began to have second thoughts after Reagan's offensive. Said one of them after what was described as a "stormy" meeting with Congressman Gramm, "Many of us are senior members of those committees [under presidential attack], and had a major voice in making those cuts. We told Mr. Gramm that we were tired of being manipulated by the White House."[108]

President Reagan recognized almost immediately that in attacking O'Neill, he made a mistake. He took prompt steps to make amends. "I am going to call the Speaker," said the president one day later. "He and I have a good relationship and I want it to continue."[109]

Reagan also had to decide what to do about the "budget substitute" he mentioned, which the administration referred to as Gramm-Latta II. As its name implied, Gramm-Latta II was a substitute reconciliation measure designed to be yet another for or against single vote on a Reagan budget. (It also carved out nearly $20 billion more in savings over the next three years.) The main purpose of the new bill was to circumvent Democrats who, in the opinion of the White House, were promulgating cuts that were specious and unworkable.

On June 17 a member of the president's staff drafted a memo for him that summarized the arguments pro and con for going ahead with Gramm-Latta II. Perhaps the main reason for backing the bill, the memo suggested, was momentum: "If we are successful with Gramm-Latta II, the perception of your leadership and commitment will be strengthened, the traditional House Democratic leadership will be weakened and the prospects of building upon the new bipartisan coalition will be enhanced." The memo also made it clear that a loss would be costly: "The votes for Gramm-Latta II are not there now, and it will take a major effort to get them . . . the strategy is risky. If it does not succeed, it will play as a major Administration loss—with an associated loss of momentum that could have adverse effects on other elements of your program."[110]

Reagan made his decision the next morning. He would go all out on behalf of Gramm-Latta II. Since the vote was to be held within less than a week, expendable items on the president's schedule were cleared to allow him to do the personal politicking necessary for Gramm-Latta II to have a chance of passing.

First, President Reagan issued a statement expressing his support for "a bipartisan amendment that would fulfill the commitment of the original Gramm-Latta resolution. . . . Let there be no doubt: We can and we will put a stop to the fiscal joy ride in Washington."[111] Next, he sent telegrams to all 253 legislators who had voted with him on Gramm-Latta I, "urgently" seeking their support again. Then, on a stop in San Antonio en route to Los Angeles, the president castigated House Democrats as "advocates of a different philosophy, manning the barricades in those puzzle palaces on the Potomac."[112] After that, he labeled as "sabotage" the Democrats' effort to thwart his spending plan by splitting the floor vote on the budget bill into six separate pieces, and thereby requiring members to take public stands on programs popular with various constituencies.[113] In Los Angeles, the president telephoned sixteen swing Democrats and several Republicans, some of them twice. Often the conversation would start out like this: "I know you're in a difficult spot, and getting a lot of pressure, but. . ." When the response was positive, Reagan would sometimes close by saying, "Well, God bless you."[114]

This telephone campaign went on late into the evening of June 24, and began again the next morning when the procedural vote was to be taken. Dozens of Republicans did their part by delaying floor consideration of the budget, thereby giving the president extra time on the phone.

Of course, the conversations were not limited to amenities. By all accounts, there was last minute dealmaking, with the president promising to support legislation in which individual members were especially interested. Said Jim Jones, "They're making deals like crazy in the cloakroom. It's like a tobacco auction back there."[115]

Congressman W. J. Tauzin, a Democrat from Louisiana, was among those who received a presidential call. When Tauzin told the president that he was concerned about the sugar price support program the administration had previously opposed, Reagan promised to reverse his position and work for its adoption. Then the president urged Tauzin to "get back on the floor and work all this out."[116] Another House member, Texas Democrat Charles Wilson, reported that he and four other Texas Democrats had been called at a party given by Texas Utilities. According to Wilson, the president asked him, "Is there anything you're really interested in that you'd like to talk about?" Wilson continued, "He asked me to stick with him. He said he knew my vote was a difficult one because I was less conservative than the others. He said that this was the only chance we had to keep his economic recovery program. He was very cordial and nice."[117]

In the clutch, then, the president relied without apparent hesitation on a persuasive combination of personal appeals, trading of favors, and compromise. Moderate Republicans were cut off at the pass by concessions on Medicare. Southern Democrats were rewarded with administration support for an expensive sugar support program that Stockman in fact considered a scandal, and with a sympathetic White House ear concerning their interest in the Fuel Use Act. Obviously such trade-offs were considered worth the cost. Several billion dollars of additional budget reductions required making some concessions on principle. As Deputy White House Press Secretary Larry Speakes blandly told reporters covering the president in Los Angeles, "Compromise is part of the political process."[118] There were "interests some members may have had" and "we were accommodating to them."[119]*

Although Stockman insisted at the time that there were no "deals made," the difference was a matter of semantics. Stockman did acknowledge that Reagan was briefed before each of his telephone calls on what issues the representative might care about. "Obviously you don't call people cold," Stockman said. The president "ought to know where the latest heartburn item is." The budget director also conceded that some "adjustments and considerations" had been granted by President Reagan adding that ever since the unveiling of the budget plan there had been hundreds of adjustments made at meetings. It was just that "a few occurred at the last minute . . . because that was the end of the tunnel."[121]

All that work paid off. Of the 16 Democrats whom President Reagan phoned, 11 finally voted in his favor on the all-important procedural issue. The House voted 217 to 210 to reject the attempt by the Democratic leadership to split the president's budget request into six separate votes. Reagan was exultant. When he first heard the news, he exclaimed, "Oh my God! You've got the news on the House vote. I just can't believe it."[122] A little later, the president told an audience of 500 in Los Angeles, "I've never felt better in these last five months than I feel in this particular moment today."[123]

*One of the Louisiana Democrats who won concessions on the sugar support program, was less euphemistic. "I went with the best deal," he said. When a reporter asked whether this meant that the congressman's vote could be bought, he responded: "No. It can be rented."[120]

But later that day, President Reagan returned to the phones. "Running scared" once again, the president made yet another seven calls to Democratic congressman on behalf of his proposed budget cuts. The next day, after a tumultuous session—Barrett called it "an orgy of bargaining and last minute amendments"[124]—the House gave President Reagan a victory on the budget by a margin of six votes. Since the Republican-controlled Senate had already adopted the Reagan budget, all that was left was for a Senate–House conference to work out the details.

It was understood at the time that it would take weeks, months, and even years to determine the full impact of what the president and the Congress had wrought with their new budget. But, as the following editorial comment from *The New York Times* suggests, the level of President Reagan's political skill was no longer in question.

> In one enormous sweep, [Mr. Reagan] has bent hundreds of laws in his ideological direction. And he has proved that the Presidency remains a pre-eminent force, provided only that its occupant knows how to combine an election victory with a sense of executive priority and bargaining skill.[125]

The Practice of Leadership

In none of the six cases discussed in this book was the opposition weaker than in this one, a point of no mean significance. But would the Democrats have been tractable in early 1981 with any Republican at the helm? Or was there something about Ronald Reagan in particular that produced compliance?

That the Democrats—especially the Democratic leadership—were unusually cooperative with Republicans in early 1981 is almost unquestioned. Their atypical quiescence was noticed from the beginning. In February, *The New York Times* worried that the Democrats were failing to articulate "general social values." In March, the paper noted that although Wright had warned his colleagues not to be "supine," neither "he nor anyone else on the Hill has thus far risen to the occasion."[126] In April, *The New Republic* accused the Democrats of responding to the "Reagan counterrevolution" with two months of "stunned silence."[127] And in May it was observed, again by *The New York Times,* that the Democratic leadership had, throughout the past months, "failed to initiate the kind of lobbying campaign for which the Democrats are famous."[128]

The behavior of key Democrats was indicative of the behavior of the party as a whole. Senate Majority Leader Byrd said that he was going to vote for the Reagan budget because the "people want the President to be given a chance."[129] During the April Easter recess, while White House lobbyists worked, leading Democrats such as O'Neill and Dan Rostenkowski (chairman of the House Ways and Means Committee) took a trip to Australia and New Zealand. On their return, O'Neill took it on himself to all but concede: "I can read Congress and I can read legislators and they go along with the will of the people, and the will of the people is to go along with the President."[130] O'Neill's concessions on legislative scheduling and the slightly peculiar behavior of Democrats on the Senate Budget Committee were further examples of the opposition's failure to resist.

There are at least four different explanations—independent of anything President Reagan actually did—for why the Democrats, as a collective certainly, did not withstand the Reagan revolution.

First, as we have seen, they lacked a leader. No one in a leadership position assumed the part of would-be spoiler; and no member of the rank and file was especially keen to be "the first one out of the box" to lay a hand on the president. Second, the budget cuts tended to hit hardest at groups with the least political power, such as the poor. Thus, the political rewards for going against the president were apt to be few, and in any case unlikely to outweigh the costs. Third, the Democrats were not entirely averse to letting the president have his way because if Reagonomics proved to be a disaster, he and his party would take the blame. Finally, more than a few Democrats were content to let the president cut the budget because he was willing to take on an unpleasant job they in fact agreed had to be done. Said one Democratic congressman who voted with Reagan half the time during the first session of the 97th Congress. "I've told many disgruntled Democrats and special interest groups that if you look at the positive side of this, we can go after the waste and better serve the programs and, quite frankly, the needs of the Democratic constituency." Said another Democratic lawmaker, "some of our programs are out of hand and we can't cut them. Reagan can and it will save us."[131]

But if it can be argued that for various reasons the Democrats had a predisposition to go along with the Reagan budget, that does not mean that the president himself was anything other than highly effective. Ronald Reagan was able to get what he wanted when he wanted it because of the nature of the times and the opposition, but also because he did many things right.

Essentially, for Reagan's budget proposal to become law, he faced four different tasks: lining up the side; formulating policy and strategy; selling the policy to the people; and engaging key members of the political elite in two-way influence relationships.

Reagan understood that for a chief executive to do a good job of lining up the side he must inspire loyal and able people to work on his behalf. Consider the examples of Meese and Stockman. Meese had worked with

Reagan in California; thus, while he was not very familiar with government at the federal level he was well acquainted with Reagan's leadership style and with what he would need in the way of staff support and organization direction.

Stockman's place in the sun was equally well deserved. The Director of the Office of Management and Budget was a fount of knowledge on the budget, an adroit and inventive strategist, and a skilled administrator. But to all appearances he was also a fervent and dedicated believer in Reaganomics. Thus, Stockman was remarkably competent, and a tireless proselytizer as well.

Of course, these were only two of the players. White House chief of staff James Baker III was, more than anyone else, responsible for setting and coordinating what turned out to be a highly effective legislative strategy. Max Friedersdorf—described as "smooth," low-keyed," and unflappable"—also did a first-rate job.[132] He arranged nearly 70 Oval Office sessions for key congressmen in Reagan's first 100 days, brought by 60 Democrats during the week before the budget vote, and on three consecutive nights before the big vote, accompanied groups of wavering lawmakers to concerts and the opera.[133]*

The team spirit that Reagan evoked was as impressive as the quality of most of his staff. Both the Executive Office of the President and the cabinet went along eagerly with Reaganomics. Obviously, Meese was careful to recruit only those who could wholeheartedly support Reagan's economic policies. But most of the credit for the internal cohesion must go to Reagan whose private manner was generally conducive to keeping those closest to him committed and in line. One is struck by the contrast in this regard between Reagan and two of his predecessors: Nixon and Carter. Nixon fought for the Family Assistance Plan against the opposition of his own vice president and most of his cabinet. Carter, by excluding his own team from almost the entire policy planning process, failed to instill in them the sense of shared mission that he might have otherwise.

Interestingly, President Reagan appears to have left a good part of task number two, the formulation of policy and strategy, for others to accomplish. Like Lyndon Johnson, he did chart the overall course and made the big policy decisions. But the detail work was left to others (especially Stockman). As Fred Greenstein writes, Reagan's strength "has been less in work-

---

*Reagan was also helped immeasurably by the strong performances of party allies in the legislative branch, especially Senate Majority Leader Baker and House Minority Leader Michel. "Their ability to maintain a majority in the Senate and remarkable unity among Republicans in the House lessened the administration's task of achieving winning coalitions and acceptable conference reports."[134]

ing with his aides to clarify policy, than in rallying them around him and his policies."[135]

Yet Reagan went further than Johnson: He left to others not only policy details, but also many of the major strategic decisions. Of course, all administration strategy was designed to further Reaganomics and to that extent, Reagan's was the guiding hand. But when it came to figuring out the specifics of what needed to be done and how to do it, Reagan was frequently content to delegate.

Reagan's aides were especially sensitive to the role of psychology in the political process. For example, their concern in the early months with maintaining momentum reflected their conviction that since the budget cuts were certain to provoke a good deal of resistance, the honeymoon period offered the best opportunity for legislative success.

A second strategy intended to gain psychological advantage—and this was one that Reagan himself confirmed on more than one occasion—was to be bold, assertive, and firm rather than timid and yielding. Buoyed in the beginning by advantages such as a convincing electoral mandate and a Republican majority in the Senate, and later by the effectiveness of Reagan's media appearances, as well as his full-speed-ahead optimism and self-confidence, the Reagan team saw little reason to compromise when it did not absolutely have to. When a "miscalculation" was revealed, the president simply ordered up to $6 billion more cut from the budget. When Jim Jones's House Budget Committee generated a Democratic alternative, the administration promptly rejected it. "Because [the alternative Democratic budget] gave the Administration at least 75 percent of what it wanted, Jones was very surprised [when] the Republicans opposed his proposal so strongly," recalled the committee's chief counsel. "But they apparently thought they could get more momentum for the later battles, especially taxes, from a total victory,"[136] Reagan's posture was similarly aggressive on the matter of Gramm-Latta II. Although he was advised that the votes "are not there now," and that if he failed, "it will play as a major Administration loss," the president nevertheless took the risk and pushed for passage.

Still another psychological ploy was to have the president communicate a dramatic break with the past. This was accomplished both substantively and stylistically. At the very start of the Reagan administration, the White House issued several decrees intended to reaffirm the new order—a freeze on federal hiring, for example, and mandates to cut certain costs and purchases. Reagan also chose to make a clear distinction between himself and his immediate predecessor on a personal level. By being ingratiating and accessible even before his inauguration, Reagan promptly showed the political elite that he was very different from Jimmy Carter.

James Baker led in formulating the substantive aspects of Reagan's political strategy. As former chief of staff for George Bush, he knew his way around Washington, and therefore quickly became unofficial head of an informal assembly of White House aides known as the Legislative Strategy Group. Baker's office thus coordinated administration efforts in the battle of the budget and assumed overall responsibility for shepherding the cuts through the Congress.

Broadly speaking, the administration's legislative strategy had four parts. The first was to whip rank-and-file Republicans into effective and loyal partisans. This was accomplished with remarkable success through the good work of Senator Baker and Congressman Michel, and by White House intervention whenever necessary and appropriate.

The second was to wean as many Democrats as possible away from the party fold. This was carried out by securing bipartisan support for the major budget bills, by having the president intervene with private and personal appeals, and by generating strong public suport that, in turn, "provided designated Democrats [and others] with the excuse they needed to vote for the administration's bill and remain in sympathy with the people who had elected them."[137] Less frequently, Democratic party contributors were contacted and urged to use their influence to persuade Democratic Congressmen to back the president's program.

The third part of the overall legislative strategy was to stay—despite all the talk of a Reagan "revolution"—close enough to the middle of the road. One of the central calculations of the budget plan was that those programs with large and politically active constituencies would escape the deepest slashes of the budget knife. Hence, the decision to exclude from immediate reductions seven basic social programs.

Finally, the administration tried wherever possible to exploit the law to its own advantage. The decision to have Gramm-Latta attach reconciliation instructions to the first budget resolution rather than only to the second, as previously, was a striking example of how the Reagan administration used several different channels to attain legislative success.

As we have seen, President Reagan almost single-handedly took on the task of selling his product to the people. Although occasionally—especially during his convalesence—there were pinch-hitters, it was the president whose name became synonymous with a major shift in economic policy, and it was he who took his own case to the American public, tying his success or failure as a leader to passage of the cuts.

In part, his success was the result of his dedication. Domestic economic policy was the issue of overriding importance to the president and, at least during his first year in office, he was almost single-tracked in pursuit of budget and tax cuts. (Reagan's single-mindedness provoked Bolling to complain: "If a President has to fight only one or two battles a year, he's very unlikely to lose. It makes the contest into a no-contest."[138])

Reagan's ability to gain support for his program must be explained as well by his skill as an educator, as a mobilizer of public opinion. Political scientist Norman Ornstein writes that in contrast to Carter

> Reagan carefully marshalled his television appearances to promote his policies. Each was dramatic, and each was followed only a short time later by a key congressionl vote. . . . The chances for success after each public appeal were enhanced, too, by a sophisticated and hard-nosed grass-roots campaign in the districts of wavering congressmen. . . . Reagan did not naively overrely on a spontaneous response.[139]

Thus, Reagan managed to create a widespread impression—among lawmakers as well as the press—of his own competence as a communicator.* He spoke to America via the tube, a medium of which he was past master; he readily met with people from all walks of political life; and he seduced the press into "a lot of kissy journalism."

Most of the time, President Reagan skillfully avoided the hard sell. His speeches were firm but not abrasive, persuasive without seeming to be hostile. He spoke of cooperation rather than conflict, of cutting waste instead of funds, of protecting the truly needy while at the same time attending to what really had to be done. Above all, his message relied on the power of positive thinking. President Reagan seemed convinced that if only we followed where he led, everything would turn out just fine.

Reagan's final task was to engage key policy makers in two-way influence relationships. The main actors in this particular drama were the president on the one hand, and moderate Republicans and conservative Democrats on the other. Once again, a president's political skills would be tested by the extent of his ability to deliver swing votes into his own column.

Reagan's special genius was that he managed to be, at once, ingratiating and persuasive. In terms of interpersonal influence in the American political culture, that constitutes a rare and powerful combination.

One of the key elements of being an ingratiating political leader is the obvious enthusiasm one brings to the leadership task. Ronald Reagan was glad to make himself available. He issued a standing order to his legislative assistants: "Tell me who you want me to call and I'll do it."[141] According to one aide, he was "willing to do pretty much what Max [Friedersdorf] recommended."[142] Once again, the contrast between Reagan and his immediate predecessor was particularly striking. Some House members claimed

---

*Greenstein makes the point that in the case of a rhetorically gifted president, the political elite is prone to observe how he makes his appeals to the public "and intuiting that a presentation they feel *should* have been effective must have been." In other words, success in this area depends as much on perception as on fact.

that they had seen more of Reagan in four months than they had of Carter in four years. During his first 100 days in office Reagan held meetings with congressman in which 467 members participated.[143] Several times he went over to Capitol Hill for such meetings, and twice he addressed the nation from there. He was especially receptive to greeting friends of the administration, for example, business groups and trade associations. "Before the president goes on television," noted one official from the White House public liaison office, "we first bring in our allies. He meets with them in private—several hundred at a time. He gives them an advance view of what he is going to do so that they can alert their allies to be prepared to go."[144]

But it was not just the quantity of Reagan's interpersonal activity that was impressive. It was the quality as well. He made it a point to avoid most of the dirty work, to leave much of the deal making and arm twisting to others. For example, Reagan's lieutenants threatened wavering Republicans with withholding campaign support in 1982. At the same time, Reagan knew how to flatter and how to make an appeal. "Repeatedly and deftly, even while criticizing Democrats, Mr. Reagan fed the insatiable congressional appetite for praise and respect."[145] One congressman who served during both the Carter and Reagan administrations recalled a meeting with Carter on proposed legislation: "We had hardly got seated and Carter started lecturing us about the problems he had with one of the sections of the bill. He knew the details better than most of us, but somehow that caused more resentment than if he had left the specifics to us." In his meeting with Reagan, the congressman reported that he was in the Oval Office for only "a couple of minutes, but I didn't feel rushed and I'm not quite sure how I was shown the door. A photographer shot the usual roll of pictures; the president gave me a firm, friendly handshake. He patted me on the back and told me how much he needed and appreciated my support. He said that I should call if I needed anything."[146]

Reagan was also adroit at small gift-giving. The flavor of these exchanges was captured in a cartoon that showed a mythical congressman dressed as a money-clutching greedy kid and boasting, "I voted for the President's budget and got these cufflinks, a White House tour and tickets to the Kennedy Center. I think the President's program is really neat-o."[147]

But all in all, it seems that Reagan's uncommonly pleasant manner was what won him so much support. Reagan is the type who might well have been voted "most popular" in high school. He is upbeat, decent to people he meets, charming, and quite funny. "He's cutting the heart out of the American dream to own a home and have a good job and still he's popular," once observed Speaker O'Neill. "He's always got a disarming story. . . . I don't know where he gets them but he's always got them, stories about the World Series, football games, everything. 'Tip, you and I are political enemies only until 6 o'clock. It's 4 o'clock now. Can we pretend it's 6 o'clock?'"[148]

The meeting between Reagan and Congressman Rinaldo is a perfect example of what worked so well. Reagan made a few gentle jokes that grew out of Rinaldo's concerns in particular; he poked fun at his own relatively advanced age; he minimized the significance of what he was asking the Congressman to do while promising to help him with his problems; and he did it all in what was described by Rinaldo later as "an extremely gentlemanly manner."

As we have seen, however, President Reagan also tended to "run scared." Among other things, that meant he was disinclined to depend on good will alone. He recognized the need for compromise, for trading, and for the provision of services. As early as March he was courting key legislators with budget decisions in their favor. For instance, he reversed the judgment of both the previous administration and Stockman by proposing an increase in funds for the Clinch River Breeder Reactor, a project that happened to be in the home state of Senate Majority Leader Howard Baker. Similarly, he rewarded his conservative supporters with proposed steep reductions or even elimination of programs advanced by liberals; the Legal Services Corporation and the Community Service Administration, both vestiges of Johnson's War on Poverty, fell into this target category. Later on—especially in June, when told that the votes were "not there" for Gramm-Latta II—Reagan unhesitatingly resorted to wheeling and dealing in order to get what he wanted. It was the June 25 "tobacco auction" that finally gave the president his victory—but only after he gave an inch or more on medical care, sugar supports, the Fuel Use Act, and no doubt other items yet to be revealed. To repeat the words of administration spokesman Larry Speakes: There were "interests some members may have had," and "we were accommodating to them."

Clearly, then, although Reagan's style was to delegate responsibility, he nevertheless knew how, when the situation required his personal participation, to skillfully employ an impressive array of political tactics. He educated the American people on Reaganomics, giving them the impression that it would reduce inflation, interest rates and taxes, while increasing employment. He gave the political elite advance notice of what he would do by stating his position quite clearly and forcefully during his campaign; and then he immediately and unceasingly followed through precisely as he had promised. He preempted some problems through early consultation and accommodation; he made extensive use of his cabinet and staff; he provided access, amenities, services, and favors; he made scores of personal appeals—in writing, on the phone, and in person; he compromised—but only late in the game, in private, and as absolutely necessary; he generated what was perceived to be strong public support; and he managed through-out to remain both impressive and appealing.

As the use of such a variety of political tactics would suggest, the president employed every available method of influence, and drew on each of his three sources of power—instrumental, authoritative, and libidinal—during his first months in office. He got followers to accept his attempts at influence by controlling their environment, persuading them that he had something to offer, providing them with material and political benefits, and presenting himself at the same time as a very appealing fellow with a stock of one-liners to boot.

The result of all this skilled political activity was no less than a change in direction of American government. Ornstein observes that by the end of the Carter administration, "generalizations had multiplied about the inability of *any* president to get things through Congress or to get our hidebound political system to act. Ronald Reagan forced us to erase . . . those generalizations. He dominated the agenda and the outcomes in Congress during much of the year, in a fashion comparable only to the first years of Franklin Roosevelt and of Lyndon Johnson."[149] Another political scientist, Bruce Russett, explored the existence of a trade-off over the last thirty years between military expenditures and social spending. He concluded that there was no systematic trade-off between the two and that, during this same period, there was no significant depressing effect on health and education expenditures by Republican administrations. Thus, the Reagan administration, under which there were "major increases in military spending and major cuts in health and education spending, emerges as exceptional." In sum, it was not "merely the presence of a Republican in the White House which made the difference, the *Reagan* presidency *is* different."[150]

It has been said that after two decades during which the American presidency has been under more or less constant attack—by bullets, jungle wars, corruption, and defeats at the polls—the people, the press, and the political elite were eager to have a chief executive emerge from at least one full term in office healthy and untarnished. In that sense, it was Ronald Reagan's good fortune to enter the national political arena at a propitious moment. Yet to his credit, he brought to the presidency both remarkable personal qualities and a readiness to employ a wide array of political tactics. The following extraordinary (if backhanded) compliments from two of the most powerful Democrats of the 1970s and 1980s make the point. In a diary kept in 1981, Jim Wright recorded the following:

> [Reagan's] philosophical approach is superficial, overly simplistic, one-dimensional. . . . Yet so far the guy is making it work. Appalled by what

seems to me a lack of depth, I stand in awe nonetheless of his political skill. I am not sure that I have seen its equal.[151]

And in a moment of exasperation later on in the Reagan presidency. O'Neill, asked whether the current occupant of the Oval Office was capable of a cynical trick on immigration policy, snapped, "He's the most political man I've seen there."[152]

The fact is that Ronald Reagan, the ultimate marketing personality,* is a consummate politician. He is a natural at tapping into the American national character, at appearing to be both democratic and friendly. It is relatively easy for him, therefore, to soften our resistance to leadership, and to sell himself and his ideas in the political marketplace. Of how many others in this book can it be said that they were able to drive a "velvet steamroller" through the Congress, and "flatten" their opponents in such a way that it was "almost painless"?

---

*Remember Fromm's claim that the "most important means of transmitting the desired personality pattern to the average man is the motion picture."

Epilogue

Presidents who benefit from a large electoral victory, party majorities in Congress, and a high level of public confidence will surely be able to lead more easily than those who lack such capital. Yet presidents *with* political capital do not necessarily know how to use it, and those *without* such advantages are not completely helpless.

As we have seen, skilled political activity goes a long way toward maximizing the capital the president has, and toward compensating for its relative absence. An array of political tactics can be used by any president with the will and skill to do so; instrumental, authoritative, and libidinal resources are available to any president motivated to draw on them.

Indeed, because leadership in America is difficult at best, political presidents will under any circumstances have an inestimable advantage: the capacity for overcoming in others the resistance to followership. Thus, political presidents are more likely to accomplish the four tasks essential to directive leadership: assembling a team both competent and committed; directing that team to develop policy and implement strategy; creating a favorable national climate; and engaging the political elite in two-way influence relationships so that policy becomes law.

If we can agree that politicking is important, we should disabuse ourselves once and for all of the notion that politics is, almost by definition, dirty. George Reedy once observed that "logrolling" is a "perjorative phrase we apply to the give-and-take process of democracy"—whereupon he settled for a much drearier description of how government works: "accommodation of different points of view."[1] But it is precisely our proclivity for sanitizing what does not need sanitizing that perpetuates the myth that the politician's trade is somehow sullied. We should not shy from terms such as "logrolling," "horse trading," "wheeling and dealing" or "dealmaking." For they merely address, inelegantly perhaps, the idea that politics in America—leadership in America—distills to influence relationships. In fact, Reedy acknowledged as much. Of Lyndon Johnson, Reedy wrote: "He knew as well as anyone that power in Washington, D.C. consists of horse-trading in commodities of political value. . . . Presidents trade in favors, in appropriations, in the distribution of the 'goodies' that are part of national management, and in the fantastic capacity of the White House to enhance egos."[2]

The trading of favors that Johnson managed so adroitly took place, of course, primarily vis-à-vis members of the political elite. One of the central arguments of this book has been that presidents benefit from having other-directed manners precisely because, in order to govern, they must negotiate with those who constitute what Nelson Polsby recently called the "inter-mediate layer"—members of Congress, state and local officials, labor lead-ers, business leaders, interest group leaders and the like.[3] How, then, can we try to ensure that future presidents have the capacity to engage in the requisite politicking?

Polsby suggests that party reform is the answer, for he argues (as I also have[4]) that the current system of presidential selection encourages candi-dates—and, later, presidents—to diminish the importance of the political elite. The idea of a political party as a coalition of interests and groups bound together by many sorts of ties is fast becoming an anachronism, Polsby notes. "Achieving financial support through mass mailings and through the public purse has displaced in importance the mobilizing of well-heeled backers and the seeking of alliances with territorially identifi-able interest groups and state party organizations." Similarly, "the stimu-lation of coverage by the mass media and the building of personal organi-zations state by state ... have been replacing dependence upon party regulars and state and local party leaders."[5] Thus, the candidates have little experience in, and even less motivation to engage in, the one-to-one kind of interpersonal activity that is the essence of politicking and, as I have argued, of leadership in America.

This leaves us with two obvious remedies. The first, as Polsby suggests, is party reform to change the presidential nominating process. But until that is accomplished, and the results are what we expect them to be, we should in any case proceed with the second alternative: careful study of the candidates' past performances with specific attention to their political skills.

The recommendation that we evaluate candidates in part on the basis of their capacity to engage in two-way influence relationships brings us finally to the question of what the ideal "political president" would look like. Throughout this book I have emphasized the fact that because the success-ful interpersonal actor in American tends to be outgoing and responsive, the effective politician would have to behave similarly. Indeed, other-directed manners are especially functional in a country that is remarkable for its heterogeneity, and for the special value it places on individualism and egalitariansim. Who better than someone sensitive to the needs and opinions of others to forge a majority—build a coalition—where there is none?

But, as we have seen, other-directedness is not enough. Gerald Ford was other-directed, but he was at least partially responsible for what he himself considered a political failure. Thus, the political president represents a departure from Riesman's typology. That person is an amalgam: other-directed in manners, but with the strong conviction and sense of direction that characterizes the inner-directed type. At least insofar as the case studies in this book are concerned, the best politicians, and the most effective directive leaders, were Lyndon Johnson and Ronald Reagan. Both were other-directed in the behavior and inner-directed in their rather fierce determination to see a very particular policy become law.

Finally, I would like to extoll the tie between leadership and politics in America. It is a virtue that presidential leadership depends so heavily on securing the cooperation of others; there is merit to a system that tends to stall unless the governor consents to negotiate with representatives of the governed. At its considerable best, politics admits change while at the same time imposing on our public life an order in keeping with the democratic ideal that power be shared. Similarly, the wellspring of presidential leadership is the exchange between the leader and those who would speak for the led.

Notes

Preface

1. *The New York Times,* January 8, 1981.
2. This was the opinion of James Fallows in a generally critical article titled "The Passionless Presidency," *Atlantic,* May, 1979, p. 34.
3. Andrew S. McFarland also writes about routine leadership. But McFarland fails to distinguish between routine leadership in routine situations and non-routine, or innovative, leadership in routine situations. That is, some decisions in routine situations involve much more than "incremental changes on a previously existing policy base." See McFarland's *Power and Leadership in Pluralist Systems,* Stanford, 1969, p. 170.
4. Originally published in 1960 by John Wiley & Sons.
5. Thomas Cronin, *The State of the Presidency,* Boston, 1980, p. 124.
6. Exceptions to this rule have been some of the biographies. See, for example, Fred Greenstein, *The Hidden-Hand Presidency: Eisenhower as Leader,* New York, 1982.
7. Aristotle's view of "the political" actually implies both science and art. "'Politics' is the scientific study of the *polis,* and of all things political, *with a view to political action* or the proper exercise of the political 'art'." Ernest Baker (ed.), *The Politics of Aristotle,* New York, 1969, p. 355.

1. Leadership in America

1. Daniel J. Boorstin notes that the worship of George Washington acquired a full cultic apparatus only between his death "in the last month of the last year of the 18th century and the outbreak of the Civil War." For the details on how this mythologizing was accomplished, see Boorstin's *The Americans: The National Experience,* New York, 1965, pp. 337–356.
2. See quote of Ralph Henry Gabriel in Donald J. Devine, *The Political Culture of the United States,* Boston, 1972, p. 126.
3. Boorstin, p. 328.
4. See, for example, Sigmund Freud, *Moses and Monotheism,* New York, 1939; Joseph Campbell, *Hero With a Thousand Faces,* Princeton, N.J., 1949; Lionel Tiger and Robin Fox, *The Imperial Animal,* New York, 1971.
5. For an elaboration of the concept of political culture see especially Gabriel Almond and Sidney Verba, *The Civic Culture: Political Attitudes and Democracy in Five Nations,* Princeton, N.J., 1963; and Lucian Pye and Sidney Verba (eds.), *Political Culture and Political Development,* Princeton, N.J., 1965. For a more contemporary discussion, see Devine, Chapter 1 and passim.

6. Erich Fromm, *Escape From Freedom*, New York, 1941, p. 305.
7. But for an excellent discussion on how even our more distant past was woven through the eighteenth and nineteenth centuries, see Louis Hartz's seminal *The Liberal Tradition in America*, New York, 1955. Hartz refers to the "master assumption of American political thought" as the "reality of atomistic social freedom" (p. 62).
8. Bernard Bailyn, *The Ideological Origins of the American Revolution*, Cambridge, Mass., 1967, pp. 302–4.
9. The quotes up to this point in the paragraph are from *ibid.*, p. 304.
10. *Ibid.*, pp. 304–18.
11. *Ibid.*, p. 306.
12. *Ibid.*, p. 319.
13. *Ibid.*, p. 319.
14. The phrase is Max Lerner's. See his *America as a Civilization*, New York, 1957, p. 718.
15. Alexander Hamilton, *The Federalist Papers*, New York, 1961, p. 423.
16. *Ibid.*, p. 422.
17. Devine, p. 143.
18. Michael Kammen, *People of Paradox: An Inquiry Concerning the Origins of American Civilization*, New York, 1972, p. 54.
19. Lerner, p. 718.
20. Alexis de Tocqueville, *Democracy in America*, New York, 1969, p. 430. James MacGregor Burns has written that Tocqueville underplayed the extent of inegalitarianism in America because of the "tendency of economic inequality to be tempered and cushioned, in both appearance and substance." For more on Tocqueville in Jacksonian America, see Burns's *The Vineyard of Liberty*, New York, 1982.
21. Samuel Huntington, *American Politics: The Promise of Disharmony*, Cambridge, Mass., 1981, p. 4.
22. *Ibid.*, p. 33.
23. Hartz, p. 111.
24. For a discussion of entrepreneurial behavior, and further insight into the fit between this behavior and a culture that idealizes freedom from conventional authority, see David C. McClelland, *The Achieving Society*, Princeton, N.J., 1961, pp. 205ff.
25. For how those who are not, in fact, autonomous, fulfill the American "dream of autonomous work," see Richard Sennett and Jonathan Cobb, *The Hidden Injuries of Class*, New York, 1972, especially Chapter V. Also see Milton Friedman's classic *Capitalism and Freedom*, Chicago, 1962.
26. Leon Sampson, "Americanism as Surrogate Socialism" in John H. M. Laslett and Seymour Martin Lipset (eds.), *Failure of a Dream?*, New York, 1974, p. 428. For a related essay on "The Frontier West as Image of American Society," see Rush Welter, *The Mind of America 1820–1860*, New York, 1975, pp. 298–328.
27. In 1979, on a scale of one to ten, the public gave the past an average rating of 6.47, the present a 4.83, and the future a 4.31. By 1983 the figures were, in turn, 5.48, 5.58, and 6.13. In *The New York Times*, January 1, 1984.
28. Richard Reeves, *American Journey: Traveling with Tocqueville in Search of Democracy in America*, New York, 1982, p. 350. Reeves argues that the main reason why we are paying less attention than ever to our political leaders is

that they no longer have exclusive access to information. With the technological revolution came an era in which everyone could know everything.

29. John Gardner, "The Antileadership Vaccine," Carnegie Foundation Report, 1965.

30. The *Gallup Opinion Index*, Political, Social and Economic Trends, No. 99, September, 1973, p. 8.

21. "Leadership: The Biggest Issue" in *Time*, November 8, 1976.

32. The *Gallup Report*, Political, Social and Economic Trends, No. 192, September, 1981, p. 3.

33. Bruce Miroff, "After Consensus: The Dilemmas of Contemporary American Leadership" in *Presidential Studies Quarterly*, Summer, 1981, p. 416.

34. David Broder, *Changing of the Guard: Power and Leadership in America*, New York, 1981.

35. Aaron Wildavsky, "The New Establishment?" in *New York Times Book Review*, August 31, 1980.

36. Broder, p. 72.

37. *Ibid.*, p. 122.

38. *Ibid.*, p. 76. For more on independence in Congress, see Richard Fenno, "What's He Like? What's She Like? What Are They Like?" in Dennis Hale (ed.), *The United States Congress*, Chestnut Hill, 1982, pp. 107–25.

39. *Ibid.*, pp. 483, 474.

40. Kammen, p. 305.

41. *Ibid.*, p. 291.

42. Lerner, p. 377.

43. Godfrey Hodgson writes: "If there is a shortage of leadership it is because people do not want to be led: they only want many things that only leadership can give them" (*All Things to All Men*, New York, 1980, p. 246). And Richard Reeves reported that "the Americans I met called for leadership, but were not willing to delegate that much to representatives or 'leaders' anymore" (p. 351).

2. Presidential Leadership

1. Andrew S. McFarland, "Role and Role Conflict" in Aaron Wildavsky, *The Presidency*, Boston, 1969, p. 3.

2. Hans Gerth and C. Wright Mills, *Character and Social Structure*, New York, 1953, p. 416.

3. *Ibid.*, p. 417.

4. Clinton Rossiter, *The American Presidency*, New York, 1956, pp. 14–40.

5. These are Cronin's terms in Thomas Cronin, *The State of the Presidency*, Boston, 1980, pp. 145–53.

6. The list is from Cronin, *Ibid.* p. 155.

7. The point is Jackson W. Toby's, quoted in McFarland, "Role and Conflict" p. 6.

8. *Ibid.*, pp. 6ff.

9. *Ibid.*, pp. 10ff.

10. The terms "role determined" and "role-determining" leaders Gerth and Mills, *Character and Social Structure*, p. 420.

11. James G. Hunt and Richard Osborn, "Toward a Macro-O Leadership," James G. Hunt et al., *Leadership: Beyond E Carbondale Ill.*, 1981, p. 201.

12. Richard M. Pious, *The American Presidency*, New York, 1979, p. 16.
13. *Ibid.*, p. 17.
14. Richard Neustadt, *Presidential Power*, New York, 1960, p. 33.
15. Paul Light, *The President's Agenda*, Baltimore, 1982, p. 14.
16. Neustadt was a believer in strong presidential government. Thus, he wrote his book to instruct on how to maximize presidential (personal) power. As elaborated below, I am less interested in asserting that presidents *ought* to maximize their personal power than in claiming that those who ignore this resource altogether will, necessarily, find their effectiveness impaired.
17. This list represents part of a list of Neustadt's propositions as paraphrased by Cronin, *The State of the Presidency*, p. 124.
18. James David Barber, *The Presidential Character*, Englewood Cliffs, N.J., 1977, p. 12.
19. Erwin Hargrove, *The Power of the Modern Presidency*, Philadelphia, 1974, p. 78.
20. This is a partial list from Ron K. Price and Rocco C. Siciliano (eds.), *A Presidency for the 1980s*, Washington, D.C., 1980.
21. Lerner, p. 377.
22. Tocqueville, *Democracy in America*, New York, 1969, p. 641.
23. Andrew S. McFarland, *Power and Leadership in Pluralist Systems*, Stanford, 1969, p. 177. For a discussion of whether America is more properly seen in terms of dialectical or multilateral conflict, see McFarland, pp. 177ff. Also see Charles Lindblom, "Another State of Mind," *American Political Science Review*, March, 1982, pp. 9–12. My use of the multilateral conflict model is not meant to suggest that I subscribe to the pluralist view of American life. It does no more than reflect my perception that the president, in any case, must cope with multilateral conflict.
24. *Ibid.*, p. 219.
25. Edwin P. Hollander, *Leadership Dynamics*, New York, 1978, p. 2.
26. *Ibid.*, p. 7.
27. In Cecil A. Gibb, "Leadership," in Gardner Lindzey and Eliot Aronson (eds.), *The Handbook of Social Psychology*, Reading, Mass., 1969, Volume IV, p. 212.
28. James MacGregor Burns, *Leadership*, New York, 1978, pp. 4, 19.
29. *Ibid.*, p. 4.
30. Dorwin Cartwright and Alvin Zander, *Group Dynamics*, New York, 1968, p. 224. On this also see Toni Falbo, "Multidimensional Scaling of Power Strategies," in *Journal of Personality and Social Psychology*, August, 1977, p. 545.
31. This section on methods of influence is taken in large part from Cartwright and Zander, *Group Dynamics*, pp. 220–23.
Falbo, "Scaling of Power Strategies," pp. 541ff.
Sigmund Freud, *Group Psychology and the Analysis of the Ego*, New York, 59.
tz in Cartwright and Zander, *Group Dynamics*, p. 226.
, *Leadership*, p. 254.
"Dependency Needs," the list of motivations affecting the follow- to comply with influence attempts is also from Cartwright and Dynamics, pp. 224–27.

37. For more on power see David G. Winter, *The Power Motive,* New York, 1973, p. 5.

38. See, for example, John R. P. French, Jr., and Bertram Raven, "The Bases of Social Power," in Cartwright and Zander, *Group Dynamics,* pp. 259–69.

39. This list is from Peter W. Sperlich, "Bargaining and Overload: An Essay on *Presidential Power,*" in Wildavsky, *The Presidency,* pp. 168–93.

40. As this paragraph suggests, I do not find Light's division of power resources into internal and external ones all that useful. We are talking, after all, about how the president gets others to go along. To this end, all his resources form a single pool from which the executive draws in different ways—depending on what might motivate others to follow.

41. For an elaboration of the distinctions between power and influence see Talcott Parsons, *Politics and Social Structure,* New York, 1969, pp. 418ff and McFarland, p. 154.

42. David C. McClelland, *Power: The Inner Experience,* New York, 1975, p. 267.

3. Political Skill in America

1. For the essence of Plunkitt, see George Washington Plunkitt, *Plunkitt of Tammany Hall,* William Riordan (ed.), New York, 1903.

2. *Ibid.,* p. 81.

3. In *The Tampa Tribune,* December 15, 1980.

4. Thomas Cronin, *The State of the Presidency,* Boston, 1980, p. 374.

5. *In Conversation* with Bill Moyers, WNET television, February 27 and March 5, 1981, p. 7 of transcript.

6. Cronin, p. 12.

7. Plunkitt, p. 45.

8. Cronin, p. 12.

9. Louis W. Koenig, *The Chief Executive,* New York, 1981, p. 15.

10. Robert Dahl, "Power," in Aaron Wildavsky, *The Presidency,* Boston, 1969, p. 157.

11. Fairlie, *Tampa Tribune.*

12. Harold J. Laski, *The American Presidency,* New York, 1980, p. 28. I used the same phrase in the Preface.

13. Clifford, *In Conversation.*

14. Some phrases in this sentence are David Riesman's. See his (with Nathan Glazer and Reuel Denney) *The Lonely Crowd,* New Haven, Conn., 1961, p. 4.

15. Quoted in Michael Kammen, *People of Paradox: An Inquiry Concerning the Origins of American Civilization,* New York, 1972, p. xi.

16. *Ibid.,* p. 97.

17. For a discussion of some of the problems with the concept of national character, see Donald J. Devine, *The Political Culture of the United States,* Boston, 1972, pp. 65ff. Devine writes that these problems have been almost exclusively methodological in nature. This is confirmed in a new book by R. A. LeVine titled *Culture, Behavior and Personality,* New York, 1982.

18. LeVine, p. 98.

19. The first quote is Karl Friedrich Moser's in Gordon Craig, *The Germans,* New York, 1982, p. 23. The second quote is Edward Eggleston's and is in Kammen, p. 97.

20. For bibliographies on the subject of American character and civilization, see Kammen, pp. 301, 302, and Max Lerner, *America as a Civilization,* New York, 1957, pp. 958, 959.

21. Alex Inkeles as quoted in Devine, p. 72.

22. For the argument that our political culture especially is essentially unchanged, see Devine, p. 47.

23. Lerner, p. 59.

24. Kammen, p. 290.

25. *Ibid.,* p. 290.

26. *The Lonely Crowd* was originally published in 1950.

27. This paragraph is based on Riesman, *The Lonely Crowd,* pp. 207, 208.

28. Talcott Parsons and Winston White, "The Links Between Character and Society," in Seymour Martin Lipset and Leo Lowenthal (eds.), *Culture and Social Character: The Work of David Riesman Reviewed,* Glencoe, Ill., 1961, p. 95.

29. In Lipset and Lowenthal, *ibid.,* p. 168.

30. "Reconsideration: The Lonely Crowd," in *The New Republic,* March 4, 1972, p. 29.

31. *Ibid.,* pp. 29, 30. See also the essay by Peter I. Rose, "David Riesman Reconsidered," in *Society,* Volume 19, No. 3, March/April, 1982.

32. William H. Whyte, *The Organization Man,* New York, 1956, p. 129.

33. Erich Fromm, *Man for Himself,* New York, 1947, pp. 68–70.

34. *Ibid.,* pp. 71, 72.

35. Lerner, p. 641.

36. I depend on such theoreticians from the 1950s as Riesman, Whyte, Fromm, and Lerner because since then little work has been done in the area of the American national character. This shift is the result of what are regarded as methodological problems in the measurement of national character and, also, changing fashions. LeVine writes: "The field of culture and personality is peculiar in that it attracted a great deal of interest in its early days . . . as an area of importance to anthropolgy, pyschology, education, and psychiatry; [it] generated sound theoretical statements and highly controversial research studies; and then lost the interest of all but those who specialize in one of its topical foci." (p. 285).

37. Lerner, p. 630.

38. Harold Lasswell, *Power and Personality,* New York, 1948, p. 108.

39. The point is made by Ralph Barton Perry. Quoted in Kammen, p. 115.

40. The point is made by Clyde Kluckholn. Quoted in Lipset, "Changing American Character," p. 171.

41. Fromm, *Man for Himself,* p. 79.

Political Skill: Tactics and Requisites

have assembled the following list from Edwards's book (San Francisco, 0, pp. 119–64); Edwards did not himself compile it in the present form.

On the subject of legislative skills also see Stephen J. Wayne, *The Legislative Presidency,* New York, 1978, especially pp. 137–68.

2. I am indebted to Leonard Grob for the concept of the teacher–leader who educates, or leads out.

3. See especially Erving Goffman, *The Presentation of Self in Everyday Life,* New York, 1959. Also see his *Behavior in Public Places* (1963), *Interaction Ritual* (1967), and *Relations in Public* (1971).

4. Edward W. Jones and Camille Wortman, *Ingratiation: An Attributional Approach,* Morristown, N.J., 1973, p. 2.

5. *Ibid.,* p. 3.

6. *Ibid.,* p. 27.

7. Some of this paragraph is based on Michael Kammen, *People of Paradox: An Inquiry Concerning the Origins of American Civilization,* New York, 1972, pp. 165, 291.

8. Larry Wayne Morris, *Extraversion and Introversion: An Interactional Perspective,* New York, 1979, pp. 5, 6. The original work on extraversion and introversion was done by Carl Jung, in *Psychological Types,* London, 1923. During the last three decades Jung's theory was considerably elaborated on by Hans Eysenck, who produced a large body of materials on the subject.

9. *Ibid.,* p. 6.

10. Riesman, *Lonely Crowd,* p. 172.

11. For more on extraverts and introverts in politics, see Barbara Kellerman, "Introversion in the Oval Office," in *Presidential Studies Quarterly,* Spring, 1983, pp. 383–99. Nixon and Carter are used as case studies.

12. Both quotes in this paragraph are from *Who Governs?,* New Haven, Conn., 1960, p. 298.

13. David McClelland, *Power: The Inner Experience,* New York, 1975, p. 267.

14. *Ibid.,* p. 253.

15. *Ibid.,* p. 260.

16. *Ibid.,* p. 263.

17. Robert J. House and Mary L. Baetz, "Leadership: Some Empirical Generalizations and New Research Directions," in *Research in Organizational Behavior,* Vol. 1, 1979, p. 352. The authors also mention the "predisposition to be influential" that I covered earlier.

18. For the details of this survey, see Ross Clayton and William Lammers, "Presidential Leadership Reconsidered: Contemporary Views of Top Federal Officials" in *Presidential Studies Quarterly,* Summer, 1978, pp. 237–45. For further discussion of the same materials see James G. Benze, Jr., "Presidential Skills," in *Presidential Studies Quarterly,* Fall, 1981, pp. 470–78.

5. Presidential Politicking

1. James MacGregor Burns, *Leadership,* New York, 1978, pp. 19, 20.

2. This paragraph is based on Edwin P. Hollander, "Leadership and Social Exchange Processes" in K. J. Gergen et al. (eds), *Social Exchange: Advances in Theory and Research,* New York, 1980, p. 118.

3. The list in this sentence is from Bruce Mazlish. For further exposition on this see his "Leader and Led: Individual and Group, in *The Psychohistory Review,* Spring, 1981, pp. 214–37.

4. Richard Neustadt, *Presidential Power,* New York, 1960, p. 58.
5. The point is made by Bruce Miroff, "Beyond Washington" in *Society,* July/ August, 1980, p. 67.
6. *Ibid.,* p. 68.
7. All the quotes in this paragraph are from Andrew S. McFarland, *Power in Pluralist Systems,* Stanford, 1969, p. 156.
8. *Ibid.,* p. 158.
9. Stephen J. Wayne, *The Legislative Presidency,* New York, 1978, p. 168.
10. *Ibid.,* p. 172.
11. George C. Edwards, III, *Presidential Influence in Congress,* San Francisco, 1980, p. 202.
12. Nor is it necessarily the case that the general types of power sources that come from the social psychological literature are impossible to define operationally; that a concept "such as reward is too broad to reflect the many types of rewards that a president may give"; that one can conclude, without examining the evidence, that "a concept such as referent power . . . is of little value to us because the president rarely has a personal relationship with Congress"; or that the social psychological materials that focus on interpersonal power relations—which is, after all, what the president's attempt to influence Congress is all about—fail, among other things, "to cover sources of indirect power, such as presidential popularity." These arguments are put forth in *ibid,* p. 50.
13. *Ibid.,* p. 190.
14. By basing his case on statistical analyses of roll call votes, Edwards skims over the areas where a president might influence the course of legislation, but where quantitative data is lacking. Political reality is far more complex, and elusive, than his statistical analysis is able to suggest.
15. Paul Light refers to this familiar pattern as the "cycle of decreasing influence." In *The President's Agenda,* Baltimore, 1982, p. 36. Valerie Bunce concludes that particular leaders "do seem to matter when they are in their honeymoons." In *Do New Leaders Make a Difference?,* Princeton, 1981, p. 229.
16. These quotes are taken from Lawrence C. Wrightsman, "The Social Psychology of Presidential Effectiveness," unpublished paper, 1982. I am grateful to Professor Wrightsman for sharing his thinking with me.
17. In a few cases, more than one policy proposal seems to meet these three criteria. Presidents have been known to declare more than one goal "most important." Where there was any doubt about what was in fact the president's highest domestic priority, as in the case of Kennedy perhaps, I made a judgment based on a combination of the president's own words and actions, and the testimony of others. With reference to another methodological decision—when to cut off the discussion of a given case—I also relied on what I trust is a sound combination of objective evidence and common sense. In the cases involving Johnson, Ford, and Reagan, the decision was easy: the story was over several months after it began because the leadership task was, in one way or another, accomplished. In the cases of Kennedy and Nixon, I halted the chronology when it first became clear that it would be difficult if not impossible for them to get what they said they wanted. I made this decision in spite of the fact that both presidents did formally resubmit their "priority" proposals in the next congressional session. In the case of Jimmy

Carter, I followed him on energy for eighteen months, the time it took him to get a compromise energy measure through the Congress.

18. Thomas Cronin, *The State of the Presidency,* Boston, 1980, p. 129. Also see, "A Symposium: Neustadt's *Presidential Power* Twenty Years Later: The Test of Time," in *Presidential Studies Quarterly,* Summer, 1981, pp. 341–63.

19. Two other differences between this book and Neustadt's are: (1) Neustadt seems to imply that the president's personal capacity to influence is all-important. By making a distinction between directive leadership and other kinds of leadership tasks, this book tries hard to refrain from giving such an impression. (2) Neustadt explores an over-arching strategy of influence whereas the interest here is in the use a president does or does not make of variously described *tactics* of influence. My concern is with the nitty-gritty of what actually happens with regard to those policy goals the president himself reports as being the most important.

6. John Kennedy and Federal Aid to Education

1. Tom Wicker, *J.F.K. and L.B.J.: The Influence of Personality on Politics,* New York, 1970, p. 25. Wicker adds that Kennedy also stood for a new minimum wage bill.

2. Theodore Sorensen, *Kennedy,* New York, 1965, p. 358.

3. *Ibid.,* p. 358.

4. Frank Thompson, Oral History Interview, John F. Kennedy Library, p. 18.

5. Hugh Douglas Price, "Schools, Scholarships, and Congressmen: The Kennedy Aid-to-Education Program," in Alan F. Westin (ed.), *The Centers of Power: 3 Cases in American National Government,* New York, 1964, p. 56.

6. Keith Ellison, unpublished 1972 Harvard College paper, on deposit at the John F. Kennedy Library, p. 1.

7. Letter to John Kennedy from Senator Joseph Clark, December 15, 1960, John F. Kennedy Library, Presidential Office Files.

8. Several points in this paragraph are made by Ellison, pp. 1, 2.

9. Wicker, p. 121.

10. Quoted in Price, pp. 56, 57.

11. Feldman File, Presidential Papers, White House Staff, Box 27, John F. Kennedy Library.

12. *The New York Times,* February 11, 1961.

13. *Ibid.,* February 21, 1961. This edition of the *Times* carried the full text of the president's message.

14. *Ibid.*

15. *The New York times,* February 26, 1961.

16. This material on the Everson case is from Harold W. Chase and Allen H. Lerman (eds.), *Kennedy and the Press,* New York, 1965, p. 38; and J. W. Gardner (ed.), *To Turn the Tide: President John F. Kennedy,* New York, 1962, p. 133.

17. *The New York Times,* March 2, 1961.

18. In Price, p. 60.

19. Wicker, pp. 129, 130.

20. *The New York Times,* March 2, 1961.

21. Alter's statement is reprinted in both Price (p. 60) and Wicker (p. 130).

22. Wicker writes that from that moment on, more than a few believed "the Kennedy school bill was dead" (p. 131).
23. Quoted in Price, p. 61.
24. *The New York Times,* March 9, 1961.
25. Wicker labels Kennedy's retreat here as "precipitous," in my opinion too strong a word.
26. Kennedy's possible retreat on the issue of loans to private schools suggested too that certain legal issues remained murky. For an elaboration of this theme see Anthony Lewis, "Constitutional Issue" in *The New York Times,* March 9, 1961.
27. White House Central Files, Box 472, John F. Kennedy Library.
28. Price, p. 64.
29. Quoted in Price, p. 66.
30. Quoted in *The New York Times,* March 14, 1961.
31. Quoted in *The New York Times,* March 15, 1961.
32. Quoted in Price, p. 65.
33. Quoted in *The New York times,* March 17, 1961.
34. Quoted in *The New York Times,* March 18, 1961.
35. *The New York Times,* March 17, 1961.
36. Quoted in Price, p. 65.
37. This correspondence is located in White House Central Files, Box 472 of John F. Kennedy Library.
38. Both O'Donnell letters are in the White House Central Files, Box 98, John F. Kennedy Library. They are dated April 20, 1961, and February 6, 1961, respectively.
39. In Box 472 of *ibid.,* and dated April 12, 1961.
40. In Box 98 of *ibid.,* and dated February 28, 1961.
41. In Box 92 of *ibid.,* and dated April 3, 1961.
42. In Box 98 of *ibid.,* and dated April 12, 1961.
43. In Box 472 of *ibid.,* and dated February 14, 1961.
44. *Ibid.*
45. Box 98 of *ibid.*
46. The events in this paragraph are listed in the President's Appointments Book, January–June, 1961, John F. Kennedy Library. This book constitutes the official schedule.
47. Arthur M. Schlesinger, *A Thousand Days,* Boston, 1965, p. 716.
48. *The New York Times,* March 16, 1961. For more on the conferences also see Harold W. Chase and Allen H. Lerner (eds.), *Kennedy and The Press: The News Conferences,* New York, 1965.
49. *The New York Times,* March 16, 1961.
50. *Ibid.,* March 17, 1961.
51. The term is Price's, p. 64.
52. Price, p. 69.
53. Powell's administrative changes were not the only factors producing conflict. Price writes that the House Education and Labor Committee has long been "notorious for its extreme partisanship, contentious members, bitter conflicts, procedural wrangling, and general lack of influence with the House membership" (p. 62).
54. Both these points were made by Ellison, p. 10.

55. Powell was also black, with a highly visible black constituency. Moreover, Powell's Education and Labor Committee also had to pass on another bill important to Kennedy—minimum wage. So Kennedy had more than one reason to keep Powell happy.
56. President's Appointment's Book, January–June, 1961, John F. Kennedy Library.
57. Presidential Papers, White House Staff File, Box 12, John F. Kennedy Library.
58. *Ibid.*
59. The Februrary 22 memo is from Claude Desautels to Larry O'Brien. In *ibid.*
60. Memo dated February 23, Presidential Office Files, Legislative Files, Box 49, John F. Kennedy Library.
61. Presidential Papers, White House Staff File, Box 12, John F. Kennedy Library.
62. *Ibid.*
63. *Ibid.*
64. From a July 19, 1961 news conference. In Chase and Lerman, p. 99.
65. April 17, 1961.
66. Quoted in *The New York Times,* March 27, 1961.
67. *Ibid.* All the information on lobbying in these paragraphs is from the same *New York Times* article.
68. *The New York Times,* March 29, 1961. For more on the legal questions, see Anthony Lewis's article in *ibid.*
69. Presidential Papers, White House Staff File, Box 20, John F. Kennedy Library.
70. Ellison, p. 15.
71. April 27, 1961.
72. Quoted in Price, p. 73.
73. *Ibid.,* p. 74.
74. *Ibid.,* p. 75.
75. *The New York Times,* May 18, 1961.
76. Price, p. 75.
77. *The New York Times,* May 18, 1966.
78. *Ibid.*
79. *Ibid.,* May 19, 1961.
80. Both letters are in the White House Central Files, Box 472, John F. Kennedy Library.
81. Price, p. 78.
82. May 26, 1961.
83. Price, p. 79.
84. June 9, 1961.
85. *The New York Times,* June 16, 1961.
86. In Price, p. 81, and *The New York Times,* June 21, 1961.
87. *The New York Times,* June 20, 1961.
88. *Ibid.,* June 21, 1961.
89. July 19, 1961.
90. Quoted in Ellison, p. 16.
91. Lawrence F. O'Brien, *No Final Victories,* New York, 1974, p. 127.
92. *The New York Times,* July 20, 1961.

93. In Box 472 of White House Central Files, John F. Kennedy Library.
94. August 2, 1961.
95. Price, p. 82.
96. *The New York Times,* August 13, 1961.
97. *Ibid.,* August 21 and 23, 1961.
98. Sorensen Papers, Box 32, John F. Kennedy Library.
99. August 31, 1961.
100. *Ibid.*
101. Arthur M. Schlesinger, Jr., *A Thousand Days,* Boston, 1965, p. 662.
102. *The New York Times,* January 12, 1962.
103. For an insider's view of the problems involved, see Secretary Ribicoff's long memorandum to the president dated October 6, 1961. Presidential Office Files, John F. Kennedy Library.
104. "It is as a formulator of programs and policies, not as a manager of them, that the presidency has gained power, visibility, and bulk" writes Lester Salamon. See "The Presidency and Domestic Policy Formulation" in Hugh Heclo and Lester Salamon (eds.), *The Illusion of Presidential Government,* Boulder, Col., 1981, p. 199.
105. Wicker, p. 82.
106. "John Kennedy and his Spectators," in *The New Republic,* April 3, 1961.
107. On this see Wicker, p. 139.
108. Gerald W. Johnson, "The Superficial Aspect" in *The New Republic,* September 18, 1961.
109. In Helen Fuller, *Year of Trial: Kennedy's Crucial Decisions,* New York, 1962, p. 101.
110. Quoted by Ellison, p. 26.
111. O'Brien, p. 111.
112. George C. Edwards III. *Presidential Influence in Congress,* San Francisco, 1980, p. 127. Thomas Cronin confirms that "John Kennedy, in spite of fourteen years in Congress, had little taste for effectively courting Congress" (*The State of the Presidency,* Boston, 1980, p. 169.) And Stephen Wayne adds that although Kennedy accepted the fact that his innovative policy proposals demanded a considerable presidential effort, he did not "necessarily relish" it (*The Legislative presidency,* New York, 1978, p. 167). A contemporary account describes the difference in this respect between Kennedy and his successor: "Where Mr. Kennedy dealt at arm's length with Congress, relying on White House aides, President Johnson uses the personal approach and direct action" (*U.S. News & World Report,* March 30, 1964).
113. Wayne, *The Legislative Presidency,* p. 147.
114. Richard Bolling, Oral History Project, John F. Kennedy Library, p. 46 of transcript.
115. *The New York Times,* July 24, 1961.
116. *Ibid.,* July 22, 1961.
117. Jim Grant Bolling, Oral History Project, John F. Kennedy Library, p. 33 of transcript.
118. Wicker, p. 146.
119. Sorensen, p. 362.
120. Presidential Papers, White House Staff File, Lawrence O'Brien, Box 4, July 11, 1962, John F. Kennedy Library.

121. Quoted in Ellison, pp. 28, 29.
122. May 5, 1961.
123. *Commentary,* December 1961.
124. Price, p. 100.
125. Lyndon Baines Johnson, *The Vantage Point,* New York, 1971, pp. 209–12. Walter Heller, Chairman of the Council of Economic Advisers under both Kennedy and Johnson, comments: "After all, federal education aid failed time and time and time again, until Lyndon Johnson got the opposing forces behind the scenes and said, 'Now look, you guys are going to kill each other if you don't get reasonable and make some compromise and then stick with it.'" (Oral History Project, p. 34 of transcript.)
126. See, for example, the previously mentioned memo to O'Donnell. And see the Oral Histories of Richard Bolling and Jim Grant Bolling, John F. Kennedy Library. Heller also comments: "On the basis of House reaction to Ribicoff's attempts at compromise, it would appear that the former Governor of the more than fifty per cent Catholic state of Connecticut did not reflect national thinking on what was negotiable with the Catholic hierarchy" (p. 103).
127. *Ibid.,* p. 45 of transcript.
128. *Ibid.,* Richard Bolling, p. 48 and Jim Grant Bolling, p. 47 of transcript.
129. "How's Kennedy Doing?" in *Saturday Evening Post,* September 16, 1961.
130. For more on Kennedy as a failed politician, see Henry Fairlie, *The Kennedy Promise,* New York, 1973.

7. Lyndon Johnson and the War on Poverty

1. Mark Gelfand writes that "records in the Johnson library leave no doubt about this Kennedy legacy." In "The War on Poverty" in Robert A. Devine, *Exploring The Johnson Years,* Austin, Tx., 1981, p. 127.
2. See memo by Walter Heller dated June 3, 1965 (EA Draft History of the War on Poverty, Legislative Background: EOA of 1964, Box 1, Lyndon Baines Johnson Library [hereafter LBJL]. The men involved in these earliest stages of the poverty program were mainly from the Council of Economic Advisors and included especially Walter Heller and Robert Lampman, previously an economist from the University of Wisconsin).
3. Walter Heller, Oral History Interview, LBJL, p. 20 of transcript.
4. *Ibid.* Kermit Gordon confirms Johnson's prompt acceptance of the idea of a poverty program: "He immediately seized on the idea as an important one ... and encouraged us to go on." Oral History Interview, LBJL, p. 5 of transcript.
5. Lyndon Baines Johnson, *The Vantage Point,* New York, 1971, pp. 69–71.
6. Jack Conway, Oral History Interview, LBJL, p. 7 of transcript.
7. James Sundquist, "Origins of the War on Poverty," in James Sundquist, *On Fighting Poverty,* New York, 1969, p. 28.
8. Gelfand, p. 128.
9. Administrative History: The Office of Economic Opportunity during the Administration of Lyndon Baines Johnson, Volume I, LBJL, p. 19.
10. Sundquist, p. 28.
11. Heller, Oral History, p. 21.

12. Doris Kearns, *Lyndon Johnson and the American Dream,* New York, 1976, p. 188.

13. In Merle Miller, *Lyndon: An Oral Biography,* New York, 1980, p. 362. Eric Goldman writes that Johnson's reasons for committing himself so fervently to the anti-poverty program were autobiographical and also ideological. "It was a key part of the President's make-up that he viewed himself with great emotional intensity as a son of poverty.... [moreover] the personalized Texas politics [of Johnson's early days] did not escape the great divide in American life in the early twentieth century between those who went along with business interests and those who wanted legislation favoring low-income groups." In *The Tragedy of Lyndon Johnson,* New York, 1969, pp. 43, 44.

14. Appointment sheet and memo dated December 2, 1963. In LE/FI 5-7 May 3, 1966, Box #51 Folder LE/FI 11, November 22, 1963–December 20, 1963, LBJL.

15. The letter is dated January 3, 1964, and it is in *ibid.,* Folder LE/FI 11, December 21, 1963–January 8, 1964.

16. In January 8, 1964, memo to the president from Jack Valenti. In *ibid.*

17. The ABA meeting would deal with economic policy generally. See two memos, both dated December 16, 1963, from Heller to the president, in Office Files of Bill Moyers, Box 39, LBJL.

18. *Lyndon B. Johnson: The Exercise of Power,* New York, 1966, p. 428.

19. *Ibid.,* p. 428.

20. *Ibid.,* p. 428.

21. Johnson, p. 73. It should be added that with regard to domestic politics, only the "War on Poverty" rates a separate chapter in that part of Johnson's autobiography that covers the year of his presidency before the 1964 election.

22. *Ibid.,* p. 74.

23. *Ibid.,* p. 74. Kermit Gordon has a less heroic version of the same story: "I think the reason it was called the War on Poverty ... was that nobody ... could think of any euphemism which didn't sound silly" (p. 3. of transcript). Gary Wills, however, writes that the phrase "Great Society" came from Richard Goodwin in *Nixon Agonistes,* Boston, 1969, p. 457.

24. Administrative History, p. 21.

25. January 9, 1964.

26. *Ibid.*

27. As I suggested, the concern with poverty had been growing in certain circles even before Johnson's State of the Union speech. Both Michael Harrington's *The Other America* and John Kenneth Galbraith's *The Affluent Society* have been credited with raising Kennedy's consciousness on the subject. But there was no widespread public awareness of poverty as a national issue until the Johnson presidency.

28. January 20, 1964.

29. January 11, 1964.

30. January 10, 1964.

31. *The New York Times,* January 16, 1964.

32. *Ibid.,* January 17, 1964.

33. January 17, 1964.

34. This paragraph is based on accounts in Gelfand and Sundquist, pp. 130 and 24 respectively.

35. Gelfand, p. 130.

36. Gelfand, p. 131.

37. It should be noted that these kinds of questions can never be answered completely and definitively. The researcher collects all the available evidence and then speculates.

38. According to *The New York Times,* February 2, 1964.

39. Administrative History, p. 25.

40. Letter dated February 11, 1964 and released to the press one day later. In EXF6 11-15, 11/22/63–11/24/64, Box 125, LBJL.

41. Administrative History, p. 30.

42. *Ibid.,* pp. 28, 29.

43. Johnson, p. 76.

44. *Ibid.*

45. Evans and Novak, p. 430.

46. Adam Yarmolinsky, Oral History Interview, LBJL, p. 8 of transcript. I am grateful to Mr. Yarmolinsky for permission to publish these materials.

47. *The New York Times,* January 21, 1964.

48. *Ibid.,* February 12, 1964.

49. Legislative Background—EOA of 1964; Box 2, Folder on Legislative History of Poverty Message, LBJL.

50. Welfare, EX WE 9, 11/22/63–3/31/65; Box 25, Folder WE 9 Poverty Program, 11/22/63–2/28/64, letter dated February 2, 1964, LBJL.

51. *Ibid.* This letter is dated January 17, 1964.

52. The letter from Meany is in Legislative Background—EOA of 1964; Box 2, Folder on Poverty Program 3/1/64–5/15/64, LBJL.

53. The letter to Quinn is dated January 22, 1964. It is in *ibid.,* folder with materials from 11/22/63–2/28/64.

54. *Ibid.* Dated January 14, 1964.

55. *Ibid.* Dated January 23, 1964.

56. *Ibid.* Dated January 18, 1964.

57. *Ibid.* Dated January 23, 1964.

58. In Legislative Background, EOA of 1964, Box 2, Folder of White House Background Programs for War on Poverty, LBJL. Dated Feburary 11, 1964.

59. Same as note 53. Dated January 24, 1964.

60. *Ibid.* Dated January 11, 1964.

61. *Ibid.* Folder 3/1/64–5/15/64. Dated March 11, 1964.

62. Office Files of Fred Panzer, Box 49D (478), Folder labeled Poverty, LBJL.

63. *The New York Times,* March 16, 1964.

64. From the press release that summarized the EOA, Office of the White House Press Secretary, March 16, 1964. In EX E6 11-15, Box 124, Folder labeled EXFG 11-15 11/22/64, LBJL.

65. Administrative History, p. 34.

66. *The New York Times,* March 17, 1964.

67. *Ibid.*

68. *Ibid.*

69. Shriver was the first to testify. See his statement before the House Education and Labor Committee, March 17, 1964. In EX E6 11-15, FG 411/E FG 999-2, LBJL.
70. March 18, 1964.
71. *The New York Times,* March 20, 1964.
72. The memo on Celebrezze is dated March 18, 1964. It is in Legislative Background—EOA of 1964, War on Poverty, Box 1, Folder on CEA Draft History of War on Poverty (3 of 3), LBJL. The memo on Wirtz is dated March 1964 and is in *ibid.*
73. O'Brien is quoted by Johnson, p. 77.
74. *Ibid.,* p. 78.
75. Gelfand, p. 133.
76. *The New York Times,* March 30, 1964.
77. *Ibid.,* March 22, 1964.
78. *Ibid.*
79. *The New York Times,* March 23, 1964.
80. Office files of Bill Moyers, Box 130 (1480), folder labeled Poverty Trip #1, Part 2 (1 of 2), LBJL. The telegram is dated April 22, 1964.
81. *Ibid.* Dated April 23, 1964.
82. The information on the South Bend stop is on two sheets in *ibid.* One is dated 4/23/64. The other has no date.
83. The information on the Pittsburgh stop is in *ibid,* in folder labeled Poverty Trip #1 4/23–4/24.
84. A copy of the entire speech is in *ibid.*
85. *The New York Times,* April 26, 1964.
86. *Ibid.,* April 25, 1964.
87. April 27, 1966.
88. From Wilson McCarthy to Bill Moyers and Jack Valenti, and dated May 6, 1964. In Office files of Bill Moyers, Box 131, folder labeled Poverty Trip #2, Part 2, LBJL.
89. Report from Jack Hight and dated May 6, 1964. In *ibid.,* folder labeled 5/7/64–5/8/64.
90. Speech delivered in Cumberland, Md., May 7, 1964, in *ibid.*
91. May 8, 1964.
92. March 24, 1964.
93. Wire from Tom Davis to Cliff Carter. (No date.) In Office files of Bill Moyers, Box 130 (1480), Poverty Trip #1, Part 2 (2 of 2), LBJL.
94. For this correspondance see Welfare, EX WE 9, Box 25, WE 9 Poverty Program, 5/16/64–6/10/64, LBJL.
95. Some of the material in this paragraph and the preceding one is taken from *Administrative History,* pp. 41, 42.
96. The memo is dated May 26, 1964, and is in Legislative Background—EOA of 1964, Box 2, folder labeled Legislative History on Poverty Message, LBJL.
97. Quotes in *ibid.,* pp. 43, 44.
98. *The New York Times,* June 17, 1964.
99. Legislation (EX LE/WE 7), Box 165, folder labeled 4/22/63–7/31/64.
100. O'Brien's covering memo is in *ibid.*
101. In *ibid.*

102. In EX E6 11-15, Box 124, folder labeled 11/22/63–11/24/64, LBJL.

103. Welfare EX WE 9, Box 25, folder labeled 5/16/64–6/10/64, LBJL.

104. It is not clear who sent this memo but it was put into the files on June 17, 1964. In *ibid.*

105. No date. In office files of Bill Moyers, Box 39 (1354), folder titled Poverty (1 of 2), LBJL.

106. The list has no date. In Legislative Background, EOA of 1964, Box 2, folder titled Legislative History and Poverty Message, LBJL.

107. In *ibid.*

108. EX LE/FI 5-7, Box 51, folder labeled LF/FI 11 11/23/63–12/20/63, LBJL.

109. *The New York Times,* July 24, 1964.

110. All the quotes in this paragraph are in *ibid.,* July 29, 1964.

111. The extent of the administration's lobbying effort is vividly illustrated by the case of Congressman Jack Flynt, a Georgia Democrat. On July 30, a two and a half page single-spaced memo was written by John Carley detailing Flynt's concerns about the EOA. These emerged after a *three hour* conversation between Carley, a spokesman for the administration, and Flynt. The memo, which was originally addressed to Yarmolinsky and Wilson McCarthy, ended up on Shriver's desk. Shriver then passed it on to Moyers with the following hand-written note scrawled across the top: "Here is an excellent summary of Flynt's worries. I also spent 2 hours with Flynt and he is 'calmed down' but perhaps not fully convinced. Sarge." In Office Files of Bill Moyers, Box 39 (1354), folder titled Poverty (1 of 2), LBJL.

112. *The New York Times,* August 5, 1964.

113. Eric F. Goldman, *The Tragedy of Lyndon Johnson,* New York, 1969, p. 186.

114. Goldman, p. 187.

115. This account of the Yarmolinsky affair is based on Goldman, pp. 187–89; Evans and Novak, pp. 432–33; and Jack Bell, *The Johnson Treatment,* New York, 1965, pp. 98, 99. Yarmolinsky remembers that at the end of the day the trade was made, Shriver came into his office saying, "Well, we've just thrown you to the wolves, and this is the worst day in my life." (LBJL, Oral History Project, p. 19 of transcript.)

116. In Goldman, p. 188, and Evans and Novak, p. 433.

117. August 11, 1964.

118. EX E6 11-15, Box 124, folder titled 11/22/63–11/24/64, LBJL.

119. August 13, 1964.

120. Johnson, p. 81.

121. *The New York Times,* August 21, 1964.

122. Johnson, p. 81.

123. Many of these problems were centered on the implementation of community action. Kenneth Clark complained that the "conflict between the newly stimulated, indigenous poor and the entrenched political power brokers . . . soon emerged as a major problem which had not been adequately anticipated or prepared for." And Wilber Cohen remarked years later that the community action program "got out of hand." It was extended from "a hundred communities to eleven hundred. And that was just too many; that just couldn't be done. We had to do it to get congressional votes for the program itself, but it was a mistake. We tried to do too much in too many

places in too short a time." Both Clark and Cohen are quoted in Miller, pp. 364, 365.

124. Gelfand, p. 132.
125. Dated July 24, 1964. Office Files of Fred Panzer, Box 490 (478), Folder labeled Press Conferences, LBJL.
126. *The New York Times,* May 10, 1964.
127. Gelfand, p. 132.
128. *The Commonwealth,* December 20, 1963. Also see *U.S. News and World Report,* December 16, 1963.
129. Joseph Kraft in *Harper's,* March, 1964. Also see Phillip Potter's article on Johnson written at the same time in *The New Republic,* March 7, 1964.
130. Kearns, p. 181.
131. *The Legislative Presidency,* New York, 1978, p. 151.
132. Heller, Oral History, LBJL, p. 35 of transcript.
133. Jack Valenti, *A Very Human President,* New York, 1977, p. 147.
134. *Ibid.*
135. *Ibid.,* p. 138.
136. Carl Albert, Oral History Interview, LBJL, p. 7 of transcript.
137. Robert Caro writes that Lyndon Johnson's size was "one factor in [his] dominance. He was, of course, over six feet three inches tall, and his arms were very long, and his hands very big," and with those long arms he made "sweeping, vigorous gestures. . . . His awkwardness was a factor . . . as was his restlessness, which kept him always in motion: sitting down, jumping up, walking, talking, never still. The drama of his appearance, which went beyond size and awkwardness, was a factor too: the vivid contrast of the coal-black hair and heavy black eyebrows against that milky white skin; the outsized nose and huge ears; the flashing smile; the flashing eyes." Caro is describing a younger man than the one I am writing about in this chapter, but the essentials remained the same. See Robert Caro, *The Years of Lyndon Johnson: The Path to Power,* New York, 1982, p. 457.
138. George Reedy, *Lyndon Johnson: A Memoir,* Fairway, Kans., 1982, p. 158.
139. For more on Johnsons's need for power, and also achievement, see David G. Winter, *The Power Motive,* 1973, pp. 212–20.
140. Kearns, p. 8.
141. *A Life in Our Time,* Boston, 1981, p. 447.
142. This sentence is a paraphrase of a quote by Robert Weaver. Weaver's statement referred primarily to urban blacks. In Miller, p. 365.
143. Quoted in Kearns, p. 112.

8. Richard Nixon and the Family Assistance Plan

1. Vincent J. and Vee Burke, *Nixon's Good Deed: Welfare Reform,* New York, 1974, pp. 9, 10. The Burkes' account of the fate of the FAP is solid and quite complete.
2. *RN: The Memoirs of Richard Nixon,* Volume 1, New York, 1978, p. 525. Nixon called his welfare reform bill his number one domestic priority throughout his first term. Also see Dan Rather and Gary Paul Gates, *The Palace Guard,* New York, 1974, p. 78.
3. Rather and Gates, p. 84.

4. Daniel P. Moynihan, *The Politics of a Guaranteed Income: The Nixon Administration and the Family Assistance Plan,* New York, 1973, p. 67. Moynihan's book is perhaps the most complete account of the history of the Family Assistance Plan and my own account inevitably draws from it. It must be pointed out, however, that as chief architect of the plan, Moynihan was—by his own testimony—hardly a disinterested chronicler.

5. Rather and Gates, p. 84.

6. Moynihan, p. 74.

7. *Ibid.,* p. 86.

8. *Ibid.,* p. 92.

9. *Ibid.,* p. 97.

10. *Ibid.,* p. 80.

11. In *ibid.,* p. 86. The two political scientists were Bill Cavela and Aaron Wildavsky. Moynihan writes: "First, [they] reasoned, 'Policies that provide unearned income run counter to widely held and deeply felt American values, such as achievement, work and equality of opportunity.' Second, great sums would have to be raised by taxation to pay for such a scheme. Third, 'Labor unions fear that a guaranteed income would render them superfluous. Militant black leaders take the same position for a similar reason.'"

12. Moynihan, p. 143. The Family Security System, in turn, grew out of a welfare reform plan that had originally been submitted to President Johnson.

13. Burke and Burke, pp. 67, 68.

14. Bernard Asbell, "Pat Moynihan: 'Too Much!' and 'Too Little!'" in *The New York Times Magazine,* November 2, 1969, p. 60.

15. Burke and Burke, pp. 13, 14.

16. Moynihan, p. 193.

17. In Moynihan, p. 201.

18. *Ibid.,* p. 213. Also see Burke and Burke, pp. 101ff.

19. Rowland Evans, Jr., and Robert Novak, *Nixon in the White House,* New York, 1971, p. 230.

20. For further discussion of the exaggerated emphasis on "workfare," see Burke and Burke, pp. 109ff.

21. *The New York Times,* August 8, 1969.

22. The quotes in this passage are taken from *Business Week,* August 16, 1964, and *The New York Times,* August 9, 1964.

23. *Business Week,* August 16, 1964.

24. August 30, 1969.

25. *National Review,* August 26, 1969.

26. Quoted in Gary Allan, *The Man Behind the Mask,* Boston, 1971, p. 326.

27. Burke and Burke, p. 125.

28. *The New York Times,* August 12, 1969.

29. *Ibid.*

30. Evans and Novak, p. 231.

31. *The New York Times,* September 2, 1969.

32. *Ibid.,* October 12, 1969.

33. *Ibid.*

34. Moynihan, pp. 412, 417.

35. *The New York Times,* November 13, 1969. Also see Moynihan, pp. 360ff.

36. *The New York Times,* November 13, 1969.

37. Quoted in Moynihan, p. 361.
38. *Ibid.,* December 3, 1969.
39. *Ibid.,* January 14, 1970.
40. *Ibid.,* January 23, 1970.
41. *Ibid.,* January 11, 1970.
42. In an article written by Tom Wicker, January 24, 1970.
43. In an article written by Ernest Van denHaag, January 27, 1970.
44. January 18, 1970.
45. *The New York Times,* January 19, 1970. This paragraph is based on a lengthy article in *The New York Times* of the same day.
46. *Ibid.,* January 25, 1970.
47. *Ibid.,* February 3, 1970.
48. *U.S. News & World Report,* February 23, 1970.
49. February 15, 1970.
50. See, for example, *ibid.*
51. See, for example, *The New York Times,* February 11, 1970.
52. *Ibid.,* November 16, 1970.
53. *Ibid.,* February 26, 1970.
54. *Ibid.,* March 6, 1970.
55. *Ibid.*
56. *Ibid.*
57. For a full description of these events, see Moynihan, pp. 428ff.
58. *The New York Times,* April 17, 1970.
59. Much of this paragraph is based on an account in *The New York Times,* April 30, 1970.
60. Moynihan, p. 439.
61. *Ibid.,* p. 469.
62. *Ibid.,* pp. 439–83.
63. *The New York Times,* May 2, 1970.
64. *Ibid.,* May 6, 1970.
65. Rather and Gates, p. 100.
66. *The New York Times,* June 14, 1970.
67. *Ibid.,* June 11, 1970.
68. *U.S. News & World Report,* June 22, 1970.
69. *The New York Times,* July 2, 1970.
70. *Ibid.*
71. Moynihan, p. 500.
72. *The New York Times,* July 21, 1970.
73. *Ibid.,* August 17, 1970.
74. The Moynihan, Finch, and Nixon quotes are in *ibid.,* August 29, 1970.
75. In Moynihan, pp. 522, 523.
76. In "The Nixon Watch," *The New Republic,* November 7, 1970.
77. Letter from J. William Fulbright to the author dated June 6, 1983.
78. Letter from Albert Gore to the author dated June 13, 1983.
79. From a telephone conversation between the author and Fred Harris on September 20, 1983.
80. Letter from Jack Miller to the author dated June 8, 1983.
81. From a telephone conversation between the author and Paul Fannin on June 16, 1983.

82. Moynihan, p. 499.

83. From a telephone conversation between the author and Carl Curtis on June 22, 1983.

84. By now, however, the administration started to recognize that time was running out. See *The New York Times,* September 18, 1970.

85. *The New York Times,* October 22, 1970.

86. Moynihan, p. 531.

87. November 20, 1970.

88. *The New York Times,* November 21, 1970.

89. The Williams quote is in a letter to the author dated July 6, 1983.

90. Moynihan's and McGrory's quote—as well as Nixon's speech— are in Moynihan, pp. 539–41.

91. All the quotes in this paragraph are in *The New York Times,* December 29, 1970.

92. Rather and Gates, p. 99.

93. *In Search of Nixon,* 1972, New York, p. 119.

94. For more on this, see Henry Hazlitt in the *National Review,* February 24, 1970.

95. In Asbell, p. 44. Also see an article titled "President's Call for Welfare Reform Breaks Long Silence on the Problem Among Political Leaders" in *The New York Times,* August 10, 1969.

96. See Osborne's collection of essays on Nixon, *The Nixon Watch,* New York, 1970, p. 145.

97. Boston, 1969.

98. William Safire, *Before the Fall: An Inside View of the Pre-Watergate White House,* New York, 1975, p. 10.

99. Rather and Gates, p. 82.

100. Safire, p. 97.

101. Rather and Gates, p. 92.

102. *Ibid.*

103. *The New Republic,* November 7, 1970.

104. Moynihan, p. 498.

105. Wills, p. 371.

106. *The New Republic,* November 7, 1970.

107. See Tom Wicker's column, *The New York Times,* December 14, 1969.

108. *The New York Times,* April 19, 1970.

109. Stephen J. Wayne, *The Legislative Presidency,* New York, 1978, p. 50.

110. George C. Edwards III, *Presidential Influence in Congress,* San Francisco, 1980, p. 127.

111. Barbara Kellerman, "Introversion in the Oval Office," *Presidential Studies Quarterly,* Summer, 1983, pp. 383–99.

112. This argument is summarized by Edwards, p. 139. Edwards draws on both Rather and Gates (pp. 114–115, 121) and Evans and Novak (p. 231).

113. Moynihan, p. 500.

114. Quoted in *U.S. News & World Report,* August 11, 1969.

115. "The Nixon Supremacy," in *Harper's,* March 1970.

116. In *The New Republic,* October 25, 1969.

117. For a cogent discussion of some underlying psychological factors that may have contributed to the erratic quality of Nixon's performance with regard

to the FAP, see the Nixon chapters in James David Barber's *The Presidential Character*, Englewood Cliffs, N.J., 1977.

9. Gerald Ford and the Tax Cut

1. Gerald R. Ford, *A Time to Heal*, New York, 1980, p. 116.
2. *Time*, January 26, 1975.
3. *The New York Times*, August 3, 1974.
4. Ford, p. 123.
5. *Ibid.*, p. 131.
6. Calls List, White House Central File (hereafter WHCF) folder "PR7-2," Gerald R. Ford Library (hereafter FL).
7. Memo, Warren S. Rustand to Kenneth Cole, November 5, 1974, WHCF, folder 'PR 7-2," FL.
8. Memo to the president from Roy L. Ash, Ken Cole, and William E. Timmons, August 15, 1974, WHCF, Folder "LE," FL.
9. *The New York Times*, August 10, 1974.
10. Ford, p. 147.
11. *The New York Times*, August 13, 1974.
12. *Ibid.*, August 29, 1974.
13. Memo, Alexander Haig to President Ford, August 14, 1974, WHCF, folder "BE 5," FL.
14. Schedule Proposal for the meeting from William J. Baroody, Jr., August 21, 1974, WHCF, folder "BE 5," FL.
15. Letter, President Gerald Ford to Senator Barry Goldwater, September 7, 1974, WHCF, folder "BE," FL.
16. "Inflation: a Presidential Catechism," September 15, 1974.
17. *The New York Times*, October 9, 1974.
18. *Ibid.*
19. The quotes in this paragraph are in *ibid*. President Ford also received private correspondence to this effect. For example, a wire was sent him by Steve Postupack, a candidate for Congress from Pennsylvania's sixth district, that read in part: "Any proposal to raise taxes on our taxpayers in the income-level proposed would be oppressive and unfair to the working man." The wire is dated October 8, 1974, WHCF, folder "FI 11-4," FL.
20. Quoted in Ford, p. 191.
21. October 9, 1974.
22. October 13, 1974.
23. *The New York Times*, October 10, 1974.
24. The draft letter is undated; a Fact Sheet with figures (which may have been attached to the cover letter) is dated October 30, 1974. Simon's letter is in the Seidman Collection, folder "Sugar Policy Review," FL; and the Fact Sheet is in the Seidman Collection, folder "Files 1974–77," FL.
25. Ford, p. 189.
26. The memorandum is in WHCF, folder "FI 11-4," FL.
27. Roger B. Porter, *Presidential Decision Making*, New York, 1980. p. 105.
28. Minutes of the Economic Policy Board—Executive Committee Meeting (EPB-ECM) Tab A, November 12, 1974.

29. Minutes of the EPB-ECM, November 6, 1974, Seidman Collection, folder "File-E.P.B. Meeting," FL.

30. *The New York Times,* November 13, 1974.

31. *Ibid.,* November 17, 1974.

32. Memo from William Simon to President Ford, November 20, 1974, WHCF, folder "FI-11," FL.

33. Memo from Alan Greenspan to President Ford, November 26, 1974, WHCF, folder "BE 5," FL.

34. Porter, p. 111.

35. From sheet titled "Possible Tax Package for January 1975." The sheet was initialed by Seidman and was probably an agenda item for a late December EPB-ECM. In the Seidman Collection, folder "Files 1974–77," FL.

36. "Possible Tax Package for 1975," December 20, 1974, Seidman Collection, folder "Files 1974–77," FL.

37. Porter, pp. 112, 113.

38. December 23, 1974.

39. Memo, Jack Marsh to the President through Don Rumsfeld, December 26, 1975, WHCF, folder "BE 5," FL.

40. Seidman Collection, Folder "E.P.B. Meeting," FL.

41. *The New York Times,* January 3, 1975.

42. *Ibid.,* January 10, 1975.

43. *Ibid.,* January 14, 1975.

44. Memorandum, Ken Cole to Don Rumsfeld, December 19, 1974, WHCF, folder "SP 2-4/1975," FL.

45. Memo from William Baroody, Jr., to President Ford, November 13, 1974, WHCF, folder "SP 2-4/1975" FL. This first State of the Union message was being taken seriously early on in the Ford administration. The Ford Library documents the extent to which the administration sought input into the speech from a fairly wide variety of sources.

46. Memo, Robert Kelly to Jerry Warren, December 14, 1974, WHCF, folder "SP 2-4/1975," FL.

47. Letter, Ron Nessen to President Ford, December 28, 1974, WHCF, folder "SP 2-4/1975," FL.

48. Memo, William Seidman, Ron Nessen, and Frank Zarb, January 4, 1975, WHCF, folder "SP 2-4/1975," FL.

49. *The New York Times,* January 9, 1975.

50. Memo, William Seidman to the EPB-EC members regarding "Schedule of Meetings with the President," January 2, 1975, Seidman Collection, folder "E.P.B. Memoranda," FL.

51. Minutes of January 6, 1975, meeting of EPB-ECM, Seidman Collection, folder "E.P.B. Meetings," FL.

52. From the minutes of what appears to be the January 8, 1975 meeting. In *ibid.*

53. January 14, 1975.

54. *Ibid.*

55. *Ibid.,* January 16, 1975.

56. *Ibid.,* January 14, 1975.

57. Memo, Jack Marsh to Max Friedersdorf, January 9, 1975, WHCF, folder "BE 5," FL.

58. Letter, Senator Hugh Scott to President Ford, WHCF, folder "FG 31-1," FL.
59. Ford's agenda for his meeting with Ulmann prepared by Max Friedersdorf, January 9, 1975, WHCF, folder "BE 5," FL.
60. Memo, Jerry H. Jones to Max Friedersdorf, January 9, 1975, WHCF, folder "SP 2-4/1975," FL.
61. Memo, Max Friedersdorf to President Ford, January 8, 1975, in *ibid.*
62. Ford's agenda for his meeting with the military leaders prepared by Max Friedersdorf, January 10, 1975, WHCF, folder "FG 31-1," FL.
63. Ford's agenda for his meeting with Russell Long prepared by Max Friedersdorf, January 13, 1975, WHCF, folder "BE 5," FL.
64. Lists of all the participants in those meetings may be found in WHCF, folder "PR 7-1," FL.
65. The complete exchange between the White House and the Black Caucus is in WHCF, folder "SP 2-4/1975," FL. Seidman was also requested to reply directly and personally to the Black Caucus.
66. Letter, president Ford to Alan Greenspan, January 10, 1975, WHCF, folder "BE 5," FL.
67. Memo, Ron Nessen to President Ford, January 15, 1975, WHCF, folder "PR 7-1," FL.
68. Memo written by Jerry O'Donnell, January 15, 1975, in *ibid.*
69. Memo, Bill Baroody and Ken Cole to President Ford, January 15, 1975, WHCF, folder "SP 2-4/1975," FL.
70. Memo, "MFW" to "Bill," January 18, 1975; also memorandum for the Record from Warren Rustand, January 17, 1975. Both are in WHCF, folder "SP 2-4/1975," FL.
71. Roudebush's letter to President Ford is dated January 17, 1975. Ford's reply is dated January 29, 1975. Both are in *ibid.*
72. Memo, Bud Littin to Gerald Warren, January 29, 1975. In *ibid.*
73. Minutes of EPB-ECM, January 23, 1975, Seidman Collection, folder "E.P.B. Meetings," FL.
74. *The New York Times,* January 20, 1975. Ford also received important support from Federal Reserve Chairman Arthur Burns. Burns gave a statement to the House Ways and means Committee—"Let me say at once that I support the principle of temporary tax cuts under current conditions"—and sent it, along with a cover letter, along to the president. Burns's cover letter must also have gladdened Ford's heart: "May I also take this opportunity to tell you that I think your recent talk before the NICB was a truly outstanding performance. I have in mind your delivery as much as the substance of your talk. In some of your earlier speeches you at times seemed to convey an impression of timidity; now you are coming through as a strong and self-assured leader of this nation." Burns's letter is dated January 30, 1975. It and a copy of his statement to Ways and Means is in WHCF, folder "FG 33-22," FL.
75. "Too Little, Too Late" is the title of Tom Wicker's column on the subject in *The New York Times,* January 24, 1975.
76. *Ibid.*
77. *The New York Times,* January 30, 1975.

78. See, for example, the President's annual Economic Report to Congress, reprinted in *The New York Times,* February 5, 1975.

79. January 30, 1975.

80. Memo, Ron Nessen to Donald Rumsfeld, February 15, 1975, WHCF, folder "BE 5," FL.

81. Memo from Doug Bennett to Max Friedersdorf, February 3, 1975, WHCF, folder "FG 33-22," FL.

82. The comparison between the two proposals is dated February 22, 1975. See WHCF, folder "FG 6-30," FL.

83. *The New York Times,* February 23, 1975.

84. *Ibid.,* February 25, 1975.

85. *Ibid.,* February 27, 1975.

86. For further details on links between the tax and energy proposals, see *ibid.,* March 1 and March 5, 1975.

87. "Memorandum for the President," from William T. Kendall through Max Friedersdorf, March 3, 1975. Both are in WHCF, folder "PR 7-2," FL.

88. "Memorandum for members of the Economic Policy Board" from William Simon, March 3, 1975, WHCF, folder "BE 5," FL. Also see the Minutes of the EPB-ECM, March 4, 1975, Seidman Collection, folder "E.P.B. Meetings," FL.

89. *The New York Times,* March 6, 1975.

90. *Ibid.,* March 7, 1975.

91. Memo, Max Friedersdorf to President Ford, March 4, 1974, WHCF, folder "FG 31-1," FL.

92. Letter, President Ford to Senator Russell Long, March 7, 1975, WHCF, folder "FI 11," FL.

93. Max Friedersdorf's "Recommended Telephone Call" sheet, March 10, 1975. There is a handwritten notation that the president "Called 3/12/75." In WHCF, folder "PR 7-2," FL.

94. *The New York Times,* March 15, 1975.

95. Agenda, prepared by Max Friedersdorf, March 15, 1975, WHCF, folder "FG 31-1," FL. The list of those present at the meeting may be found in WHCF, folder "PR 7-1," FL.

96. Proposed Questions and Answers on a sheet dated March 16, 1975. The responses appear to have been prepared by the Executive Committee of the EPB. The Question and Answer sheet is in WHCF, folder "FG 6-30," FL. Also see "Economic Policy Board Procedural Guidelines," March 24, 1975, Seidman Collection, folder E.P.B. Memoranda," FL.

97. Memo, Max Friedersdorf to President Ford, March 20, 1975, WHCF, folder "FI 11," FL.

98. Letter, Ron Nessen to Senator Mike Mansfield, March 22, 1975, WHCF, folder "FI 11-4," FL.

99. See paper titled "Consensus" and stamped "The PRESIDENT HAS SEEN. . . ." It is dated March 22, 1975 and located in WHCF, folder "(FOA 48 (A)." FL.

100. Memo, "Cap" Weinberger to President Ford, March 23, 1975, WHCF, folder "FI 11-4," FL.

101. *The New York Times,* March 24, 1975.

102. *Ibid.,* March 23, 1975.

103. This letter was apparently sent to the House and Senate Leadership, and also to members of the joint House–Senate Conference Committee. It is certain that the letter went to Senators James Eastland, Mike Mansfield, Hugh Scott, Russell Long, and Paul Fannin. It also went to Representatives John Rhodes, Thomas O'Neill, Jr., Herman Schneebeli, and Al Ullman. Copies of the letter can be found in the Seidman Collection, folder "Files 1974–77," and also WHCF, folder, "FI 11," FL.

104. The quotes in this paragraph are all from *The New York Times,* March 27, 1975.

105. Ford, p. 251.

106. Memo, Max Friedersdorf to President Ford on "Tax Reduction Bill," March 27, 1975, WHCF, folder "PR 7-2" FL.

107. The list was probably compiled by Max Friedersdorf or a member of his staff. It is dated March 27, 1975, and is in *ibid.*

108. Ford, p. 252.

109. Memo, Max Friedersdorf to President Ford on "Bob Michel/Herman Schneebeli/Barber Conable/John Rhodes, March 27, 1975, WHCF folder "FI 11," FL.

110. Memo, William Kendall and Patrick O'Donnell to Jack Marsh on "The Tax Reduction Act of 1975," March 28, 1975, in *ibid.*

111. Letter, Senator Mark Hatfield to President Ford (no date), WHCF, folder "FI 11-4," Fl.

112. Memo, William Seidman to President Ford, March 28, 1975, WHCF, folder "FI 11," FL.

113. This is Ford quoting Simon in Ford, p. 251.

114. Memo, Casper Weinberger to President Ford, March 27, 1975, WHCF, folder "FI 11-4," FL.

115. Ford, p. 252.

116. Memo, Ron Nessen to President Ford, March 28, 1975, WHCF, folder "FI 11," FL.

117. Memo, Ron Nessen to President Ford March 28, 1975, WHCF, folder "FI 11-4," FL.

118. The draft of the veto statement is in the Seidman Collection, folder, "Files 1974–77," FL.

119. *The New York Times,* March 30, 1975.

120. Brock Brower, "Under Ford's Helmet," *The New York Times Magazine,* September 15, 1974.

121. *Ibid.* The persistence of a public perception is astonishing. As late as June 1983, Hamilton Jordan wrote, "Johnny Carson still gets laughs with jokes about Gerald Ford bumping his head." In "Mondale's Choice," *The New Republic,* June 6, 1983.

122. *Ibid.*

123. Quoted in Robert Peabody, *Leadership in Congress,* Boston, 1976, pp. 119, 120.

124. *Ibid.,* p. 119.

125. Brower.

126. Peabody, p. 119.

127. *Ibid.*

128. Richard Neustadt, *Presidential Power,* New York, 1960, p. 64.

129. Porter, p. 118.

130. *The New York Times,* January 16, 1975.

131. Quoted in Stephen J. Wayne, *The Legislative Presidency,* New York, 1973, p. 54.

132. George C. Edwards III, *Presidential Influence in Congress,* San Francisco, 1980, p. 127.

133. Memorandum to the President, Subject "Tax Cut Bill." It is unsigned and there is no date. It may well have been prepared by Seidman and was almost certainly written on March 27 or 28, 1975. In the Seidman Collection, folder "Files 1974–77", F.L.

134. Memos, Vernon C. Loen to President Ford through John Marsh, Don Rumsfeld, Max Friedersdorf, March 28, 1975. In WHCF, folder FI 11 3/ 27/75–3/31/75, FL.

10. Jimmy Carter and the Energy Package

1. Haynes Johnson, *In the Absence of Power,* New York, 1980, p. 187.

2. Jimmy Carter, *Keeping Faith,* New York, 1982, p. 91.

3. Carter, pp. 124, 125.

4. Carter, p. 91.

5. *Ibid.,* p. 93.

6. *The New York Times,* January 31, 1977.

7. *Ibid.,* February 21, 1977.

8. *Ibid.,* February 24, 1977.

9. Johnson, p. 188–90.

10. *Ibid.,* p. 188.

11. April 2, 1977.

12. *The New York Times,* March 4, 1977.

13. *Newsweek,* April 18, 1977.

14. Carter, pp. 96, 97.

15. *Ibid.,* p. 97.

16. *Time,* March 7, 1977. The speaker is quoted in Nelson W. Polsby, *Consequences of Party Reform,* New York, 1983, p. 109.

17. *Ibid.,* and also see John Osborne, "Carter and Congress," *The New Republic* March 5, 1977.

18. *The New York Times,* April 19, 1977.

19. *Ibid.*

20. This list is based on one in *ibid.*

21. *The New York Times,* April 22, 1977.

22. James Reston, *The New York Times,* April 22, 1977.

23. *Ibid.*

24. In Johnson, p. 192.

25. *Ibid.*

26. *The New York Times,* April 22, 1977.

27. *Newsweek,* April 25, 1977.

28. See, for example, "Energy and National Will" in *The Nation,* April 30, 1977.

29. The phrase is Senator Lloyd Bentsen's, *The New York Times.* April 21, 1977.
30. *Nesweek,* May 2, 1977.
31. *Time,* May 2, 1977.
32. May 2, 1977.
33. May 2, 1977.
34. *Time,* May 2, 1977.
35. The list is drawn from *U.S. News & World Report,* May 2, 1977.
36. *The Nation,* May 7, 1977.
37. *Newsweek,* May 2, 1977.
38. For details on the Ad Hoc Committee, see the 1977 *Congressional Quarterly Almanac,* pp. 721 ff.
39. Carter, p. 97.
40. *Time,* May 2, 1977.
41. *The New York Times,* May 4, 1977.
42. *Ibid.*
43. *Ibid.,* May 5, 1977.
44. *Ibid.,* May 8, 1977.
45. *Ibid.,* May 20, 1977.
46. *Ibid.,* May 25, 1977.
47. June 11, 1977.
48. June 13, 1977.
49. Carter, p. 99.
50. *The New York Times,* June 12, 1983.
51. Johnson, pp. 192, 193.
52. *The New York Times,* June 14, 1977.
53. *The New York Times,* June 19, 1977.
54. *Ibid.*
55. *The New Republic,* June 25, 1977.
56. *The New York Times,* July 1, 1977.
57. *Ibid.,* July 6, 1977.
58. See the *National Journal,* July 16, 1977, p. 1125, for a description of the conference.
59. *The New York Times,* July 10, 1977.
60. *Ibid.,* July 31, 1977.
61. *Ibid.,* August 2, 1977.
62. *Newsweek,* August 15, 1977.
63. *National Journal,* July 30, 1977, p. 1196.
64. *Newsweek,* August 15, 1977.
65. *The New York Times,* August 7, 1977.
66. *National Journal,* August 30, 1977, p. 1306.
67. *The New York Times,* August 7, 1977.
68. *National Journal,* July 9, 1977, p. 1068.
69. *The New York Times,* September 1, 1977. Also see *National Review,* July 2, 1977, p. 1050.
70. *Ibid.,* September 27, 1977.
71. Johnson, p. 221.
72. *Ibid.,* pp. 222.
73. *The New York Times,* October 2, 1977.

74. *Ibid.*
75. *Ibid.,* October 7, 1977.
76. Hedrick Smith, "Problems of a Problem Solver," *New York Times Magazine,* January 1, 1978.
77. *Time,* October 17, 1977.
78. October 22, 1977.
79. *The New York Times,* October 14, 1977.
80. *Ibid.*
81. *Ibid.,* October 22, 1977.
82. *Time,* October 31, 1977.
83. *Ibid.*
84. This paragraph is a slightly condensed version of three paragraphs in *ibid.*
85. *The New York Times,* October 21, 1977.
86. *Ibid.,* October 18, 1977.
87. *Ibid.,* October 20, 1977.
88. *Ibid.,* November 1, 1977.
89. *Time,* November 7, 1977.
90. *The New York Times,* November 11, 1977.
91. This paragraph is based on an account in *ibid.,* November 14, 1977.
92. *Ibid.,* November 23, 1977.
93. *Ibid.,* November 24, 1977.
94. *Ibid.,* December 1, 1977.
95. *Ibid.,* December 13, 1977.
96. See transcript of December 15 presidential press conference in *ibid.,* December 16, 1977.
97. Carter, p. 105.
98. *The New York Times,* January 15, 1978.
99. *Ibid.,* January 13, 1978.
100. *Ibid.,* January 20, 1978.
101. *Ibid.,* May 13, 1978.
102. *National Journal,* March 18, 1978.
103. Carter, p. 103.
104. *Ibid.*
105. This paragraph is based on an account in the *National Journal,* March 18, 1978, pp. 421–23.
106. *The New York Times,* April 6, 1978.
107. See, for example, his response to a question about conservation in *ibid.,* April 12, 1978.
108. August 5, 1978.
109. *The New York Times,* Supplementary Material, September 6, 1978.
110. Carter, p. 106.
111. The quotes in this paragraph are taken from the account in the *National Journal,* September 30, 1978, pp. 1556–59.
112. *Time,* October 9, 1978.
113. George C. Edwards, III, *Presidential Influence in Congress,* San Francisco, 1980, p. 178.
114. *Time,* September 11, 1978.
115. *Time,* October 9, 1978.
116. *Ibid.*

117. *National Journal,* September 30, 1978.

118. *The New York Times,* Supplementary Material, October 5, 1978.

119. *Ibid.,* October 11, 1978.

120. Carter, p. 106.

121. *National Journal,* October 21, 1978, p. 1682.

122. *The New York Times,* October 14, 1978.

123. Carter, p. 106.

124. *The New York Times,* November 10, 1978.

125. *Ibid.*

126. Edwards, *Presidential Influence in Congress,* p. 195. Whether changes in Congress do indeed hamper presidential leadership is a matter of debate. Polsby argues that a democratic president in particular would now have "an increased potential for favorable" results if he were "willing to work with the congressional leadership in establishing legislative priorities and strategies" (p. 113).

127. Paul Light, *The President's Agenda,* Baltimore, 1982, p. 51.

128. On the larger issue of feeding Carter too much too soon, see Ben Heineman and Curtis Hessler, *Memorandum for the President: A Strategic Approach to Domestic Affairs in the 1980s,* New York, passim. Heineman and Hessler's book is in good part an attack on what they consider the bad strategic planning of the Carter administration. On the other hand, Light argues that Carter "proposed not much more than Kennedy and much less than Johnson. However, Congress has become more sensitive to competetion for agenda space" (p. 54).

129. James Fallows, "The Passionless Presidency," in *Atlantic,* May, 1979, p. 40. See Heineman and Hessler for a discussion of how the energy plan might ideally have been developed.

130. *U.S. News & World Report,* October 24, 1977.

131. This paragraph is based on an account in *The New York Times,* April 24, 1977, titled "Carter Shaped Energy Plan with Disregard for Politics."

132. The phrase appeared in *ibid.*

133. *National Journal,* July 2, 1977, p. 1050.

134. *Ibid.*

135. Fallows, "The Passionless Presidency."

136. Betty Glad, *Jimmy Carter: In Search of the Great White House.* New York, 1980, p. 439.

137. Richard Neustadt, *Presidential Power,* New York, 1980 edition, p. 215.

138. *National Journal,* August 20, 1977, p. 1303. Also see article titled "O'Neill's Imprint on Energy Bill," *The New York Times,* August 1, 1977.

139. In Hedrick Smith, *New York Times Magazine,* January 8, 1978.

140. *The New York Times,* October 14, 1977.

141. A November 25, 1977 editorial in *The New York Times* encouraged Carter to make just such a compromise.

142. The phrasing is Ward Just's in the *Atlantic,* January, 1978.

143. For a further discussion of Carter's natural distaste for politicking, see Barbara Kellerman "Introversion in the Oval Office," *Presidential Studies Quarterly,* Spring, 1983, pp. 383–99.

144. The observation is by a former aide in Morton Kondracke, "Mondale on Mondale" in *The New Republic,* August 4, 1983.

145. In "The Passionless Presidency" Fallows writes the "Carter performance on first meeting was something special."

146. In Kondracke, "Mondale on Mondale."

147. This paragraph is based on Glad, p. 421.

148. In Califano's *Governing America,* New York, 1980, p. 415.

149. See article titled "Lobbyists Are Putting the Blitz on Carter's Energy Program" in *National Journal,* November 26, 1977, pp. 1836–40.

150. For more on this, see Charles O. Jones, "Keeping Faith and Losing Congress" in *Presidential Studies Quarterly,* forthcoming.

151. Erving Goffman makes the pertinent point that the information we *initially* acquire about people is very important. It is on the basis of this initial information that we start to define the situation and plan our response. This notion should serve as a special caution to presidents who, on taking office, are relatively unknown to Washington insiders. See Goffman's *The Presentation of Self in Everyday Life,* New York, 1959. p. 10.

152. These sentences are based on Elizabeth Drew, *The New Yorker,* May 23, 1977, p. 114.

153. In *ibid.,* p. 117.

154. Fallows, "The Passionless Presidency," p. 41.

155. *Business Week,* October 31, 1977.

156. *Ibid.*

157. Edwards, p. 175.

158. Johnson, p. 298.

159. *Ibid.,* p. 41.

160. In Polsby, p. 109.

161. For more on this see Glad, pp. 417ff.

162. Edwards, p. 175.

163. *Ibid.,* p. 173.

164. Light, p. 37.

165. This point was made by Professor Charles O. Jones at the 1983 American Political Science Association Convention in Chicago.

166. This is one of the main points made by Heineman and Hessler.

11. Ronald Reagan and the Budget Cuts

1. For more on this, see Fred Greenstein, "The Need for an Early Appraisal of the Reagan presidency," and Hugh Heclo and Rudolph Penner, "Fiscal and Poltical Strategy in the Reagan Administration" in Fred Greenstein (ed.), *The Reagan Presidency: An Early Assessment,* Baltimore, 1983.

2. In *Reagan,* New York, 1982, p. 321.

3. The sentence is based on Laurence I. Barrett, *Gambling with History: Reagan in the White House,* New York, 1983, pp. 48–50.

4. Timothy B. Clark, "The President Takes On the 'Iron Triangles' and So Far Holds His Own," in *National Journal,* March 21, 1981, p. 515.

5. *Ibid.*

6. In *Vital Speeches of the Day,* August 15, 1980, Southold, N.Y., 1983, p. 644.

7. In Barrett, pp. 133, 134.

8. Dick Kirschten, "White House Strategy," *National Journal,* February 21, 1981, p. 300.
9. November 3, 1980.
10. November 24, 1980.
11. Barrett, pp. 137, 138. The chapters in Barrett's book titled "Seduction and Blitzkrieg" and "In Search of Great Expectations" have provided considerable background material for this chapter.
12. Barrett, p. 143.
13. Kirschten, pp. 300, 302.
14. *Ibid.*
15. *Ibid.*
16. Barrett, pp. 80–82.
17. Stephen J. Wayne, "Congressional Liaison in the Reagan White House: A Preliminary Assessment of the First Year," in Norman J. Ornstein, *President and Congress: Assessing Reagan's First Year,* Washington, 1982, p. 50.
18. Kirschten, p. 303.
19. Wayne, p. 51.
20. Kirschten, p. 303.
21. Barrett, p. 38.
22. Cannon, p. 322.
23. Heclo and Penner, p. 27.
24. Barrett, p. 84.
25. *The New York Times,* February 5, 1981.
26. *Ibid.,* February 6, 1981.
27. *Ibid.*
28. *Ibid.,* February 7, 1981.
29. *Ibid.*
30. This sample is taken from a list in Rowland Evans and Robert Novak, *The Reagan Revolution,* New York, 1981, pp. 127, 128.
31. *The New York Times,* February 16, 1981.
32. *Ibid.,* February 18, 1981.
33. *Ibid.,* February 16, 1981.
34. *Ibid.,* February 18, 1981.
35. Evans and Novak, p. 43.
36. *Ibid.,* February 19, 1981.
37. Timothy B. Clark, "Reagan's Budget Cuts: The Reasons Why," *National Journal,* February 21, 1981, p. 305.
38. *The New York Times,* February 19, 1981.
39. *U.S. News & World Report,* March 2, 1981.
40. February 21, 1981.
41. *The New York Times,* February 20, 1981.
42. *Ibid.*
43. Cannon, p. 333.
44. *U.S. News & World Report,* March 2, 1981.
45. *Ibid.* Even three years later, it is argued that Reagan "has survived the assaults of the press better than any President in decades." See Sidney Blumenthal's "Reagan the Unassailable" in *The New Republic,* September 12, 1983.
46. February 6, 1981.

47. *U.S. News & World Report,* May 2, 1981.
48. Michael Kramer, "Taking a Hard Look at Those Budget Cuts," *New York,* March 2, 1981.
49. *Business Week,* March 2, 1981.
50. *The New York Times,* February 20, 1981.
51. *Ibid.,* February 12, 1981.
52. *The New York Times,* February 18, 1981.
53. *Ibid.,* February 21, 1981.
54. *Ibid.,* February 28, 1981.
55. *Ibid.,* March 3, 1981.
56. *Ibid.,* March 7, 1981.
57. *Ibid.,* March 4, 1981.
58. *Ibid.,* March 7, 1981.
59. *Ibid.,* March 1, 1981.
60. *Ibid.,* February 28, 1981.
61. *Ibid.,* March 5, 1981.
62. *Ibid.,* March 8, 1981.
63. *Ibid.,* March 10, 1981.
64. *National Journal,* March 14, 1981.
65. *The New York Times,* March 13, 1981.
66. *Ibid.,* March 22, 1981.
67. *Ibid.,* March 11 and 12, 1981.
68. Barrett, p. 147.
69. *The New York Times,* March 20, 1981.
70. *Ibid.,* March 21, 1981.
71. *Ibid.,* March 20, 1981.
72. "The Reagan Cannonball" was the title of a *New York Times* editorial on March 22, 1981.
73. *Ibid.,* March 17, 1981.
74. *Ibid.,* March 18, 1981.
75. *Ibid.,* March 21, 1981.
76. *Ibid.,* March 23, 1981.
77. Barrett, p. 124.
78. For further details, see relevant chapters in Barrett and Cannon.
79. *Ibid.,* p. 404.
80. *The New York Times,* April 27, 1981.
81. *Ibid.,* April 24, 1981.
82. *Ibid.,* April 28, 1981.
83. *Ibid.*
84. *Ibid.,* April 29, 1981.
85. *Ibid.*
86. *National Journal,* April 18, 1981.
87. Barrett, p. 153.
88. *The New York Times,* April 29, 1981.
89. May 11, 1981.
90. *U.S. News & World Report,* May 11, 1981.
91. *Ibid.,* May 18, 1981.
92. *The New York Times,* May 1, 1981.
93. *Ibid.,* May 3, 1981.

94. *U.S. News & World Report,* May 18, 1981.
95. *The New York Times,* May 6, 1981.
96. *Ibid.,* May 8, 1981.
97. May 15, 1981.
98. May 16, 1981.
99. May 10, 1981.
100. *National Journal,* May 16, 1981.
101. These two paragraphs are based on "How the Budget Cutters Cracked the Whip" in *Fortune,* August 10, 1981, pp. 169–74.
102. *Ibid.*
103. *The New York Times,* May 15, 1981.
104. Barrett, p. 159.
105. *Ibid.,* June 17, 1981.
106. *Ibid.*
107. *Ibid.*
108. *Ibid.,* June 18, 1981.
109. *Ibid.*
110. The memo and the account are in Barrett, p. 160. The events of the week of June 17 are described slightly differently in Cannon.
111. *The New York Times,* June 20, 1981.
112. Barrett, p. 161.
113. *The New York Times,* June 25, 1981.
114. Barrett, p. 161.
115. *The New York Times,* June 26, 1981.
116. *Ibid.*
117. *Ibid.*
118. Cannon, p. 334.
119. *The New York Times,* June 27, 1981.
120. Cannon, p. 334.
121. *The New York Times,* June 27, 1981.
122. Barrett, p. 162.
123. *The New York Times,* June 26, 1981.
124. Barrett, p. 162.
125. *The New York Times,* June 28, 1981.
126. March 22, 1981.
127. April 21, 1981.
128. May 3, 1981.
129. *Ibid.*
130. *Ibid.*
131. In Cannon, p. 410.
132. Wayne, p. 60.
133. *Newsweek,* May 18, 1981.
134. Wayne, p. 64.
135. "Reagan and the Lore of the Modern Presidency: What Have We Learned?" in Greenstein, p. 180.
136. *National Journal,* May 16, 1981.
137. Wayne, p. 58.
138. *The New York Times,* June 17, 1981.

139. In "Assessing Reagan's First Year," in Ornstein, *President and Congress,* p. 95.
140. "Reagan and the Lore of the Modern Presidency," p. 174.
141. Cannon, p. 333.
142. *Newsweek,* May 18, 1981.
143. Cannon, p. 333.
144. Wayne, pp. 54, 55.
145. Tom Wicker, *The New York Times,* May 1, 1981.
146. In Allen Schick, "How the Budget Was Won and Lost," in Ornstein, p. 24.
147. In Cannon, p. 333. The cartoon was drawn by Ben Sargent and appeared in the *Austin American Statesman.*
148. In Cannon, p. 406.
149. In "Introduction," Ornstein, p. 1.
150. "Defense Expenditures and National Well-Being," *American Political Science Review,* Vol. 76, 1982, pp. 767, 776.
151. In Barrett, p. 15.
152. *Time,* October 17, 1983.

Epilogue

1. *In Lyndon Johnson: A Memoir,* Fairway, Kan., 1982, p. 7.
2. *Ibid.,* p. 133.
3. Nelson W. Polsby, *Consequences of Party Reform,* New York, 1983, p. 127.
4. See my "Introversion in the Oval Office," *Presidential Studies Quarterly,* Summer, 1983, pp. 383–399.
5. Polsby, p. 133.

Index